Saddles

J.A. ALLEN & CO. LTD., LONDON S.W.1

Saddles

BY RUSSEL H. BEATIE

FOREWORD BY DEAN KRAKEL

DRAWINGS BY NANCY KAY NILES AND JUDY OSBURN

Library of Congress Cataloging in Publication Data

Beatie, Russel H. 1915–
  Saddles.

  Bibliography: p. 365
  Includes index.
  1. Saddlery.   I. Title.
SF309.9.B42   685'.1   79–6708

ISBN: 085131.365.5

This book is dedicated to

LOU AND ALICE CHERBENEAU

of Estes Park, Colorado

for their great help during its birth

and to

my very patient, long-suffering wife

JULIA MARIE BEATIE

who has put up with a saddle-nut husband for many years

On Day Herd. Drawing by Lee M. Rice.

Foreword

I got my first saddle when I was about twelve. My mother gave it to me. My saddle was made by Charles P. Shipley, of Kansas City, Missouri. The saddle had belonged to my grandfather, Joseph F. Cross. He rode the saddle sometime after the turn of the century from Texas County, Missouri, to northeastern Colorado, where he took up a homestead claim about six miles from the little prairie town of Keota. My grandfather had divorced and remarried. He brought with him a new wife and five daughters (one of whom was my dear mother) by his first marriage. Granddad and his daughters drove a small herd of cows and horses ahead of the wagon. My step-grandmother drove the wagon, filled with their few possessions left from a sale and settlement. The sisters took turns driving the buggy.

Granddad told me he bought his saddle from Charles P. Shipley, the maker whose shop and store was right next to the big stockyards in Kansas City. He had sold a small herd of cows and plunked down silver for the saddle—Shipley number 210.

I loved my grandfather because he made me feel I was someone special. He was a teller of tales. He let me do such wild things as shoot his 38-caliber revolver and drive his old Buick car. He wanted me to go to law school and hoped I would be a tobacco chewer. I failed him on both scores.

I cherish the saddle because of its family history, the tough times of pioneering it represents. Granddad rode in that saddle "all them six or seven hundred miles," he said, "just so's we could go real broke farming in a dry country." This saddle is among my collection of western stock saddles by various makers, some of whom are the great craftsmen of the saddle-making industry.

My Shipley saddle is in good condition because it has been cleaned and oiled every year since Mom gave it to me. I had a stand made with a half-barrel rack to place it on. It has a special place in my library. Hardly a day goes by that I don't look at that old Shipley. I have always appreciated the smell of real saddle leather; the old-time saddle has a shine and finish to it unlike anything else man ever created. My saddle is almost ninety years old. It has all the beautiful classic characteristics of western stock-saddle art: high cantle, narrow open A fork, assorted rosettes and straps, solid horn, short jockeys and skirts, an economy of stirrup leathers, metal-covered oxbow stirrups. The pattern stamped into the leather all over is basket weave.

Thus my interest in saddles, like Russel Beatie's, goes back a long way. Through the years I have studied saddle makers—trying to determine where they had their shops, when were their most productive years, how their saddles differed from one another. As a result of my interest I have a fine collection of saddle-makers' catalogs and saddles. To a cowman and a cowboy, a western stock saddle constituted a cherished possession and was bought with the same care one would buy a bed or an easy chair. For the working cowboy who works several months each year from his saddle cinched to a horse, a saddle is a personal piece of property, an item included in most real cowboys' wills. An object to be formally disposed of. While I'm not a cowboy of any sort, I am willing my Shipley to my son Jack because he shares my affection for it.

The time I could devote to my saddles, other than caring for them and preparing a catalog card on each one, has been limited. After reading Mr. Beatie's manuscript, I am more appreciative of all saddles and so can more fully catalog my own collection. Russel Beatie traces the history and evolution of the saddle from all parts of the world to the Spanish conquistador and on to Texas and the Great Plains.

The author's bibliography and method of citing nomenclature are outstanding. The National Cowboy Hall of Fame has more than 150 saddles in its collection. This book will be of great service to our catalogers.

A story my granddad told me shortly before he died in 1940 was about a roundup he worked on when he was a young man. It may illustrate a point: in rounding up the calves for branding, the cowboys gathered a fully saddled horse. The horse was locoed, having eaten the weed by the same name. On close examination the cowboys found that hanging from a stirrup was a boot that contained part of a human leg. The horse had dragged the rider to death bucking and stomping and separated the body from a leg at the knee. While the story made me half sick, my grandfather closed with, "There was almost no way you could tear one of them old-time stock saddles apart."

Dean Krakel
Executive Vice-President
National Cowboy Hall of Fame

Contents

Preface

My association with horses and their gear began at a very early age, on the Kansas farm of my wonderful grandfather. A stockman-farmer, he owned almost a section of good Kansas land thirty-five miles southwest of Wichita. There one day I walked back to the farmhouse, dripping wet, from an outing on my grandfather's gentle riding horse—who had just lain down and rolled in the middle of Slate Creek, with me aboard. He had left his hapless young rider in no danger of drowning in the knee-deep water, but wet and mortified. That horse had never done anything wrong in his life until he met up with a greenhorn from town.

In spite of—or perhaps because of—that first encounter, horses continued to interest me on into young adulthood, during a hitch in the army, college days, the pursuit of a career, and the founding of a business. In time my interest began to focus on saddles, about which there was, it turned out, very little recorded information.

The more I complained about the lack of information, the more my friends encouraged me to "write a book." I've heard that that is how a lot of books get written—out of the reader's frustration in not being able to find one on the subject that absorbs him. Finally, gradually, I embarked on what became a seven-year research project during which I traveled thousands of miles and spent uncounted hours reading and researching in libraries, museums, patent records, and individual collections and repositories.

It came to be that when I set out on automobile business trips I took along my collection of material, which as it grew I sorted into loose-leaf notebooks. Before long the trunk and back seat of my car began to look like a mobile library. My car and its contents excited a lot of comment, some of it amused.

With the help of people from all walks of life, from library reference specialists to ranch hands, my knowledge grew piece by piece. I acquired a library of my own; the Bibliography in the back of the book is made up largely of works in my own collection. Librarians and book dealers helped me find rare items. Catalogs of saddlemakers and suppliers proved to be of particular value. Catalog compilers realize that when they put together an aggregation of materials they may be setting down history. Saddle catalogs from the old days are hard to come by (how many people save outdated Sears catalogs?)—and are becoming valuable. One of the best catalog collections is that in the National Cowboy Hall of Fame, in Oklahoma City. The museum graciously allowed me to reproduce illustrations from catalogs in its holdings that I did not have in my own collection.

The research broadened over the years—each new bit of information led into new areas. What I had originally envisioned as a modest subject grew like Topsy into an all-consuming venture. For how can you talk about saddles without delving into the subject of the trees on which they are built? And how can you talk about the leathers without devoting some space to what you've by now learned about the uniquely American art of saddle leatherwork? And so the project grew.

Some of the most enjoyable aspects of my research were the many interviews I had with the most erudite historians, horse trainers, saddle collectors like me, museum enthusiasts. I had engaging visits with old-time saddlemakers or their descendants, who were pleased that a family craft was at last being accorded its place in history. Those whom I could not meet in person corresponded with me; the letters on which much of this book is founded would fill another volume.

Despite all the research some intriguing questions that have long teased historians still remain unanswered: Who (or what) was the Hope of the Hope saddles? Who designed the Morgan saddle? Who was Sam Stagg, and where did he work? When did the steamed-and-bent wooden stirrup originate? And so on. There is a lot yet to be done on stirrups, bits, and bridles, subjects that need to be dealt with in detail that is beyond the scope of this book.

Though I have sought to avoid bias, the discerning reader will detect here and there my views on the controversial subject of saddle-seat design, and I have tried to convey what I sincerely believe to be the best advice available on matching rider, horse, and saddle, though

I make no pretense at being a professional in horse training or riding. Plenty of good books are available on those subjects. Nor do I expect anyone to be able to design and build a saddle after reading these pages. But the novice can learn a lot about what he wants in a saddle and how to take care of it, and the saddlemaker will learn something about the history of his craft.

It is also my hope that after reading these pages the reader will go out to the barn or garage and take down that old, long-disused saddle hanging on a nail, clean it up with some saddle soap and neat's-foot oil, and take another look at it. It just might be a collector's gem— a genuine artifact of American history. Much of that history, after all, was made on horseback.

Russel H. Beatie

Wichita, Kansas

Acknowledgments

For their very generous help in time and knowledge, I wish to express my appreciation to the following individuals, museums, and companies:

Hank Ack, of Danville, California, well-known trainer-instructor, whose suggestions were of great value.

J. K. Anderson, Department of Classics, University of California, Berkeley, California, author of *Ancient Greek Horsemanship* and a most helpful authority on the early history.

Earl Bain, Instructor in Leatherwork and Saddles at Oklahoma State Tech, a branch of Oklahoma State University, Okmulgee, Oklahoma.

Garnet Brooks, of Shamrock, Texas, collector of western paraphernalia and historian, formerly with the National Cowboy Hall of Fame and Western Heritage Center, Oklahoma City.

Jack Carroll, of Carroll Saddle Company, McNeal, Arizona, a very knowledgeable, experienced maker of well-designed saddles.

Pierce A. Chamberlain, of Tucson, Arizona, Chief Curator of the Arizona Historical Society, who read the manuscript and offered corrections.

Major Charles Chenevix-Trench, of Tipperary, Eire, author of *A History of Horsemanship* and a great help to me.

Reba Collins, Curator of the Will Rogers Memorial Museum, Claremore, Oklahoma, who researched and provided pictures of Will Rogers's saddles.

Lou and Alice Cherbeneau, of Estes Park, Colorado. He is an astute western buff, and she has been a valuable proofreader and monitor of style.

John Cornelison, of Cheyenne, Wyoming, formerly Curator of the Wyoming Historical Museum, Cheyenne.

Dale Durham, of the Fort Sill Museum, Lawton, Oklahoma, who has much knowledge on the restoration of old saddles.

Henry Davis, Jr., of California, formerly Curator of the Fort Riley Cavalry Museum, near Junction City, Kansas.

Robert Moorman Denhardt, of Arbuckle, California, a historian of great merit and an interesting correspondent.

Herb Endres, of Tulsa, Oklahoma, a western buff and friend who spent many hours discussing points with me.

Jim Eskew, Jr., of Ardmore, Oklahoma, the late son of Colonel James Eskew (an old-time rodeo producer) and world's champion roper.

Dr. L. E. Evans, of the School of Veterinary Medicine, Oklahoma State University, Stillwater, Oklahoma. He loaned me books and gave advice; his wife, who of French birth, translated for me all my letters from overseas.

Johanna C. Fallis and Fallis Custom Made Saddlery, Inc., Elbert, Colorado, who provided me with outstanding photographs.

W. Sidney Felton, an attorney and author of the informative *Masters of Equitation*.

Dallas W. Freeborn, Topeka, Kansas, consulting engineer and military historian, whose specialty is McClellan saddles.

C. R. ("Slim") Gieser, of Wichita, Kansas, my friend and saddle repairman, a young man with a wealth of saddle knowledge.

Gillett Griswold, Director of the Fort Sill

Museum, Lawton, Oklahoma, and nationally known authority on United States military and western history.

J. Evetts Haley, of Canyon, Texas, an erudite western historian, author of many excellent books, and a fascinating man to spend time with.

Kay Halverson, of Cheyenne, Wyoming, Curator of the fine Wyoming Historical Museum, who was extremely helpful to me.

J. David Hamley, of Pendleton, Oregon, the third-generation proprietor of the famous saddlemakers Hamley and Company. He too was very helpful to me.

Sarah Greeley Hubbs.

Walter H. (Buddy) Jones, Assistant Curator of the Fort Sill Museum, Lawton, Oklahoma. He is a western buff as well as a trained military historian.

H. Kauffman & Sons, New York, who generously provided photographs.

Robert L. Kaupke, of Braman, Oklahoma, a collector of and dealer in western paraphernalia, who loaned me many items for drawings.

Dean Krakel, Director of the National Cowboy Hall of Fame and Western Heritage Center, Oklahoma City, who had faith in this book.

Tom and Andrea Leach, of Gentry, Arkansas, trainers and friends who offered many suggestions.

Mrs. Mary Aiken Littauer, widow of Captain Vladimer Littauer, and an extremely knowledgeable historian in her own right, who was most helpful to me.

Phil Livingston, a fine artist, author of many saddle articles, and a helpful friend.

Mrs. Esther Long, Librarian of the National Cowboy Hall of Fame and Western Heritage Center, Oklahoma City, who generously provided assistance every time I entered the library.

Bob Love, former Curator of the Will Rogers Memorial Museum, Claremore, Oklahoma.

Dale Lucas, of Gund Arabians, Bixby, Oklahoma, for his moral support—and for riding a flat-seated saddle for years.

W. Charles Maple, former Advertising Director of Wyeth Hardware & Manufacturing Company, St. Joseph, Missouri, an old-line saddlemaking company which has now discontinued saddle manufacture.

Tad Mizwa, of the *Western Outfitter,* Houston, Texas. He is an outstanding collector as well as publisher in the field.

Miller's Inc., of New York, who generously provided photographs.

Dr. Robert L. Morin, of Clinton, Illinois, whose help in obtaining old magazines was invaluable.

Dr. Tom Monin, of the School of Veterinary Medicine, Oklahoma State University, Stillwater, for his ideas and his answers to my many questions.

Aliph Moss, of Norman, Oklahoma, a knowledgeable horse trainer, who provided able editorial assistance with text and a myriad of illustrations.

Helmut Nickel, Curator of the Arms and Armor Division of the Metropolitan Museum of Art, New York, a very knowledgeable historian who was of much help to me.

Mrs. Sheila Ohlendorff, of the University of Texas, Austin, who was in charge of the Dr. Edward Laroque Tinker Foundation items in the University of Texas Museum. She was kind enough to abstract a very helpful start on the bibliography contained in this book.

Schneider's, Cleveland, Ohio, for generously providing illustrations.

Dr. J. S. Palen, of Cheyenne, Wyoming, a retired veterinarian and collector of western items and literature, who was very helpful to me in my research.

Harold Porter, of Tucson, Arizona, for the time he took to discuss the meanderings of his grandfather, N. Porter.

William N. Porter, of Phoenix, Arizona, another grandson of N. Porter, who was very helpful on various points of history.

Gregor de Romaszkan, author of *The Horse and Rider in Equilibrium,* who reviewed and made worthwhile suggestions on the section on riding.

Paul A. Rossi, of Woodland Park, Colorado, eminent sculptor-historian and author and former director of the Thomas Gilcrease Institute of American History and Art, Tulsa, Oklahoma, for allowing me to use photographs of his saddle bronzes, and to his wife, Florence, for her encouragement.

Ryon's Saddle and Ranch Supplies, Inc., Fort Worth, Texas, for generously supplying illustrations.

Dr. Samuel W. Sabin, of the Department of Animal Science, Cornell University, Ithaca, New York, for allowing me to use parts of his fine pamphlets on horses.

Rudy Terrell, of the Bully Good Saddle Shop, Muskogee, Oklahoma, for the interesting discussions we had and the items he loaned me for drawings.

TexTan Western Leather Company, Yoakum, Texas, and the staff of the Advertising Department, for providing many photographs.

Sy Vogt, Curator of the J. M. Davis Gun Museum, Claremore, Oklahoma, whose saddle collection and help were very useful to me.

Mitch Willour, of Enid, Oklahoma, an excellent trainer, for patiently answering my many questions while I was researching this book.

Fay E. Ward, of Prescott, Arizona, author of the fine *Cowboy at Work,* for allowing me to reproduce drawings from his work.

Dr. Arthur Woodward, knowledgeable historian of Patagonia, Arizona, for many years associated with the Los Angeles County Museum of Natural History, for the time he and his pleasant wife gave me and his help in reviewing parts of my book.

Most of the drawings were made by Nancy Kay Niles. Other illustrations, including the saddle drawings that appear on the part-title pages, were drawn by Judy Osburn, of Norman, Oklahoma, a horsewoman and talented artist in her own right.

To all of these and to museum staffs across the land, I am deeply grateful.

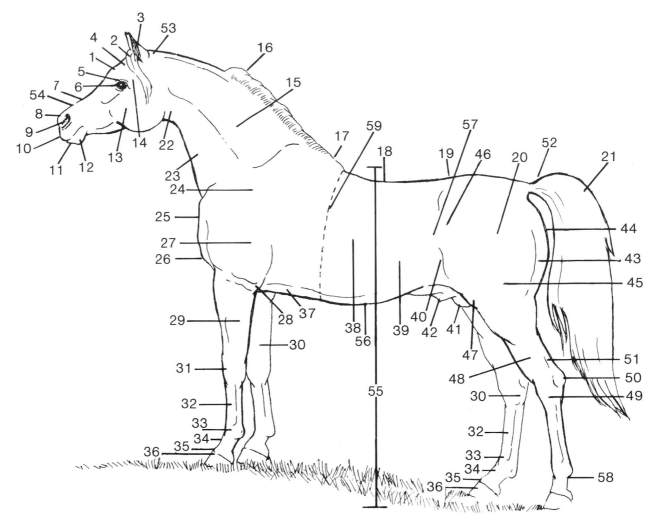

THE PARTS OF THE HORSE

1. Forehead	21. Tail	41. Testicles
2. Forelock	22. Throat-latch area	42. Sheath
3. Ear	23. Cervical groove	43. Buttock (hind quarter)
4. Supra-orbit	24. Shoulder	44. Point of buttock
5. Eyebrow	25. Shoulder point	45. Thigh
6. Eye	26. Breast	46. Haunch (point of hip)
7. Nose	27. Upper arm	47. Stifle
8. Nasal peak	28. Point of elbow	48. Leg or gaskin
9. Nostril	29. Forearm	49. Hock
10. Upper lip	30. Chestnut (night eye)	50. Point of hock
11. Lower lip	31. Knee	51. Tendon Achilles, or hamstring
12. Chin	32. Cannon	52. Dock
13. Cheek	33. Fetlock joint	53. Poll
14. Temple	34. Pastern	54. Bridge of nose
15. Neck	35. Coronet	55. Height (in hands)
16. Crest (nape)	36. Foot (hoof)	56. Underline
17. Withers	37. Brisket	57. Coupling
18. Back	38. Rib area	58. Ergot
19. Loins	39. Abdomen	59. Heart girth
20. Croup (rump)	40. Flank	

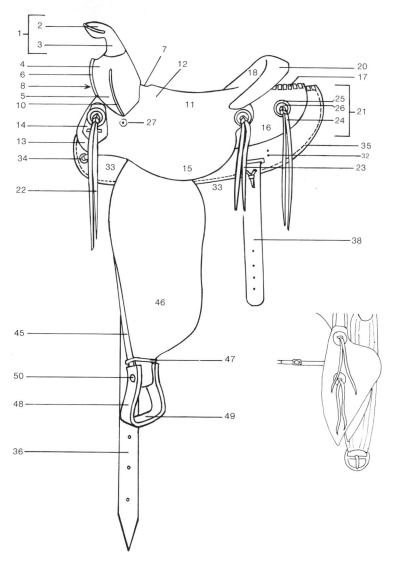
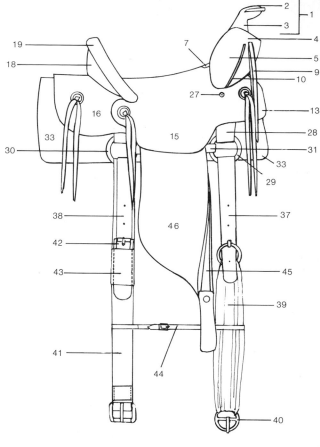

THE PARTS OF THE MODERN WESTERN SADDLE.

Left: Near-side view, California skirt.

Right: Off-side view, Texas skirt.

1. Horn	18. Cantle	35. Buckstitch
2. Horn cap or head	19. Cantle bead	36. Cinch strap (near side)
3. Horn neck	20. Cheyenne roll	37. Off strap (front billet, off side)
4. Fork	21. Saddle-string assembly	38. Flank cinch billet
5. Swell (of fork)	22. Saddle string number one	39. Cinch
6. Fork binding	23. Saddle string number three	40. Cinch ring or buckle
7. Hand hole	24. Saddle string number four	41. Flank cinch
8. Gullet	25. Rosette	42. Flank cinch buckle
9. Rope strap	26. Concha	43. Stationary leather keeper
10. Welt	27. Screw-and-ferrule assembly	44. Cinch connector strap
11. Seat, full-extended	28. Rigging straps (leathers)	45. Stirrup leather
12. Throat of seat	29. Front rigging ring	46. Fender
13. Front jockey	30. Rear rigging ring	47. Stirrup-leather keeper
14. Cinch-strap holder	31. Rigging-ring connector strap	48. Stirrup
15. Side jockey	32. Rear rigging plate	49. Stirrup tread
16. Back jockey	33. Skirt	50. Stirrup roller, or bolt
17. Laced seam connecting back jockeys	34. Breast strap D	51. Tapadero

PART I   The History and Development of the Saddle

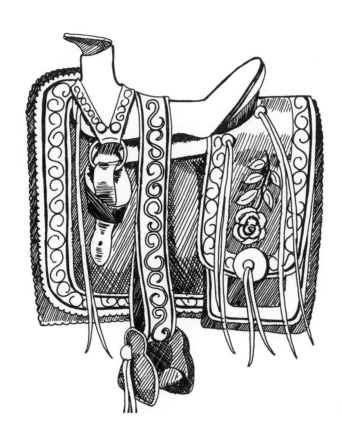

CHAPTER 1

Prehistoric Times

To put the relationship of the evolution of the horse and that of man in proper perspective, it is necessary to know certain facts of history, and even beyond—of prehistory (for the early evolution of the horse, see Willoughby, 1974; and Simpson, 1951). The term *prehistoric* does not necessarily refer to the age of the dinosaurs; it simply means "before written history." To learn about prehistoric man and his culture, including the domestication of the horse, we must go to the evidence he left behind, such as pottery, drawings, and carvings; pieces of ivory; and artifacts of stone and bone. Such evidence is available for a time as far back as the Paleolithic (Old Stone) Age, in the form of chipped stone tools. The Neolithic (New Stone) Age— approximately ten thousand to five thousand years ago—is represented by ground and polished stone tools. In some areas of the world this age lasted longer, as in Britain and, surprisingly, China, where it lasted to about 2500 B.C. (J. K. Anderson, letter).

Then came the age of metals. The Chalcolithic (Copper-Stone) Age began in some parts of the world in 6500 B.C. It was followed by the Bronze Age, which was in full flower by approximately 3000 B.C. In the Bronze Age came such inventions as metal axles and wheel rims for chariots and metal swords, shields, and tools.

Following the Bronze Age came the Iron Age, which dawned about 1200 B.C. With it came the ability to utilize hard, durable iron, a much more abundant metal than copper. Tribes with iron armaments could wage and win battles. What was ultimately even more important, they could become farmers.

Until man developed farming implements, he either lived a nomad's life, moving about from place to place to secure food, or had to live in an area where abundant food was assured. With metal tools, man became an agriculturalist, in approximately 5000 B.C.

CHAPTER **2**

The Evolution and Domestication
of the Modern Horse

We know, of course, that grain-fed horses grow larger than grass-fed horses. With the start of agriculture—man's developing ability to cultivate grains for his animals and his growing knowledge of selective breeding—must have begun the horse's great increase in stature, which it accomplished in a relatively short time compared with the sixty million years of its earlier evolution.

The last migrations of the small preagriculture horses from the North American continent across the Bering Strait to Asia took place during the Pleistocene Epoch (Simpson, pp. 145–47). After the migration of Equus, modern species of horses began evolving in north-central Asia. Some Equidae migrated to Africa, where they evolved into zebras. The Asiatic wild horses appeared following this period; the tarpan and Przevalski's horse are direct descendants of the original Asiatic horse. For some unexplained reason all the horses in the Western Hemisphere died out. There were to be no more until they were brought back by Columbus on his second voyage in early 1494.

Horses spread from northern Asia throughout the Asiatic and European continents by three main routes: (1) eastward, where they evolved into the Chinese and other horses of the Orient, (2) westward into Europe, (3) and southwest into Asia Minor and beyond.

There are drawings of horses in the caves of Cro-Magnon man in southern France and northern Spain dating 25,000 to 30,000 years ago. At that time the horse had not yet been domesticated but, along with other animals, was hunted as food. His hide was used for shelter.

We come now to the question when the horse was first domesticated. The word "domesti-

cated" can have several connotations. It can mean raised for food, raised as a draft animal, raised for riding, or raised as a pet. For our purposes here it is sufficient to assume that the word means "tamed," for whatever purpose.

Horses were mentioned in the clay tablets of Mesopotamia in the third millenium B.C. under the name "ass of the mountains" (J. K. Anderson, p. 2). They also first appeared as domesticated animals about 3000 B.C., and invaders from the north rode them into the valleys of the Tigris and the Euphrates as early as 2000 B.C. Models of chariots of an earlier time that appear to be drawn by horses are actually being pulled by onagers, or wild asses (see Fig. 3.1).

The literature is full of conjectures but no precise information about when and where the horse was domesticated. One writer says that the domesticated horse probably arrived in northwestern Europe about 1700 B.C. (Chenevix-Trench, p. 9).

Nor do we know whether the horse was first ridden or was first used as a draft animal. We do know that oxen were used as draft animals as early as 5000–4000 B.C. (Chenevix-Trench, p. 10) and that chariots with solid wheels were being drawn by onagers around 3000 B.C. So it is logical to believe that the horse with his great speed was early used for pulling chariots in battle.

The horses of Asia Minor in 2000 B.C. were no more than four feet (twelve hands) tall. Oxen would be strong enough to pull some type of sled with considerable weight on it, but the small horses would have neither the weight nor the strength to pull heavy sleds. Many of us have seen very heavy sled loads being pulled by small horses at fairs or in contests. We must remem-

8

ber that this is possible only by equipping the horses with calked iron shoes for traction. In 2000 B.C. iron shoes had not yet been invented.

It was not until the invention of the wheel that the lightweight horses could be used as draft animals.

CHAPTER 3

The Chariot

The invention of the wheel was one of the most important achievements of early man. The first wheels were made of solid wood, and such wheels were used in Mesopotamia on carts drawn by oxen and later by onagers. The light war chariot with spoked wheels appears to have been invented after the first half of the second millennium B.C. (Yadin, p. 39). At some time during this period the speedier horse began replacing the onager as the chariot steed.

With various modifications the chariot spread to Eighteenth Dynasty Egypt, Hittite Anatolia,

FIG. 3.1.   Onagers drawing a quadriga, about 2600 B.C. Courtesy of Oriental Institute, University of Chicago.

FIG. 3.2.   Early chariot wheels from Kish. Field Museum of Natural History, Chicago. From Robert T. Boyd, *Tells, Tombs, and Treasures.* (Note: Full citations to published works are given in the Bibliography.)

FIG. 3.3. Replica of chariot drawn by onagers in use in Mesopotamia in the first half of the third millennium. Courtesy of Oriental Institute, University of Chicago.

FIG. 3.4.   Light spoked-wheel chariot driven by Rameses II at the Battle of Kadesh, 1296 B.C. Bas-relief in Thebes Museum. From Miklos Jankovich, *They Rode into Europe.*

FIG. 3.5.   A modern conception of Persian chariot wheels and axles with scythes as described by Xenophon. From *Xenophon's Anabasis,* edited by Maurice W. Mather and Joseph William Hewitt.

Minoan Crete, and Mycenean Greece. It continued and survived as a major weapon of war until the ninth or eighth century B.C., when it was gradually replaced by mounted cavalry, though heavy chariots with scythed wheels and axles continued to be used occasionally by the Persians, and light chariots survived in the Celtic West until the Roman conquest.

CHAPTER 4

Riding and Cavalry

It is not known when the horse was first used as a conveyer of man. Surviving representations of riding in Mesopotamia date from about 2000 B.C., and textual references to riding appear at least as early as the seventeenth century B.C. In a Sinai mine is a carving from about the same period showing a rider sitting sideways on an ass that is being led by a ring in its nose. There are representations of a rider on a horse on Eighteenth Dynasty Egyptian temple walls. Such riders were called "scouts" (Schulman, pp. 263–71). There are no representations in Egypt of

FIG. 4.1. Rider from the tomb of Horemheb (1332–1306 B.C.). Courtesy of Musèo Cívico Archeològico, Bologna, Italy.

horseback riding before that time—that is, before about 1580 B.C. The earliest pictures of men riding good-sized horses are those in the tomb of Horemheb, a fourteenth century B.C. pharaoh (Chevenix-Trench, p. 13, see Fig. 4.1).

About 1360 B.C., Kikuli, a Mittari, wrote a work for the Hittites on horse training and conditioning on four surviving cuneiform tablets and a fifth very fragmentary one. There are also two extant shorter but similar Middle Assyrian texts ascribed to the same period (Mary Aiken Littauer, letter). These tablets, inscribed "Handbook for the Treatment of the Horse," were discovered during excavations at Boghaz-koy, the site of Hattussas, the ancient capital of the Hittites in Anatolia. They were published in part in 1931.

It is interesting to note that the rider shown in Horemheb's tomb is seated well back on the haunches of the animal. For some reason even to this day onager and donkey riders sit in this position. It would be logical that onager riders would begin riding horses that way. By the eighth century B.C. the Assyrian riders of Tig-lath–Pileser III (747–727) were riding well forward (see Fig. 5.1).

FIG. 4.3. Syrian riding sidesaddle style. The scene, from a relief at Karnak, depicts the victory of Rameses II over the Syrians (thirteenth century B.C.). From Cecil G. Trew, *The Accoutrements of the Riding Horse.*

There are other scattered references to riding in remote times: Babylonian riding horses are mentioned during the time of the reign of Nebuchadnezzar I, around 1200 B.C. (Jankovich). A rock drawing from Ladak, at the west end of the Tibetan Plateau, also estimated to date from about 1200 B.C., shows a mounted archer (see Fig. 4.2).

Chariots were usable only on the open plains; therefore, as the art of horsemanship improved, the extreme mobility and speed of cavalry as an effective instrument of war on many kinds of terrain began to be recognized. According to Anderson, however, the Greeks continued to use chariots in war as late as 700 B.C., and chariots were used well past that period for racing and ceremonial purposes.

The Assyrians began using mounted fighters in the ninth century B.C. (Chevenix-Trench, p. 16). The first authentic reference to Assyrian cavalry dates from 890 B.C. Two Assyrian kings, Assur-Nasir-Pal II (884–59 B.C.) and Shalmaneser III (859–24 B.C.), employed mounted troops (Chevenix-Trench, p. 16). A relief in the palace of Assur-Nasir-Pal II shows mounted nomads in warlike posture—shooting arrows backward

FIG. 4.2. Rock drawing from Ladakh, Kashmir, India, about 1200 B.C. From Jankovich, *They Rode into Europe.*

15

from their horses (Jankovich, p. 43). Many of the early riders were so adept and so well balanced on their horses that, when retreating, they could turn around and shoot their arrows backward off the horse. From this practice comes the modern expression the "Parthian shaft"—a parting verbal shot when leaving.

The Scythians, a group of warlike nomads, appeared on the Russian steppes in the seventh century B.C. They and the Sarmatians, who lived east of them, are sometimes—incorrectly, I believe—called the earliest peoples to ride. These nomads all but lived on horseback, and this might be considered the real beginning of the horse culture. The horse was an integral part of their existence.

At first the cavalry was an unorganized group. Later the Macedonian mounted phalanx was the first to use a triangular formation made possible by the riders' very long lances. From this beginning, cavalry developed into highly organized, specialized corps of armies—heavily armored cavalry and a highly mobile, lightly armored cavalry.

The origin of one piece of riding gear, the martingale—the tie-down from the cinch to the noseband or bridle reins—is unknown. On reliefs from the palaces of the Assyrian kings is shown a remarkable anticipation of the modern martingale. It is a weighted tassel on the reins of Assyrian horses of the seventh century B.C., which appears to have had somewhat the effect of a martingale. There was, however, no tie-down strap from the bridle to the girth. This tassel was not used, as far as Anderson knows, by any other peoples (J. K. Anderson, p. 11).

Denison wrote, "In the years 722 to 705 B.C., in the representations of the reigns of Sargon (722–705 B.C.) and Sennacherib (705–681 B.C.), the cavalry . . . largely increased and [were] continually shown in the scenes of battle" (p. 12). Their seat in the earliest figures is very remarkable: the knees are drawn up as high as the horse's back and are pressed close against the neck and withers. The legs and feet are naked and hang close to the shoulders. This shows that the mounting of the horse was a new

idea and that the riders had not yet discovered the proper and natural way of sitting (Denison, p. 12).

In Greece, horsemen, a few of whom were armed and even fighting on horseback, appeared in increasing numbers in Attic and Boeotian art from the late eighth century B.C. (J. K. Anderson, p. 75). An Etruscan vase painting of the seventh century B.C. shows a mounted army on the march (Chenevix–Trench, p. 35). In the sixth century B.C. military superiority passed to the Persians because of their larger, stronger horses (Chenevix–Trench, p. 35). The Persian King Darius (522–486 B.C.) had the first recorded pony express; it helped hold his kingdom together from India to the Caucasus Mountains.

Philip II of Macedon, who ruled from 359 to 336 B.C., was a master of cavalry and cavalry tactics. When Philip was assassinated in 336 B.C., his son, Alexander III (Alexander the Great) succeeded him. Alexander, born in 356 B.C., was only twenty years old when he took over the Macedonian cavalry. He won three victories over his enemies the Persians largely by the use of his cavalry, which he led in person. In 326 B.C., at the Battle of the Hydaspes River in Kashmir (now the Jhelum River of Pakistan), Alexander defeated a numerically much superior force with brilliant cavalry tactics. Before his death in 323 B.C., he had conquered most of the known world, from Macedonia into India and Egypt.

Bucephalus, Alexander's famous horse, was a high-spirited animal (Fig. 4.4). The story is told that Bucephalus was being shown to Philip, Alexander's father. The boy Alexander noticed that every time the horse saw his shadow he became uncontrollable. Alexander begged for the horse. Philip said that Alexander could have him if he could ride him. Alexander turned the horse so that his shadow was not visible to him, mounted, and rode him. Bucephalus carried Alexander through many battles. Once Bucephalus was stolen but was returned under threat of extreme reprisals by Alexander. Bucephalus was mortally wounded at the Battle of Hydaspes but carried Alexander to safety before dying.

FIG. 4.4.   Alexander the Great on Bucephalus. Courtesy of British Museum, London.

In his memory the city Bucephala was founded where the Kashmir road crossed the Hydaspes in Pakistan.

Hannibal, ruler of Carthage, in Africa, lived from 247 to 183 B.C. The Punic Wars were waged between Carthage and Rome during Hannibal's time. The Numidian light-horse cavalry of Hannibal's army was very effective (Chenevix–Trench, p. 19). Hannibal defeated the Romans at the Battle of Cannae (216 B.C.) because of his much better cavalry. The Romans learned their lesson and improved their own cavalry. Under Scipio's leadership, they defeated Hannibal at the Battle of Zama in 202 B.C. The Roman cavalry played an important role in the victory.

CHAPTER 5

The Saddle Cloth

After this brief history of the early domestication of the horse, from draft animal to riding animal, it seems appropriate to describe the early accouterments of the horse, beginning with the saddle-type cloth or pad.

The cavalry of the Assyrian Tiglath-Pileser III (747–27 B.C.) rode well-bred horses a good 14.2 hands tall (Fig. 5.1). Assyrian cavalry before this and after rode on fringed cloths with breast collars and cruppers (Chenevix–Trench, p. 16). The cavalry of Sennacherib (705–681 B.C.) rode cinched, quilted pads in the same position as the present-day saddle (Chenevix–Trench, p. 16). Note that there appear to be

FIG. 5.1.   Cavalry of Tiglath-Pileser III, eighth century B.C. Note that the riders are now riding well forward. Courtesy of British Museum.

FIG. 5.2. Sennacherib's horses with pad saddles, seventh century B.C. Courtesy of British Museum.

two cinches on the pads shown in Fig. 5.2. We do not encounter these again until illustrations from the days of chain-mail armor.

Pliny the Elder (A.D. 23–79) in his *Natural History* declared that Pelethronius, a Thessalonian, was the first to put a cover between the horse and rider; however, that appears to be legend. As Anderson says, the Greeks and Romans of this era wanted everything to have an exact beginning, especially if it began with one of their forebears (Anderson, letter). But the Greek historian and soldier Xenophon (434–355

B.C.) wrote essays on horsemanship that were masterpieces of their kind, in which he ridiculed the Persians for putting "coverlets on their horses" (J. K. Anderson, p. 81).

The Parthenon Frieze, carved under the direction of Phidias about 440 B.C., shows Greek mounted men; however, it does not show any cloths between the riders and the horses (Fig. 5.3). According to Anderson, there is no evidence for saddlecloths on the Greek mainland until the fourth century B.C. (p. 79), but by the second century B.C., "Antiphanes, a Greek

FIG. 5.3.   Greek riders, Parthenon Frieze. Courtesy of British Museum.

whose plays were performed in public for the first time towards the close of the second century B.C., alludes to 'coverlets for a horse,'" (Tozer, p. 38).

Rudenko's research in 1951 on the frozen burial graves of the central Asian nomads at Pazyryk

produced actual examples of two types [of saddles], the simpler consisting merely of two felt cushions designed to lie on each side of the horse's back-

bone and the latter and more elaborate having padded wooden frames to act as pommel and cantle. They were used on top of large gaily decorated saddlecloths and secured by breastband, girth and crupper. [J. K. Anderson, p. 81]

These graves were made in the fifth and fourth centuries B.C., leading one to the assumption that the saddle with frame was in use that long ago.

FIG. 5.4.   Pazyryk leather-and-felt pad saddle from tomb at Altai (USSR), fifth century B.C. From Charles Chenevix-Trench, *A History of Horsemanship*.

CHAPTER 6

Saddles with Frames

One knowledgeable researcher has indicated that the rigid saddle dates back as far as 980–960 B.C., but I did not have access to his information. The earliest rigid saddle that I have found recorded is the saddle pad found by Rudenko in the burial ground at Pazyryk. It consists of a felt pad on either side of the spine, united by wooden bows. The construction of this saddle shows an awareness of what we all now know—that the rider should not contact the backbone of the horse.

This type of saddle is shown on the Chertomlyk Vase, dated fourth century B.C. On a frieze on the vase is a Scythian hobbling his horse. On the horse is a pad saddle (see Fig. 6.1).

Saddles with rigid frames (without stirrups) first appeared in China during the Han Dynasty (206 B.C.–220 A.D.) and in Roman Gaul during the first century A.D.

In a letter to me J. K. Anderson provided a great deal of clarification on the subject of early saddles:

FIG. 6.1. Scythian hobbling his horse. Chertomlyk vase (Greek), fourth century B.C. From Chenevix-Trench, *A History of Horsemanship.*

FIG. 6.2. Roman funerary monument to an officer of Julius Caesar. *(A)* Bas-relief on south face of base. *(B)* Bas-relief on north face of base. *(C)* From north face. *(D)* From south face. From H. Rolland, *La Mausolée de Glanum.*

FIG. 6.3.   Emperor Theodosius, showing saddle. From Basil Tozer, *The Horse in History.*

"Sella" is Roman for saddle or seat. It seems first to be used in the Theodosian code: writers of the Augustine period—and earlier, Julius Ceasar in his "Bellum Gallicum" 4.24—used the Greek ephippium, one would suppose a mere saddle cloth (or shall we allow a lion-skin for Emperors?), were it not for the abundant sculptural evidence to the contrary. Fig. 6.2 shows what is nowadays generally supposed to be a Roman funerary monument of a retired officer of Julius Caesar's, from St. Remy in the South of France. Approximate date the 30's B.C. Details of horses and harness from the battle scenes that are on the 4 sides of the plinth (base) are shown on "Face Nord 6" [Fig. 6.2C] and "Face Sud" [Fig. 6.2D].

These being riderless, (they) show particularly

clearly saddles with high pommels and cantles. (Compare the photograph of plinth Face Sud [Fig. 6.2D], extreme left, and the photograph of plinth Face Nord. [Fig. 6.2B].

Ceasar (in the passage cited above) says that the Germans always rode bareback and despised people who used "ephippia"—implying that Gauls and Romans did so habitually, so that there was no need to mention the fact. Whether the word in Caesar means saddles, pads, or both one cannot say: at least the St. Remy evidence makes it clear that it could be saddles. A little later, saddles seem to be standard Roman cavalry equipment. J. Kromayer and G. Veith-Heerwesen, in their *Kriegfuhrung der Griechen und Romer* [Munich, 1928], Figs. 113, 114, show two cavalry men's tombstones from the Rhineland: there are lots like them in Britain, date between 50 A.D.—200 A.D.: best estimate 75—125 A.D. Also from Kromayer–Veith is a picture I can date precisely. It shows Trajan's army crossing the Danube at the opening of the first Dacian war in 101 A.D. The picture is from Trajan's Column in Rome, erected 10 years later. (These reliefs are of course published in a lot of these places and you will find there saddled horses, including the Emperor's own charger.) [J. K. Anderson, letter]

Demmin wrote in 1877 that "John Zonaras, a Byzantine historian who lived in the twelfth century, is the first to describe a saddle, properly so called, in giving an account of a combat fought in the year A.D. 340 between Constans and his brother Constantine" (Demmin, p. 355). Tozer, in 1903, mentioned that by A.D. 380 the cavalrymen of Theodosius I, who ruled from A.D. 379 to 395, were mounted on horses with a true saddle with a tree showing a front and rear bow (Tozer, p. 81). They had no stirrups, however.

In the Hippodrome of Constantinople the column of Theodosius I had what has been considered the first representation of the true saddle. The column erected in A.D. 385, was demolished around 1500, but a few of the reliefs that decorated its shaft have survived.

Emperor Theodosius II (A.D. 401–50), grandson of Theodosius I, published the Theodosian Code about 438. The code limited the weight of the saddle and bridle to sixty pounds. From such a heavy weight limit it would appear that frame saddles had been developed to some degree by that time (Fig. 6.3).

CHAPTER 7

Stirrups

In the art of warfare the invention of the stirrup, possibly in the late second century B.C., was comparable in importance to the invention of gunpowder. It was just as important in the development of transportation. One wonders that it took so long for man to devise the stirrup, which so greatly improved his stability on the back of his horse, among other benefits. The old literature reports that one of the occupational hazards of the nomadic barbarian horseman was hernia caused by the legs dangling loosely down the sides of the horse for hours on end. The invention of the stirrup relieved that problem. Certain peoples did not accept its use for a while because they considered it effeminate. Sooner or later, however, everybody adopted this useful invention.

Ms. Gladys Brown Edwards, in an interesting letter to me, suggested that the invention and use of the stirrup were dependent on the development of the cinch. The saddle had to be well anchored so that the weight of a rider mounting a horse would not turn the saddle on the horse's back.

Before the advent of stirrups, mounting a horse was a problem to all but agile young riders. Xenophon advised that the groom should "know how to give a leg up in the Persian manner." The "Persian manner" was not explained; it may have been simply having someone kneel down and act as a mounting block, as the Persians' captured enemies are shown being compelled to do on monuments (J. K. Anderson, p. 83). Sapor, who reigned from A.D. 241 to 271 forced the conquered Roman emperor Valerian to do this (Tozer, p. 43).

Mounting blocks were noted by Plutarch (A.D. 46–120) on the beautiful new roads in Italy built by Gaius Gracchus: ". . . stones at small distances from one another, on both sides of the way, by the help of which travellers might get easily on horseback without wanting a groom" (J. K. Anderson, p. 83). Another method of mounting was to train the horse to kneel so that the rider could step onto his back. Having the horse sit was a less acceptable method, because a horse has difficulty rising from that position. The commonest method of mounting was to vault onto the horse's back, sometimes with the aid of a spear used as a vaulting pole. In some references a spear is shown with a loop attached to the handle, into which the rider placed his foot, which allowed him to step up onto the horse.

FIG. 7.1. Roman mounting with the aid of a loop on his spear. Drawing by Nancy Kay Niles. Except where otherwise noted, drawings in this book are by Nancy Kay Niles.

FIG. 7.2.   Emperor Anastasius I, ivory diptych, sixth century A.D., in the Louvre, Paris. From W. F. Volbach, *Early Christian Art.*

27

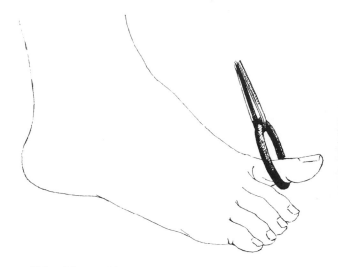

FIG. 7.3. How a big-toe stirrup might have looked. From Trew, *The Accoutrements of the Riding Horse.*

The first stirrup, a loop for the big toe, was used in India late in the second century B.C. (see Fig. 7.3). By the fifth century A.D. the booted Chinese had expanded the big-toe stirrup. Another source (Bivar) states: "The first evidence of a stirrup as such is in the biography of a Chinese officer who lived in A.D. 477. He said that it was invented by the Huns. There is questionable evidence that the stirrup was invented before this." The foot stirrup had reached Korea by the fifth century (see Fig. 7.4). It arrived in Japan and some central Asian countries in the sixth century A.D.

In 1846, Beckman wrote:

"The first certain account of stirrups, as far as I have been able to learn, is in a book by Mauritius (A.D. 286) respecting the art of war, where the author says that a horseman must have at his saddle two iron *scalae*. This work, commonly ascribed to Mauritius, is supposed to have been written in the end of the sixth century. [Beckman, p. 440]

There seems to be some discrepancy between the time in which Mauritius lived and the time when Beckman believed the work was written.

The Juan-Juans, a powerful group in central Asia, apparently suffered a rebellion of their

FIG. 7.4. One of the earliest stirrup representations, fourth century A.D., on jug from Silla Kingdom. From Chevenix-Trench, *A History of Horsemanship.*

Turkish subjects in the middle of the sixth century A.D. A group of Juan-Juans was driven out of Asia and moved across southern Russia to settle between the Danube and the Theiss. They became known as the Avars ("exiles"). They became a source of anxiety to the Byzantine Empire and its emperor, Maurice Tiberius, who in about 580 published a detailed military

FIG. 7.5. Miscellaneous antique stirrups. *(A)* T'ang Dynasty (A.D. 607–907) stirrups, the earliest found by the author. Courtesy of Metropolitan Museum of Art, New York City. *(B)* Anglo-Saxon (tenth- or eleventh-century) iron stirrups inlaid with bronze wire on the hoop and side plates in a spiral pattern. Height, 23.9 cm. Collected from the Thames River at Battersea. Courtesy of British Museum. *(C)* Antique stirrups. From Auguste Frederic Demmin, *A History of Arms and Armor*. *(D and E)* Primitive iron stirrups without slots for

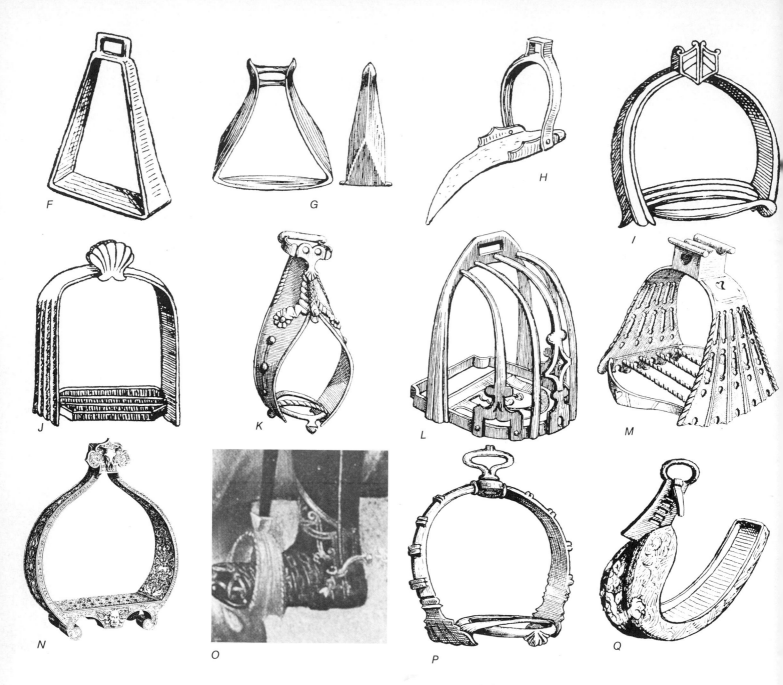

the leather. In the Naples Museum. *(F and G)* Early French stirrups of forged steel. *(H)* Stirrup for the long, pointed shoe of the Middle Ages. *(I)* Stirrup described in 1550 as "the perfect stirrup." *(J)* Stirrup described as "the evil stirrup." *(K)* Fifteenth-century stirrup shaped to prevent the foot from slipping through. It was forged and had a chiseled ornament. *(L)* Cage stirrup, designed to prevent the foot from slipping through and to protect it from sword cuts. The term "stirrup window" is derived from this design. *(M)* Stirrup of the heavy-armor period, with twisted bars to prevent the foot from slipping. It was unsatisfactory because of the difficulty of disengaging the foot. *(N)* Stirrup made in 1546 for Charles V by Antonio Bartolomeo Campi, of Pesaro, a famous armorer. It is of steel, damascened with gold and silver. In the Victoria and Albert Museum, London. *(O)* Detail from a portrait of Francis I, king of France, 1515–47. From Anthony Dent, *The Horse Through Fifty Centuries of Civilization. (P)* Stirrup dated 1430, rounder than the earlier forms and made of delicately forged iron. *(Q)* Seventeenth-century Japanese stirrup made of iron inlaid with brass and silver, weighing about four pounds. In Victoria and Albert Museum. *(D–N, P, Q)* from Trew, *The Accoutrements of the Riding Horse.*

manual known as the *Strategikon,* which among other things required the use of iron stirrups (Bivar).

The Vikings, who came in contact with the Avars, took their stirrups west and north, from there they were introduced into England and Norman France. There is no definite proof that stirrups were in France during the time of Charles Martel, who defeated the Moors in the Battle of Poitiers in 733, or even during the time of his grandson, Charlemagne (742–814), but logic would say that they were, and many sources agree.

Again there is no definite proof that the Moors took the stirrup across the northern edge of Africa and on to Spain, but descrip-tions of the battles between the Moors and Charles Martel lead one to conclude that the Moors were riding with stirrups. It is to be hoped that future researchers will be able to clarify this point.

The Battle of Hastings, fought in England in 1066, was the subject of the Bayeux Tapestry (now in the Bayeux Museum in France), created shortly after the battle. In many battle scenes on the tapestry, mounted, armored soldiers are shown riding with long stirrups in the fashion we now call *a la estradiota.* Several earlier authors cited the stirrups on the tapestry as the earliest real evidence of the first use of stirrups, a premise that we now know is incorrect.

CHAPTER 8

Saddles Through the Dark and Middle Ages

The Dark Ages commenced in the fifth century, more precisely in A.D. 410, with the fall of Rome to the barbarians. The period lasted until the emergence of medieval chivalry nearly seven centuries later. This age is rather poorly named; actually it was a period of much change and growth in human society. The name came about because of the lack of surviving information about this period. During the Dark Ages the accumulated knowledge of the world was held for safekeeping in the monasteries. The Venerable Bede (673–735), an English monastic, wrote that the English first began saddling horses about the year 631 (Tozer, pp. 88–89).

THE EIGHTH TO TENTH CENTURIES

The Moors successfully invaded Spain about 710, overrunning the country on light, very fast horses. They were less successful in France, where they were defeated at the Battle of Poitiers, mentioned above. Some authorities believe that at the time of this important battle the French had not yet accepted the stirrup as a part of the saddle. Jankovich pictures a contemporary statuette of Charlemagne, about which he writes: "It was damaged and restored in the sixteenth century, but it seems fair to assume that if the original had shown stirrups, the reproduction would have had them also." The statuette shows no stirrups.

Jankovich continues:

The Avar nation disappeared without trace, and their territory was divided among the Slavonic tribes under petty princes. The only traces remaining today of their rule in Central Europe [which lasted two and a half centuries], are graves of their horsemen from which stirrups—perhaps among the first seen in Europe—were often found. The saddle and the stirrup are what they bequeathed to European horsemanship. [P. 56]

The Avars were assimilated into the Frankish realm by their last treaty in 805. By the tenth century all western European horsemen had adopted the stirrup (Jankovich, p. 83).

THE ELEVENTH CENTURY

In the Battle of Hastings in 1066, when William the Conqueror defeated Harold, cavalry played a very important part, as shown on the Bayeux Tapestry. The knights shown in the tapestry and in later illustrations are shown riding in the typical *a la estradiota* position—with their legs extended straight out and down, a position that caused them to lean heavily against the cantle. The age of knighthood, of which horsemanship was an indispensable part, was introduced into England by the French at the Battle of Hastings (Vernon, p. 151). Jankovich commented:

The West European institution of "Chivalry" [which originally had the same meaning as "cavalry"] grew up around the nucleus of a school of horsemanship that owed something to Near Eastern and much to Germanic influence. The Knight of France—Norman pattern—became the typical figure of Western Christendom in the Middle Ages. [Jankovich, p. 72]

THE TWELFTH CENTURY

Tozer pointed out that toward the end of the twelfth century the Norman hauberk (chain-mail tunic) began giving way to heavy, all-encompassing mail armor, called the "perfect

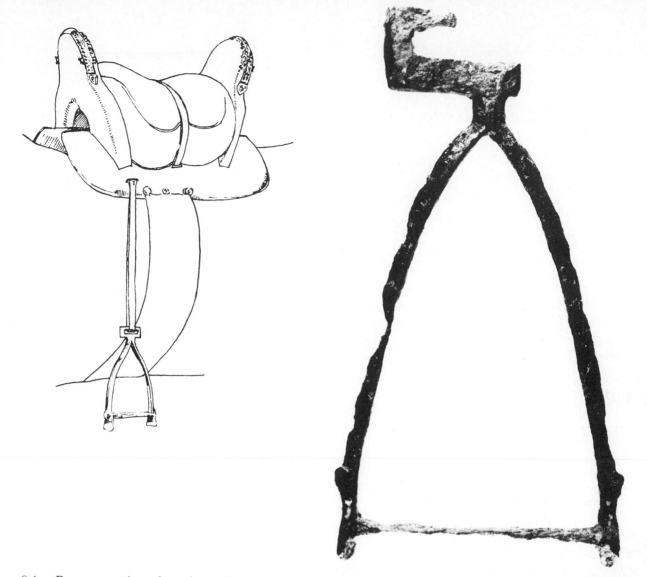

FIG. 8.1.   Reconstruction of an eleventh-century Polish saddle and stirrup. From Chenevix-Trench, *A History of Horsemanship*.

armor." Horses with much stamina were needed to carry men armored in mail. The invention of the crossbow lessened the protection of mail armor, which was replaced with plate armor in the fourteenth and fifteenth centuries. In the sixteenth century the invention of gunpowder in turn lessened the protection of this kind of armor, which finally disappeared.

Tylden (p. 22) described the saddle used with mail armor as having a rectangular wooden tree with no points to the arches, often two girths, and always a breastband. Jankovich says:

The saddle of chivalry consisted of two enormous rigid "bows," the hinder one of which "embraced" the pelvis of the rider, united by wooden bars which were more like planks. The seat was stuffed, as was the inside of the saddle next to the horse. The high, wide pommel rose sheer in front of the rider's stomach, with only just room between it and the cantle . . . Most saddles used on the march, for traveling and for hunting, seemed to be of the same pattern. They were not really practical or comfortable for either horse or rider, but in comparison with Roman models, they did represent a technical advance. [Jankovich, pp. 75–76]

Chenevix-Trench has written:

It is impossible to charge home with couched lance unless one is sitting securely in a saddle with a high cantle. Stirrups can, perhaps, be dispensed with in a charge where horse, rider, and lance are not required for hand–to–hand fighting in a mêlée but simply make up a single missile, directed straight at the enemy, to overthrow him by weight and impetus. But a saddle, with a proper saddle-tree shaped into a high cantle behind the rider, is necessary: without it, he will simply be forced, by the terrific shock of impact, back over his horse's croup and tail. The Sarmatians must have used a saddle with a solid wooden tree and high cantle; and, sure enough, contemporary, eyewitness illustrations of these vigorous barbarians show just such a saddle. [Chenevix-Trench, p. 58]

The difference between the seat of the armored knight on horseback and that of the mobile Moslem light-cavalryman is striking. As mentioned above, the armored knight rode *a la estradiota,* with long stirrup leathers, his legs straight and pushed forward, sitting with his back flush against the high cantle so that the shock of contact would not force him off the back of the horse. The Moslem cavalryman rode *a la jineta,* with very short stirrups and with his knees bent almost as if he were sitting in a chair. From this position he rose out of the saddle to use his weapons. He was lightly armored and therefore extremely fast and mobile. Since it was impossible for such lightly armored horsemen to combat a charge of heavily armored knights, the Moslems adopted hit-and-run guerrilla tactics.

Riding *a la estradiota* was thus practiced mostly by heavily armored cavalry for several centuries. The light cavalry was not introduced into Europe until the seventeenth century "under pressure from the invading Turks and through the perfection of firearms that could be effectively handled by horsemen" (Nickel,

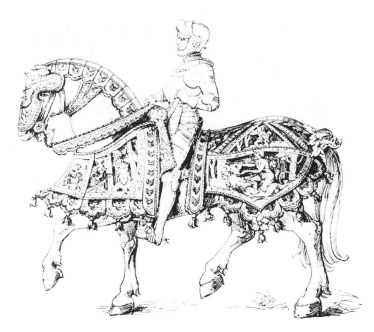

FIG. 8.2.   Armored horse and rider. From Robert M. Denhardt, *The Horse of the Americas.*

letter). The literature often incorrectly calls this riding style *a la brida,* which is, according to Arthur Woodward, guiding by reins and knees and refers only to light cavalry.

THE THIRTEENTH CENTURY

An interesting anecdote about the English Saddlers' Guild appears in an account of the companies, or guilds of London:

There is, in possession of the chapter of Westminster, a parchment agreement as to masses, etc., between the convent and the gild of Saddler's: undated, but probably made about 1154—not later than 1216: and, from its language, it seems very likely that the Saddler's gild was than an ancient body, dating from Saxon times. It is not enumerated among the adulterine gilds in the list of 1180. A charter was granted by Edward I in 1272; not to the London gild specially, but to the general body of Saddler's throughout the kingdom. . . .

The first charter to the Saddler's of London as a separate body was granted by Richard II in 1364/5. [Kent]

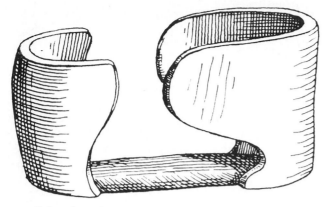

FIG. 8.3. Jousting saddle. From Trew, *The Accoutrements of the Riding Horse.*

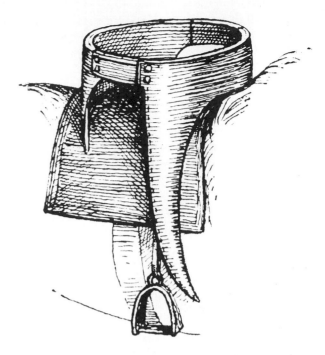

FIG. 8.4. A jousting saddle that completely encircles the rider. The side pieces are hinged and buckled. From Trew, *The Accoutrements of the Riding Horse.*

The invention of the crossbow began the transition from medium-sized cavalry horses to sturdier horses fitted with heavy saddles. The invention of firearms completely reversed this trend. Armor disappeared, and the light, mobile horse came back into its own.

The powerful English longbow was developed in Wales in the thirteenth century. Contrary to statements made by many historians, an arrow from a longbow would not penetrate mail armor. The value of the longbow lay in its distance-carrying power: many longbowmen firing many arrows could stop a cavalry charge by killing the horses.

THE FOURTEENTH AND FIFTEENTH CENTURIES

For many hundreds of years successions of barbaric nomads of the Russian and Asian steppes invaded and overcame more civilized, sedentary people who had learned to live in permanent homes and had become agriculturists. The conquering nomads, who had lived under extremely difficult climatic conditions, retained their mobility until in time they themselves became civilized and sedentary—only to have another group of nomads repeat the process. This process of conquest and absorption repeated itself constantly under various strong leaders, and the process changed only after the advent of gun-

FIG. 8.5. Fourteenth-century war saddle. From Trew, *The Accoutrements of the Riding Horse.*

FIG. 8.6.   The "steel wall of Western chivalry," from *Le Roman de Tristan,* 1468. The knights are riding *a la estradiota.* From Jankovich, *They Rode into Europe.*

powder, cannons, and guns. It was only then that the sedentary people were able to stand up to and defeat mounted barbarians.

The earliest recorded European gun dates from about 1360. The matchlock gun, of which the harquebus was one, was developed about 1450. This was the gun used by the conquistadors in the New World. With the advent of handguns and field artillery by the end of the fifteenth century, the day of the warrior knight was over (Rudorff, p. 277). From about the middle of the fifteenth century onward the light-horseman replaced the armored knight. A brilliant example was Oliver Cromwell's Ironsides, formed about 1643. They were a force of highly mobile cavalry with very light armor, mounted on light, agile horses. By their victories the Ironsides contributed greatly to the decline in the use of heavy armor.

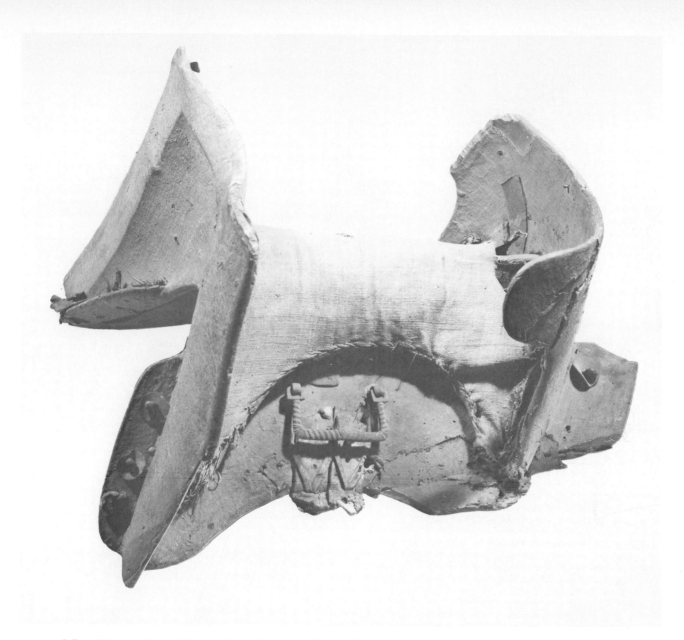

FIG. 8.7.   The saddle of Henry V of England (1387–1422). Courtesy of Westminster Abbey, London.

FIG. 8.8   Common saddle of the fifteenth century, Gervase Markham's "perfect saddle." Woodcut by Salomon de la Broue. From Trew, *The Accoutrements of the Riding Horse.*

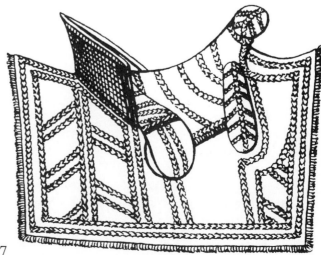

FIG. 8.9. *General Gattamelata,* bronze statue by Donatello (1382–1466). From Lady Viola (Meeking) Apsley, *Bridleways Through History.*

FIG. 8.10. *Bartolomeo Colleoni in Venice,* statue by Berrochio (modeled 1479–88, erected in 1496). From Trew, *The Accoutrements of the Riding Horse.*

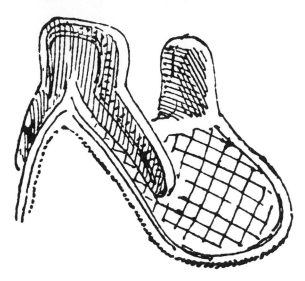

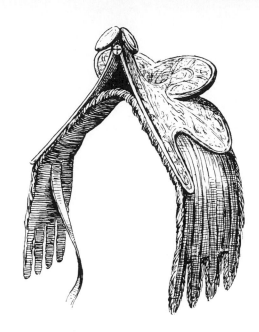

FIG. 8.11.   Italian war saddle, copied from Colleoni's statue (Fig. 8.10). From Demmin, *A History of Arms and Armor.*

FIG. 8.12.   Fifteenth-century French saddle, with two-lobed seat and two disks on the pommel to prevent the reins from falling when released. The style is suggestive of the American western saddle. From Trew, *The Accoutrements of the Riding Horse.*

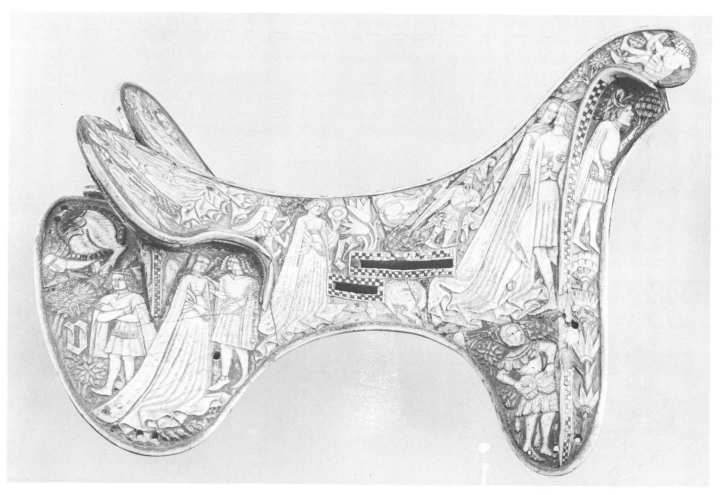

FIG. 8.13.   Ivory-covered saddle, fifteenth century. Courtesy of Metropolitan Museum of Art.

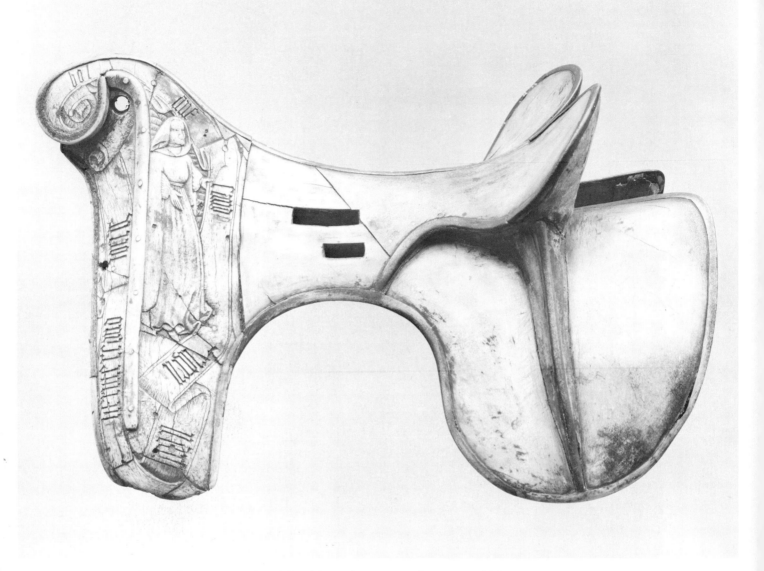

FIG. 8.14.   Ivory-covered saddle, fifteenth century. Courtesy of Metropolitan Museum of Art.

FIG. 8.15.   Detail from *The Vision of Saint Hubert* (fourteenth century), by the Master of Werden. From Chenevix-Trench, *A History of Horsemanship.*

CHAPTER 9

From the Time of Columbus and the Conquistadors to 1800

Columbus is credited with the reintroduction of the horse into the Western Hemisphere. Embarking on his second voyage in 1493, Columbus left Spain with the first horses to enter the Western Hemisphere in ten thousand years. He left Spain late in 1493 with twenty light-horsemen with lances and five mares and arrived in the West Indies before the end of the year. He cruised around for some time looking for a promising place to land and finally settled on Port Isabella, in what is now the Dominican Republic, on January 2, 1494.

When Columbus and later the Spanish conquerors arrived in the Western Hemisphere, there were no unloading docks. The horses were either driven overboard and forced to swim to shore or were unloaded in slings (Figs. 9.1 and 9.2). On coastal trips the men found ingenious ways to take their mounts with them (Fig. 9.3).

There is no evidence that any of Columbus's horses survived or left descendants in the New World. Ashton says that "the first horses to be reintroduced to the North American continent which survived were brought to Mexico by Hernando Cortes in 1519, when he conquered the Aztecs" (Ashton, 1944, p. 44).

The saddles that were brought to the Western Hemisphere in the early sixteenth century were primarily Spanish war saddles (see Fig. 9.7). This saddle was essentially the saddle of the Knights and crusaders, with a high cantle to prevent the warrior from being pushed over the back of his horse and with a high protecting fork. The rigging was of the centerfire type. A breast strap on the front and either a crupper or breeching in the rear held the saddle in place. The stirrup leathers hung directly behind the

fork, much as they do on the present-day saddle, and the rider rode *a la brida,* with long stirrup leathers and his legs in a straight position as had the knights of old (Livingston). The replica of Coronado's man (Fig. 9.8) is riding *a la brida.*

FIG. 9.1. Probably the first illustration of the early method of loading livestock on boats. At unloading, the animals were forced to jump overboard and swim ashore. From a seventeenth-century publication. From Robert M. Denhardt, "The Southwestern Cow-Horse," part 1, *Cattleman,* December, 1938.

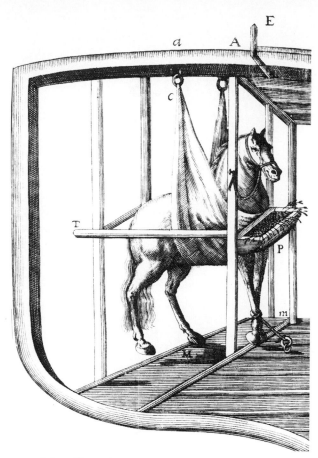

FIG. 9.2. How the conquistadors took their horses to the New World. From Chenevix-Trench, *A History of Horsemanship.*

FIG. 9.4. Aztec temple stormed by Spanish soldiers during the Conquest. From a sixteenth-century manuscript. From Jankovich, *They Rode into Europe.*

FIG. 9.3. Boating horses across rivers and bays. From an early book published in Mexico. From Denhardt, "The Southwestern Cow-Horse," part 2, *Cattleman,* January, 1939.

FIG. 9.5. Hernando Cortés, conqueror of Mexico, and his warhorse, El Morzillo (The Black One), in armor. Culver Pictures, Inc.

FIG. 9.6. The spread of the horse in North America. From Denhardt, *The Horse of the Americas.*

FIG. 9.7. Sixteenth-century Spanish war saddle, a type that may have been brought to America by the conquistadors. In the Royal Armor Museum, Madrid, Spain. Photograph courtesy of Paul Rossi, Woodland Park, Colorado.

The rider in the sixteenth-century drawing (Fig. 9.4) appears to be riding *a la jineta.* According to Pierce Chamberlain, if they rode without armor, they rode with short stirrup leathers, *a la jineta.* When riding with armor they rode with long stirrup leathers and straight legs, *a la brida.*

A stirrup probably brought by the Spanish conquistadors was the flat bronze stirrup that had originated in Turkey (Fig. 9.9). This stirrup had a broad footplate and high sides and weighed up to ten pounds (Stalter).

One of the early stirrups made in North America was the wrought-iron cruciform stirrup with an opening in the center of the cross for the rider's foot. The one shown in Fig. 9.10 is eighteen inches high and thirteen inches wide. Such stirrups weighed as much as eleven pounds.

There appears to be a disagreement among authorities about whether these early American

44

FIG. 9.8.   A replica of "Coronado's man." Courtesy of Los Angeles County Museum of Natural History.

stirrups were made in America by the conquistadors or were developed later—as late as the first half of the eighteenth century. None of them are found in the art or literature of the Old World until after their appearance in the New World. The following statement by R. Zschille is apparently the basis of the controversy:

The oldest stirrups of Mexico are extremely large and very heavy; they are in the form of a cross and therefore are called *estriberas de Crux*—"cross stirrups." . . . No doubt, the note of Francisco López de Gómara in his *Historia de la Conquistas de Hernando Cortes,* published in 1826 by Carlos de Bastamente, refers to the enormous stirrups: ". . . that the Spanish leaders cut down the Aztecs who had not yet fallen under the blows and thrusts of their swords and lances in the battle of Otumba, with their huge iron stirrups, called *mitras,* whose form resembled more that of a cross than a bishop's miter and were very heavy." This note dates from the time of the wars of Hernando Cortes against the Aztecs between 1519 and 1521 and this gives us some clues about the approximate age of these stirrups. [Quoted in Hotz, p. 152]

Ford E. Smith, eminent lawyer and stirrup collector-historian of Seattle, Washington, says that in Guatemala this stirrup is known as the "Cruz de Alvarado" (Alvarado was the conquistador sent by Cortes about 1520 to conquer and pacify the area south of Mexico). According to Smith, the priests pointed out to the natives that Alvarado was a holy man, as evidenced by his cross-shaped stirrups.

Contradicting these statements is the sixteenth-century drawing of an Aztec temple being stormed by Spanish soldiers and a cavalryman (Fig. 9.4). The horseman is not using the cruciform stirrup. Of course this is not positive proof one way or another, since we do not know whether the drawing was done by an artist who was present or whether the artist had an eye for such details.

Alan Probert has proposed that the cruciform stirrups originated in the Middle Americas. In a letter to King Carlos III (r. 1759–88) the bishop of Ciudad Real De Chiapa, Mexico,

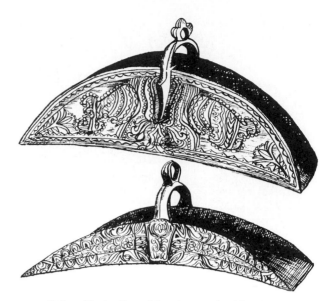

FIG. 9.9. Early Spanish stirrups in North America. Marcile Weist Stalter, "The Mexican T-shaped Stirrup," *Western Horseman,* January–February 1946.

pointed out that the stirrups were in the shape of a bishop's miter, which caused the king to issue an edict on July 20, 1778, to the governor of Guatemala to abolish this profane custom. These stirrups then went underground and be-

FIG. 9.10. Middle-American cruciform stirrup of the seventeenth and eighteenth centuries. This stirrup is 18 inches high and 13 inches wide. It belonged to Emperor Maximilian I, who sent it to Austria not long before his death in Mexico. From Demmin, *A History of Arms and Armor.*

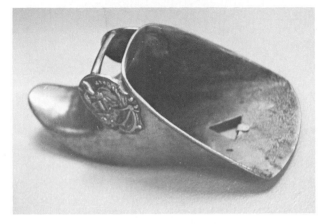

FIG. 9.12.   Solid-brass Spanish colonial shoe stirrup, the style used in South America. Courtesy of Smith Collection, Seattle.

was a sand-cast brass stirrup of shoelike design (Fig. 9.12). But because of the shortage of metals in the New World and the increasing demand for saddles, North American Spanish stirrups were soon being hand-carved from flat, solid, single pieces of wood (Figs. 9.13 and 9.14). Some

FIG. 9.11.   Cruciform stirrup (missing brass knob), known as Cruz de Alvarado in Guatemala. The stirrup weighs 11 pounds. Courtesy of Ford E. Smith Collection, Seattle, Washington.

came hard to find. They are now valuable collectors' items. According to Stephen W. Grancsay:

The best-known "document" showing such stirrups is an oil painting representing the main square of Mexico City in the year 1767, with the Committee of the Viceroy, the Marquis de Croix, proceeding from the palace to the Cathedral. In this painting similar cross-shaped stirrups may also be seen suspended in several metal merchants' shops.

Probably the favorite replacement for the crosslike stirrup in Central and South America

FIG. 9.13.   Early North American Spanish wooden stirrup with tapadero. From Paul A. Rossi, "The Vaquero," *American Scene,* vol. 11, no. 4.

FIG. 9.14. Early North American Spanish wooden stirrup, without tapadero, showing ornate carved detailing. From Rossi, "The Vaquero," *American Scene,* vol. 11, no. 4.

FIG. 9.15. An old print showing a Spanish caballero roping a steer. Note that the other end of the rope is tied to the horse's tail. Miguel Bracho, "Schools of Riding in the New World—a Jineta," *Western Horseman,* September, 1950.

were made of cottonwood. Through the center was cut a toehold, with a stirrup-leather slot cut in the top. Later the front was covered with a round sheet of hand-tooled leather and still later with a tapadero. Ford E. Smith has in his collection one of these stirrups, which came from Guatemala. He believes that it is carved of tough quebracho. It measures 4½ inches from front to back, and was obviously suspended from a rope instead of leather, as shown by the rope grooves worn in the stirrup-leather slot.

Once the Spaniards had assured their hold on the New World, their attention shifted from military conquest to colonial development. In many parts of the Spanish Americas cattle raising was the dominant pursuit. The Mexican vaquero (cowboy) saddle of the 1700s was developed when the vaqueros discovered that the old Spanish war saddle was not practical for working cattle in the wide-open spaces of the Americas. The vaquero saddle consisted of a hide-covered tree with a rather low cantle, a

rigging in the Spanish (single) style, and a much lowered fork with no horn.

After the Spaniards in America discarded pike poles and hocking irons in handling cattle, they revived the use of the lariat. The lariat is very old; it goes back at least to the ancient Scythians and the Asiatic nomads, as well as to the Hungarian hussars.

After a cow was roped, there had to be some place to tie the home end of the lariat. The vaqueros at first hard-and-fast-tied it to the horse's tail (Figs. 9.15 and 9.16). That was too brutal, and they began tying it to the cinch ring or to a D ring anchored firmly behind the cantle on the fan of the bar. The high fork was lowered, the cantle was shortened, and the rigging was moved forward, forming what we now call the Spanish style (Livingston). The saddle was rawhide-covered only. Later a small triangular piece of leather was tacked to the top of the bars, the apex of the triangle being tacked halfway up the front side of the cantle. This seat was called a *half-rigged seat* (it has never been called a "half seat"). There were no skirts on these saddles, and the stirrup was cut from one solid piece of oak. This early Spanish saddle design was used, with only minor modifications, for two hundred years.

The history of the saddle in the New World is tied directly to the development of the trade

FIG. 9.16. Roped steer, showing lasso tied to horse's tail. Once caught, the steer was moved by being pulled in this manner. From Bracho, "Schools of Riding in the New World—a Jineta." From *Western Horseman,* September, 1950.

routes. Therefore, a short history of colonial expansion is useful at this point. After the Spaniards settled Mexico, they began to expand their colonies into what is now the United States.

Santa Fe, New Mexico, was founded in 1610 under Pedro de Peralta. Taos was established in the eighteenth century. San Antonio was established on May 1, 1718, by a Spanish military expedition from Monclova in northern Mexico. The mission priests ranged north from Baja California to San Francisco, which was founded in 1775. Where the Spaniards rode, their saddles went with them.

Meanwhile, the Americans started their trek west of the Allegheny Mountains in 1770, after Daniel Boone opened the way. Saint Louis had been founded by the French in 1764 as a main trading post on the Mississippi River. The Americans who rode came west on their flat English saddles and continued to use them during the frontier period.

The Conestoga wagon was used from 1750 to about 1850 on the long migrations to the West. The wagon was quite often pulled by a three-team unit and was driven by a rider who rode a typical Conestoga saddle on the back of the near wheel horse.

FIG. 9.17. Detail from painting by Félix Achilles Saint-Aulaire in 1821, showing the banks of the Ohio at an unspecified location. The saddle is a type of English "flat saddle." From Robert G. Athearn, *Young America,* American Heritage New Illustrated History of the United States, vol. 5.

CHAPTER 10

From 1800 to 1849

The purchase from France in 1803 of the Louisiana Territory annexed to the United States a great area of land west of the Mississippi to the Rocky Mountains. Meriwether Lewis and William Clark, starting from Saint Louis, made their famous westward exploration of this territory from 1804 to 1806. Lieutenant Zebulon Pike began exploring west and southwest of Saint Louis, arriving in Santa Fe in 1807.

In the very early 1800s the saddle that was being used from Santa Fe to California was a development of the colonial Mexican saddle. The tree was of native wood covered with rawhide. Horned saddles were used in Europe in the seventeenth century, and an illustration of the Villasur Expedition of 1720 shows what is probably a European horned saddle (Hotz). New World saddles did not have horns until between 1820 and 1835. On saddles before that time the pommel (fork) and cantle protruded through slits in the *mochila,* or tree covering. The mochila was removable and frequently had large pockets on each side of the fork. Behind the mochila was the anquera. The anquera was originally a piece of leather armor used by Spanish frontier troops. By the 1800s it was serving as a rumble seat. It was attached to the top side of the rear rigging strap as it passed over the fan of the bars and was used to protect a señorita's dress when she rode double behind her Californio. There were no skirts on this saddle. The rigging, in the three-quarter position, was single. The one-piece hand-carved wooden stirrup was usually covered with a distinctive three-piece tapadero, which allowed only toe room. There were no fenders on the stirrup leathers.

Zebulon Pike, during his scouting trip in New Mexico in 1807, described a horned saddle that he had seen there, but paintings and drawings made during that period do not show such a saddle (the earliest photographs showing horned saddles date from 1854, taken during the Crimean War). There is a common misconception that what has been termed the "horned Santa Fe saddle" was in existence at that time, but, as mentioned above, it has been established that the horn did not come into being until sometime between 1820 and 1835. Beginning in 1837, artists were painting saddles with horns. A saddle of the type described by Pike could not have existed before 1860 or 1870. This misconception has arisen from the works of famous western artists of the period from 1870 to 1890 who depicted such saddles in paintings of subjects of a much earlier day. There is thus a close resemblance between the Hope saddle as we believe it to have appeared and the Santa Fe saddle the artists drew. It is possible that the Santa Fe saddle was an offshoot of the Hope saddle.

From 1821 to 1844 traders from Missouri, especially from Saint Louis, traded goods to Santa Fe and brought back goods, among which were saddles (Carmichael). Most of the trappers rode flat saddles or dragoon saddles, over which was thrown a buffalo robe, held in place by a surcingle. Though this fact distresses some proponents of the "western cult," it has been documented by paintings by artists who lived and painted during the early 1800s.

Saddle horns were common by the 1850s. The horns on early Spanish saddles, unlike the large knobs or flat, platterlike horns that came later, had thin necks with relatively small horn caps (Fig. 10.4). A few years later came the

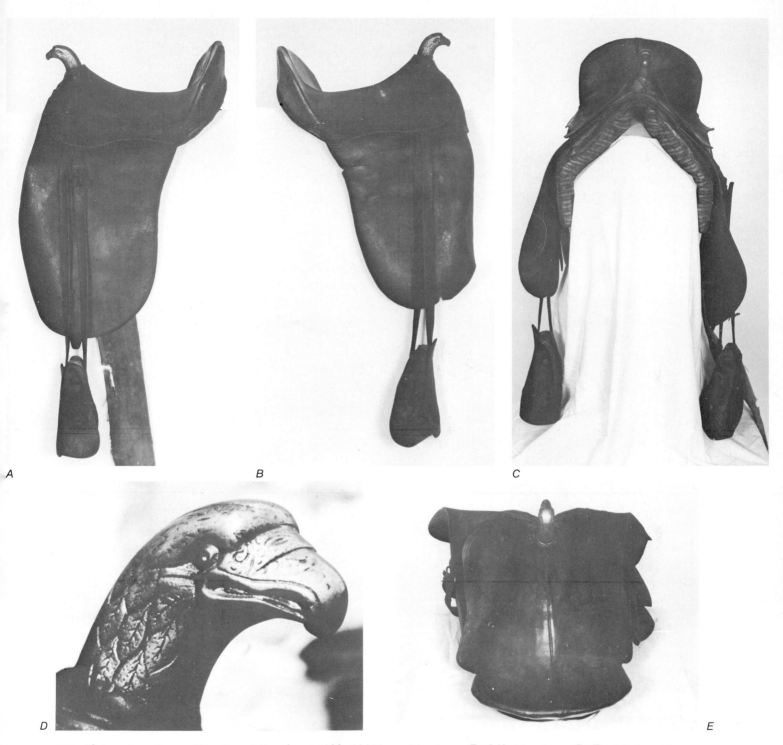

FIG. 10.1.   American officer's saddle, about 1830. *(A)* Near-side view. *(B)* Off-side view. *(D)* Eagle's head brass horn. *(C)* Front view. *(E)* Top view. Courtesy of Fort Sill Museum, Fort Sill, Oklahoma.

FIG. 10.2.   General Antonio López de Santa Anna in military dress, Mexico, 1847. From *Gleason's Pictorial Drawing Room Companion,* May 15, 1852.

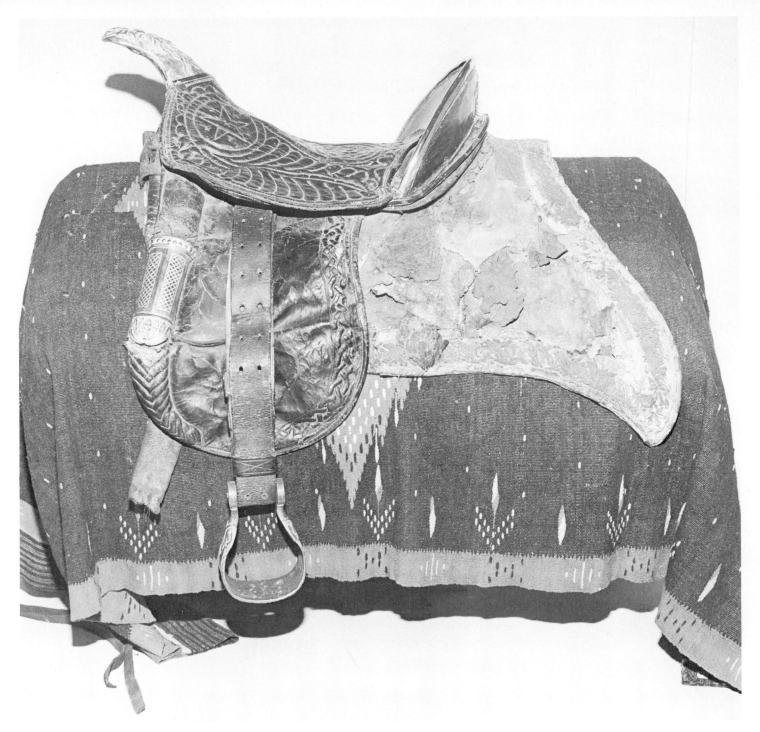

FIG. 10.3.   The saddle General Santa Anna rode into Texas at the head of his army to put down the Texans' rebellion. After his defeat at the Battle of San Jacinto in 1836, when Texas gained its independence, his saddle was taken as spoils of war, and the general was made to walk home to Mexico. General Sam Houston's men bought the saddle for $850 and presented it to him. It is decorated with inlaid gold and platinum. According to Houston's correspondence, the stirrups are not the original ones. Courtesy of Sam Houston Museum, Huntsville, Texas.

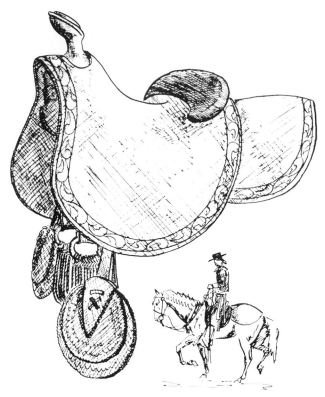

FIG. 10.4.   Early California saddle with mochila and anquera, after 1835. Drawing by Phil Livingston. From *Appaloosa News,* January, 1972.

Hope saddle, with its short, stubby neck and large, flat horn cap.

Not much information about the Hope saddle can be found. It appeared in Texas around 1846 (Woodward), and several saddles were copied from it. The saddle was not much more than a tree with a horn. The California variety was rawhide covered with a mochila. It had no skirts and no jockeys. There was nothing to soften the impact on the tree but blankets between the tree and the horse and blankets or robes between the tree and the rider.

The Hope saddle was used experimentally by the First and Second U.S. Cavalry regiments between 1855 and 1858 (Haley, n.d.). In 1856, General Joseph E. Johnston, commanding the Second Cavalry, reported that all his officers who were able to do so bought Hope saddles

for their own use (his own Hope saddle is shown in Fig. 10.5). Four hundred Hope saddles were ordered by the army from Rice and Childress of San Antonio in 1857.

Tapaderos as we know them today go back to the 1830s. Centerfire rigs appeared in California long before the gold rush in 1849. Both round and square skirts were used. The round skirt later became so common that the terms *round skirt* and *California skirt* became synonymous (Shipman, 1962).

FIG. 10.4*A*.   Conestoga saddle. The rider rode on the near wheel horse to control the wagon.

FIG. 10.5. *(opposite)*   Hope or Hope-style saddles. *(A)* Off-side, front, and top views of Hope saddle. Courtesy of Fort Sill Museum. *(B)* General H. J. Kilpatrick's Hope saddle. Courtesy of Smithsonian Institution, Washington, D.C. *(C)* General Joseph E. Johnston's Hope saddle. Courtesy of Museum of the Confederacy, Richmond, Virginia. *(D)* Hope-style saddles in the Museum of the Horse, Patagonia, Arizona. Courtesy of Ms. Ann Stradling.

A

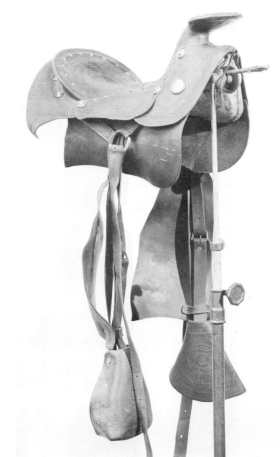

B

C

FIG. 10.6.   Saddle made by James Marshall, a saddlemaker who lived in Kelsey, California, from the late 1850s to his death in 1885. Marshall was the man who discovered gold at Sutter's Mill and started the California gold rush in 1849. Marshall and Sutter were bilked out of everything by squatters. Courtesy of Sacramento State Parks, West Sacramento, California.

CHAPTER 11

From 1850 to 1869

In the 1850s the mochila was still the preferred alternative to a raw tree. The mochila was removable and could be slipped on or off the saddle skeleton (Fig. 11.1). By the early 1860s the Mother Hubbard saddle had appeared. It was an outgrowth of the saddle on which the mochila was adhered permanently to the saddletree with saddle strings. The Mother Hubbard had squared corners and did not have skirts underneath the bars or fenders on the stirrup leathers. The stirrups were still of the one-piece, hand-carved wooden type, although occasionally iron rings were used instead. By 1866 the Mother Hubbard was being used on long trail drives by most Texas cowboys (Carmichael).

The Yorktown corus (mochila) saddle (see Fig. 12.15) was popular from the 1850s through the 1870s (Haley, 1938). There were no double-rigged saddles during the Civil War, as far as can be determined (Haley, 1938).

The large, flat Mexican horn caps appeared after 1860, and all of them were in Mexico; they had not yet been adopted in the United States (Woodward, 1961, p. 37). Such horns, referred to as "dinner-plate horns," never had much acceptance in the United States except for parade and show use.

The Morgan saddle, which had much the same appearance as the Hope saddle, was used by middle-western farmers and southern plantation owners (Figs. 11.5 and 11.6). It appeared in the late 1860s or early 1870s.

Steamed bent-wood stirrups were in existence at least by 1860 and perhaps much earlier, though 1860 is the earliest date I have been able to document. They replaced the one-piece hand-carved Spanish stirrups. Regulation 1612 of *The Revised Regulations for the Army of the U.S.,* 1861 specified "two stirrups (hickory or oak, made of one piece bent." The *U.S. Army Ordnance Manual of 1862* shows steamed bent-wood stirrups on the model 1859 McClellan cavalry saddle. It also shows fenders on the stirrup leathers.

In the history of the American West the pony express has been built into a legend out of all proportion to its importance or duration. The first pony-express ride began at Saint Joseph, Missouri, on April 3, 1860. The completion of the transcontinental telegraph line in October, 1861, ended the need for the express. It officially ceased operations on October 26, 1861, and the last mail was delivered to San Francisco in November of that year (Settle and Settle). But the pony express lasted long enough to develop its own saddle!

The pony-express saddle was well adapted to the job. It was a light, skeleton-rigged saddle that stayed with the horse. The removable mochila had a locked mail pouch at each of the four corners (Fig. 11.13). When the rider galloped into a station, the mochila was removed and put on a fresh horse, and the mail continued on. Many of these saddles were made by Israel Landis in Saint Joseph, Missouri.

After the Civil War ended, full double rigging began appearing on Texas saddles (Haley, 1938). The front and rear rigging rings were connected with a connector strap to give the rigging more strength and rigidity. The flank cinch had arrived. The mochilas that covered the saddletree were squared at the corners, and the stirrups were made of steamed and bent pieces of flat wood. The original wooden stirrup of this type was called the *box* or *box car* because of its large, square shape (Fig. 27.2[A]). Skirts as we know them appeared around 1868.

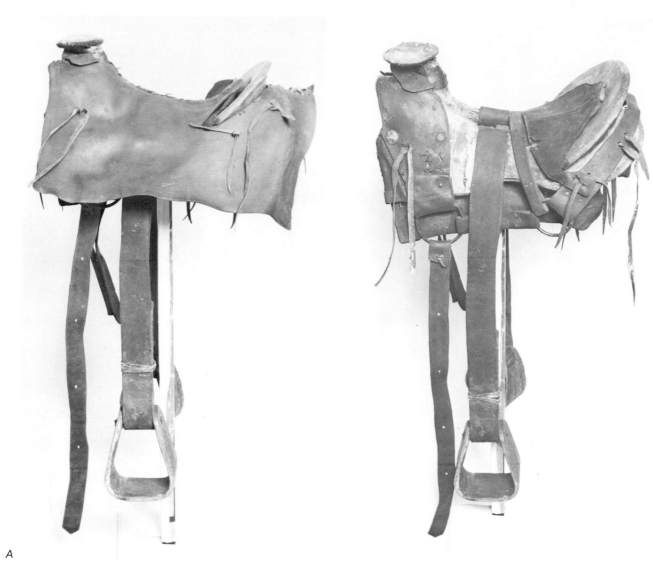

A   B

FIG. 11.1.   Texas saddle. *(A)* With mochila covering. *(B)* Without mochila, showing saddle construction. Courtesy of Fort Sill Museum.

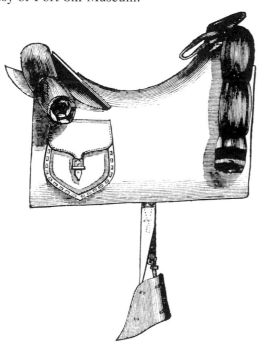

FIG. 11.2.   California saddle, late 1850s. From Randolph B. Marcy, *The Prairie Traveler.*

58

FIG. 11.3.   California ranchero saddle with removable mochila, about 1855. Courtesy of Los Angeles County Museum of Natural History, Los Angeles, California.

FIG. 11.4. Main & Winchester's Saddlery and Harness Warehouse, at the corner of Battery and Richmond streets, San Francisco, 1862. From *California Farmer,* September 12, 1862.

FIG. 11.5. Morgan saddles, 1894–95. From Smith-Worthington, catalog, ca. 1905.

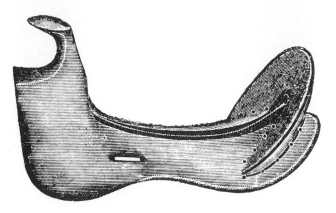

FIG. 11.6. Morgan saddletree. From L. D. Stone Company, San Francisco, catalog, ca. 1905.

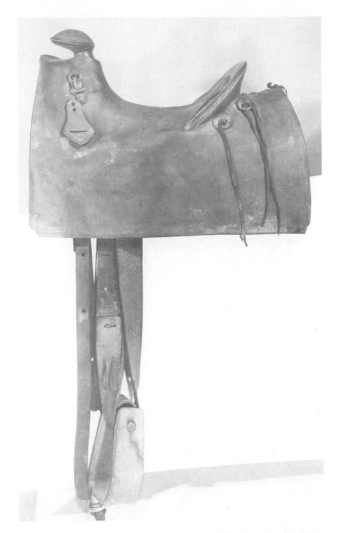

FIG. 11.7. Applehorn Mother Hubbard saddle, 1860s. Courtesy of Phil Livingston.

A

FIG. 11.8. Saddle of General Eugene A. Carr. *(A)* Three-quarter front view. *(B)* Three-quarter rear view. Courtesy of Idaho State Historical Society, Boise, Idaho.

FIG. 11.9. Another saddle of General Eugene A. Carr. Courtesy of Museum of New Mexico, Santa Fe.

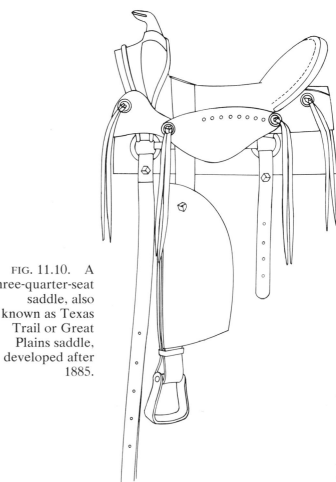

FIG. 11.10. A three-quarter-seat saddle, also known as Texas Trail or Great Plains saddle, developed after 1885.

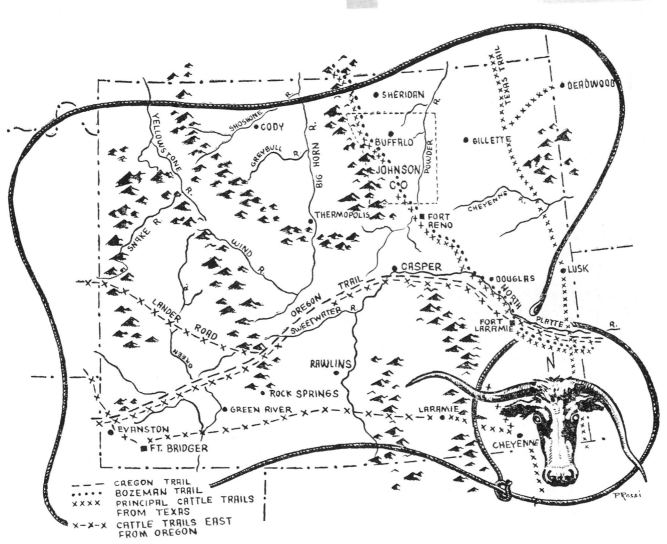

FIG. 11.11. Principal cattle-drive trails to the north from the Texas area. From James E. Serven, "Cattle, Guns, and Cowboys," *Arizona Highways,* October, 1970.

FIG. 11.12. Cattle-drive trails into Wyoming. Courtesy of Maurice Frink, *Cow Country Cavalcade,* Wyoming Cattlemen's Association.

FIG. 11.13. Replica of the original pony-express saddle and mochila. Courtesy of Pony Express Museum, Saint Joseph, Missouri.

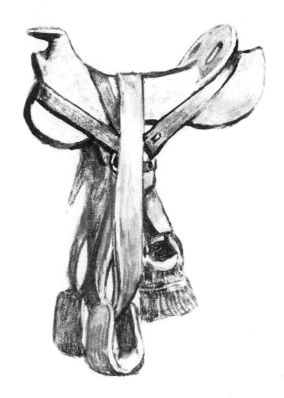

FIG. 11.14. Pony-express saddle without mochila. From Nick Eggenhofer, *Wagons, Mules, and Men: How the Frontier Moved West.*

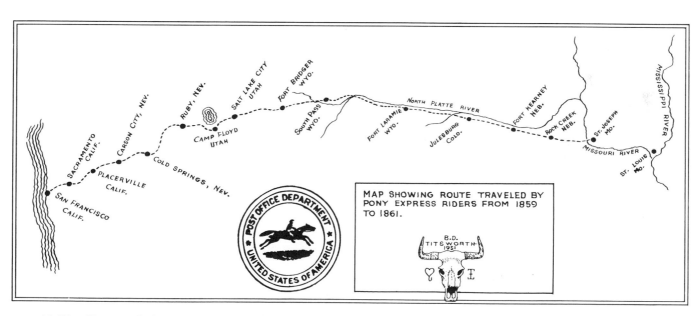

FIG. 11.15. Route of the pony express. From W. H. McNeal, "The Pony Express," *Western Horseman,* December, 1951.

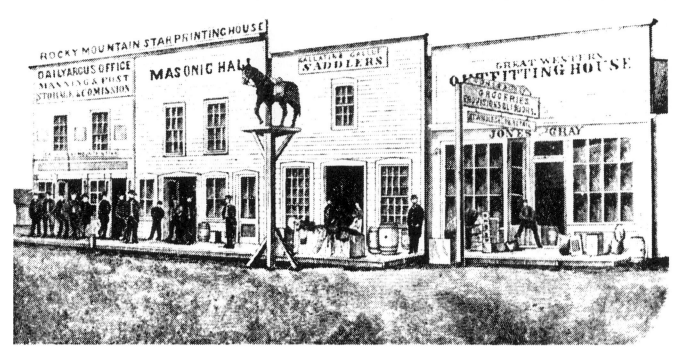

FIG. 11.16. Cheyenne, Wyoming, 1868. Gallup and Gallatin's Saddler's Shop is in the center. Courtesy of Wyoming Historical Society, Cheyenne.

FIG. 11.17. This saddle was presented to Major General Philip H. Sheridan by a Mexican officer in 1866. It is a typical nonmilitary, gentleman-rider's charro saddle. The saddle maker was Felipe del Aguilar. Courtesy of Smithsonian Institution.

FIG. 11.18. Theodore Roosevelt's saddle, made by E. L. Gallatin, Cheyenne, Wyoming Territory. Courtesy of Theodore Roosevelt National Memorial Park, Medora, North Dakota.

CHAPTER 12

From 1870 to 1899

The date of the first use of the steel horn on a saddletree is still a matter of some conjecture. Until that time the saddle horn and the fork were cut from one piece of wood. Unfortunately, the wooden horn had a tendency to break off when a heavy animal hit the end of the lariat, making the saddle useless for roping or working cattle. At first these useless saddles were sold to Indians at a cheap price. Sometime, probably in the 1870s, replacement horns of steel became available. Some writers claim that the steel horn was made as early as the 1860s, but I have been unable to document the earlier date.

At about the same time, fenders made their appearance on the stirrup leathers. They had not been needed with the Mother Hubbard saddle, although some later models of this saddle have them.

The California saddles of this period were modified with a slightly swelled fork with a high steel horn bolted to it. This horn, with the cap pitched back, was ideal for the dally man (Fig. 12.1). The cantle of the new saddle was higher and had less slope than the Texas saddle of the same period. The fork-and-cantle combination formed a deeper seat, which made the saddle popular for riding "bad" horses. It was the forerunner of the swell fork.

The rigging was usually in the centerfire position (although in the Northwest, especially in Montana and Wyoming, the three-quarter was preferred) and was nailed to the tree under the fork cover. The skirts, usually square, were lined with wool to help hold the saddle blanket in place. Sheepskin linings were first seen by Kellner in 1881 (Haley, 1938). The *corus rig* had appeared in Texas in the 1870s (Haley,

1938). Also by 1870 the Mother Hubbard saddle, which had been so common throughout the central plains and on the cattle trails from Texas, had been replaced by the three-quarter-seat saddle (Fig. 12.3). This saddle, even as late as the early 1880s, had no seat jockey. The fenders were long and hung high and were used until the seat jockey was devised, around 1885

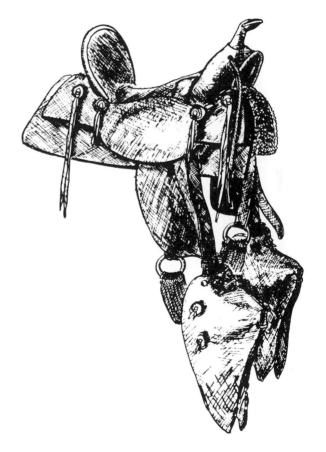

FIG. 12.1. California saddle, ca. 1900. Courtesy of Phil Livingston.

FIG. 12.2. Page from Main and Winchester's 1882 catalog. From A. Sheldon Pennoyer, *The Last American Frontier.*

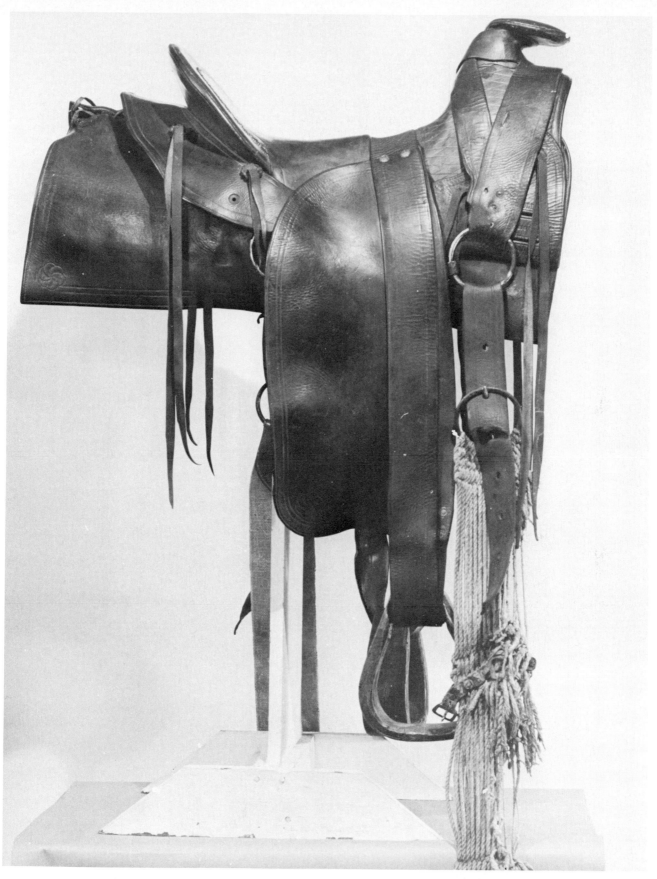

FIG. 12.3.   A. J. Collins saddle with a three-quarter seat, early 1870s. It has no side jockeys. Courtesy of Wyoming Historical Society.

FIG. 12.4. Frank Meanea saddle with a three-quarter seat, after 1885. It has a side jockey. Courtesy of Wyoming Historical Society.

(Fig. 12.4). This saddle had a back jockey (Rice, 1974). All the three-quarter-seat saddles had slick forks.

In the literature on the saddle appear many references to the *Sam Stagg rigging* (Fig. 12.5).

FIG. 12.5. Sam Stagg rigging around the horn. From Fay E. Ward, *The Cowboy at Work.*

In this type of construction the front rigging leather is looped around the horn and goes down each side of the slick fork to a rigging ring. It is made of one piece of leather. In later styles this rigging consisted of two front rigging leathers, one going from the rigging ring up and over the front of the fork of the saddle in front of the horn, with the second front rigging leather looped around the horn in Sam Stagg style. This was often accomplished with only one piece of leather, properly slit lengthwise so that the rear, narrower piece could be wrapped around the horn, as was done by Gallatin in 1862 when he made Colonel Leavenworth's saddle (Fig. 40.1).

In all my research and review of the literature I have never been able to learn exactly who Sam Stagg was. Lee M. Rice has written:

Sam Stagg and his saddle rigging has long been an unsolved mystery for students of western saddlery. No doubt he operated a small one-man saddle shop somewhere in the Southwest, most likely in Texas. The Sam Stagg rigging came into use after the "Mochila" [Mother Hubbard] was discarded and was widely used by many saddleries east of the "Rockies" up to about 1900. After that date it was only made up on special orders. Around 1900 the swell fork was gaining wide favor which put an end to the rigging over the fork.

Before the days of taxes, few small saddle shops kept books and therefore left no written records. The history of the Sam Stagg rigging can only be arrived at by deduction. The first American saddle

forks were whittled from the natural fork of a small oak tree. The distance in front of the horn was too short to hold a rigging of sufficient strength. Using a wider strip of leather, splitting both ends from both sides of the horn, then giving the narrow strips a half turn around the horn gave the rigging more strength as well as holding it in place.

As no record of Sam Stagg has yet been found, this is my conclusion gained from my long experience with the western stock saddle. [Rice, 1974]

Paul A. Rossi, the noted sculptor, artist, and researcher of the American West, has a comment on Sam Stagg: "I have long felt that we may never know who Sam Stagg was. It is just a name that has come down the line, even though I keep hoping someday that I, or some

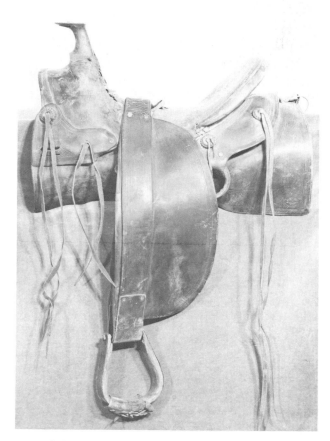

FIG. 12.6. Saddle said to have been used on the ranch of the Marquis de Morès, at Medora, North Dakota Territory. Courtesy of State Historical Society of North Dakota, Bismarck.

one, will blow the dust off an old document, article or what have you, and there will be Sam Stagg" (Rossi, 1974).

The roll cantle, which later became the *Cheyenne roll,* apparently was first made in Frank Meanea's shop. It was shown in his catalog of 1874 (Rice, 1974). The addition of the roll was strictly ornamental.

The California round skirts appeared in California in the early 1870s (Fig. 12.7). Because

of their great popularity there, they are associated with that state (Rice, 1948). Until then the Californians had used both round and square skirts.

The Texans liked square skirts (Fig. 12.8).

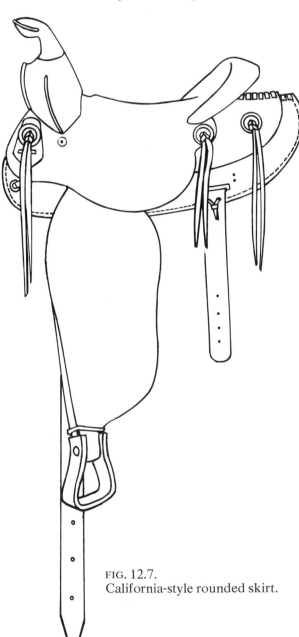

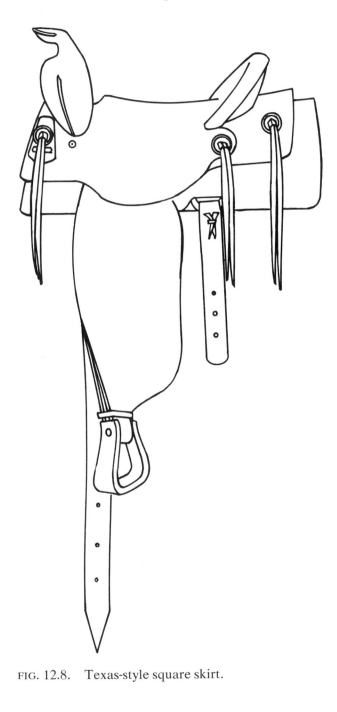

FIG. 12.7.
California-style rounded skirt.

FIG. 12.8.   Texas-style square skirt.

They were so popular there that the square skirt is still known today as a Texas skirt. Saddles made in Pueblo, Colorado, had square skirts because many of them were purchased by Texans.

Doghouse (wooden) *stirrups* were first made in the 1860s or 1870s. Turner steel stirrups were used on Gallup and Frazier saddles in the 1880s (Rice, 1974).

In 1877, H. C. and J. R. Still patented a cast-iron steel fork with an integral steel horn (Fig. 12.9). The horn was cast hollow to lighten the weight. On top of the horn was a wooden cap.

Another steel-fork patent was issued to E. B. Light in 1879. Instead of a solid casting, this fork was wood reinforced with a steel strap on the underneath side of the gullet, countersunk into the fork and bolted down at the lower edges of the fork. On top of the fork was a hollow-steel horn. The hollow neck of the horn was placed over the outside of a neck of wood on top of the fork. This arrangement was bolted together from a countersink in the top of the horn, down through the neck, and through the steel reinforcing strap on the underneath side of the gullet (Fig. 12.10).

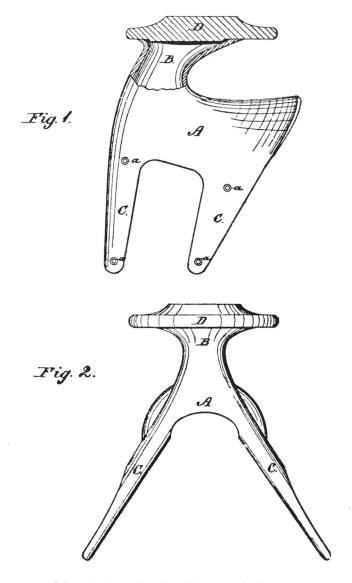

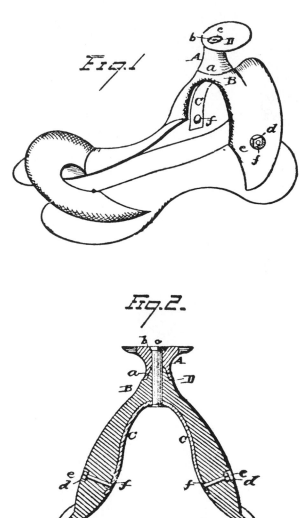

FIG. 12.9. H. C. and J. R. Still steel fork, patented September 18, 1887.

FIG. 12.10. E. B. Light's steel fork, patented December 9, 1879.

The cast-steel fork patented by the Stills in 1877 necessarily had a steel horn. The same was the case with the fork patented by Light in 1879. It was obvious that the day of steel horns in one form or another had arrived.

The L. D. Stone Saddlery, as shown in its catalog of approximately 1905, sold a patented steel fork (Fig. 12.11). This fork had wooden

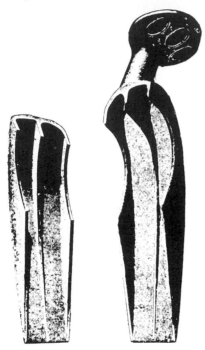

FIG. 12.11. L. D. Stone's steel fork, inside view. The manufacturer claimed that it would withstand a 2,000-pound pressure. The fork is countersunk into and fits close to the bars, fastened to them with wrought-iron nails. From Stone, catalog, ca. 1905.

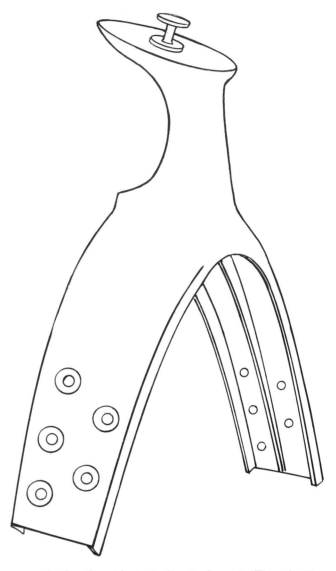

FIG. 12.12. Steel fork similar to Stone's (Fig. 12.11).

attachments on both the front and the back sides to form out the entire fork.

In 1882, Theodore E. Meanea, Frank Meanea's brother, who had a saddletree shop in Denver, patented a saddletree with a steel horn. The neck of the wooden horn was left on the fork, and the steel horn he patented covered the wood and greatly strengthened it. His steel horn was not only screwed to the sides of the fork with horn points, somewhat as horns are mounted today, but also bolted through the top of the

horn cap down through the fork to the top side of the gullet (Fig. 12.13).

I have seen another reinforced fork in which a steel rod had been placed diagonally internally in each side of the fork. It was intended to serve as a reinforcing bar, much as a bar is used in concrete. Today steel forks have disappeared, and their period of use was very short, probably because they tended to work loose. The name "steel-fork saddles" continued to be used for some time by various saddlemakers to designate saddles with steel horns.

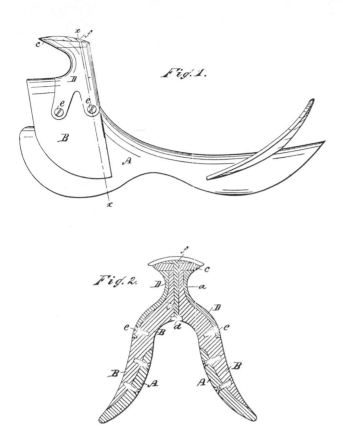

FIG. 12.13. T. E. Meanea's steel-horned saddletree, patented July 18, 1882.

Rice (1974) states that by 1885 most saddle shops had steel horns, which they used to replace broken wooden horns (Fig. 12.14). Steel horns were standard on saddles by 1890. With the use of steel horns it was no longer necessary to use a wooden fork that could be shaped into both the fork and the horn as a single unit. The fork could be designed by itself and the steel horn attached to it in any size or shape desired. Later it was common practice to make the fork of two separate pieces of wood jointed at the top of the gullet underneath the steel horn.

Today some saddle manufacturers, using the latest techniques for strength of construction, make the fork of laminated pieces of wood, each layer having the grain running in an opposite direction. This also allows more variation in styling.

The corus-rigged Yorktown tree of the 1880s had an iron horn with wood on the top. It came

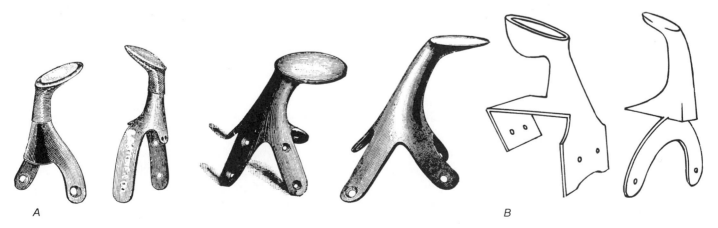

FIG. 12.14. Replacement horns. *(A)* From Stone, catalog, ca. 1905. *(B)* Left to right: Baldwin patented horn, 1905; modern; Sampson.

to be known as the *"applehorn* saddle" (Figs. 12.15 and 12.16). J. Frank Dobie, in an undated note to J. Evetts Haley, stated that "Walter Billingsley claims his father made 'the first' applehorn saddle in South Texas at Refugio, 1869" (Haley, n.d.). The name of the first maker of the Yorktown saddle is unknown; however, a letter in Haley's possession states that he was a German who had a shop in Yorktown, Texas (Haley, n.d.).

Quilted, padded seats go back to the period of the Spanish-Mexican saddles, and on western saddles they go back to the 1880s. The cowboys disliked them, however, because after a rain they would not dry rapidly, and the seat was uncomfortable (Rice, 1974).

The *loop seat* was an extended seat with squares cut out of the seat revealing the tops of the stirrup leathers where they went over the

FIG. 12.16. Applehorn saddles. From J. Evetts Haley, "Texian Saddles," *Cattleman,* June, 1938.

tree (Fig. 12.17). One obvious reason for the design was to allow easy cleaning and oiling of this normally difficult-to-reach stress area on the stirrup leather. Harold Porter, of Porter's

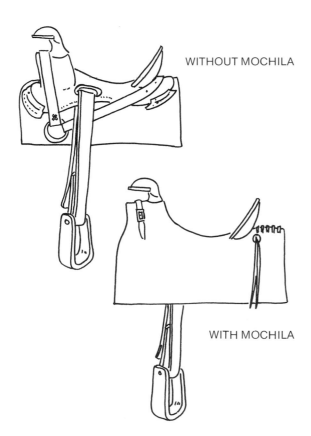

WITHOUT MOCHILA

WITH MOCHILA

FIG. 12.15.   Applehorn saddle shown with and without mochila. Drawing by Phil Livingston.

FIG. 12.17.   Loop-seat saddle with Texas skirt.

Swells on forks were originally made by attaching some kind of bucking roll around the fork (Figs. 12.19 and 12.20). It could be a slicker,

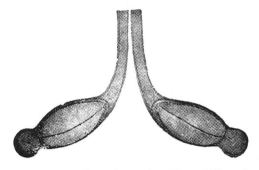

FIG. 12.19. Bucking rolls. From Riley & McCormick, Calgary, Alberta, Canada, catalog, November, 1940.

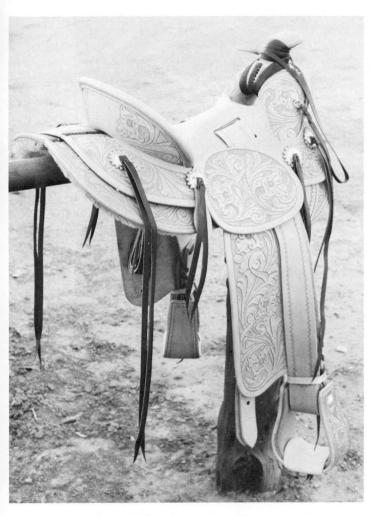

FIG. 12.18. "Dick Foster" saddle, a modern loop style designed by Jack Carroll. Courtesy of Jack Carroll Saddle Company, McNeal, Arizona.

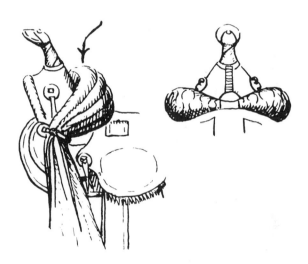

FIG. 12.20. Bucking roll on fork. From Ward, *The Cowboy at Work*.

of Tucson, says that the holes were there because the stirrup leather used then was so stiff that it could not have been removed and replaced without the aid of the cut-out areas. Porter owns an original N. Porter saddle built by his grandfather in 1875, as shown by the saddlemaker's stamp. It was made at Tharall (now spelled Thrall), Texas. His grandfather was at Tharall for only six months before moving to Taylor, Texas.

The loop seat was on D. E. Walker's saddles as early as 1885; it became popular around 1895 and was common up to around 1920.

a coat, or even a stick or an ax handle tied across the fork just behind the horn (Carmichael). Later it was a leather roll stuffed with hair (Adams). Jack Carroll, of the Carroll Saddle Company, says that the reason for the bucking rolls "was to keep the rider's pelvis from slamming forward on a pitching horse and banging against the fork" (Carroll, letter). Later the rolls were buckled onto the fork and, finally, were made as an integral part of the fork (Fig. 12.21).

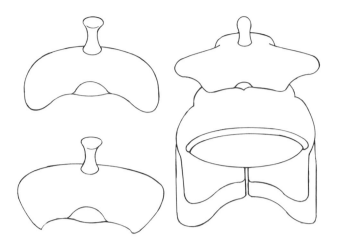

FIG. 12.21.   Swell forks.

it easier for the cowboy to ride a bucking horse. Like other fashions this one eventually went to the extreme, with a fork that was twenty-four inches wide. The cowboys called these exceptionally wide forks "freaks." Carmichael credits the first swell fork to Coggshall but does not give any date. It is known that the Visalia Stock Saddle Company had swell forks on some of their saddles in the late 1890s.

The first recorded swell fork came from the shop of T. W. Farrel in Ellensburg, Washington, in 1892 or 1893. It was designed by Earnest Boucher, one of the saddlemakers in the shop (Rice, 1950a). The swell fork (Fig. 12.22) made

FIG. 12.22.   The California stock saddle used from 1878 to 1919 by the Canadian forces. From Major G. Tylden, *Horses and Saddlery*.

CHAPTER 13

From 1900 to 1919

The John Clark Saddlery, of Portland, Oregon, patented a bucking roll in 1901 (see Fig. 13.1). The bucking roll was used by those who did not have one of the new swell-fork saddles.

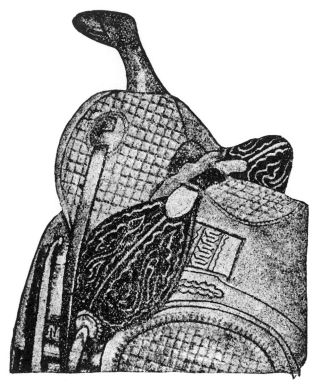

FIG. 13.1. Clark's patented bucking roll. From Stone, catalog, ca. 1905.

Cast-iron steel forks continued to be listed in saddlemakers' catalogs around 1905. They were lighter than hardwood forks. Nickel and brass horns also arrived on the scene in the very early 1900s.

The full-extended seat arrived about 1900.

This seat fully covered the seat of the saddle and lacked the cut-out squares of the loop seat.

Fashions—and what we are accustomed to —die hard. The three-quarter-seat saddle was still listed in Frazier's catalog of 1905 with the statement that "this has been one of our best sellers for 20 years." The loop seat was continued until about 1920 (Rice, 1974). Another proof that fashions die hard is that Thompson and Swope in western Colorado made Mother Hubbard saddles until 1920. An interesting attempt at improvement and simplification is shown in F. J. McMonies and J. J. Hamley's patent drawing of a cable rigging for saddles (Fig. 13.7). Another interesting patent was issued to McMonies and Hamley in 1915 on an odd-shaped D ring (Fig. 13.8).

The deeply undercut swell was developed in Oregon about 1910, when the swell was at its peak of popularity. Another attempt to improve the security of the rider's seat was a backward bulge on the back of the fork (Fig. 16.3). Apparently not too many of these were made; a saddle with this feature on it is somewhat scarce today.

Because of the use of "freak" saddles in the bucking contests, the rodeo associations decided to make the contests both more difficult and fairer by adopting what later became known as the *Association saddle* (Fig. 13.11). It is possible that the acceptance of the Association saddle by the major rodeo groups had much to do with the demise of the extremely wide-swell fork saddle, which could no longer be ridden in rodeo competition.

Probably the best way to explain how this change came about is to quote from a letter to

FIG. 13.2. Picture from late 1903 of a deputy sheriff and Arizona ranger, possibly taken in Greenlee County in east-central Arizona. The saddle appears to have a separate side jockey, but it is uncertain whether it is a three-quarter seat. It has a high-back cantle, a dally horn, a limited-swell fork, Wilson steel stirrups, Texas skirts, and a rope strap on the near side, though the rider is right-handed. Courtesy of Arizona Historical Society.

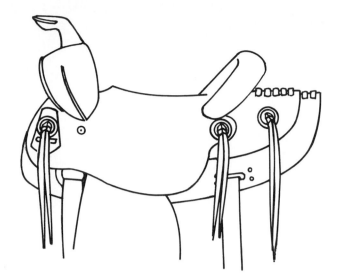

FIG. 13.3. Full-extended seat.

me, dated January 9, 1975, from J. David Hamley, president of Hamley's, of Pendleton, Oregon. Hamley wrote as follows:

Just following the Pendleton Round-Up, in September, 1919, and to bring about standardization of the Bucking Contest Saddle, a representative of the management of each of the shows at Pendleton, Boise, Cheyenne and Walla Walla, Washington, met with representatives of Hamley & Company in the Hamley offices in Pendleton. Among the committeemen attending were George Drumheller of Walla Walla, S. R. "Sam" Thompson of Pendleton. They, along with the representatives from Cheyenne and Boise, met with J. J. Hamley, L. H. Hamley, John M. Hamley and F. J. McMonies, who was then a member of the firm of Hamley & Company. As a committee, they unanimously agreed to adopt and officially recognize a bucking saddle which would be a modification of what was then known as the "Ellensburg" tree. The Ellensburg fork was changed slightly, but the other specifications of the tree remained the Ellensburg type.

The saddle itself was made with round skirts, 3/4 single "E-Z" rigging [a 1915 Hamley patent], and had a flank rigging set further back than the rear dee of a regular double rigged saddle. This saddle was later designated the "Association," and at present, and for many years, has been referred to as the "Association Saddle." I might say that the saddle was first referred to as a "Committee Saddle."

FIG. 13.4. Mexican saddle with "platter" horn cap.

The original Association Saddle had a straight-up 5" cantle, and a 14" swell fork [as it does today], but for about 37 years now, this 5" cantle has been made "laid back" to about 4 1/4". The fork, in almost every respect, has remained identical to the original fork of the 1919 "Committee Saddle."

The original trees developed by this committee in the offices of Hamley & Company in Pendleton, Oregon, were made in the Hamley Saddle Tree Shop, and the Hamley Association subsequently became known as the "Original Contest Bucking Saddle," which reputation it has maintained over all these years.

81

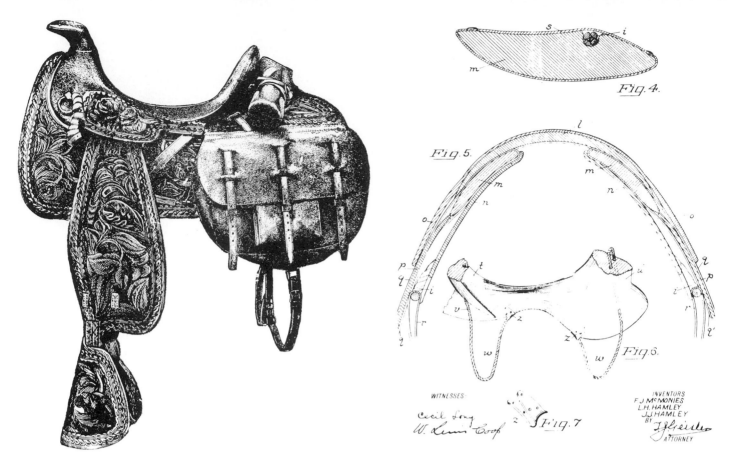

FIG. 13.5.   Whitman modified Mexican saddle, an example from the catalog of the Mehlbach Saddle Company, New York, 1907. From Dent, *The Horse Through Fifty Centuries.*

FIG. 13.7.   Cable rigging for saddles, patented March 11, 1913, by F. J. McMonies and L. H. and J. J. Hamley.

FIG. 13.6.   San Francisco after the 1906 earthquake and fire. At the immediate right is 510 Market Street, for many years the home of the Visalia Stock Saddle Company.

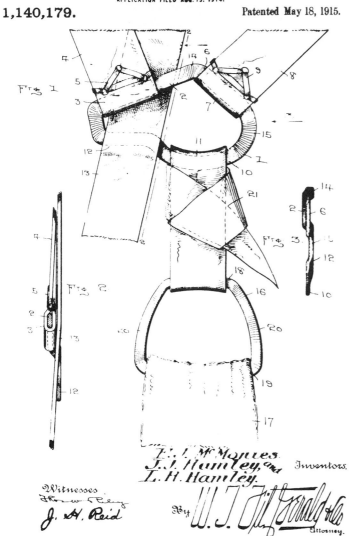

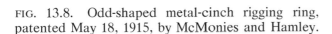

FIG. 13.8. Odd-shaped metal-cinch rigging ring, patented May 18, 1915, by McMonies and Hamley.

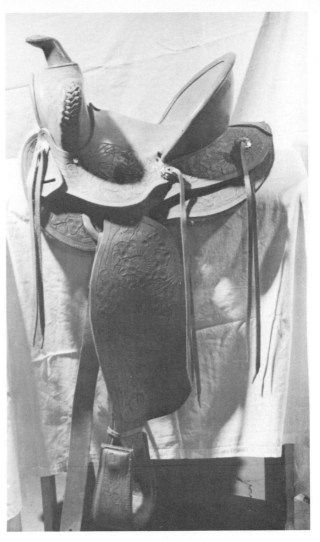

FIG. 13.9. Old bronc saddle.

Most Association Contest Saddles are today made without the horn, since most of the cowboys were cutting the horn off their saddles, not only to eliminate the "hazard" of the horn but also the temptation to grab on to it.

One of the first of the original Association Saddles made following the 1919 meeting was for a real old-timer named Earl Monahan of Hyannis, Nebraska, who remained a very staunch friend and customer of ours over a long span of years.

Steel stirrups lost popularity around 1914 because they were cold to the rider's feet and also because they hurt much more when they hit a rider than did the wooden stirrup. They were still listed in saddlemakers' catalogs much later, however.

Visalia was still showing a loop seat and some saddles with separate side jockeys in its 1917 catalog.

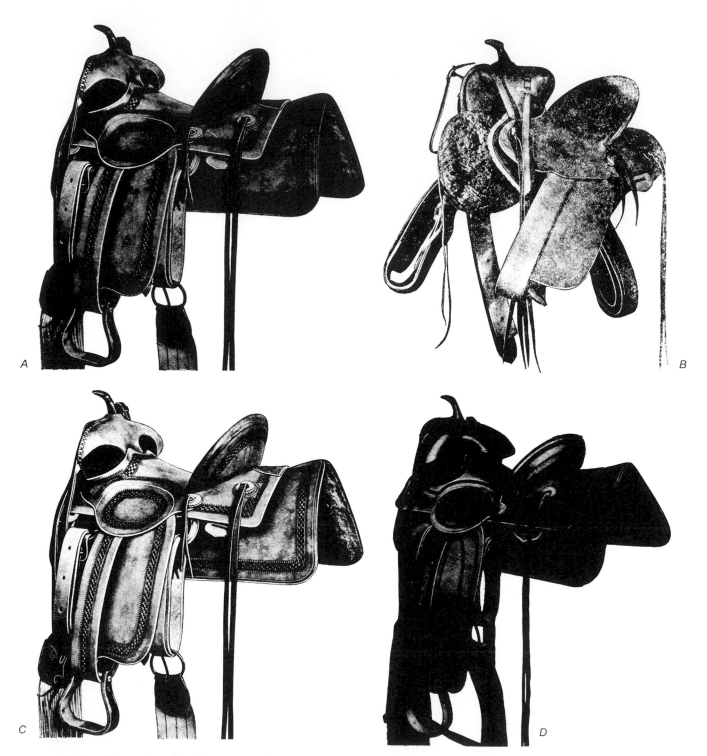

FIG. 13.10.   Examples of undercuts on the swell fork. *(A)* Courtesy of Hamley Company, Pendleton, Oregon. *(B)* Courtesy of Fred Mueller Saddle and Harness Company, Denver, Colorado. *(C)* and *(D)* From Wyeth Hardware & Manufacturing Company, Saint Joseph, Missouri, catalog no. 220, 1939.

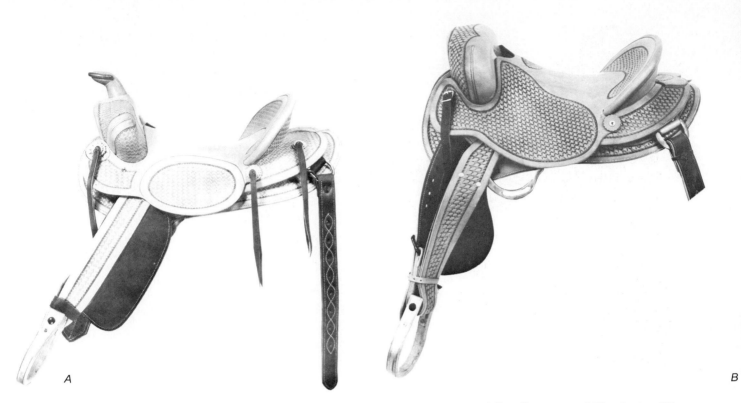

A   B

FIG. 13.11.   Two styles of Association saddles. *(A)* Horned Association saddle. Courtesy of Hamley's. *(B)* Muley Association saddle. Courtesy of Tex Tan Western Leather Company, Yoakum, Texas.

CHAPTER 14

From 1920 to the Present

The front jockey and side jockey were commonly one piece by 1920, though the design had been tried much earlier (Fig. 14.1). Cutting

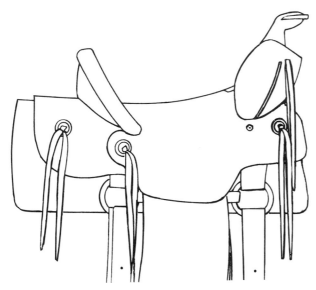

FIG. 14.1. Front jockey, side jockey, and seat, all in one piece.

the front jockey and the side jockey from one piece of leather made the assembly job easier; moreover, in some of the wide-swell saddles there was no place to put the saddle string underneath the swell, and it had to be attached to the saddletree by some other method. This brought about the use of the screw and ferrule. When the screw and ferrule began replacing the number 2 saddle string beneath the fork, the result was the six-string seat.

The popularity of the wide-swell fork peaked in the early 1920s (Rice, 1974). By the mid-1930s it had begun to disappear. Also by the mid-1930s the height of the cantles had dropped

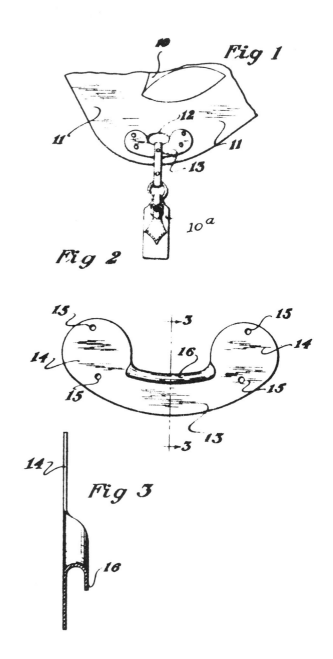

FIG. 14.2. Flat-plate, on-tree rigging, patented July 21, 1925, by L. H. Hamley.

from the old five- and six-inch-high backs to something more like the present-day height of three inches or less.

The excessive slanting upward of the seats to the fork began in the early 1930s. Like all other excesses of fashion, the slant increased to the point that today saddles have seats with such ridiculous angles that the rider finds it impossible to stay away from the cantle. Fortunately this fad appears to be dying away.

The first example of *flat-plate on-tree rigging* that I have found is the Hamley flat plate in Hamley's catalog no. 22, published in 1922. This effective innovation was patented on July 21, 1925, by L. H. Hamley (Fig. 14.2). This type of rigging plate appeared later in N. Porter's catalog no. 20, published in 1932. The E. O.

Wilson flat-plate rigging first appeared in the Denver Dry Goods catalog in the summer of 1936 (Figs. 14.3 and 14.4). W. D. Allison was issued a patent in 1950 for an adjustable flat rigging plate installed in rigging leathers (Fig. 14.5).

In-skirt rigging was developed by the N. Porter Company after some time of trial. It was first shown in Porter's catalog no. 36, published in 1951, and was trademarked as "Rig-In-Skirt." Another in-skirt-rigging patent was issued to D. O. Diaz, a saddlemaker with the N. Porter Company, in 1954 (Fig. 14.6). According to Bill Porter, within six months other saddlemakers

April 14, 1936.　　　E. O. WILSON　　　2,037,406

RIGGING FOR SADDLES

Filed May 25, 1935

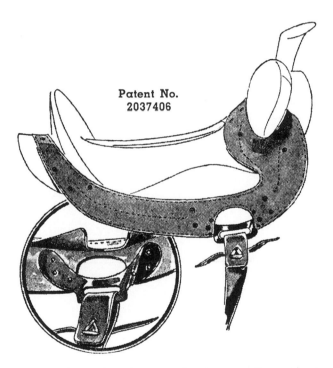

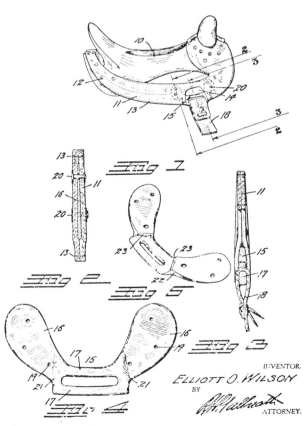

FIG. 14.3. Advertisement for Denver Dry Goods Company's "Powder River" on-tree plate rigging, invented by "Mr. Wilson, one of the best and most experienced makers of good saddles in the West." The rig eliminated the side bulge. The plate was fitted between the rigging leather and was hand-riveted, with a special latigo slot. The manufacturers guaranteed the rigging to withstand any strain. From Denver Dry Goods Co., spring–summer catalog, 1937.

FIG. 14.4. On-tree plate rigging, patented April 14, 1936, by E. O. Wilson.

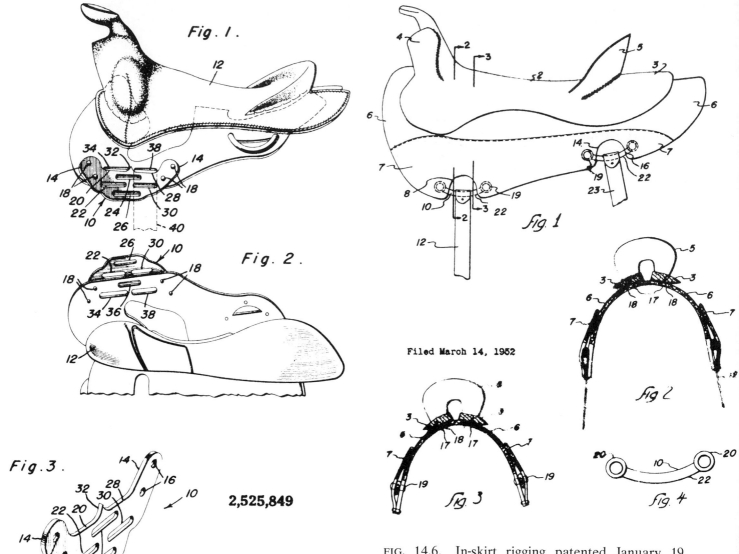

2,525,849

FIG. 14.5.   Adjustable saddle rigging plate, patented October 17, 1950, by W. D. Allison.

Filed March 14, 1952

FIG. 14.6.   In-skirt rigging patented January 19, 1954, by D. O. Diaz.

were offering in-skirt rigging without previous experience with it, and the errors they committed accounted for the questions that arose in many riders' minds about the value of this worthwhile development.

Cheyenne rolls appeared in N. Porter's catalog no. 17 in 1930 and again in Porter's catalog no. 20 in 1932. This roll had previously been called a *leather-roll binding,* and the catalogs jump back and forth between the two terms, which makes one wonder whether the name Cheyenne roll had not been copyrighted. The Cheyenne roll had not taken over completely in the catalogs by 1950; the cantle bead binding was still used. I confess that I am still partial to the bead-type binding.

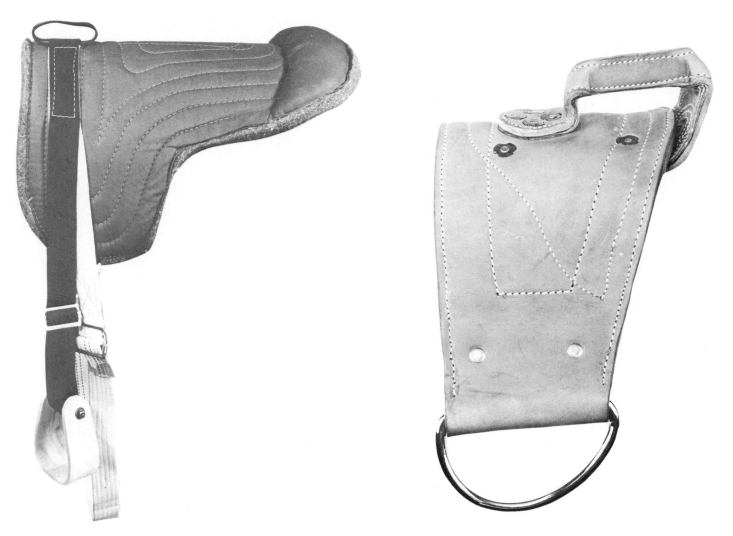

FIG. 14.7.   Specialized bareback riding equipment. Left: popular bareback pad used by many young riders. Right: bareback bucking rig used in rodeos. Courtesy of Tex Tan Western Leather Company.

Basic saddle designs have changed relatively little from 1950 to the present. In-skirt rigging has been well accepted, the Cheyenne roll has almost completely taken over as the cantle binding of choice, and the back-slanted seat still appears in most catalogs. The artistic appeal of saddles has been improved, however.

For a drawing of what I consider a correct modern saddle see Fig. 36.17.

PART II   The Parts of the Saddle and Accessories

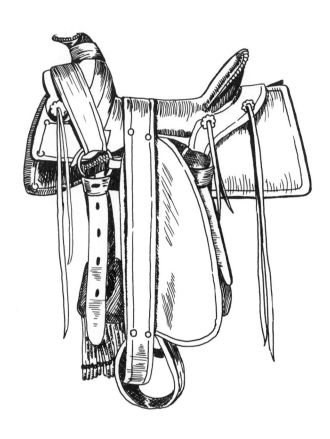

HIGH GRADE SADDLE TREES WITH STEEL FORKS

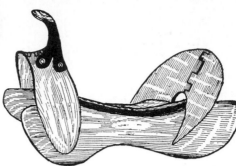

This illustration shows the construction of all our high-grade trees. We use the best grade of hardwood.

This illustration shows the inside view of the steel fork used in our high-grade trees. It will stand a 2000 pound pressure. Owing to its construction, it is impossible for it to spread, spring or break with anything like fair usage. The fork is countersunk into and fits closely to the bars, fastened to same with wrought iron nails.

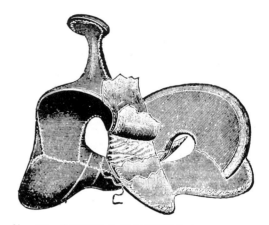

No. 19.—DOUBLE RAWHIDE COVERED.

Each.................................. $ 20 00

This tree, being covered with two layers of heavy rawhide and made of the very best hardwood, is the strongest tree made.

Any high-grade tree made double rawhide covered at above price.

This tree furnished on any saddle listed in this catalogue at $50.00 or more, for $10.00 advance on list price.

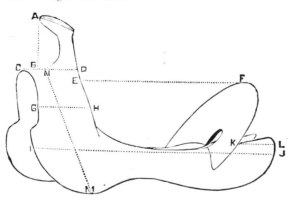

TREES MADE TO ORDER.

We can make any style tree desired. If you do not see just what you want illustrated in this catalogue, send us the dimensions according to your ideas, measured as shown in the above diagram, and we will make it to order for you. An average tree measures 15 inches from D to F.

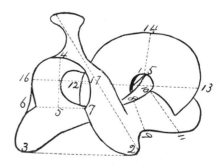

FRONT MEASUREMENTS.

Stone's improved steel horn tree has all the requirements of a first = class easy = riding tree.

FIG. 15.2. Page 127 of Stone catalog, ca. 1905.

CHAPTER 15

Trees

The *saddletree,* so called because its components originally came from a tree, is the foundation on which the saddle is built. For many hundreds of years men rode saddle pads on which there were no saddletrees. The usefulness of the horse was greatly advanced when man learned to put a rigid frame inside his saddle pad. The only other invention in saddlery that was as important was the stirrup.

The tree is an assembly of various component parts, which are glued and screwed together and then covered with wet rawhide, which is sewed tightly over the components (Fig. 15.1).

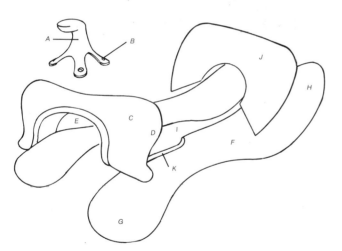

FIG. 15.1.   Parts of the saddletree. *(A)* Horn. *(B)* Points of horn (4). *(C)* Fork. *(D)* Swell of Fork. *(E)* Gullet. *(F)* Bar (2). *(G)* Bur of bar. *(H)* Fan of bar. *(I)* Channel. *(J)* Cantle. *(K)* Stirrup-leather groove.

As the rawhide dries, it shrinks, forming a vise-like covering. The combination of dry rawhide and tree parts makes an extremely durable, rigid frame. The use of rawhide in this way can be compared to the greatly increased strength of concrete when reinforcing bars are put inside the concrete and the water evaporates. The two together have much greater strength than either one has alone.

Rawhide-covered wooden trees, while extremely strong, have a certain amount of flexibility, which allows them to conform somewhat to the horse's outline.

Bull hide is one of the best sources of uniform rawhide because it has the least number of weak, thin, or uneven spots. A tree covered with this material is capable of withstanding the shock and the hard use of roping and accidents. Beef hide and then steer hide rank next in strength. Canvas or cheesecloth is used to cover cheaper trees that are used only for riding.

Trees have been made from materials other than the ponderosa pine commonly used today. In the past there have been attempts to make trees of steel, aluminum, and, more recently, molded fiberglass. About the only material other than wood that has found any long-term acceptance is molded fiberglass; however, it is still somewhat new, and only time will tell whether it is here to stay as the basic material of the tree. The main problem of casting fiberglass is economic—it is expensive to cast all the many shapes and sizes of trees required to fit different horses and riders; therefore, it lends itself mostly to production-line saddles.

The *bars* are the long pieces on each side of the tree. They are the actual bearing surfaces on the horse's back. It is impossible to design one shape of bar that will fit all horses. Some horses are high-withered, and some are flat-backed; some have long backs, and others have short backs. Such conformations determine the shape, length, set angle, and flare of the bars. The secret to the fit of a saddletree is the way the bars conform to the curves of a horse's back. The statement that no one saddle will correctly fit all types of horses is as true as the statement that one pair of shoes will not fit all feet.

The *set angle* of the bars is too often ignored by saddle buyers (Fig. 15.3). It is a big mistake

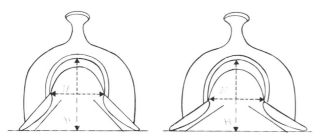

FIG. 15.3. Set angle of bars on high- and low-withered horses (angle exaggerated).

to buy a saddle because it is attractive without knowing whether or not it will fit the horse. If the set angle is too narrow, then only the edge of the bar is making contact with the horse. If the set angle is too flat, then only the top inside of the bars is making contact with the horse. The weight of the rider rests on one area and is not distributed evenly over the horse's back. This is readily apparent when one examines a diagram showing the girths of two different-shaped horses (Fig. 15.4). The different horse breeds have certain inherent characteristics of girth conformations, but horses within a breed have different girth conformations too. The procedure outlined in Fig. 31.12 shows how to make a pattern that the saddle buyer can show the saddle maker to determine the correct set angle and flare of the bars.

The proper *length* of the bars has been a subject of much discussion for many generations. One theory holds that a long bar distributes the weight of the rider over a much greater area of the back and is easier on the horse. Another theory, much discussed in the cavalry, was that

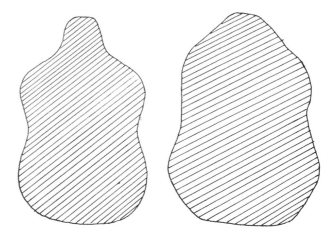

FIG. 15.4. Cross section through the withers of two types of heart girths, showing top-line shape. Drawing by Judy Osburn.

long bars tend to gall the horse at the back end (Fig. 31.7) and that a shorter bar distributes the weight so that it can be correctly supported by the horse's bone structure (Fig. 31.6). Despite the theorizing, there has been too little research on the bar's relationship to the bone structure and musculature of the horse, as well as to the horses' "innards."

The *flare* of the bars is another important factor in the conformation of the tree to the horse's back. The shoulder below the withers and the back area are on two different planes. The bar must be so shaped that it lies flat against these points and as much of the points between as possible. The bars under the fork (which is over the withers) must be set at a much more acute angle than the bars over the much flatter back under the cantle. The *flare angle* of the bars is the difference between the narrower set angle of the bars under the fork and the flatter set angle of the bars under the cantle.

The *channel* between the bars—the open area separating the bars at the top—has a definite purpose. Nothing on the saddle should ever rest against the horse's backbone to do it any damage or interfere with its movement. Everything must be designed to allow free movement of air in this area, just over the backbone.

Wooden trees have been constructed of white

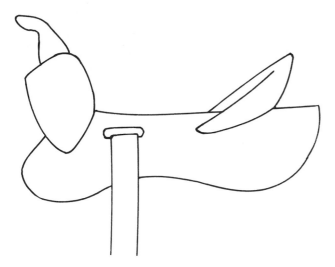

FIG. 15.5. Saddle bar, showing stirrup leather slot.

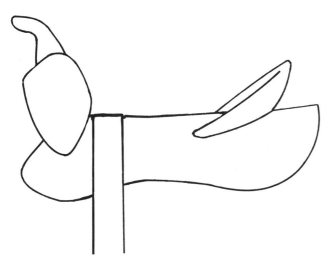

FIG. 15.6. Saddle bar, showing stirrup leather resting in the groove on the tree.

ponderosa pine, beechwood, ash, walnut, cottonwood, hard mesquite, oak, buckeye, laurel, willow, and Douglas fir. While the sturdiest trees have been covered with rawhide for many years, less expensive and less-hard-used saddletrees have been covered with canvas or cheesecloth. On an old 1885 highback saddle in my collection the tree is covered with burlap.

Saddletrees have changed very much as horses' conformation changed, from predominantly high-withered to generally low-withered with flat backs. Some well-known older saddletrees are the Ellensberg, Friseka (the correct spelling, per Woodward), Goodell, Ladesma, Nelson, Portland, Taylor, Tipton, Visalia (perfected by Ricardo Mattlé, or Mattley), White River (California), and White River (Thompson, in Colorado).

Earlier in this century there appeared what was called the free-swing method of attaching stirrup leathers to the bars (Fig. 15.7). The

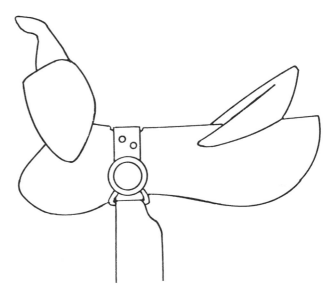

FIG. 15.7. Saddle bar, showing free-swinging stirrup-leather attachment.

attaching point was a swivel mechanism. Its purpose was to give an easier swing to the stirrups for positioning under different conditions encountered while riding. This method had an inherent weakness at the point of attachment, according to saddlemakers, and for the last ten years it has been little used.

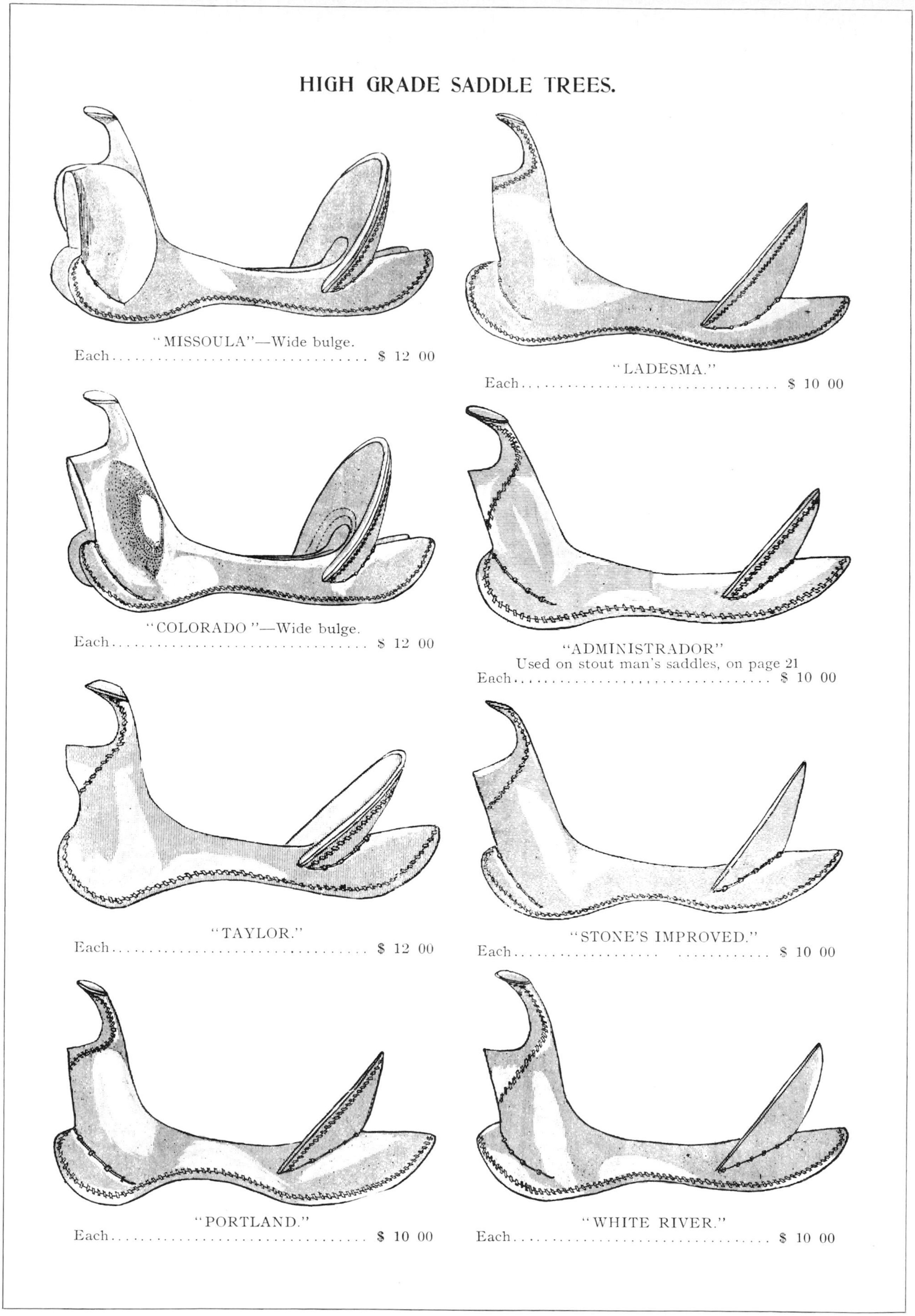

HIGH GRADE SADDLE TREES.

"MISSOULA"—Wide bulge.

Each.................................. $ 12 00

"LADESMA."

Each.................................. $ 10 00

"COLORADO "—Wide bulge.

Each.................................. $ 12 00

"ADMINISTRADOR"
Used on stout man's saddles, on page 21
Each.................................. $ 10 00

"TAYLOR."

Each.................................. $ 12 00

"STONE'S IMPROVED."

Each.................................. $ 10 00

"PORTLAND."

Each.................................. $ 10 00

"WHITE RIVER."

Each.................................. $ 10 00

FIG. 15.8.   Page 128 of Stone catalog, ca. 1905, showing a wide variety of saddletrees.

CHAPTER 16

Forks

The *fork* is the strong, upright piece attached at the front of the saddle near the front end of the bars. The horn is attached to the upper center of the fork. The fork was so named because in the old days the saddlemaker made this part of his saddle from the fork of a tree. In those days the horn and the fork were cut out of one piece of wood. A strong fork of a deer's antler was also occasionally used, which led to the name "horn." In an effort to standardize the terminology of the western saddle, this part of the saddle will be referred to here as *fork,* never as *pommel.* The word *pommel* is closely associated with the English saddle, and the word *fork* is never used in speaking of an English saddle.

Figure 16.1 shows the frontal outlines of various styles of forks, from the old, easily ridable slick fork to the monstrous twenty-four-inch swell fork, which even in its heyday was called a "freak."

The style of the fork went through an evolutionary period because of the uses to which saddles were put and also the preferences of the riders. From the original A fork, whose topside angled almost straight up from the

tree bar to the attachment point of the horn, the style began to widen. The fork then went into the "narrow-fork" stage, though it did not go farther out laterally than the point of attachment to the bar. Then came the era of bronc busting. The riders found that if the outsides of the fork were extended beyond the attachment place to the bar they could get a better seat on a gyrating horse by putting their knees in under the outward extension, called the *swell* (the fork itself is not a swell).

If a line is drawn perpendicularly from the outside attachment point of the fork to the bar and the fork does not extend outside this line, it is a *narrow fork.* Anything that extends outside this line is referred to as the *swell on the fork,* and the whole unit is a *swell fork.* Arbitrary dimensions of the A fork, the narrow fork, and the swell fork are as follows: A fork, 9 inces wide or less; narrow fork, between 9 and 14 inches wide; swell fork, 14 to 24 inches wide. (Fig. 16.2). When a rider can get a grip with his legs underneath the fork, he is riding a swell fork. Hamley and Company undercut the backside of the swelled fork and trademarked the new fork in 1929 as the Form Fitter. One

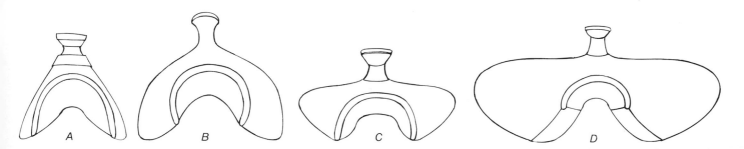

FIG. 16.1.   Front view of various forks, from the 8-inch "slick" fork to the 24-inch "freak" wide fork. *(A)* A, or slick, fork. *(B)* Narrow fork. *(C)* Swell fork. *(D)* Wide-swell, or "freak," fork.

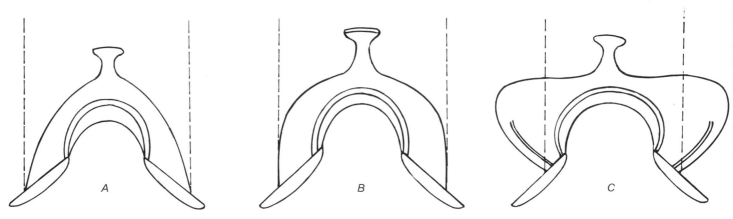

FIG. 16.2.   Types of forks. *(A)* A fork, or slick fork. *(B)* Narrow fork. *(C)* Swell fork showing vertical determination lines for fork type.

type of swelled fork was puffed out on the backside; this was called a *back swell* or *back bulge* (Fig. 16.3). It was intended to give the rider a firmer seat on a bronc.

Another bronc saddle was the *bear trap* (Fig. 16.4). This saddle had a very wide swell, but the swells were Vd backward from the horn so that a rider was literally in a trap between the old

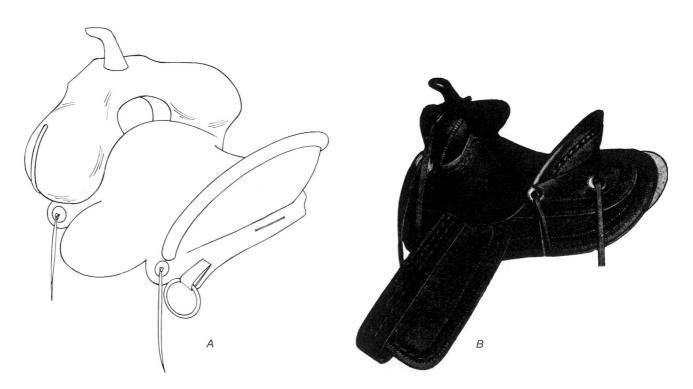

FIG. 16.3. Saddle with backward bulge on the fork. *(A)* From author's collection. *(B)* From Muellers, catalog no. 88, 1950.

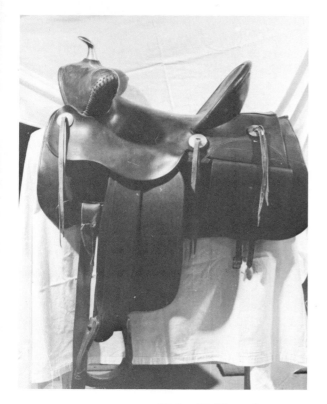

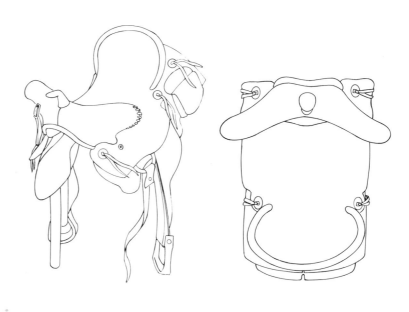

FIG. 16.4.   T. Flynn bear-trap saddle, three-quarter near-side and top-side views.

high-back cantle and a backward Vd fork. It was excellent for staying in the saddle but almost an impossibility to get out of should the horse fall with the rider. It was commonly considered a dangerous saddle.

Ropers did not like the wide-swell saddles because the rope could catch under the swell. Professional ropers also disliked it because the wide swell cut down the speed of their dismount.

Forks can be attached to the bars at different angles from a vertical position. A slight slope from the bars up to the top of the fork is considered a *no-slope fork*. If the angle becomes a little more obtuse, it is considered a *medium-slope fork,* and if the obtuse angle is increased a few more degrees, it is considered a *full-slope fork* (Fig. 16.5).

Now we come to another important part of the fork, the *gullet.* This is the cut-out under-

neath side in the center of the fork that goes over the withers of the horse. It is extremely important that the gullet allow plenty of room (two fingers edgewise minimum) for clearance of the fork above the withers of the horse. A short gullet will rub the horse raw on top of his withers. If the gullet is too wide, the bars

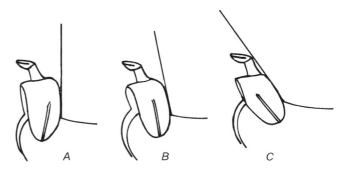

FIG. 16.5.   Forks showing different slopes: *(A)* Straight up (no slope). *(B)* Medium slope. *(C)* Full slope.

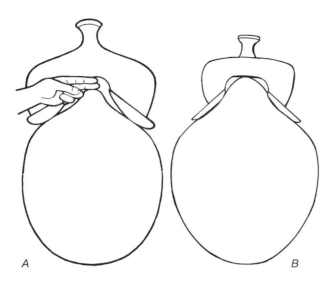

FIG. 16.6. Cross section of a horse's withers in relation to the gullet. *(A)* Good gullet clearance, at least two fingers. *(B)* Gullet too short; will injure the horse's back.

set too far down on the horse's sides, and the gullet rubs a sore spot on top of the horse's withers (Fig. 16.6).

The correct relationship of the height of the gullet and the set angle of the bars is important in purchasing the correct saddle for a horse. The width of the gullet is measured straight across from the point where the bars join the fork to the same point on the opposite side. The height of the gullet is measured when the tree bars are resting on a flat surface. The distance from this surface (the lowest part of the bars) to the center spot at the front of the gullet (directly under the front tip of the horn) is the height of the gullet (Fig. 16.7).

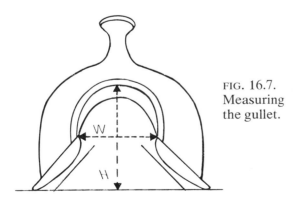

FIG. 16.7. Measuring the gullet.

Because each breed of horse has a somewhat consistent conformation in withers and back, saddlemakers tend to produce an "Arabian saddle," a "Quarter Horse saddle," and so on. This practice does not take into account both the largest horses of the specific breed and the smallest ones, the overfed horses and the underfed ones, the overworked horses and the family pets. It is obvious that the breed of the horse is no real criterion to use when buying a saddle.

The width and shape of the fork are dictated by the rider's personal choice and the use to which the saddle will be put. The width is measured directly across the back of the fork at the widest point of the swell (Fig. 16.8).

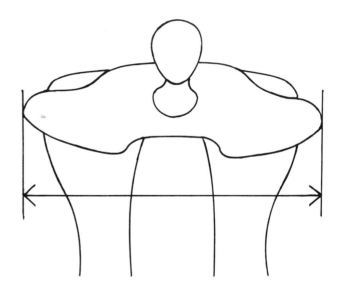

FIG. 16.8. Measuring the fork width.

The bead-type fork binding is made by sewing together the leather covering the gullet and the leather covering the outside of the fork itself (Fig. 16.9). Sometimes the leather covering the fork is merely turned in underneath to cover the gullet and nailed, leaving a smooth appearance (Fig. 16.10).

The leather of wide-swell forks must have a seam on the outer edge of the swell to bring together the front and back coverings of the fork into a neat, tight cover; this seam may be

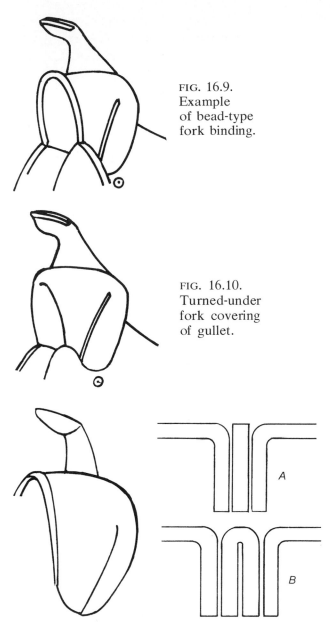

FIG. 16.9. Example of bead-type fork binding.

FIG. 16.10. Turned-under fork covering of gullet.

FIG. 16.11. Location of the welt on the fork. *(A)* Single welt. *(B)* Turned welt.

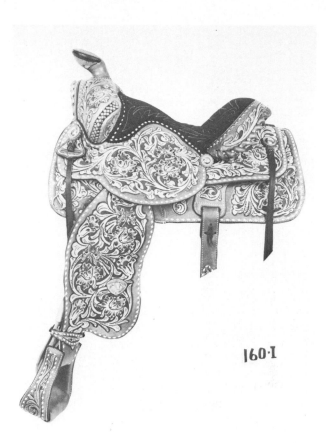

FIG. 16.12. Laced seam on a swell fork. Courtesy of Tex Tan.

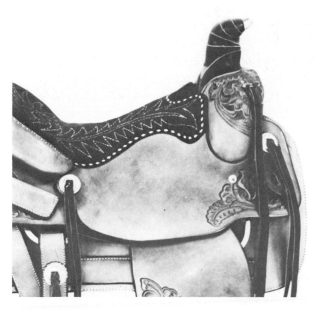

FIG. 16.13. Rope strap on the off side of the fork. Courtesy of Tex Tan.

welted (single or turned, Fig. 16.11), stitched in the seam, or laced together (Fig. 16.12). Less expensive saddles have a single welt, while more expensive ones have a turned welt.

The *rope strap* is the narrow strap usually attached to the upper off side of the fork or to its front off side. Its purpose is to hold the lariat. Occasionally a rope strap is shown on

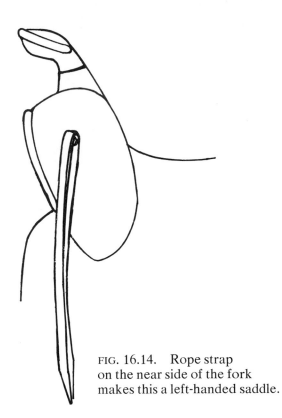

FIG. 16.14.   Rope strap
on the near side of the fork
makes this a left-handed saddle.

both the near and the off side of the fork. If
there is a single rope strap on the near side, the
rider is a left-handed roper, and the saddle is
known as a *left-handed saddle.*

For a rope strap working riders prefer a
looped thong, a "fail-safe" device should the
horse fall and the rider become entangled in
the rope.

CHAPTER 17

Horns

Horns have come in as many shapes and styles as there have been ingenious designers (Fig. 17.1). Horn styles have been dictated by their use—as snubbing posts for lariats or reatas. The length and style of the *horn neck* and the *horn cap* were determined by whether the roper was a *dally roper,* who snubbed his reata around the horn neck one or two times in a half hitch and then played out the rope to absorb much of the shock as the steer hit the end of the rope, or a *hard-and-fast-tie roper,* who worked with the lariat secured to the horn at all times with a horn knot. The dally roper's horn neck (Fig. 17.2) must be thicker and longer than the hard-and-fast-tie horn neck (Fig. 17.3). At one time the cap on the dally horn sloped upward from back to front, but today some are flat, making it easy for the dally roper to wind his rope around the horn (Fig. 17.4).

The *pitch* of the *horn cap* (the head) is usually determined by preference. It has no real significance except in dally roping, where it is flat today (Fig. 17.5).

Needless to say, the strength of the steel horn and the flexibility the metal allowed in design and type made it the horn of preference from its introduction. Because of its tendency to rust, the steel horn was covered with leather; however, around 1900 solid-brass and solid-nickel horns were introduced. They were used by hard-and-fast-tie ropers, not by dally ropers. The base of the steel horn *(horn points)* is attached with screws or bolted to the fork.

For proper measuring when ordering a specific type horn, see Fig. 17.8. When ordering horns on trees, it is important to specify the type and shape desired (Fig. 17.8).

In the old days the adherents of each of the two methods of roping, the hard-and-fast-tie method and the dally method, would die vowing that theirs was the "only" method. The hard-and-fast-tie cowboys mostly came from Texas, while the dally ropers came from California and points west of the Rocky Mountains. The two methods met in Wyoming and Montana.

The hard-and-fast-tie ropers used a shorter lariat, around thirty-five to forty feet long, and tied the end of the lariat fast to the horn. Their territory was one of mesquite and heavy brush. They might get only one chance at the critter, and they did not want to waste time dallying or take a chance on letting the catch get away. The disadvantage of this method was apparent when the roped critter went around one side of a tree and the horse went around the other side. A collision was inevitable.

The hard-and-fast-tie ropers rode full-double-rigged saddles, so the saddle would not stand on end when a heavy animal hit the end of the rope.

The more open areas of the Far West were the ranges of the dally roper. He used a longer lariat, sixty to eighty feet long. When the catch was made, depending on the weight of the animal, he took a quick one or two turns (half hitches) around the horn and played the rope to take the shock, and also to wear out the cow. When equilibrium was reached, he could secure the rope by making a clove hitch on the horn (Figs. 17.9 and 17.10).

Jack Carroll says that on Mexican saddles covered only with rawhide the dally roper played his rope much as a fisherman does his fish to wear it out. Smoke would curve up from it sometimes, as the rider slipped his dallies. A ranch replacement for the worn rawhide was

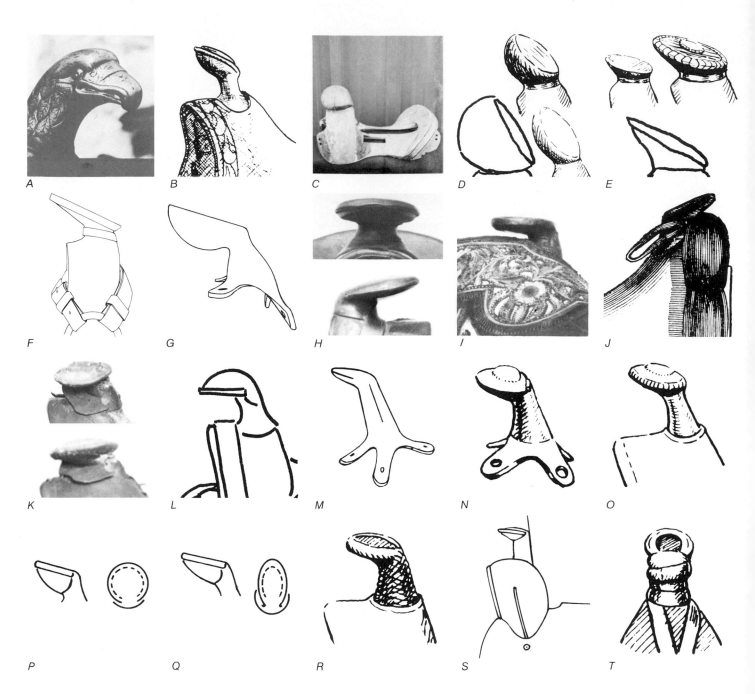

FIG. 17.1.   Saddle horns. *(A)* American officer's saddle horn, 1830. Courtesy of Fort Sill Museum. *(B)* Spanish horn, after 1835. Courtesy of Phil Livingston. *(C)* Early Mexican gourd horn. Courtesy of Garnet Brooks. *(D)* Later gourd horns. From Bracho, "Schools of Riding in the New World—La Jineta." *(E)* Later large, flat-capped Mexican horns. From Bracho, "Schools of Riding in the New World—La Jineta." *(F)* Late large, flat-capped Mexican horn. *(G)* Modern Mexican brass horn. *(H)* Hope saddle horns, 1850. Courtesy of Fort Sill Museum. *(I* and *J)* California saddle horns, 1850s. *(K)* Texas saddle horns, 1860s. Courtesy of Fort Sill Museum. *(L)* Applehorn, 1860s. Courtesy of Phil Livingston. *(M)* Modern steel horn, regular. *(N)* Button-top horn. From Ward, *The Cowboy at Work. (O)* Button-top horn mounted. From Ward, *The Cowboy at Work. (P)* Pelican horn. Courtesy of Tex Tan. *(Q)* Egg-shaped horn. Courtesy of Tex Tan. *(R)* Braid-wrapped horn. From Ward, *The Cowboy at Work. (S)* Dally horn. *(T)* Dally wrapped horn. From Ward, *The Cowboy at Work.*

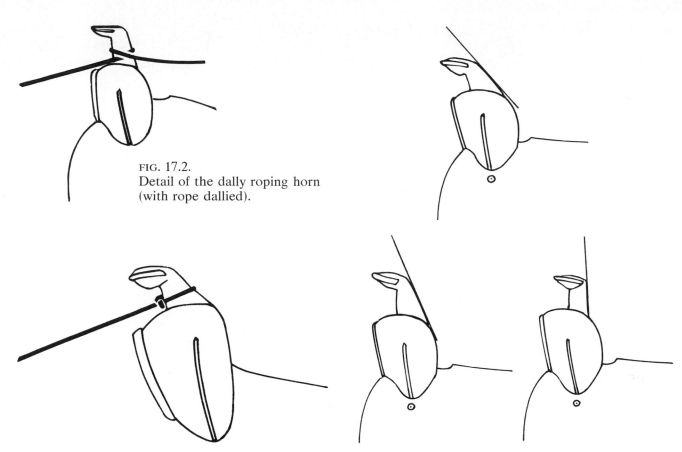

FIG. 17.2.
Detail of the dally roping horn
(with rope dallied).

FIG. 17.3. Detail of the hard-and-fast-tie roping
horn (with rope tied).

FIG. 17.4. Slopes of the horn.

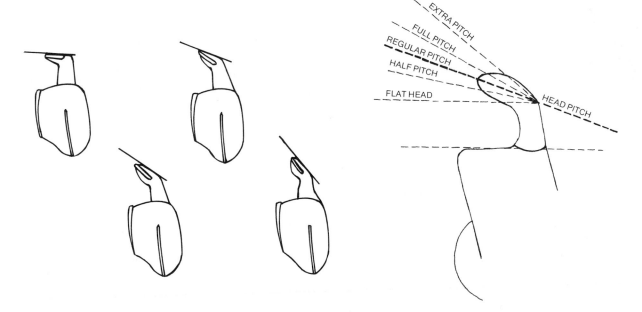

FIG. 17.5. Pitches of the horn cap (head). Drawing at right by Judy Osburn.

105

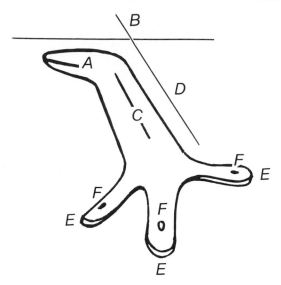

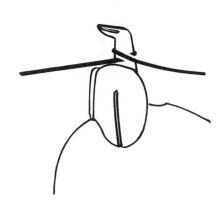

FIG. 17.9. Detail of half hitch around the horn.

FIG. 17.6. Detail of horn. *(A)* Cap (head). *(B)* Pitch of cap. *(C)* Neck. *(D)* Slope of neck. *(E)* Points. *(F)* Screw or bolt holes.

FIG. 17.7. Attaching the horn.

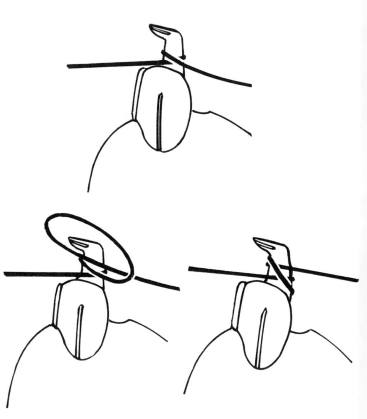

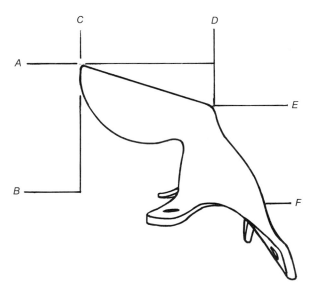

FIG. 17.8. Measuring saddle horns. Measure from *(C)* to *(D)* for the size of the head. Measure from *(A)* to *(B)*—top of fork to front edge of horn cap —for the height. Measure from *(E)* to *(F)* for the horn neck.

FIG. 17.10. Detail of clove hitch around the horn.

the scrotal sack off a castrated bull, which was shrunk over the horn to cover it.

The old dally roper rode a centerfire saddle. One of the occupational hazards of dally roping becomes apparent when occasionally you meet

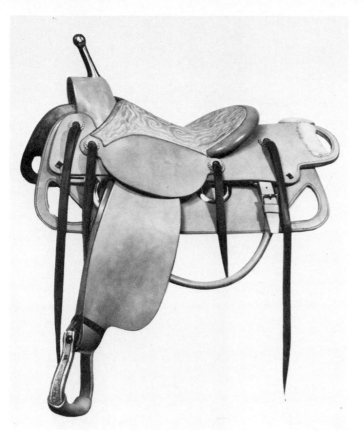

FIG. 17.11. Trick rider's saddle horn. Courtesy of Hamley's.

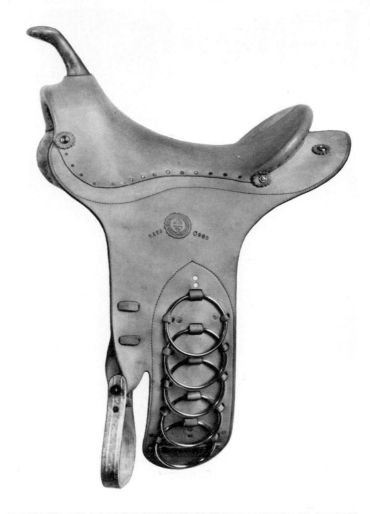

FIG. 17.12. Quick-change relay saddle with special cinch. Courtesy of Hamley's.

an adherent of this method who is minus a thumb, one or more fingers, or even all the fingers on one hand.

In dallying, the slickness of an uncovered steel or wooden horn or of smooth leather is greatly diminished by covering the horn neck with soft cotton rope or rubber cut from an old inner tube. This gives the rope something on which to get a "bite." The horn cap must not be too wide, but a 3-inch cap is good, and the pitch should preferably be flat.

The horn neck should not slope forward. A right-handed roper usually dallies around the horn counterclockwise with his thumb up.

Sometimes the horn neck is wrapped with a 1-by-36-inch-long piece of inner tube cut circularly around the tube. It should be wound in such a way that the "bite" of the dallying rope tightens it rather than unwinding it.

An unusual horn is the one on a trick rider's saddle. It is usually about 6 inches high and 3/4 inch in diameter with a round knob 1 1/2 inch in diameter on top of the horn (Fig. 17.11).

CHAPTER 18

Cantles

The *cantle* is the upright portion at the back of the saddle that prevents the rider from going off the back end of the horse. It also affords the rider a comfortable support to lean against during long rides or when the horse is standing quietly.

The cantle has evolved through a series of repeats. In medieval days the cantle was high and covered the back of the mailed knight or jouster very securely so that he could not be pushed backward off his horse. After the Span-

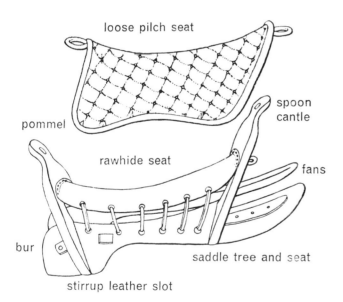

FIG. 18.1.   Hussar military saddletree of 1805 with spoon cantle. From Tylden, *Horses and Saddlery.*

ish war saddle with its high-backed cantle was brought to this country, the cantle was redesigned and cut down to approximately the same height as that of the cantle on the Mexican saddle today. This cantle has undergone very

little change since 1700. Later, as the horseback trips grew longer and the hours in the saddle became days on end, the cantle again increased in height, up to the six-inch "highback cantle." Today a cantle over three inches high is unusual.

Somewhere along the line military saddles developed the *spoon cantle* (Fig. 18.1, 2). The

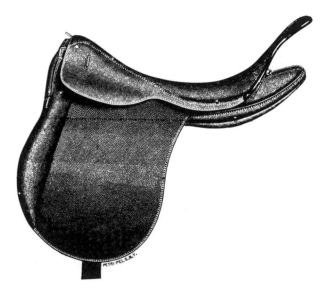

FIG. 18.2. Shifting-panel military saddle with spoon cantle. From *Moseman's Illustrated Guide for Purchasers of Horse Furnishing Goods.*

spoon was used as the forward anchor for the crupper, as well as a convenient, sturdy place to tie articles the cavalryman needed during a war campaign.

The *leather roll cantle* had a flat plate extending backward and somewhat angled downward from the top back side of the cantle (Fig. 18.3). It was apparently first made in Frank Meanea's

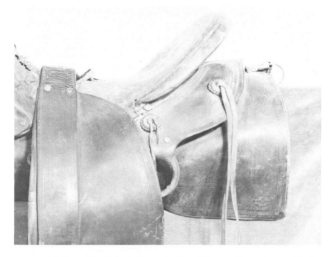

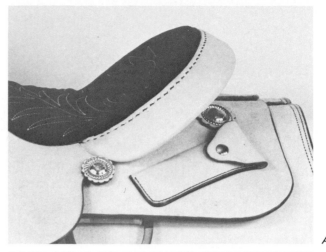

FIG. 18.3. Early roll cantle. See also FIG. 12.6. Courtesy of State Historical Society of North Dakota, Bismarck.

FIG. 18.4. Cheyenne roll cantles. *(A)* Standard roll. Courtesy of Tex Tan. *(B)* Roll with rope edge. Courtesy of Hamley's.

saddle shop in Cheyenne, Wyoming, in the 1870s. Because no particular purpose for the roll has been discovered, it should probably be considered mostly ornamental. The roll fashion faded out around 1890 to 1900, giving way to bead cantle binding. In my antique-saddle collection, the most comfortable saddle to ride is an old re-covered 3/4-seat saddle that was probably made in the late 1880s. It has a leather roll cantle.

Around the mid-1930s the roll cantle now known as the *Cheyenne roll* again became fashionable. It is now used almost universally on saddles. The Cheyenne roll (Figs. 18.4, 18.5) is usually about 1 1/2 inches wide. It can be considered a safety feature for the rider who is likely to be jolted backward out of the saddle seat and come down on the cantle. It is also designed to keep spurs from hanging up on the cantle in the fast dismounts necessary to timed rodeo events.

Another cantle binding is the *bead binding,* a rounded bead over the top of the cantle (Fig. 18.6).

Somewhere around the early 1920s the height of the cantle began to lower to about the height it is today on most saddles. The reason given

for the reduction in the cantle height is that when a roper wishes to dismount rapidly from his horse with the least obstruction he can get his leg over the present-day low cantle easier and faster. According to Harlan Webb:

Movies proved that when [the cowboy] got off, his leg would have cleared a 4" cantle with room to spare. He got into a deeper seat [in front] with a 13" front and 3" cantle and his roping improved immediately. Now when his horse breaks out of the box, my friend is able to *ride his horse,* rather than fighting to stay in the saddle.

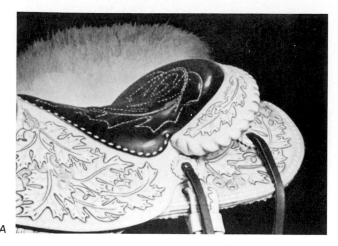
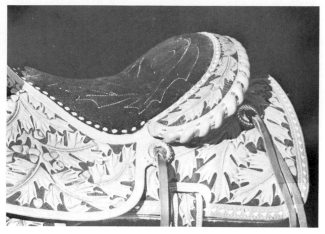

FIG. 18.5.   Elephant-ear Cheyenne rolls. *(A)* Courtesy of Fallis Saddlery. *(B)* Roll with silver-laced rope edge. Courtesy of Fallis Saddlery.

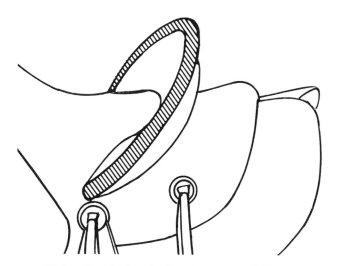

FIG. 18.6.   Cantle bead trim. Courtesy of Hamley's.

Like forks, cantles can be attached to the bars, so they have varying pitches, or slopes. There is a steep-sloped cantle, a medium-sloped cantle, and a low-sloped cantle (Fig. 18.7). The front side of the cantle can be either flat or dished out into a cuplike shape, depending on the rider's preference. The shape of the cantle can be *regular,* in an approximate half circle, or *flat-topped,* somewhat rounded at the corners (Fig. 18.8).

On the back of many of the old highback cantles in the buffalo-hunting and Indian-fighting days was often a small leather pocket used to

STEEP

MEDIUM

LOW

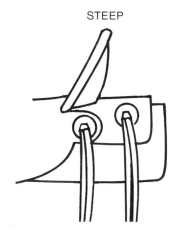
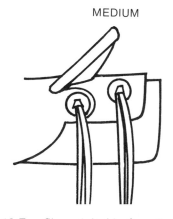
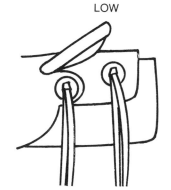

FIG. 18.7.   Slope (pitch) of cantles.

110

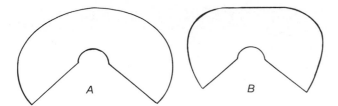

FIG. 18.8. Cantle shapes. *(A)* Oval. *(B)* Comfort.

carry bullets. In later years it often held fence staples, and it is now referred to as *staple pocket.*

The proper way to measure cantle height and width is shown in Fig. 18.9. The width is from one extreme outer edge to the other extreme outer edge crosswise. The height is measured from the top of the back jockey to the top of the cantle binding.

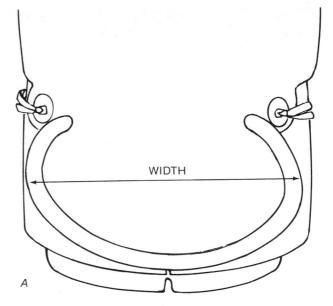

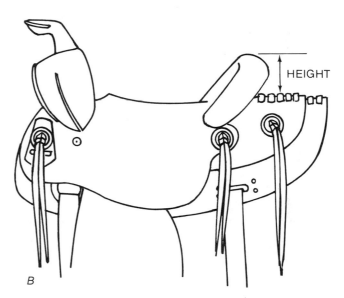

FIG. 18.9. Cantle measurements. *(A)* Width. *(B)* Height.

CHAPTER 19

Seats

The *saddle seat,* like everything else on the saddle, has gone through a series of modifications. The early saddles of North America were rawhide-covered only, sometimes with blankets or bearskins thrown over and under them. Later they were partly leather-covered. Then came the *mochila,* a loose single piece of leather that slipped down over both the fork and the cantle, covering the entire saddle. Finally came the permanent coverings over the seat and the rest of the saddle (Fig. 19.1).

One of the earliest seat shapes was the *half-rigged seat* (Fig. 10.1*B*). This seat was an approximate equilateral triangle of leather with the base of the triangle tacked down to both bars and the apex of the triangle tacked approximately one-third to halfway up the front side of the cantle.

Next came the *three-quarter seat* (Fig. 19.1*E*). This seat covered all of the front side of the cantle, and the leather of the seat extended forward, completely covering the bars and the channel to the back of the stirrup-leather grooves in the bars. The stirrup leathers were exposed on the three-quarter seat. This design was very prominent from about 1870 until the early 1900s. On the three-quarter seat the side jockeys were separate from the seat itself; however, in the early 1880s the three-quarter-seat saddles had no side jockeys.

The next evolutionary stage was the *loop seat* (Fig. 19.1*F*). A single piece of leather covered the front of the cantle and extended forward to the fork, entirely covering the seat except for a rectangular slot cut out of the seat over the position where each of the stirrup leathers went over the bars in the stirrup-leather grooves. This exposure of the stirrup leathers made it easy to examine, clean, and if necessary change them. A Coggshall saddle in my collection has a seat of this type (see Appendix, "Early Saddlemakers," Montana). The side jockeys and the seat are a single piece of leather. The loop seat was common from the early 1900s to the 1920s.

Next came the *full seat,* or *full-extended seat* (Fig. 19.1*G*). A single piece of leather covered the front of the cantle and the entire seat. The side jockeys were one piece with the seat. In later evolution of this seat came the front jockeys, the side jockeys, and the seat were all one a later evolution of this seat the front jockeys, the side jockeys, and the seat were all made from one piece of leather. Generally a screw was used at the base of the fork to hold down the leather. It replaced the number 2 saddle string, which had previously been used in this position.

In some saddles, such as the McClellan cavalry saddle, the leather did not cover the channel between the bars but extended around each bar individually. This type of seat is called a *slotted seat* (Fig. 19.2).

We tend to think of padded seats as a somewhat recent innovation for comfort. In the early 1900s, however, there was a ladies' astride saddle, called a *spring seat* or *spring-bar seat* (Fig. 19.3), which had a heavily padded seat. A distinctive feature that usually accompanied the spring seat was a heavily padded, fairly large round roll, sometimes called a *squaw roll.* On the western saddle it was placed over the top and the sides of the fork and cantle. On the English saddle it was placed not only over the cantle but also around the top side of the front of the pommel.

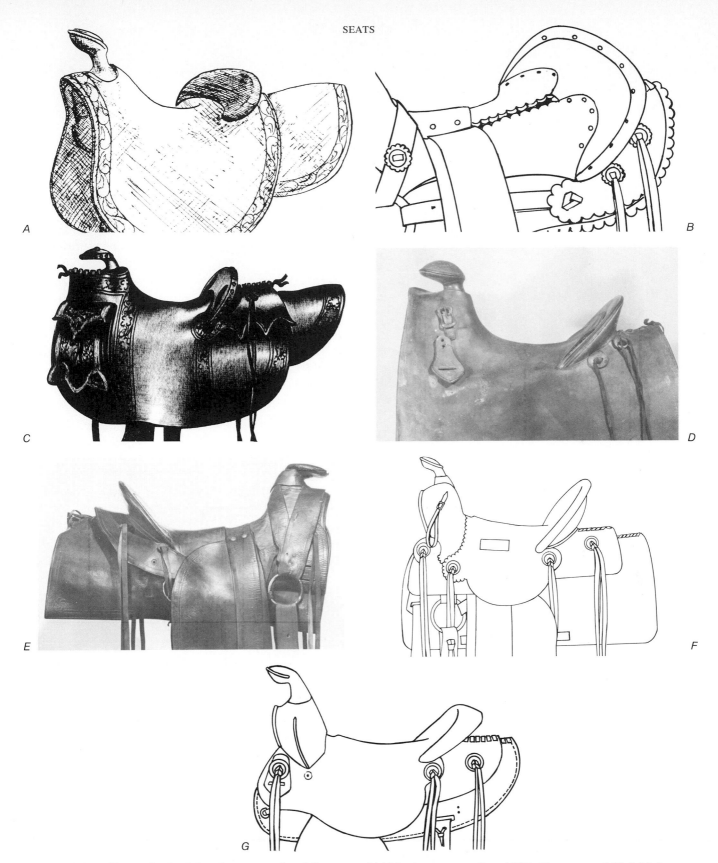

FIG. 19.1.   Chronological development of saddle seats. *(A)* Mexican seat, after 1835. Courtesy of Phil Living-ston. *(B)* Half-rigged seat on Mexican saddle. *(C)* Mexican with removable mochila seat. Courtesy of Paul Rossi. *(D)* Mother Hubbard with permanently attached mochila-type covering. Courtesy of Phil Livingston. *(E)* Three-quarter seat. Courtesy of Wyoming Historical Society. *(F)* Saddle with loop seat. *(G)* Full-extended seat with California skirt.

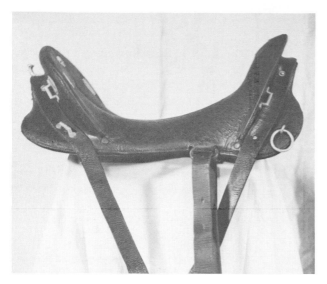

FIG. 19.2. Slotted seat on McClellan saddle. Courtesy of Fort Sill Museum.

Very few western saddles were padded until the 1930s. Padding then began to appear frequently. Some of the padding is quilted, and the quilting may be inlaid or overlaid.

When the base is built for a seat, a leather *bar riser* is added to the wooden tree. It goes on top of the bar at the base of the fork to give the seat its foundation in front. On top of the *channel,* the space between the bars, is placed the *metal strainer* (Figs. 19.4 and 19.5). The strainer prevents the seat from collapsing into the channel, losing its shape, and becoming uncomfortable to both horse and rider. The curvature of the strainer varies depending on the style of the tree and on how high and narrow the front of the seat is to be. On top of the strainer are placed larger pieces of leather to finish forming the foundation for the seat covering. As all these components are added, the saddlemaker must keep in mind that the stirrup leathers are to be placed over the *outside* of the bar and pulled down *inside* the bar in the stirrup-leather groove.

The *slope* of the seat has much to do with the position of the rider with regard to the center of gravity of horse and rider combined. Obviously, after having ridden for a while, the

A   B   C

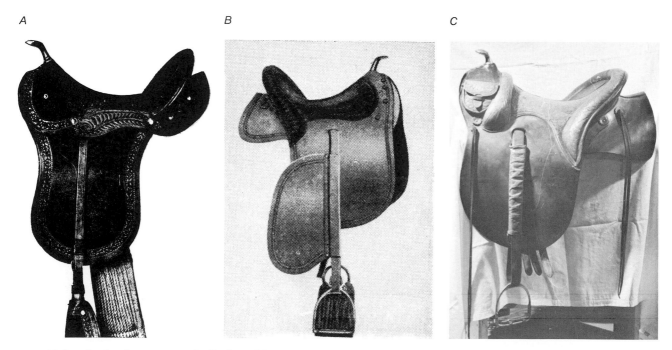

FIG. 19.3. Spring-bar seat on ladies' astride saddles. *(A)* From Wyeth catalog, 1939. *(B)* Ladies' Canby astride saddle. From Kauffman, catalog no. 757, 1927. *(C)* Ladies' astride saddle. Author's collection.

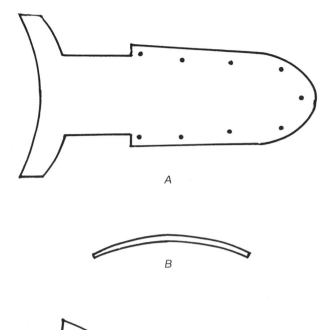

A

B

C

FIG. 19.4. Metal strainer. The curvature of the strainer varies, depending upon the style of tree and the height and width of the seat in front. *(A)* Top view. *(B)* Front view. *(C)* Side view.

rider will position himself in the lowest part of the seat because the natural movements of the horse will move him into this position. If the seat is flat, the rider can easily move his position relative to the horse's center of gravity (Fig. 19.6). If the seat is somewhat semi-circular (concave), the rider will be pushed into the center of the saddle (Fig. 19.7). If the seat is sloped downward from the fork back toward the cantle, the rider will be pushed against the cantle (Fig. 19.8). I believe that the flat seat is preferable to the others.

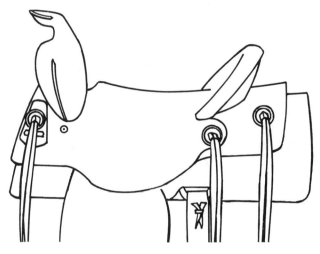

FIG. 19.6. Flat seat.

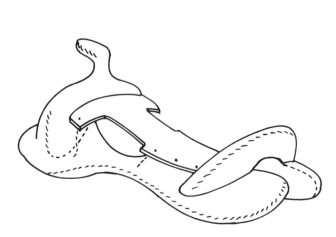

FIG. 19.5. Metal strainer over channel, raised above location on the bars. It is directly nailed to the bars. Courtesy of Phil Livingston.

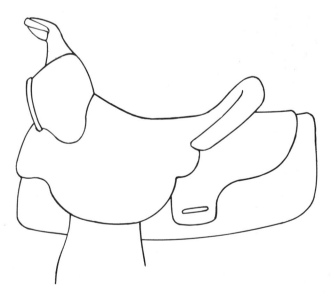

FIG. 19.7. Center seat.

115

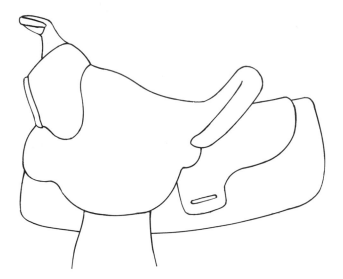

FIG. 19.8.   Backward-slant seat.

The customary method of measuring a seat is to measure the distance from the fork at the base of the horn to the top center of the cantle (Fig. 19.9). An extra one-half inch should be

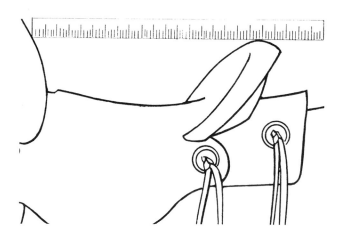

FIG. 19.9.   Customary method of seat measurement.

added to the length of the seat if it is padded or quilted. This method of seat measurement leaves much to be desired, because the slope of the fork and the slope of the cantle are not taken into account. Because of the extreme

variations in the slope angles of both the fork and the cantle, the standard method of measuring the length will show a two- to three-inch variation in the length of the seat. A more accurate method is to measure the seat as shown in Fig. 19.10. This method measures

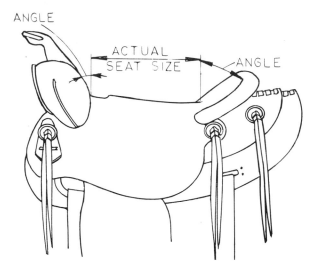

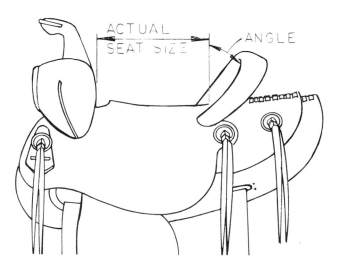

FIG. 19.10.   Improved method of seat measurement. The actual seat size of both saddles is identical; however, their measurements differ by about two inches because of the slopes of the fork and the cantle.

the exact seat length from the base of the fork to the base of the cantle (in the center of the seat). By drawing perpendicular lines upward from these two points, one can measure the slope angle of the fork and the slope angle of the cantle. This will give the actual "availability" room in the seat.

The only way to lengthen the seat of a western saddle is to move the cantle farther back on the bars, away from the fork, or to slope the cantle. The fork's location is set and can be varied only slightly.

For rider comfort a very important measurement that is ignored by customary seat-measurement systems is the distance horizontally from the lower back of the swell fork to the outside lower front of the cantle. This distance determines the leg room available to the rider. On an A-fork, narrow fork, or form-fit saddle this measurement is not important because there is nothing in front to hinder the leg's forward movement.

CHAPTER 20

Skirts

The *skirts* are the large sheets of leather attached to the underneath side of the bars. They extend outward from the bars and down the sides of the horse, and are held in place by the saddle-string assembly. The purpose of the skirt is to protect the horse's back from the bars, which would otherwise ride directly on its back. It also keeps the horse's sweat off the rider. A skeleton saddle without skirts appears rather bare. The old Mexican saddles were of this type.

The heavy leather skirt is lined on the underneath first with a thin protective lining of leather, called a *sudadero* by the Spaniards and old-time cowboys. This name has often been improperly used to refer to the *fender,* or *rosadero.*

The bottom layer of the completed skirt is a layer of sheepskin (Fig. 20.1). The sheepskin

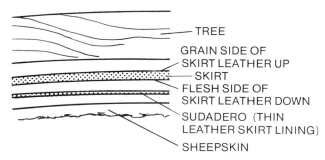

FIG. 20.1.   Cross section of a skirt (on the near side).

provides some friction between the saddle's slick leather and the saddle blanket to help prevent the saddle from shifting. It also gives a soft, comfortable layer between the saddle and the horse.

Skirts have two main shapes: the rounded *California skirt,* so called because of its popu-larity in California (Fig. 12.7) and the large, square *Texas skirt* (Fig. 12.8), so called because of its popularity in Texas. The Texas skirt is made large to protect the sides of the horse against mesquite, cactus, and brush. The width of the skirt is normally one-half the length; narrow skirts tend to crawl on the horse's back. Originally the skirt was made in one piece; however, it did not leave an air channel along the backbone of the horse. Because of this and, of course, because it is easier to obtain smaller pieces of leather, all skirts today are made in two pieces.

Many skirts have a small D ring near the forward edge about one-third of the way up. This is the *breast collar* D *ring,* to which the rig strap of the breast collar is attached. In place of a D ring some saddles have a slot cut through the skirt where the breast-collar rig straps attach (Fig. 20.2).

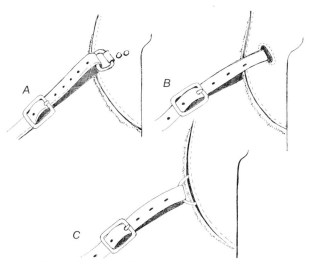

FIG. 20.2.   Breast-collar attachments. *(A)* D ring on skirt. *(B)* Slot style in skirt. *(C)* D ring between skirt edges. Drawings by Judy Osburn.

CHAPTER 21

Jockeys

The *jockeys* are the coverings for the exposed upper side of the saddletree bars except that part covered by the seat. Jockeys are cut to shape to accomplish this purpose and yet blend in with the over all needs of the saddle. They not only cover the bars but also protect them. Jockeys are also called *housings.*

Each of the three jockeys covers a particular area. The *front jockey* covers the *bur,* the bar from the fork forward. The *side jockey,* also known as the *seat jockey,* covers the exposed part of the bar between the fork and the cantle. The *rear jockey* covers and protects the *fan,* the bar from the back of the cantle backward to the end.

On the old eight-string-seat saddle (a saddle with eight strings, four on each side, Fig. 21.1) the *number 1,* or *forward, string* held the front jockey to the skirt ahead of the fork. The *number 2 string* was at the base of the fork and held the skirt to a back corner of the front jockey and a forward corner of the side or seat jockey. The *number 3 string* held a rear corner of the side jockey and a forward corner of the rear, or back, jockey. The *number 4 string* held the rear jockey and the skirt together.

In the early days saddles had three separate jockeys, as exemplified on the three-quarter-seat saddle of the late 1880s and 1890s (Fig. 21.2). This saddle was also known as the *Texas Trail saddle* or *Great Plains saddle.* In later years the jockeys underwent many changes. The first change was combining the seat and the side (seat) jockey into one piece of leather (Fig. 21.1). Later the seat, side jockey, and front jockey were all cut from one piece of leather (Fig. 21.3). Combining the side and front jockeys with the seat eliminated the need for a

FIG. 21.1.   Eight-string saddle showing seat and side jockey in one piece. From Frazier, catalog no. 37, 1935.

saddle string to hold the two together and to the skirt underneath the fork of the saddle. On many saddles the saddle-string assembly was replaced with a screw concha or a screw-and-ferrule assembly.

119

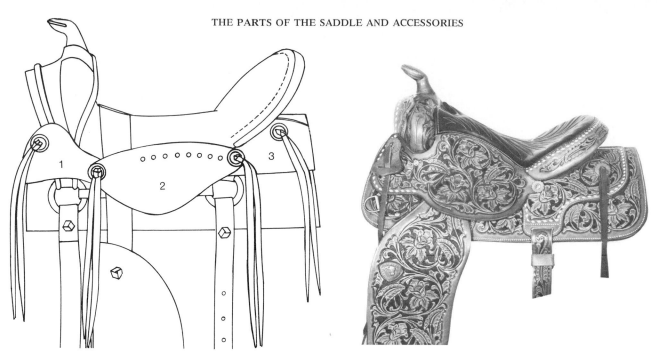

FIG. 21.2.   Three-quarter-seat saddle with three separate jockeys and eight strings.

FIG. 21.4.   Four-string seat. Courtesy of Tex Tan.

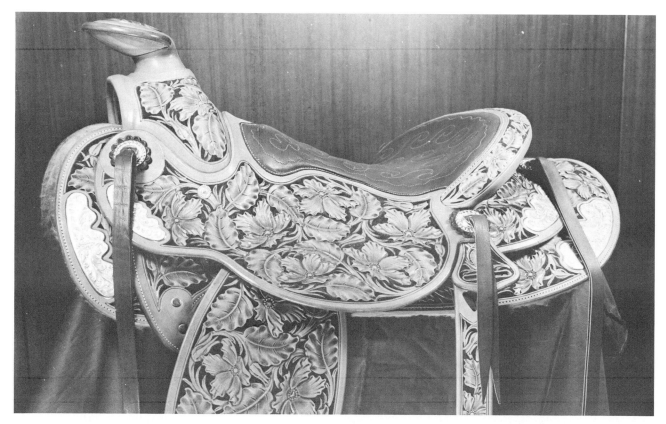

FIG. 21.3.   Six-string seat, the Pitchford, made in 1952 by Hamley. The seat and front and side jockeys are one piece. The screw at the base of the fork replaces saddle string no. 2. Courtesy of Hamley's.

The rear jockeys are usually separate and are joined at the upper center of the back of the saddle, either laced together with leather thongs (Fig. 21.7) or connected to each other by the

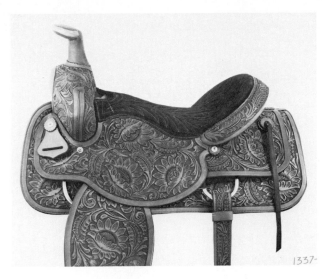

FIG. 21.5. Two-string seat. Courtesy of Tex Tan.

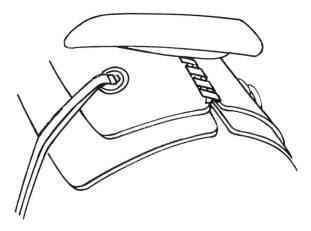

FIG. 21.7. Back jockeys laced.

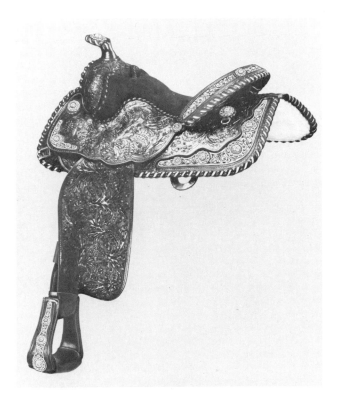

FIG. 21.6. Modern no-strings saddle (Billy Royal). Courtesy of Schneiders, Cleveland, Ohio.

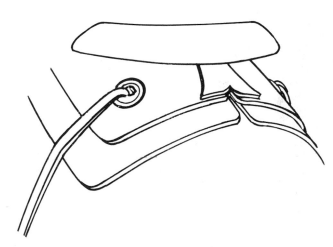

FIG. 21.8. Back-jockey connector plate.

back-jockey connector plate, a leather plate covering the connecting line between the two jockeys. This plate is stitched to each jockey (Fig. 21.8).

CHAPTER 22

The Saddle-String Assembly

The *saddle-string assembly* holds together the loose pieces covering the saddletree bars. It anchors the skirts to the underneath side of the bars and the jockeys and the loose ends of the seat leather to the top of the bars.

The saddle-string assembly (Fig. 22.1) con-

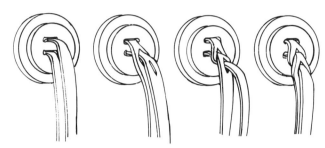

FIG. 22.2. Slit-braid tie.

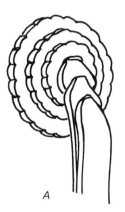

FIG. 22.1. Saddle-string assembly *(A)* With tiered-leather rosettes. *(B)* With leather rosette and metal concha.

sists of a *saddle string,* a long leather thong; a leather *rosette* (or rosettes), a round, slotted piece of leather, often with a serrated or scalloped edge (Fig. 22.8); and a concha (fig. 22.11). The saddle string starts at the skirt and is run through two slots of the rosette and the slots of the metal or silver concha or through a tiered series of two or three rosettes, each smaller from bottom to top. The saddle string is tied by the slit-braid-tie method (Fig. 22.2), which makes it a solid, substantial anchorage.

The standard saddle-string tie is almost always used, although in the past there have been other styles of saddle-string knots, one

of which was the *rose tie* (Fig. 22.3). Another style was a square knot in which the strings were twisted as the knot was made so that the same sides (flesh or grain) showed. The long, loose ends of the saddle strings were used to tie packages, equipment, and so on, to the saddle for transportation, leaving the rider's hands free.

As mentioned earlier, when the seat, side jockey, and front jockey were made from one piece of leather, saddle string number 2 was replaced with a screw and a ferrule. The saddle was then a six-string saddle (three strings on each side, Fig. 21.3).

As the need to transport articles diminished, saddle string number 3 at the base of the cantle

FIG. 22.3. Old-fashioned "rose" tie knot.

was also replaced with a screw and ferrule, and the saddle became a four-string seat. Finally, as saddles were used more and more for pleasure riding and show and less for work, the remaining two saddle strings on each side were removed, and the screw-and-ferrule method of anchoring the leather became common (Fig. 22.4).

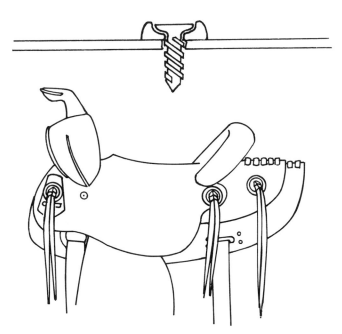

FIG. 22.4. Screw-and-ferrule replacement for saddle string number 2.

Because the screw and ferrule are not very attractive adornments, saddlemakers began covering them with an ornamental concha (Fig. 22.7). The problem with the concha is that it makes it difficult to disassemble the saddle to oil the underneath side of the leathers.

Saddle strings still have their purposes, and on many modern saddles a small D ring is attached to the screw-and-ferrule concha arrangement, and a saddle string may be hung from it (Fig. 22.5). Quality saddles are made in such a way that the saddle string on the underside of the skirt is underneath the sheepskin lining, not on top of it.

A cross section of a standard saddle-string assembly is shown in Fig. 22.6. The cross section

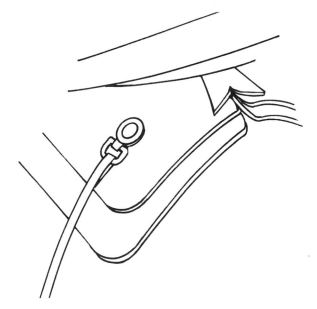

FIG. 22.5. D ring on screw concha.

of the ferrule-screw-concha arrangement is shown in Fig. 22.7. Conchas are shown in Figs. 22.9 to 22.11.

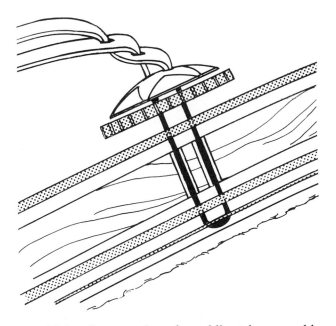

FIG. 22.6. Cross section of a saddle-string assembly through the tree.

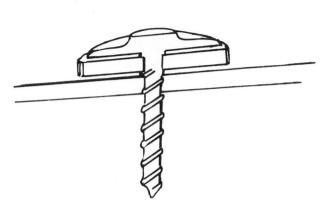

FIG. 22.7. Cross section of a screw concha with decorative rosette.

FIG. 22.8. Graduated scalloped-leather concha rosettes.

FIG. 22.9. Metal or nickel-silver conchas.

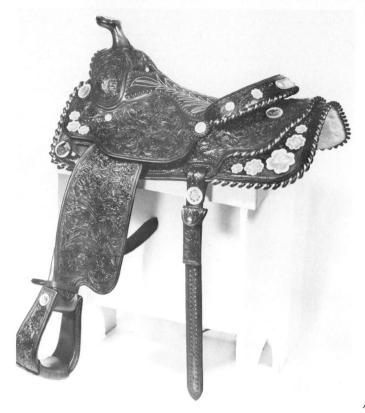

A

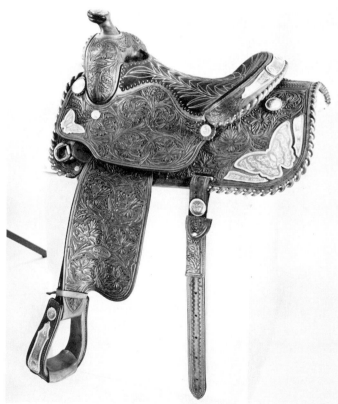

B

FIG. 22.10. Show saddles with sterling-silver screw conchas featuring dome pattern that matches silver trim. *(A)* Cloverleaf. Courtesy of Ryon's, catalog no. 66, 1978. *(B)* Monarch. Courtesy of Ryon's.

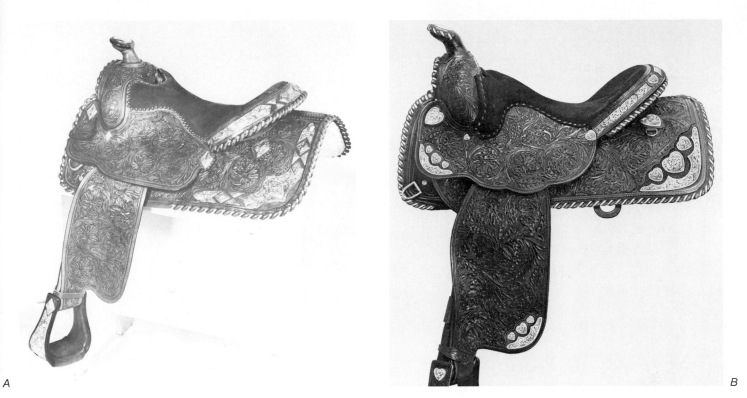

A

B

FIG. 22.11. Show saddles with sterling-silver screw conchas that match decorative silver trim. *(A)* Diamonds. Courtesy of Ryon's. *(B)* Hearts. Courtesy of Schneiders.

CHAPTER 23

Rigging

The *saddle rigging* is the assembly to which the cinch is anchored to hold the saddle firmly in place on the horse's back. It consists of the rigging leathers, which are attached at the bottom end by either a circular or a D ring. To the bottom of the rigging ring is attached the *cinch strap,* or *billet,* which attaches to the cinch. This is called *conventional,* or *on-tree, rigging* (Fig. 23.1). This type of rigging adds

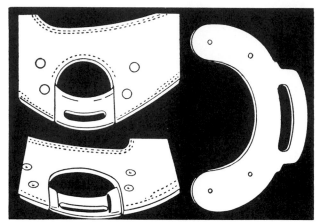

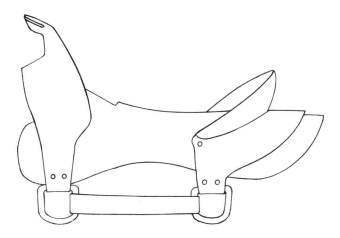

FIG. 23.1.   Conventional rigging on the tree.

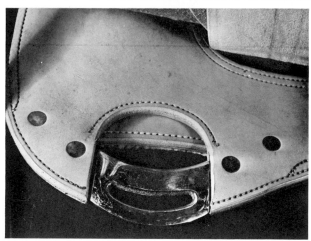

FIG. 23.2.   On-tree rigging. From Hamley's, catalog no. 53, 1953.

weight and bulk under the rider's thighs and knees.

In 1925 a new style of rigging appeared in which a plate with a slot for the cinch strap replaced the rigging ring in the rigging leathers (Fig. 23.6). This style is still used by many saddlemakers.

In 1952, N. Porter registered and trademarked the Rig-in-Skirt, a style that is today known as *in-skirt rigging* (Fig. 23.2). In this style the rigging-ring replacements (plates) are attached directly to the skirts of the saddle (Fig. 23.4). This style has had increasing acceptance. Instead of a flat rigging plate in the skirt the conventional D rings or circular rings may be attached to the skirts (Fig. 23.5).

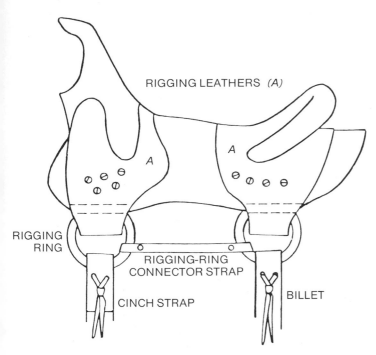

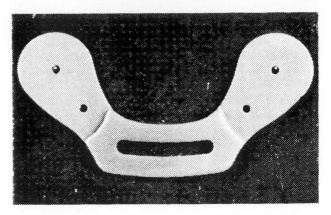

FIG. 23.6. In-skirt flat rigging plate. From Tex Tan, catalog no. 82, 1973.

FIG. 23.3. Conventional full double rigging showing parts.

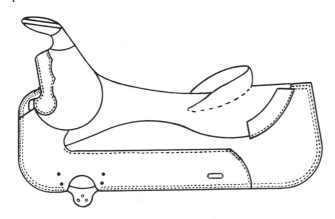

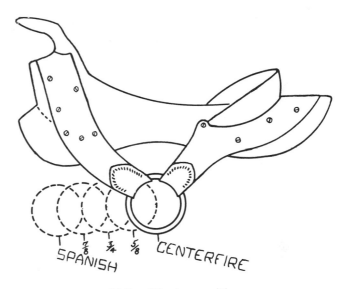

FIG. 23.7. Rigging positions.

FIG. 23.4. Built-in in-skirt flat-plate rigging. From N. Porter's, Phoenix, Arizona, catalog no. 37, ca. 1959.

Bulkless rigging came into popular use after 1954 with the development of the Monte Foreman Balanced Ride® saddle (Fig. 36.20), which eliminated much of the under-saddle bulk.

There are as many proponents of one or another style of rigging as there are riders of horses. Valid reasons can be given for adopting a specific type of rigging for the particular work for which the saddle is to be used.

The various styles of conventional rigging can be grouped as follows:

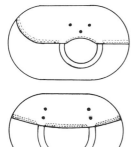

FIG. 23.5. Conventional D ring used in in-skirt rigging. From N. Porter's, catalog no. 37, ca. 1959.

127

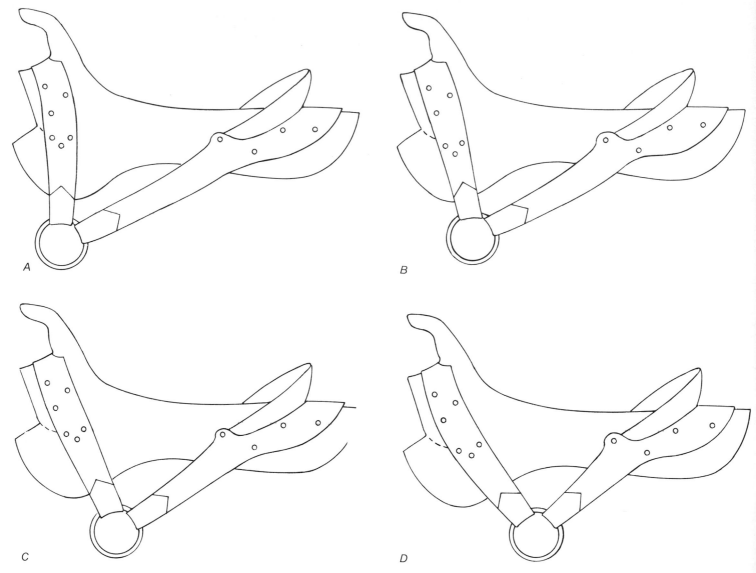

FIG. 23.8.   Rigging styles. *(A)* Spanish rigging (full). *(B)* Seven-eighths rigging. *(C)* Three-quarter rigging (Montana). *(D)* Five-eighths rigging (Arizona).

Single rigging:
  1. Spanish (Fig. 23.8*A*)
  2. Seven-eighths (Fig. 23.8*B*)
  3. Three-quarter (Montana) (Fig. 23.8*C*)
  4. Five-eighths (Arizona) (Fig. 23.8*D*)
  5. Centerfire (California) (Fig. 23.8*E*)

Double rigging:
  1. Full (rimfire) (Fig. 23.8*F*)
  2. Seven-eighths (Fig. 23.8*G*)
  3. Three-quarter (Fig. 23.8*H*)

In early days *Spanish rigging* (Fig. 23.8*A*) was the predominant rigging style in California. It was later replaced by *centerfire,* or *California, rigging* (Fig. 23.8*E*). The method of dally roping used by Californians never created the tremendous pull on the saddle that occurs in the hard-and-fast-tie-roping style used by Texans. Therefore the Spanish rig and the centerfire rig were very well suited to their purposes. Centerfire rigging was used primarily in flat country and

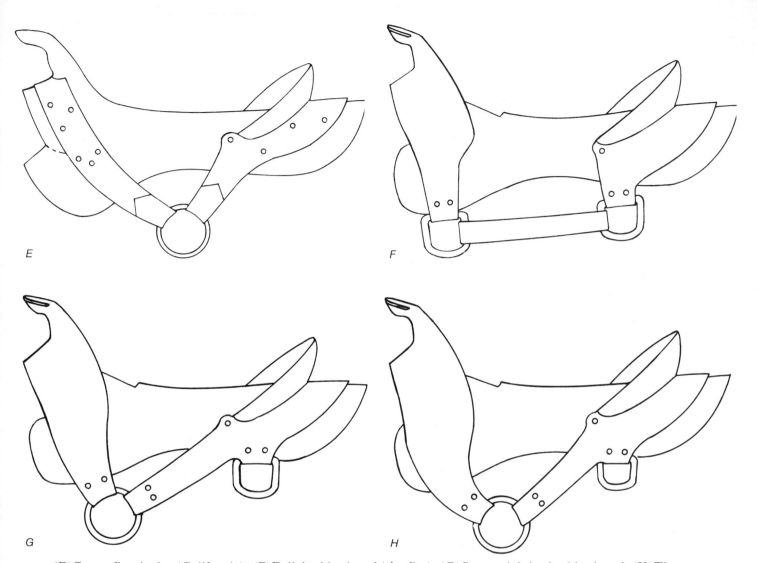

(E) Centerfire rigging (California). *(F)* Full double-rigged (rim fire). *(G)* Seven-eighths double-rigged. *(H)* Three-quarter double-rigged.

was not designed for heavy roping. It was used with a wide cinch. It was and is best used on a horse with good withers (Holes, 1949).

The hard-and-fast-tie rope used by Texans was about forty feet long, whereas the dally rope was about sixty feet long. The home end of the hard-and-fast-tie rope was tied securely to the saddle horn. When the cow or bull hit the end of the rope, it gave a tremendous jerk to the saddle. To keep the saddle from tilting up-

ward, a second cinch, the *flank cinch,* was added to the back of the saddle. This brought about the full double rig (Fig. 23.8*F*). From a full double rig evolved the seven-eighths double rig and then the three-quarter dougle rig. Neither centerfire nor five-eighths double rigging was used.

Saddles used in rodeo roping and bulldogging contests are full-double-rigged. These rigging positions are approximately 1 1/2 inches apart on a 12-inch seat to 2 inches apart on a 16-inch seat.

There are several variations of single rigging. Originally it was the Spanish rig with the single rigging ring in the full position, or directly below the fork. Then came the centerfire position, where the small rigging ring was suspended halfway between the base of the fork and the base of the cantle. Then came variations of the single rigging, such as the seven-eighths (Fig. 23.8*B*), the three-quarter, or Montana (Fig. 23.8*C*), and the five-eighths, or Arizona, rigging (Fig. 23.8*D*).

The Sam Stagg rigging common in the 1880s has been discussed previously.

Proponents of in-skirt rigging say that, contrary to the fears of the early cowboys, it is as strong as the conventional styles. In-skirt rigging makes a saddle "sit well" on a horse: the saddle conforms to the horse's shape, the rider is nearer his horse, and the rigging rings are not under the rider's knees. In-skirt rigging eliminates bulk in this area, but some say that it may restrict air circulation between the skirt and the horse.

There are two styles of in-skirt rigging, *built-on* and *built-in.* Built-on rigging is merely a

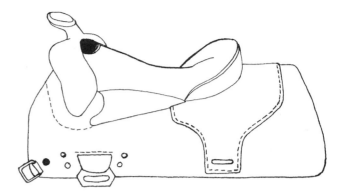

FIG. 23.10.   Ryon's built-in in-skirt rigging. Drawing by Judy Osburn.

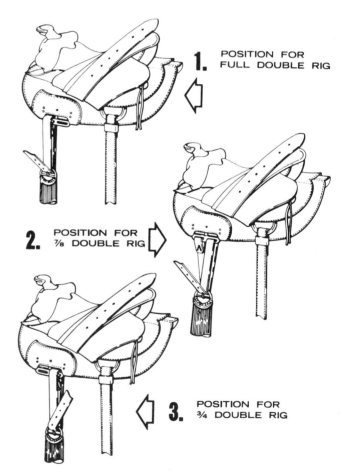

1. POSITION FOR FULL DOUBLE RIG

2. POSITION FOR ⅞ DOUBLE RIG

3. POSITION FOR ¾ DOUBLE RIG

FIG. 23.11.   Built-in rigging, adjusting to one of three positions. *(A)* Full double rig. *(B)* Seven-eighths double rig. *(C)* Three-quarter double rig. From J. V. Wilson Leather Company, Belle Fontaine, Mississippi, catalog no. 73, 1973.

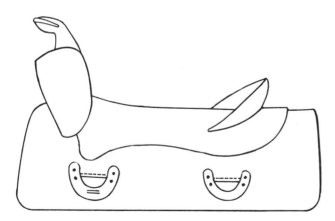

FIG. 23.9.   Built-on in-skirt rigging.

plate attached to the surface of the skirt. This is the usual style on inexpensive saddles that will not have hard use. Built-in rigging has a

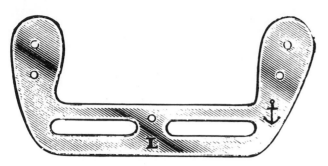

FIG. 23.12.   Three-way rigging plate. From Wilson, catalog no. 73, 1973.

FIG. 23.13.   Rear rigging plate, in-skirt style. From Wilson, catalog no. 73, 1973.

plate on the surface of the skirt over which is sewed another piece of leather with the rigging plate attached firmly between the two. This

style of rigging is good for almost any kind of heavy-duty work, including roping.

CHAPTER 24

Rigging Rings, Ds, Bars, and Plates

Rigging rings are made of steel, brass, or aluminum and are generally made in one of two shapes viewed in a cross section. One shape is made of round, heavy wire. The other shape is made of a teardrop-shaped oval with the sharp edge of the teardrop on the outside diameter of the rigging ring. The ring is either

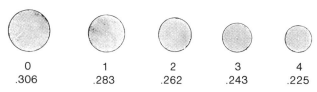

0	1	2	3	4
.306	.283	.262	.243	.225

FIG. 24.1. Rigging-ring wire sizes and gauges. From Ruwart Manufacturing Company, Denver, Colorado, catalog, 1963.

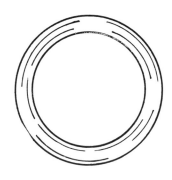

FIG. 24.2. Circular-wire metal rigging ring.

FIG. 24.3. Circular-wire D ring.

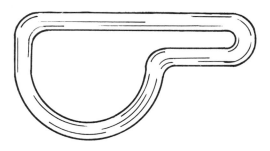

FIG. 24.4. Extended D ring, circular wire.

FIG. 24.5. Leather-covered ring, or D.

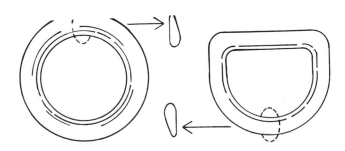

FIG. 24.6. Flat metal rigging ring and D (available in steel or brass).

132

FIG. 24.7. Pear rigging ring, used with a single-rigged saddle only.

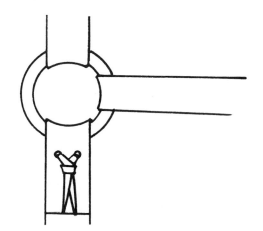

FIG. 24.8. Rigging ring with attached mounting.

circular, with a 2-to-4-inch inside diameter, or in the shape of a D, 3 to 4 inches across.

The circular steel-wire rigging rings were often leather-covered to extend their life in heavy-duty service. The teardrop-shaped rings are called *flat rigging rings,* while the round wire rings are called *wire rigging rings.* They are available both as circular rings and as Ds. Flat D rings, rings with two flat sides, are not recommended (Holes, 1949).

The rigging rings of all saddles should be exactly opposite each other and at the same height. Even a 1/4-inch variation will allow the saddle to "crawl" on the horse's back.

To reduce the bulk under the rider's thighs the flat rigging bar was developed by Hamley in the early 1920s. This bar is still in use today, with many modifications (Fig. 23.2).

In-skirt rigging may use wire or flat rigging rings, but more often rigging plates are used (Fig. 23.10). These plates are attached to the skirt as described earlier.

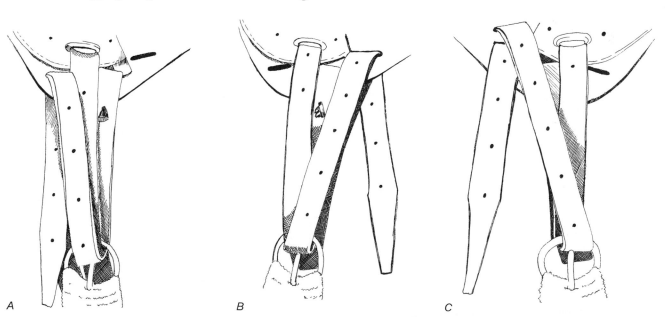

FIG. 24.9. Three different ways of tying bulkless rigging. *(A)* Near side. *(B)* Near side. *(C)* Off side. Drawings by Judy Osburn. Courtesy of Fallis.

133

CHAPTER 25

Cinches, Rings, Straps, and Billets

The purpose of the *cinch* is to anchor the saddle to the horse as comfortably as possible, in the position in which the rider wishes it to stay. The cinch should not interfere with the horse's action any more than necessary. Cinches are made of webbing or cords of horsehair, canvas, leather, and so on. With centerfire rigging a wide cinch is used. With a full double-rigged saddle a narrow cinch is generally used to reduce the possibility of galling.

It is my belief that the use of *girth* (pronounced "girt" by cowboys) in referring to the western *cinch* is incorrect. Technically *girth*

refers to the outside circumference of the horse at a given point, not to the equipment that goes on the "outside" to hold the saddle in position (the word girth is correctly used in referring to English saddles).

Probably the longest-lasting cinches were those made of horsehair (hair from a horse's mane, not from the tail). Many of the old cavalry cinches made of horsehair are still in existence and even usable. Today a horsehair cinch is almost prohibitively expensive, and not many are offered in catalogs (Fig. 25.2).

Canvas cinches are more commonly used

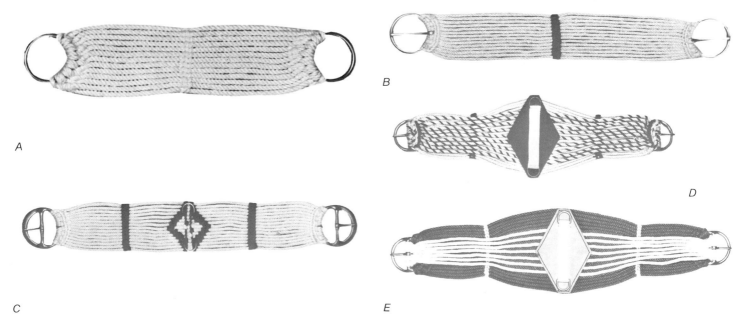

A

B

C

D

E

FIG. 25.1.   Styles of cinches. *(A)* Cinch with cinch rings. *(B)* Cinch with two tongue-style buckles and crossbar. Also available with tongue-style buckle on one side and plain ring on the other. *(C)* Cinch with center-bar rings, tongue-style buckles, crossbar, and center Ds. *(D)* Roping cinches with center-bar rings, tongue-style buckles, and center Ds. Courtesy of Tex Tan.

FIG. 25.2. Horsehair cinch. Mane hair, not tail hair, is used.

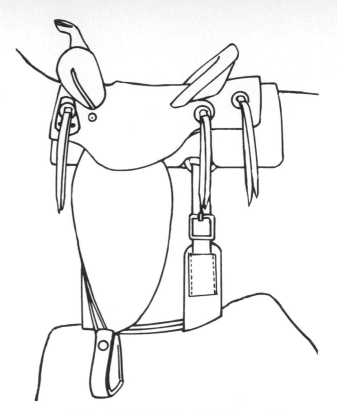

with English saddles, less often with western saddles. Leather cinches are commonly used for the flank cinch, less commonly for the front cinch (Figs. 25.3 to 25.6). A roper's flank cinch

FIG. 25.5. Flank cinch buckled (near side).

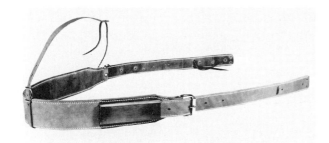

FIG. 25.3. Flank cinch with attached cinch connector strap. Courtesy of Tex Tan.

FIG. 25.4. Cinch connector strap. Courtesy of Tex Tan.

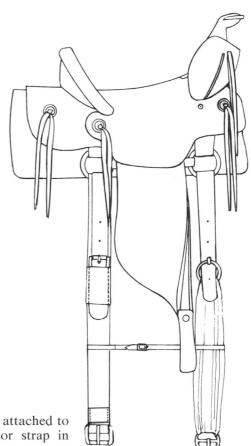

FIG. 25.6. Front cinch and flank cinch attached to the saddle, off side, showing connector strap in place.

135

has a long *stationary (tunnel) keeper* on each end to prevent the ropes from being caught on the loose end of the flank billet.

The *spider* is a second, reinforcing rigging strap over the fan of the tree attaching at each end of the rear rigging ring (Fig. 25.7).

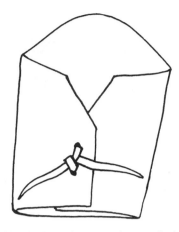

FIG. 25.8. Cinch-ring chape (rub guard), full leather.

FIG. 25.7. Roping saddle with spider. From Tex Tan, catalog no. 86, 1976.

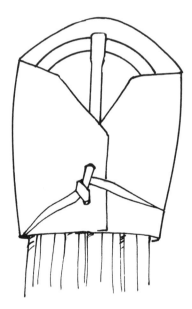

FIG. 25.9. Safe (assembled cinch ring and chape) full leather.

The most widely used cinches are the cord, or webbing, cinch. The cord cinch usually has 15 to 17 cords per inch; a roping cinch may have 14 to 27 cords per inch. Cord cinches are made of several kinds of material, including mohair, rayon, nylon, and cotton or a combination of these.

At each end of the cinch is a *cinch ring,* with or without a buckle tongue. Through these rings the cinch is anchored to the saddle by the cinch

FIG. 25.10. Round chape. Courtesy of Tex Tan.

136

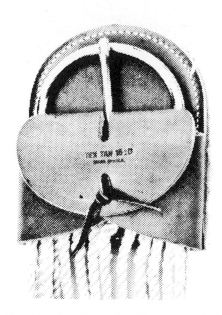

FIG. 25.11.   Full leather safe. Courtesy of Tex Tan.

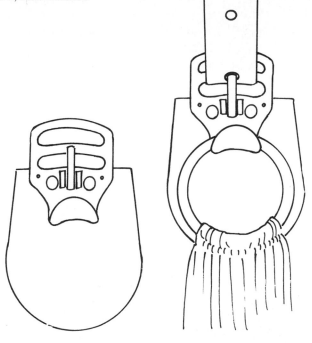

FIG. 25.13.   Tackaberry cinch buckle with chape. *(A)* Detail. *(B)* In use.

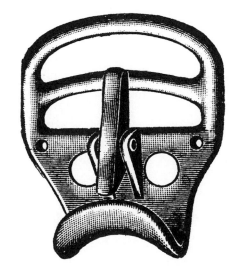

FIG. 25.12.   Tackaberry cinch buckle. From Stockman-Farmer Supply Company, Denver, Colorado, catalog no. 44, 1934.

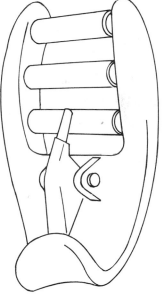

FIG. 25.14. Garner's safety saddle buckle (no longer available).

strap. Cinch rings are made in three styles: without a buckle tongue, with a buckle tongue, and with a crossbar across the ring to which a buckle tongue is attached (Fig. 25.1).

Everybody has a pet peeve, and mine is the sale of improperly sized cinches. The standard 30-inch cinch is too short for most horses ridden with seven-eighths or full double rigging. A 30-inch cinch places the cinch ring directly behind the horse's elbow and in a position to interfere with its action, as well as gall the horse. Even on a 14-hand horse a 34-inch cinch is required to clear this point (Fig. 25.16).

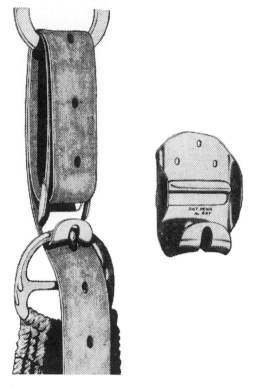

FIG. 25.15. Al Ray cinch hook. The hook saves taking down the cinch strap to cinch or uncinch and eliminates bind and bulk over the rigging ring. The cinch rivets to the hook and buckles with the cinch tongue. *(A)* Detail. *(B)* In use. From Western Saddle Manufacturing Co., Denver, catalog, 1951.

The length of the cinch is measured from the far end of one cinch ring to the far end of the other cinch ring (Fig. 25.18). Cinches stretch 1 to 2 inches in use, and this should be taken into account.

I once watched a western class at an Arabian show in Oklahoma City. Of the eighteen entries only two had their cinch rings in the proper position. The saddles were all full-double- or seven-eighths-rigged.

The cinch ring on all but five-eighths- and centerfire-rigged saddles should be in a position that will not interfere with the elbow and should be even on both sides of the horse (Fig. 25.17). More will be said about this in Chapter 33, "Saddling a Horse."

I have purposely avoided using *buckle* as a noun in speaking of cinch rings. In these pages the word *buckles* is used to denote square-ended or rectangular buckles rather than rounded cinch rings with buckle tongues or with center-bar and buckle tongues.

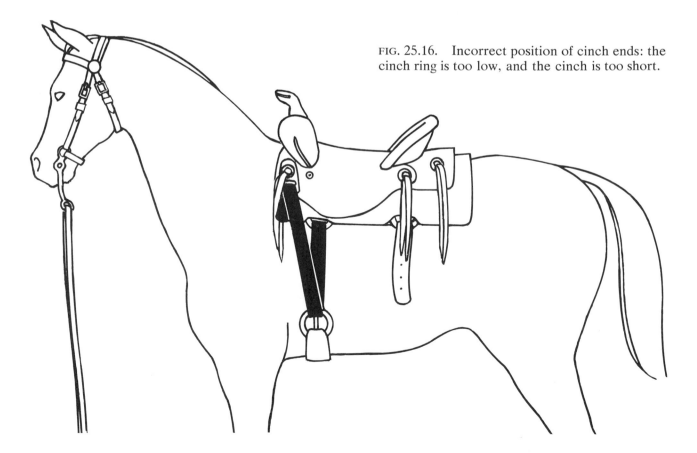

FIG. 25.16. Incorrect position of cinch ends: the cinch ring is too low, and the cinch is too short.

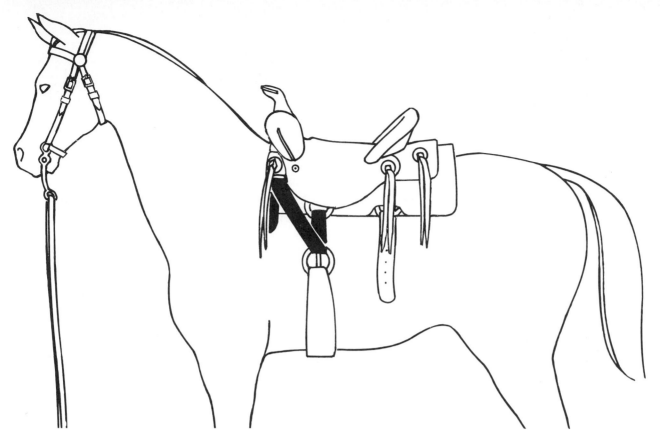

FIG. 25.17. Correct position of cinch ends. The rings are clear of the horse's elbows.

For a long time *latigo* has been used incorrectly to denote *cinch strap* (Fig. 25.19). *Latigo* actually refers to a dyeing process. Most cinch straps are leather, although straps of nylon webbing are gaining acceptance.

The purpose of both cinch straps and *billets* is to anchor the saddle on the horse's back through their attachment from the saddle rigging rings to the cinch rings. The cinch strap is tightened so that the saddle will not work loose on the horse's back or slip sideways with the rider or pull forward when a heavy steer is roped. Tightening up the cinch so that the saddle is properly and securely positioned on the horse is called *cinching up*.

Many horses have a bad habit of swelling up when the rider begins tightening the cinch. This will cause the cinch to be dangerously loose after the horse has moved a bit. The cinch should be tightened gently. Then the horse should be walked fifteen or twenty steps to

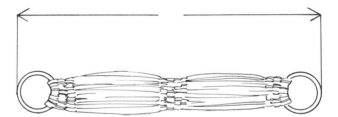

FIG. 25.18. Measuring a cinch.

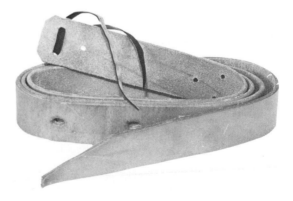

FIG. 25.19. Cinch strap. Courtesy of Tex Tan.

un-track him, after which the cinch should be tightened again. After about a quarter mile, the rider should reach down and check the cinch's tightness. He may save himself a spill. The cinch should not be too tight. The rider should be able to get three fingers side by side under the cinch on the horse's belly.

A cinch strap is usually rather long, from at least 30 inches up to 6 feet long when it is used in a double or triple wrap-around style. It is attached to the lower part of the rigging ring. It can be used with cinches that have either cinch rings or cinch rings with buckle tongues at the ends.

Since the final cinching up is always accomplished on the near side, the cinch strap on the near side is anchored with a buckle tongue on the cinch ring, with the loose end of the cinch strap anchored in a cinch-strap holder usually near the front jockey (Figs. 25.20 and 25.21).

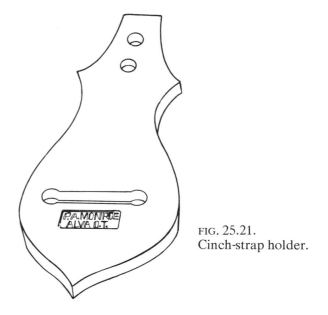

FIG. 25.21.
Cinch-strap holder.

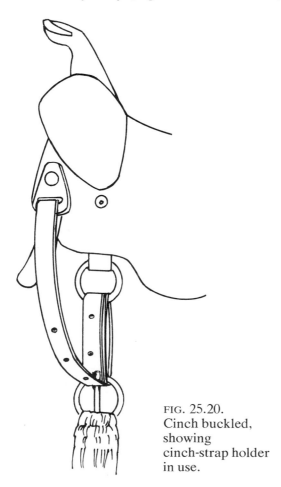

FIG. 25.20.
Cinch buckled,
showing
cinch-strap holder
in use.

The cinch strap can also be tightened by means of a *cinch hitch* on the near-side front rigging ring (Fig. 25.22). On the off side a "billet-to-cinch" buckle is generally used. A "cinch-strap-to-cinch-buckle" arrangement can be used on the off front rigging ring, but this side is usually cinched up by means of a cinch hitch because there is seldom a cinch-strap holder on the off side of the saddle.

Another method of tying the cinch strap to the cinch is called the *Montana knot.* It is accomplished by putting the cinch strap through the cinch ring and rigging ring *twice* and then turning the strap around and pulling a length of it back through the rigging ring from the underneath back side. Even though the strap is not totally anchored, this is a very effective way of cinching up the horse (Fig. 25.23).

Another method of anchoring the cinch to the rigging ring on the off side is by means of a billet, which in this position is called the *off front billet.* Because of the strength required in this position, this billet is doubled (Fig. 25.24) over the front rigging ring and can be used only with a cinch with a buckle tongue on that side (Fig. 25.25).

Another form of billet, called the *half-breed billet,* is used when exceptionally heavy work

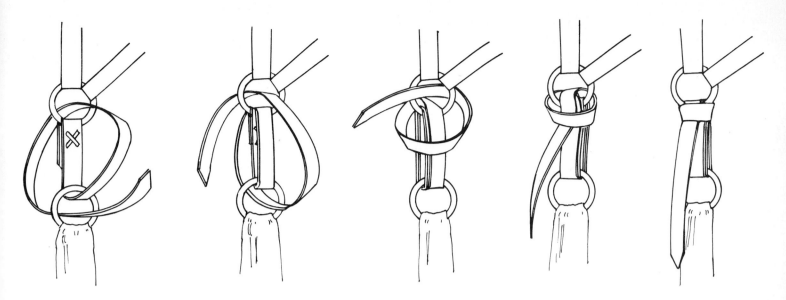

FIG. 25.22.   Tying the cinch hitch.

FIG. 25.24.   Off-front billet, double ply.

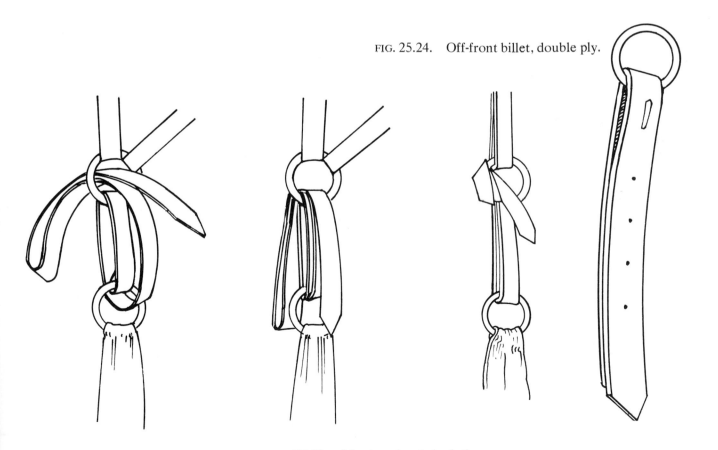

FIG. 25.23.   Montana-knot cinch tie.

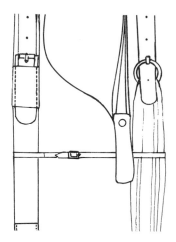

FIG. 25.25. Off-front billet, buckled.

is to be done or there is available only a light piece of leather that needs additional strength. The half-breed is a doubled strap; the doubling starting at the cinch buckle, with the double strap put through the rigging ring from the front, pulled down behind the first strap through the cinch buckle, and buckled at that point (Fig. 25.27). It can be used on the off front rigging ring or on either of the rear rigging rings.

Cinch straps are seldom used on flank cinches, although they can be. The flank cinch has nothing to do with how well a saddle stays in place during pleasure riding. Its purpose is to prevent the saddle from tilting up in the back during roping or fast stops. Because they require less work, billets are customarily used. They may be doubled, or they may be a single strap anchored at the rear rigging ring. The flank cinch is usually leather and has a buckle at each end.

A *keeper* is a rectangular loop of leather used to anchor the loose piece of leather that extends past a buckle. A *free keeper* slides up and down the leather strap. It is also used on

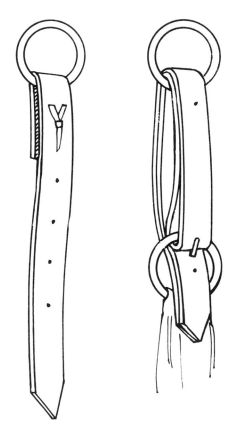

FIG. 25.26. Flank billet, single ply.

FIG. 25.27. Half-breed off billet.

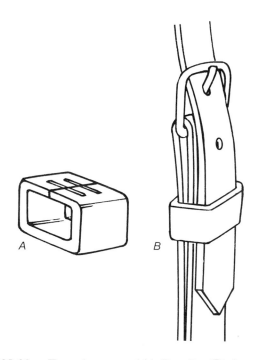

FIG. 25.28. Free keeper. *(A)* Detail. *(B)* In use.

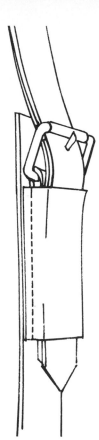

FIG. 25.29. Stationary tunnel keeper stitched over buckle strap.

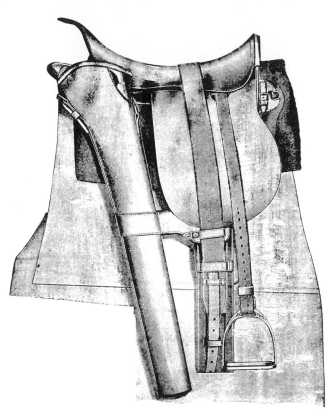

FIG. 25.31. British military saddle showing surcingle around the saddle. From William H. Carter, *Horses, Saddles, and Bridles.*

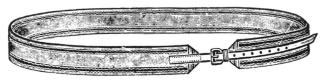

FIG. 25.30. Surcingle for saddle. From Wyeth, catalog no. 220, 1939.

the cheekpiece of a bridle, on curb straps, and on other pieces of tack. A *stationary keeper,* or *tunnel keeper,* is a keeper with the back piece stitched on the back of a piece of leather with a buckle on the end. On a saddle with a tongued buckle on the stirrup leather there may be a stationary keeper below the buckle on the buckle end of the stirrup leather. It is often used on a flank cinch also.

The *surcingle* is a strap that completely encircles the horse, going over the seat of the saddle (Figs. 25.31 and 25.32). It was often used on saddles in the old days, especially on military saddles, and is still used on racing saddles. Although it acted as a secondary safety should the cinch give way, its primary purpose was

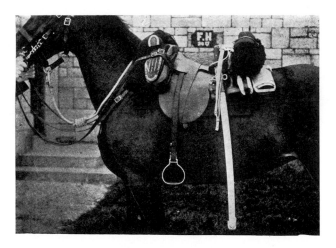

FIG. 25.32. Surcingle around the saddle on the horse. From Carter, *Horses, Saddles and Bridles.*

to keep the saddle firmly in position. Earlier in this century *surcingle* was often incorrectly used for *cinch strap.*

143

CHAPTER 26

Stirrup Leathers and Fenders

The *stirrup leathers* are the straps that attach the stirrups to the saddletree. Some older trees, such as those used in Morgan saddles, had a slot through the bars through which the stirrup leathers were placed. I have such a tree in my collection. Before the appearance of the stirrup-leather slot through the bars, an iron loop attached to the bars was the home end for stirrup leathers (Woodward, conversation).

A stirrup leather can be any size from a heavy 1-inch-wide strap on military and English saddles to the 3-inch-wide straps on some western saddles. Twenty-ounce stirrup leather 3 inches wide and 67 inces long is generally used on heavy-duty saddles, such as those used for roping. On barrel-racing and pleasure saddles 16-ounce, 2- or 2½-inch-wide stirrup leather is more often used.

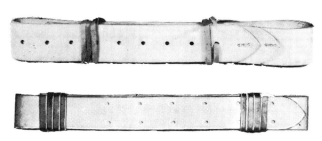

FIG. 26.1. Stirrup leathers. From Tex Tan, catalog no. 82, 1973.

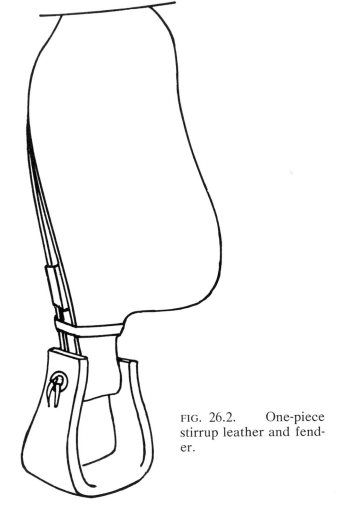

FIG. 26.2. One-piece stirrup leather and fender.

The stirrup leather may be a single strap with a separate fender attached to it, or the stirrup leather and fender may be cut out of one piece of leather so that the fender is an integral part of the stirrup leather.

Riders who spent long, tedious hours in the saddle found themselves wondering how it could be made more comfortable. Someone decided that by reducing the thickness and weight of the half double stirrup leather there would be less tension against the stirrup, making it easier hold the foot in and less bulky between the rider's

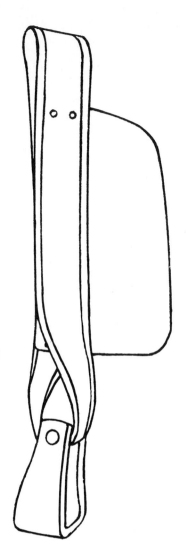

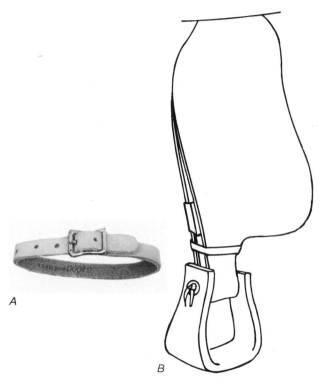

FIG. 26.4. Stirrup-leather keeper. *(A)* Detail. *(B)* In use. Courtesy of Tex Tan.

FIG. 26.3. Two-piece fender and stirrup leather. The stirrup leather is one piece, turned around the stirrup on one end and over the tree bars on the other end and buckled together underneath the fender.

leg and the horse. Thus the single stirrup leather was developed. The fender does not lie on top of the stirrup leather but is used in place of the outside portion of the stirrup leather.

Over the years many ways of attaching the stirrup leathers to the saddle have been tried. The *free-swing method* is one (Fig. 26.6). It was discontinued about ten years ago, accord-

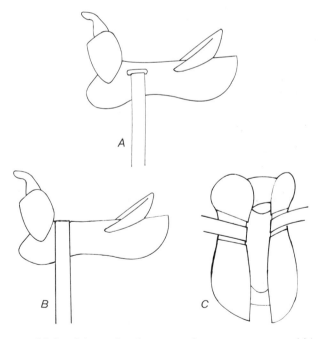

FIG. 26.5 Stirrup-leather attachments to tree. *(A)* Through slot in bar. *(B)* In groove on inside of bar. *(C)* Bottom view of tree, showing stirrup leather in groove.

145

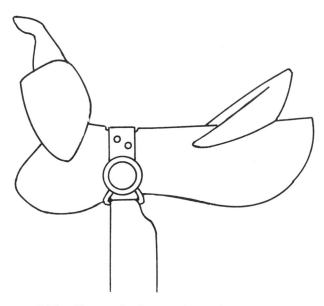

FIG. 26.6.   Free-swinging method of attachment to bars.

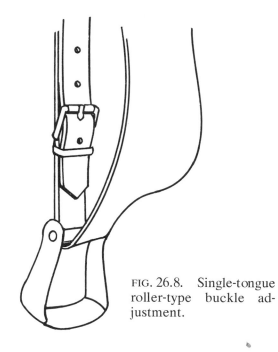

FIG. 26.8.   Single-tongue roller-type buckle adjustment.

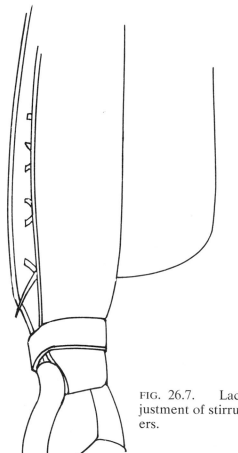

FIG. 26.7.   Lacing adjustment of stirrup leathers.

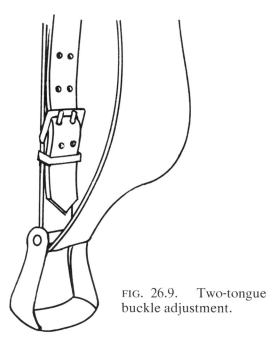

FIG. 26.9.   Two-tongue buckle adjustment.

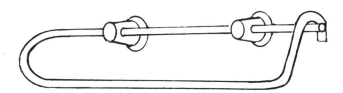

FIG. 26.10.   Speedy stirrup pin to replace lacing.

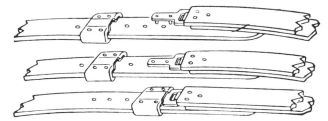

FIG. 26.11. Blevins Quick Change stirrup buckle. From Hamley's, catalog no. 77, 1974.

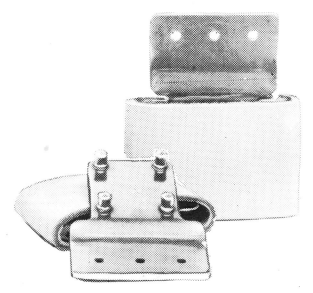

FIG. 26.12. Improved four-prong Blevins Quick change buckle. From Tex Tan, catalog no. 82, 1973.

FIG. 26.13. Al Ray Quick Adjustable stirrup-leather buckle. From Tex Tan, catalog no. 82, 1973.

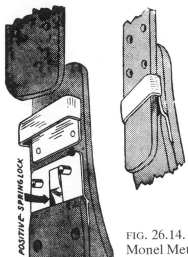

FIG. 26.14. Al Ray Improved Monel Metal stirrup-leather buckle. From Ruwart, catalog, 1963.

ing to Jack Carroll, because it made for weak construction.

Stirrup leathers must have some means of length adjustment. The old method of adjusting the length by lacing together the stirrup-leather ends with strong leather thongs had a practical reason: the leathers could be repaired in the field without tools, an especially important advantage to cowboys and the horse soldiers.

The *single-strap stirrup leather* was designed many years ago; a modification is used today on the Foreman Balanced Rider saddle made by Fallis Saddlery, in Colorado. The idea is to eliminate all unnecessary leather between the horse and the rider's leg. The single stirrup leather with separate fender is shorter than a doubled one. The lower extension of the one-piece fender is sewed or riveted at the stirrup end of the strap to join the two pieces. This doubled part is just long enough to provide the bend in which the stirrup hangs; the doubled part is then laced to the long stirrup strap, forming a loop for the stirrup. The top of the fender is then attached to the long length of the stirrup strap so that it lies smoothly against the strap. The upper end of the stirrup strap is inserted under the saddle seat and over the tree bar in the regular way, but the end of the strap reaches

147

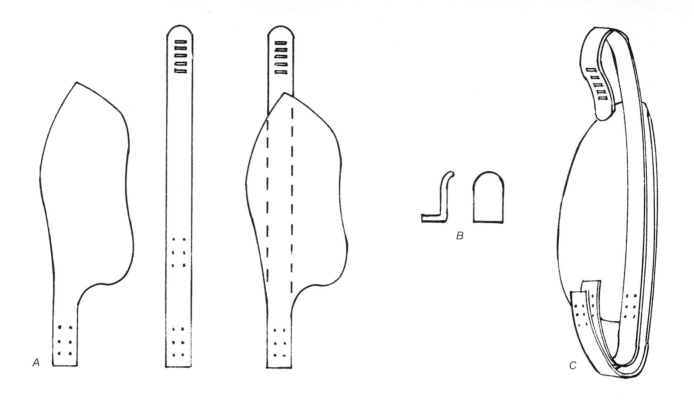

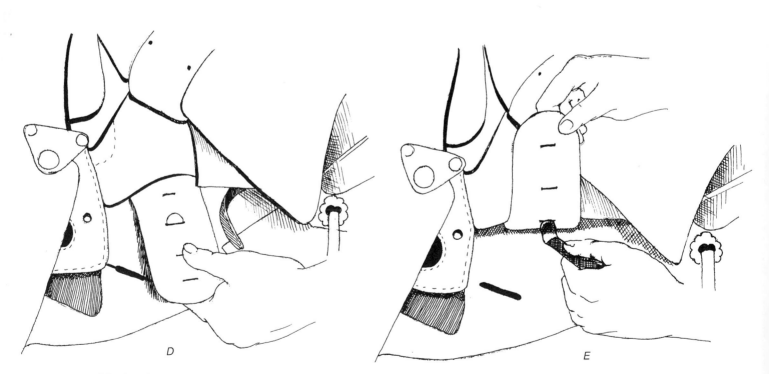

FIG. 26.15.   Single-strap stirrup leather. If desired, the stirrup loop can be made to stay twisted. *(A)* Front detail. *(B)* Hook to go in slots against lower tree edge. *(C)* Back detail. *(D)* Pulling out the leather to free the

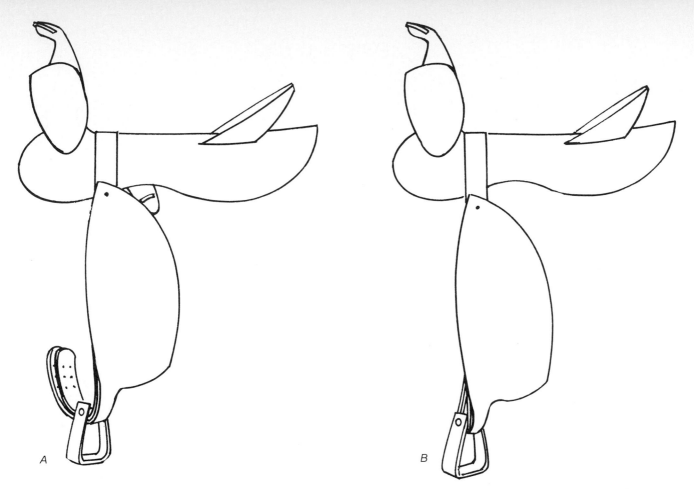

FIG. 26.16. Single-strap stirrup leather on saddletree. *(A)* Attached under tree. *(B)* With slot adjustment shown against the lower tree edge.

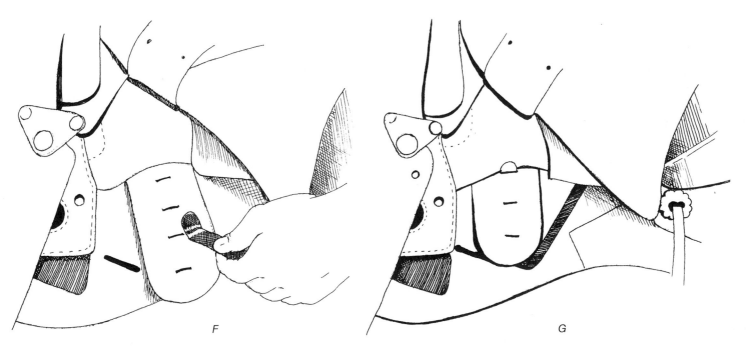

hook. *(E)* Freeing the hook to place where needed. *(F)* Replacing the hook. *(G)* Hook anchored in position against the tree. Drawings *(D–G)* by Judy Osburn.

FIG. 26.17. Fender shapes. (A) Arizona fender. (B) Pear-shaped fender. (C) Phoenix fender. (D) Other variations.

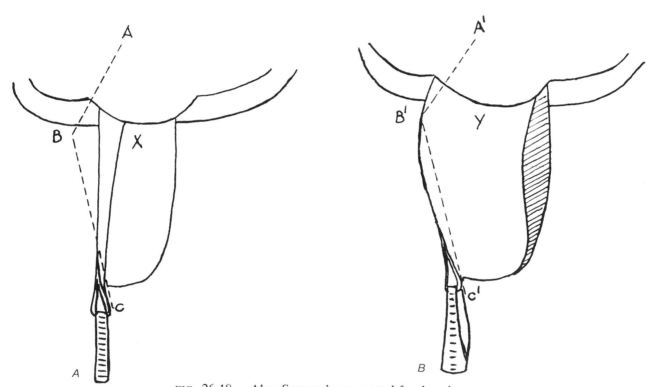

FIG. 26.18. Alex Swaney's suggested fender shape.

(A) Popular fender shape. This fender, X, represents a common straight-cut type. The angle 1–2–3 represents the front side of the inner leg contacting the saddle and horse. Note that the knee at 2 will be well in front of the leather because of the thickness of the fender and stirrup leathers at the front of the fender; discomfort will result when knees are close to the horse where they should be. (B) Swaney's fender shape. Fender Y represents a newer type which largely overcomes the defects of fender X.

The angle 1–2–3 represents the front of the inner leg making contact with the saddle. At the knee, point 2, the leather is curved well forward and should contact the inner side of the knee when it is close to the saddle. Some fenders are cut too wide in Swaney's opinion. The leg rarely if ever contacts the shaded portion shown at the rear of the fender, Y, and that portion might well be eliminated. From Alex Swaney, "The Balanced Seat in the Stock Saddle," *Western Horseman,* May–June, 1943.

only six to eight inches below the tree bar and lies on top of the skirt. The strap end under the tree bar is punched with adjustment slots, through which a small metal bar (or strip) is inserted to keep the strap from pulling back up under the tree bar. Thus there is no length of stirrup strap going back down to join the other end to form a loop for the stirrup.

Changing the stirrup-strap length for different riders of the same saddle takes just a little more time than some of the buckle systems do, but this type of stirrup strap eliminates one layer of leather and is ideal for the rider who does not have to share his saddle with others. Naturally the stirrup strap must be strong to minimize stretching; some riders find that harness leather works well for this purpose.

Fenders, also called *sweat leathers,* prevent the horse's sweat from getting on the rider. Any shape or size that accomplishes this and causes no discomfort to the rider's knee is acceptable. Fenders may be made separate from the stirrup leathers and then attached to them, or the fender and the stirrup leather may be cut from a single piece of leather (Figs. 26.2 and 26.3). Fender shapes are shown in Figs. 26.17 and 26.18.

To make the stirrup hang facing forward so that it is easily available to the rider's foot, the stirrup leathers may be laced backwards; otherwise the stirrup and fenders must be set (Figs. 26.19 to 26.22; see also Chapter 30).

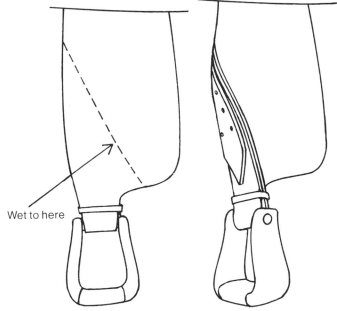

FIG. 26.19. Wet-setting stirrup leather for proper stirrup angle.

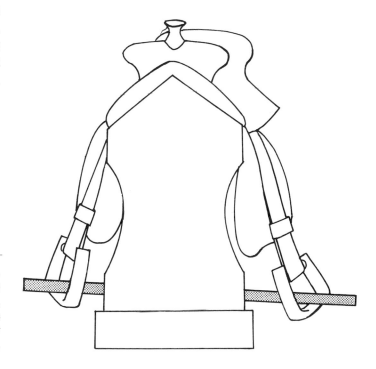

FIG. 26.20. Setting stirrup leather for stirrup angle. This home-built stirrup turner will keep the stirrup leathers in place for more comfortable riding. First, use a generous application of saddle soap on the area to be set, moistening it well. Then put a narrow board, dowel, or broom handle through the stirrups.

151

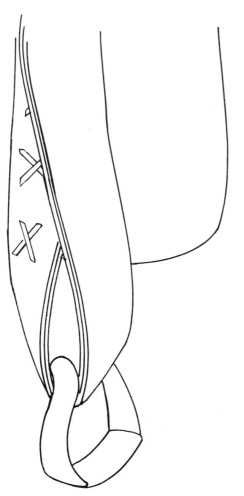 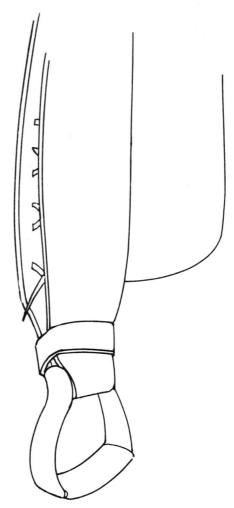

FIG. 26.21. Old-style lacing for dry-setting the proper stirrup angle.

FIG. 26.22. Conventional lacing before setting stirrup leather.

CHAPTER 27

Stirrups

The early carved stirrup of the Spaniards and Mexicans has been discussed earlier (see Figs. 9.14 and 27.1). The stirrup made of a flat piece

FIG. 27.1. Examples of early Spanish and Mexican one-piece hand-carved wooden stirrups. From Bush, "Those Amazing Stirrups," *Horseman,* April, 1974; and Fay E. Ward.

of wood, oak, or hickory bent to the desired shape appears to be strictly an American design that appeared around 1860 (Fig. 27.2). According to Ford E. Smith flat pieces of wood were soaked in water, and after they were steamed and treated with uric acid, they could be shaped with ease.

The *box stirrup* was the original stirrup of this kind (Fig. 27.2). At first it had a wide tread, up to 8 inches wide. Saddlemakers began experimenting with it, narrowing the sides and finally the tread. Around 1890 to 1900 the *oxbow stirrup* began to replace the box stirrup. The oxbow stirrup with its rounded tread has received wide

acceptance because, no matter what position the foot is in, it is still on the rounded tread. It is now the commonly accepted rodeo stirrup for bronc riding (Fig. 27.4*C*).

Still later saddlemakers began covering the outside of wooden stirrups with galvanized sheet iron. This trend would eventually lead to the beautiful brass-covered wooden stirrup. A metal-bound stirrup is shown with its component parts in Fig. 27.5.

The next improvement was to cover the tread of the wooden stirrup with leather to reduce wear. Finally the whole stirrup was covered with leather, because many horsemen wanted their stirrups encased in rawhide to add strength as it did to the tree. It is of little value in determining the age of a saddle to use the age of the stirrup as a guide, because stirrups wear out faster than the saddle does and are frequently replaced.

A later development in stirrup covering is the *tapadero,* or *tap,* a leather hood for the front of the stirrup, also called *toe fender.* The original purpose of tapaderos was to protect the boots of the rider from being scratched by mesquite or heavy brush. They also kept his feet warmer and prevented his feet from turning in the stirrups. The rider could also slap a tapadero against the horse's neck to get him to turn when the rider's hands were otherwise occupied in training. Like all useful saddle items, the tapadero was in time ornamented and was then lengthened to extend below the stirrup for eye appeal. The extreme exaggeration in length was 28 inches. Only extremely long tapaderos had any real effect on balance in riding.

A letter from Jack Carroll gives a different

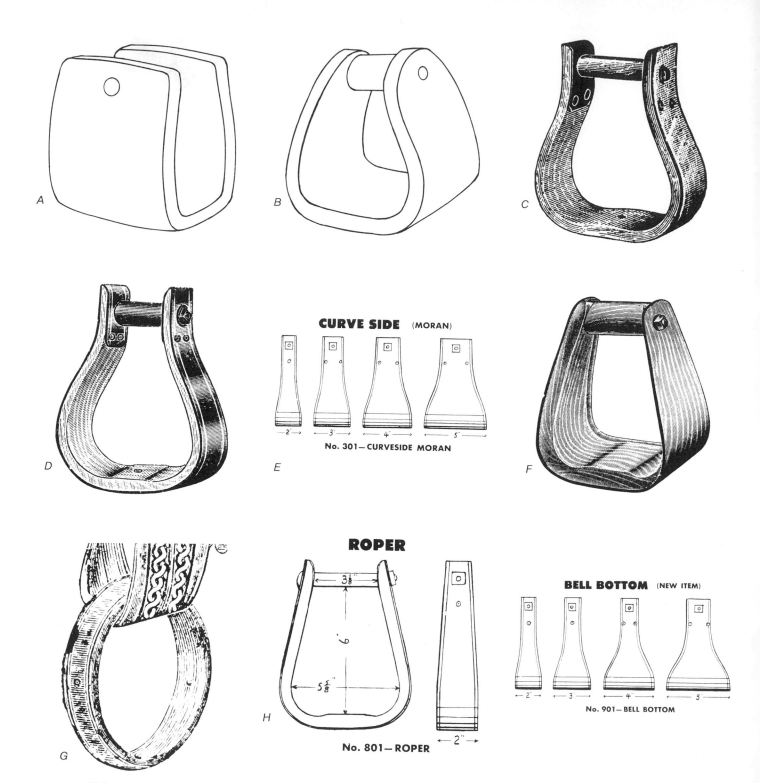

CURVE SIDE (MORAN)

No. 301—CURVESIDE MORAN

ROPER

No. 801— ROPER

BELL BOTTOM (NEW ITEM)

No. 901— BELL BOTTOM

FIG. 27.2.   American steamed and bent wooden stirrups. *(A)* Box stirrup. *(B)* Satinwood stirrup. *(C)* Visalia stirrup. From Wilson, catalog no. 73, 1973. *(D)* Moran pattern, brass-bound stirrup. From Wyeth, catalog no. 220, 1940. *(E)* Curved-side Moran stirrup, four sizes. From Ruwart, catalog, 1963. *(F)* Tarkio stirrup. From Wyeth, catalog no. 220, 1939. *(G)* Gilham's patented white-ash round stirrup with 5½-inch spread. From Stone, catalog, ca. 1905. *(H)* Roper's stirrup, two views. From Ruwart, catalog, 1963. *(I)* Standard curved-side bell-

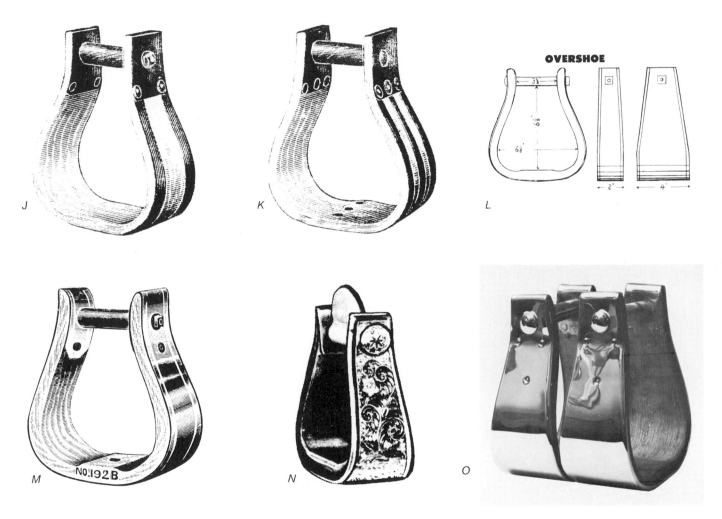

bottom stirrup, four sizes. From Ruwart, catalog, 1963. *(J)* Two-strap iron-bound stirrup. From Smith-Worthington, catalog, ca. 1905. *(K)* Three-strap iron-bound stirrup. From Smith-Worthington, catalog, ca. 1905. *(L)* Overshoe stirrup, two sizes. From Ruwart, catalog, 1963. *(M)* Hagelstein brass-bound stirrup. From Wyeth, catalog no. 220. *(N)* Silver-overlaid wooden stirrup. From Carroll, catalog no. 37, 1977. *(O)* Monel no-rust stirrups, highly polished. Courtesy of Schneiders.

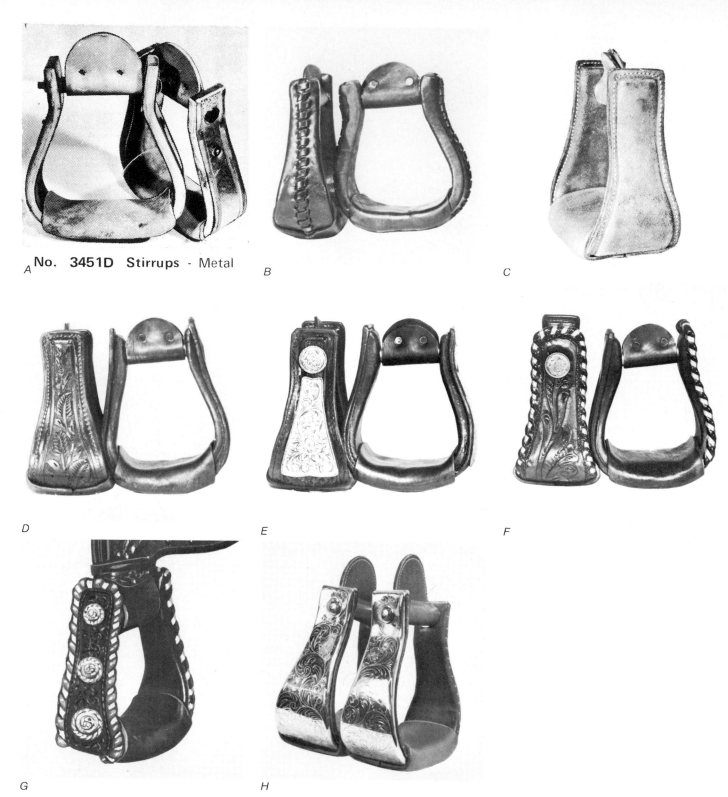

No. 3451D Stirrups - Metal

A

B

C

D

E

F

G

H

FIG. 27.3.   Leather-covered wooden stirrups. *(A)* Stirrups with wear leathers on bolt and tread. From Tex Tan, catalog no. 84, 1974. *(B)* Full-leather-covered stirrups, plain, laced. Courtesy of Schneiders. *(C)* Full-leather-covered stirrups with rough-out skirting leather. From Tex Tan, catalog no. 84, 1974. *(D)* Full-leather-covered stirrups embossed with floral design. Courtesy of Schneiders. *(E)* Full-leather-covered stirrups with sterling-silver concha and trim. Courtesy of Schneiders. *(F)* Stirrups sterling-silver-laced on edges with concha. Courtesy of Schneiders. *(G)* Full-leather-covered stirrups with graduated round conchas. Courtesy of Schneiders. *(H)* Stirrups with engraved sterling silver mounted on Monel. Courtesy of Schneiders.

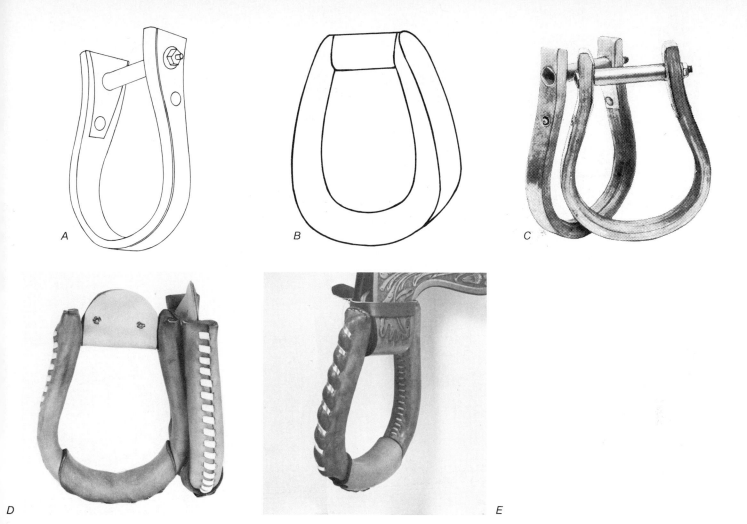

FIG. 27.4.   Wooden oxbow stirrups, showing differences between rodeo and regular stirrups. *(A)* Flat wood. *(B)* Round wood. *(C)* Contest. From Tex Tan, catalog no. 84, 1974. *(D)* Full-leather-covered and laced oxbow. Courtesy of Tex Tan. *(E)* Sterling-silver-laced oxbow. Courtesy of Ryon's.

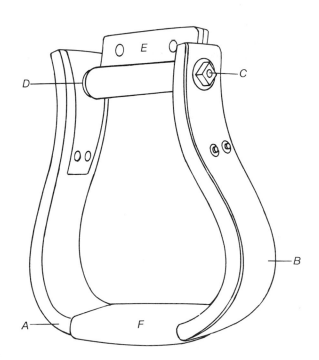

FIG. 27.5.   Wooden stirrup, metal-bound, showing parts. *(A)* Tread (thicker wood than sidepieces under wear leather). *(B)* Sidepieces (may have outside covering of galvanized iron, sheet brass, or leather). *(C)* Bolt. *(D)* Roller (under wear leather). *(E)* Bolt wear leather. *(F)* Tread wear leather.

157

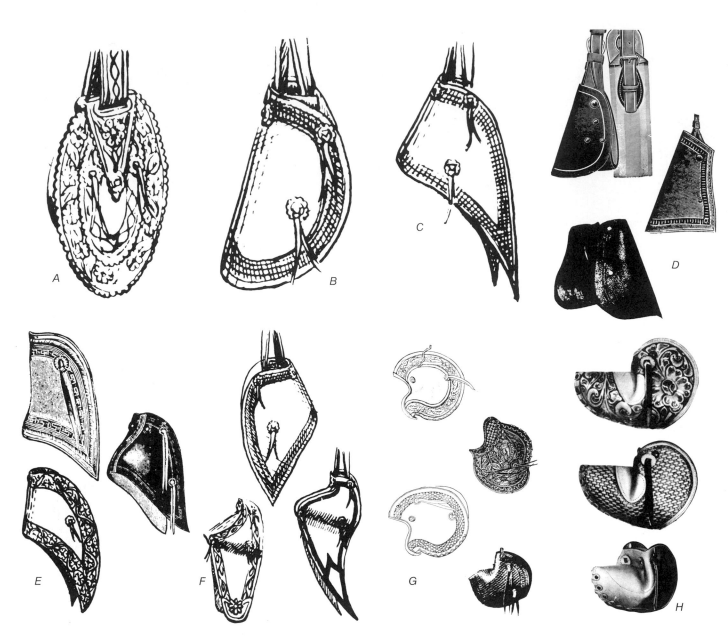

FIG. 27.6. Tapaderos. *(A)* Early Spanish. From Ward, *The Cowboy at Work. (B)* Early California. From Ward, *The Cowboy at Work. (C)* Early Texas. From Ward, *The Cowboy at Work. (D)* Hooded, dragoon-type tapaderos. From top to bottom: Courtesy of Wyeth; from R. T. Frazier Saddlery, catalog no. 37, 1935; and from Montgomery Ward, catalog, 1894–95. *(E)* Shield tapaderos. Top to bottom: From Marcy, *The Prairie Traveler;* two from Stone, catalog, ca. 1905; and Ward, *The Cowboy at Work. (F)* Bull-nose tapaderos. From Ward, *The Cowboy at Work. (G)* Bulldog tapaderos. Top to bottom: three from Stone, catalog, ca. 1905; one from Visalia Stock Saddle Company, San Francisco, catalog no. 101, 1974. *(H)* Monkey-face tapaderos. From Casa Zea, Juárez, Mexico, catalog no. 1, 1963.

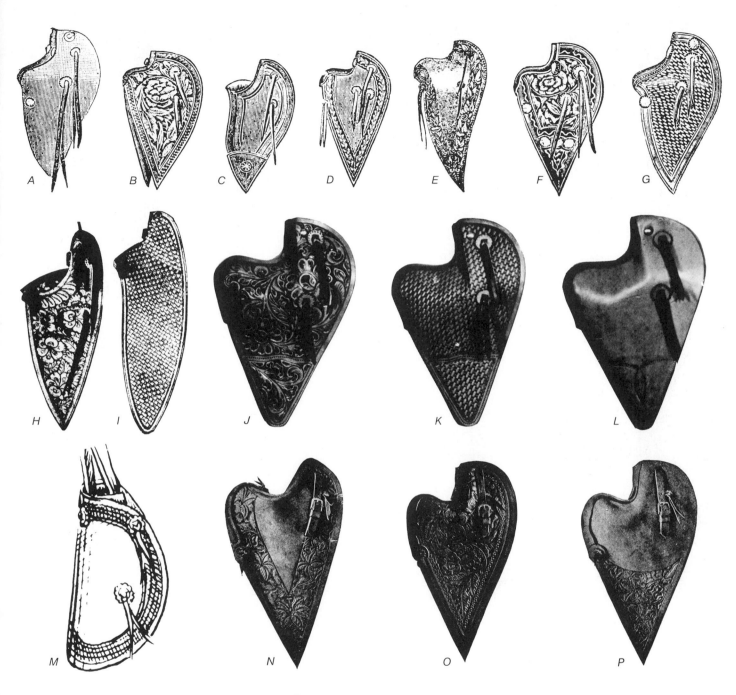

FIG. 27.7.   Monkey-nose tapaderos. *(A–G)* From Stone, catalog, ca. 1905. *(H and I)* From Visalia, catalog no. 101, 1974. *(J–L)* From Casa Zea, catalog no. 1. *(M)* From Ward, *The Cowboy at Work.* *(N–P)* From R. T. Frazier Saddlery, Pueblo, Colorado, catalog no. 37, 1935.

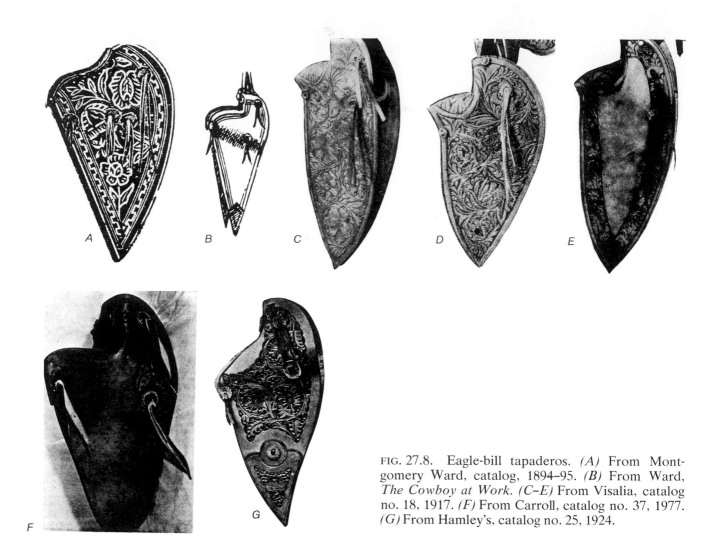

FIG. 27.8. Eagle-bill tapaderos. *(A)* From Montgomery Ward, catalog, 1894–95. *(B)* From Ward, *The Cowboy at Work. (C–E)* From Visalia, catalog no. 18, 1917. *(F)* From Carroll, catalog no. 37, 1977. *(G)* From Hamley's, catalog no. 25, 1924.

reason why the Mexican cowboys use taps: "Charros wear low heels on their botins (boots). Charro saddles are sold with taps for safety (prevents the foot going through the stirrup and getting hung up)."

Tapadero styles were named for their appearance: there are *bulldog tapaderos, eagle-bill tapaderos, mule-ear tapaderos, monkey-nose tapaderos, hog-snout tapaderos,* and others (Fig. 27.6). The nomenclature of tapaderos is confused, and the examples shown in the literature overlap in appearance. It is almost impossible to identify some tapaderos precisely.

The ingenuity of the American businessman and his willingness to use readily available material brought the saddlemaker to the use of tough steel for stirrups, beginning about 1890. Since that time steel stirrups have been made in many shapes and sizes, ranging from heavy wire rings to strap steel formed in the shape of a stirrup. to latticework stirrups, to sheet-steel stirrups with angles in the sidebars of the stirrup to conform to the position of the foot, and even to safety breakaway stirrups (Fig. 27.9). Steel stirrups might have a tread covered with leather, and on some of the lattice-

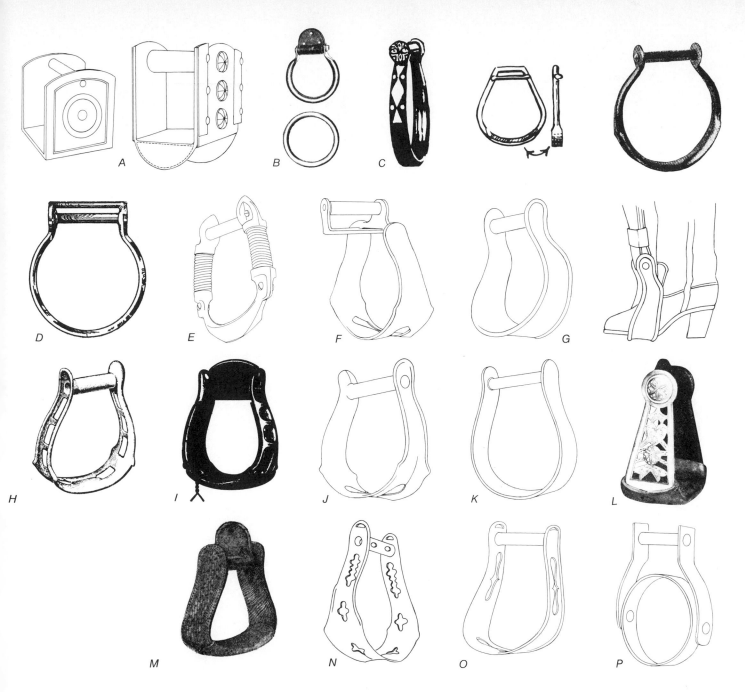

FIG. 27.9. Steel, iron, and brass stirrups. *(A)* Mexican steel box. Courtesy of Rudy Terrell, Bully Good Saddle Shop, Muskogee, Oklahoma. *(B)* Tubular brass or steel ring. From Visalia, catalog no. 18, 1917. *(C)* Forged steel. Left to right: two from Ward, *The Cowboy at Work;* one from Stockman-Farmer, catalog no. 31, 1927–28. *(D)* Heiser Patent safety bar. From Stockman-Farmer, catalog no. 31, 1927–28. *(E)* Acme patented coil-spring steel safety stirrup. Courtesy of Robert L. Kaupke. *(F)* Stockman. Courtesy of Robert L. Kaupke. *(G)* Wilson stirrup patented in 1897. Left to right: Detail and foot positioned in stirrup. *(H)* Turner stirrup. *(I)* Improved Turner stirrup with bolt and wear leathers with lace trim. From Wyeth, catalog no. 220. *(J)* Patented Ellis steel stirrup. Courtesy of Robert L. Kaupke. *(K)* Uncovered strap steel. *(L)* Ornate silver-inlaid steel. From Visalia, catalog no. 18, 1917. *(M)* Full-leather-covered steel. From Visalia, catalog no. 18, 1917. *(N)* Gschwend steel stirrup. Courtesy of Robert L. Kaupke. *(O)* Bantz steel stirrup. Courtesy of Robert L. Kaupke and S. R. and I. C. McConnell. *(P)* J. E. Collins swiveling-steel-ring stirrup. Courtesy of Robert L. Kaupke.

work stirrups, such as the Turner, an ornamental strap of leather was laced through the latticework.

The common complaint against the steel stirrup was the coldness of the metal to the rider's foot in wintertime and its bruising weight when it hit a rider. It lost favor and was little seen after 1914, perhaps because steel was in short supply during World War I. Hamley continued to catalog steel stirrups into the 1930s, and a Frazier catalog of about 1935 pictured a steel stirrup with heavy coiled springs in place of sidepieces.

The high heel, called a *riding heel,* on the old-time cowboy boot was to prevent the foot from going through the stirrup and catching in such a way that the rider could be dragged by a runaway horse. It was also useful for digging in when holding a roped animal.

The correct position of the foot in the stirrup is a matter of much discussion. The old-time cowboys rode with their boots *homed* or *all the way home* in the stirrups, with the boots far enough into the stirrups that the front of the boot heels rested against the stirrup treads. Some say that it is less tiring to ride this way, but it is harder to get the feet loose in the event of trouble. Resting the ball of each foot on the tread is safer and allows the rider to take some of the jolts of a rough-riding, rough-trotting horse with the springlike action of the rider's ankles (Fig. 36.7).

CHAPTER 28

Leatherwork

Saddlemaking is an art, and among other requirements of the art is skill in leatherwork. Many kinds of leather are available to the saddlemaker—so many that a discussion of them is beyond the scope of this book (the Bibliography contains some excellent references on the subject).

Finished leather has a *grain* (smooth) side and a *flesh* (rough) side. For appearance' sake the smooth side is generally on the outside, although some riders prefer what they call a *roughout saddle,* a saddle built with the flesh side of the leather out. The rough leather gives the rider a more secure seat (Fig. 28.1*A*). Similarly, designs on the smooth side of the leather of a saddle are not just for ornamentation. The roughness of the designs creates friction between the rider and the saddle, giving the rider a more secure seat.

Leather has a unique attribute in that it will receive permanent impressions or indentations on the grain, or smooth, side to make designs. There are two methods of decorating leather: embossing and hand carving. Embossing can be done in two ways: (1) the tool, which is a negative of the design, is struck on the face of the leather, leaving a raised design (Fig. 28.2); (2) the design is raised on the tool, which is placed on the underside of the leather, and the leather is worked down from the top side around the design. Embossing can be accomplished by either hand tooling or machine-stamping.

The carving method involves hand-cutting the design outline into the grain surface of the leather with a swivel knife. Various striking tools are then used to bring the design into relief. It is easy to distinguish a hand-tooled or hand-carved design from machine stamping. It is impossible for the hand artist to be perfectly uniform, whereas the machine-stamped design is the same in every dimension (Fig. 28.3). Because of the many hours of work required for hand-tooling or hand-carving designs, not many saddles are decorated that way today except custom-made and show saddles.

Among the stamp designs commonly used are the rosette, leaf, sunburst, pine tree, oak, acorn, horseshoe, box weave, basket weave, flower, and arrow. Certain patterns have been popular in certain areas, and some old-time saddlemakers used designs of flowers or trees or other objects that symbolized the region in which they lived. Each saddlemaker had his own preferences, and they were many and varied. One who is familiar with the saddlemakers' design characteristics can identify their work (Figs. 28.4 and 28.5).

When a piece of leather is cut to size, the edges are rough. They can be given a smooth finish by beveling and rubbing one direction with a *rub rag,* a light piece of canvas that has been dampened with much saddle soap rubbed in on both sides and allowed to dry. When the rag is dry, the edges of the leather are dampened and then rubbed in one direction. Because of the labor costs only very good, usually expensive saddles have hand-rubbed leather edges. On most saddles this work is done on a burnishing machine.

The leatherworker may finish the saddle by leaving it the natural russet color, antiquing it, dyeing it, inlaying colors, staining it, or oiling it, and so on.

Leather can be stitched together in several ways. One method is to butt two pieces of leather edge to edge and lace a narrow thong

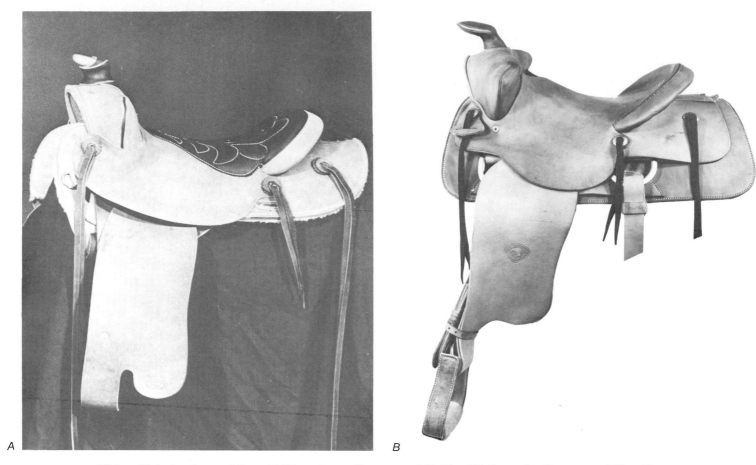

FIG. 28.1.   Plain-leather saddles. *(A)* Roughout. Courtesy of Fallis. *(B)* Smooth. Courtesy of Tex Tan.

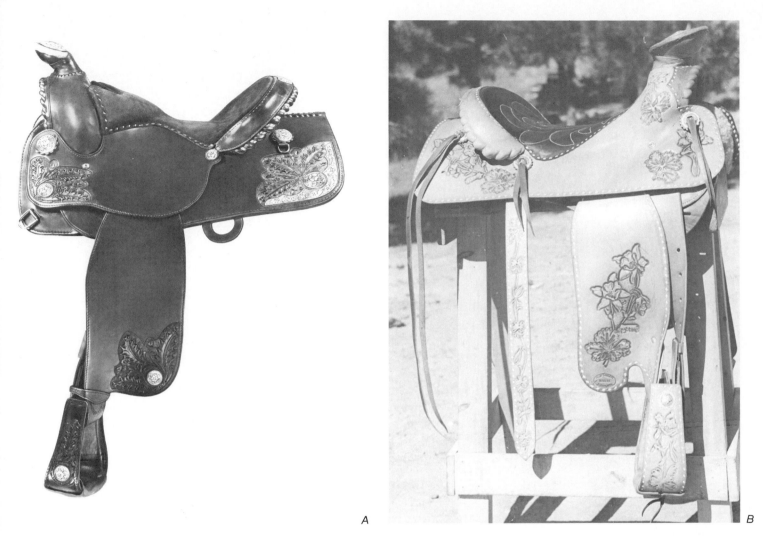

A   B

FIG. 28.2.   Examples of unique corner-stamp trim, showing overlaid quilted, padded seats. *(A)* Corner stamp with sterling silver mounted trim on California-style saddle with roughout, quilted, built-up seat. Courtesy of Schneiders. *(B)* Corner stamp on modern Mother Hubbard–style saddle with smooth-leather-quilted level seat. Courtesy of Fallis.

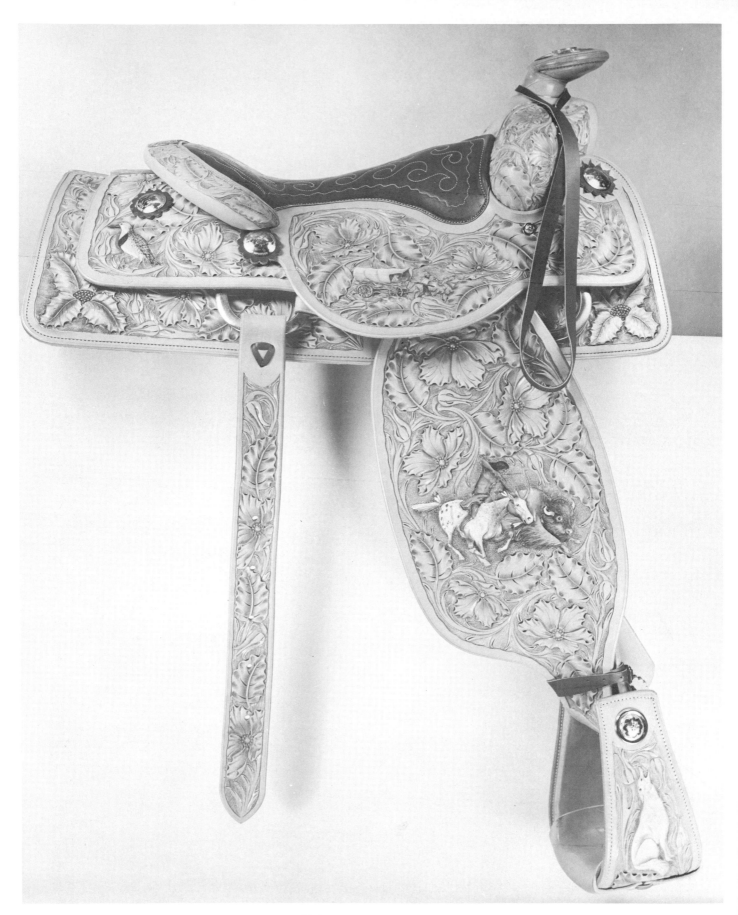

FIG. 28.3. Trophy saddles. *(A)* Over-all tooled. Courtesy of Hamley's.

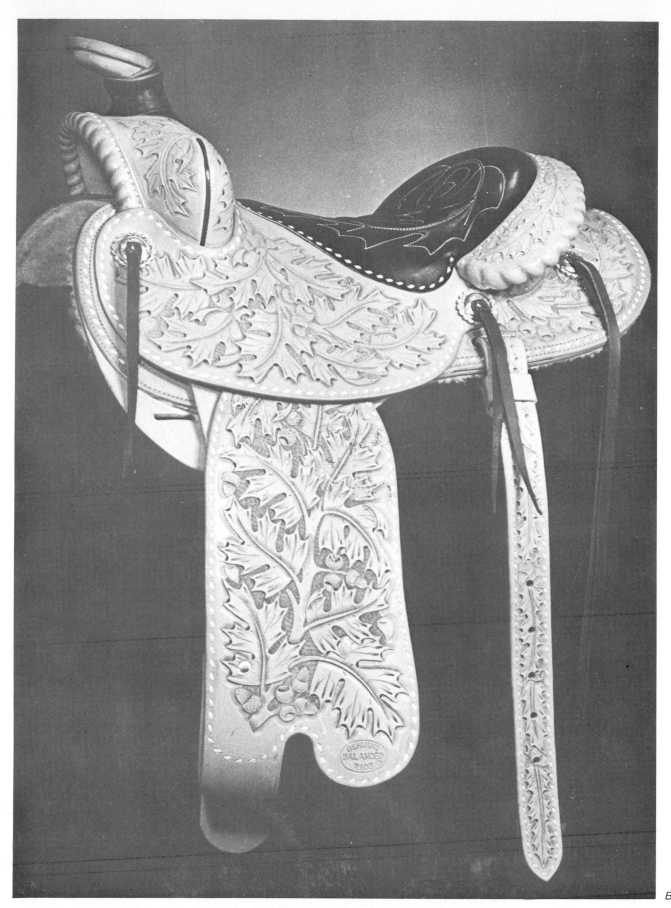

(B) Over-all stamped. Photograph by Johanna C. Fallis. Courtesy of Fallis.

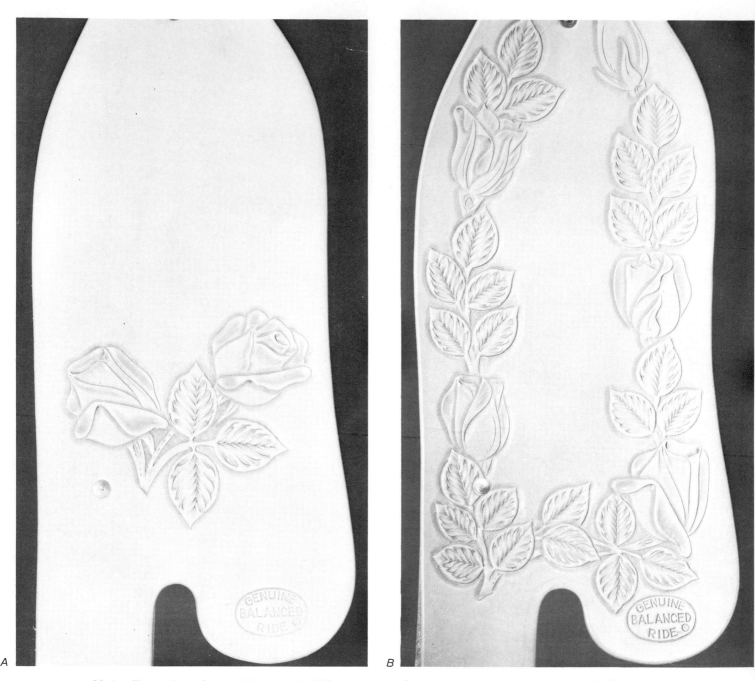

A

B

FIG. 28.4.   Examples of a saddlemaker's different uses of one pattern, the tame rose. *(A)* Single or corner.

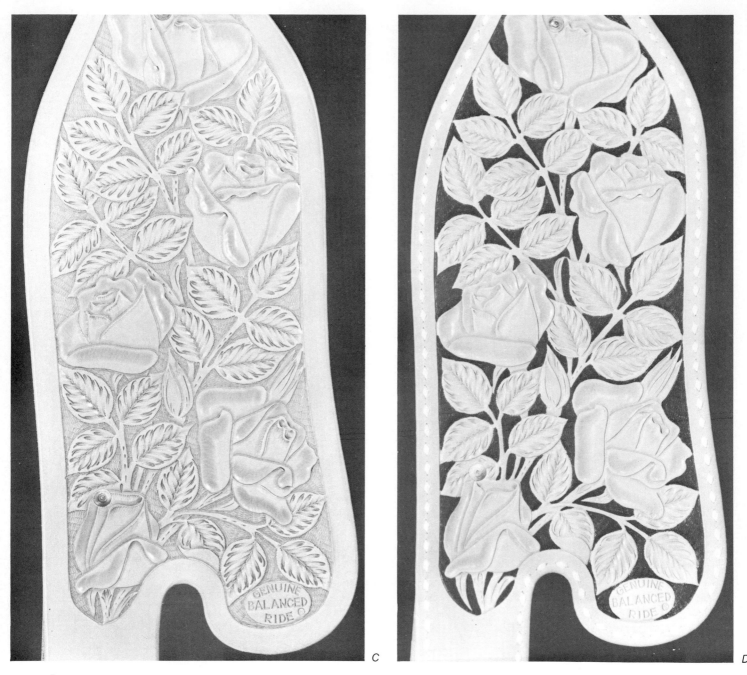

C

D

(B) Border. *(C)* Over-all stamp, available with or without the border. *(D)* Over-all stamp, dyed background with buckstitching. Courtesy of Fallis.

169

FIG. 28.5.   Popular tooling patterns used on custom-made saddles. *(A)* Poco Oak. *(B)* Ryon Floral. *(C)* Chip Flower. *(D)* Multi Flower. *(E)* California Rose. *(F)* Mighty Oak. *(G)* Trophy Oak. *(H)* Murray Flower. *(I)* Lewis Flower. *(J)* Oak Leaf Supreme. *(K)* Basket Weave. *(L)* Tilo Flower. Courtesy of Ryon's.

back and forth between them, much as a shoe-string is laced in a shoe (Fig. 21.7). Two pieces of leather can also be joined in the standard fashion, one laid on top of the other and the two stitched together. The two pieces can also be *blind-stitched:* the leather to be stitched is slit on the edge just below the grain surface approximately one-quarter inch into the leather. The smooth-finished surface is lifted back, and the rough underpart is stitched to other leather. The smooth-finished surface leather is then flattened in its original position and glued down. The edge is rubbed smooth, and the stitching is hidden.

A *split seam* is a kind of seam made to reduce wear between two pieces of leather stitched together. A cross-section view of a split seam shows that the two pieces of leather to be stitched together have a third piece of leather separating them. The seam is cross-stitched to give it more strength. A *welt* is one type of split seam (Fig. 16.11).

Buckstitching is an ornamental, light-colored narrow thong woven in and out of darker leather in an attractive design. It can be used as an edging or other decoration. The contrasting light-and-dark colors give buckstitching its aesthetic appeal (Fig. 28.6).

Padding is not new to saddlemaking. Its obvious purpose is to make the seat more comfortable. The old-time cowboy would have looked with disdain at anybody riding a padded seat. They disliked the padding because it took so long to dry after a ride in the rain or a river crossing. Today, however, comfort being highly prized, most saddle seats are padded. There are two kinds of padded seats, the *overlaid padded seat* and the *inlaid padded seat*. On the overlaid seat the pad covering is sewed on the surface of the seat leather. On the inlaid seat the existing seat leather is cut out where the pad is to go and the pad cover inlaid into the area. The inlaid pad has nothing extra between it and the tree. Obviously an inlaid pad is smoother than an overlaid pad, but few saddle paddings are inlaid on saddles made today. The

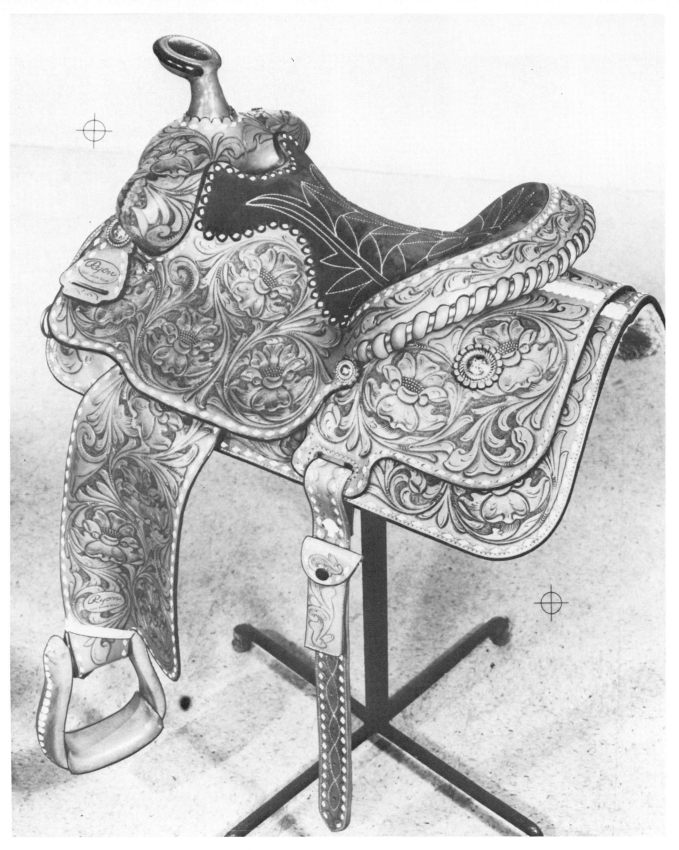

FIG. 28.6.   Buckstitching on saddle. Courtesy of Ryon's.

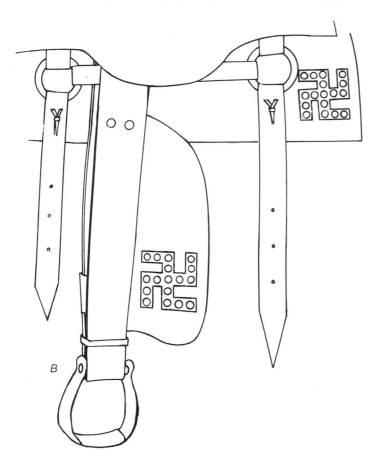

ination a plain saddle or bridle could be dressed up with them (Fig. 28.7). The spots had two sharp prongs on opposite sides. The prongs pierced the leather and were bent down on the underneath side to hold the spot in place.

For those interested in the restoration of old, hard, brittle leather to a soft, pliable condition, I recommend John W. Waterer's *A Guide to the Conservation and Restoration of Objects Made Wholly or in Part of Leather,* and Per E. Guldbeck's *The Care of Historical Collections,* which has a section on leather. Both books are listed in the Bibliography. British Museum leather dressing can be obtained from the Fisher Scientific Company, Pittsburgh, Pennsylvania. Before using the dressing, it is necessary to clean the leather with Toluene (use care: Toluene is highly inflammable). Another leather restorer is Neutralfat SSS Leather Restorer, obtainable from the Ventron Corporation, Danvers, Massachusetts. Instructions for the use of these products can be obtained from the suppliers.

On the following pages are shown examples of the saddle leatherworker's art, from the early decades of the twentieth century.

FIG. 28.7. Brass or nickel spots. *(A)* Detail of bright-metal pronged leather decorations. From Muellers, catalog no. 88, 1950. *(B)* Fender and skirt ornamented with spots.

padding is quilted to keep it in place so that it will not shift around.

Several years ago people liked to adorn their saddles with small half-round metal circles called *spots*. They were available in either brass or nickel and ranged in diameter from 1/4 to 5/8 inch. The most commonly used size was approximately 3/8 inch in diameter. With a little imag-

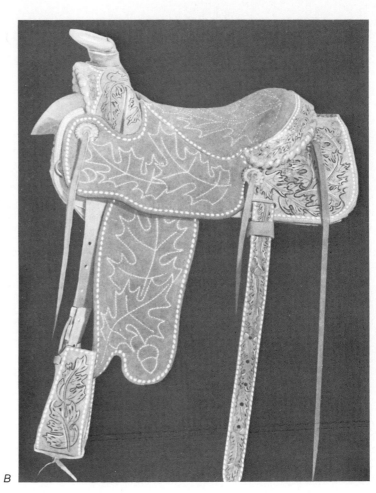

B

FIG. 28.8.   *(A)* Black-dyed border design with matching overlaid quilted seat, lacing, and strings. *(B)* Overlaid quilted seat, jockeys, and fenders. Courtesy of Fallis.

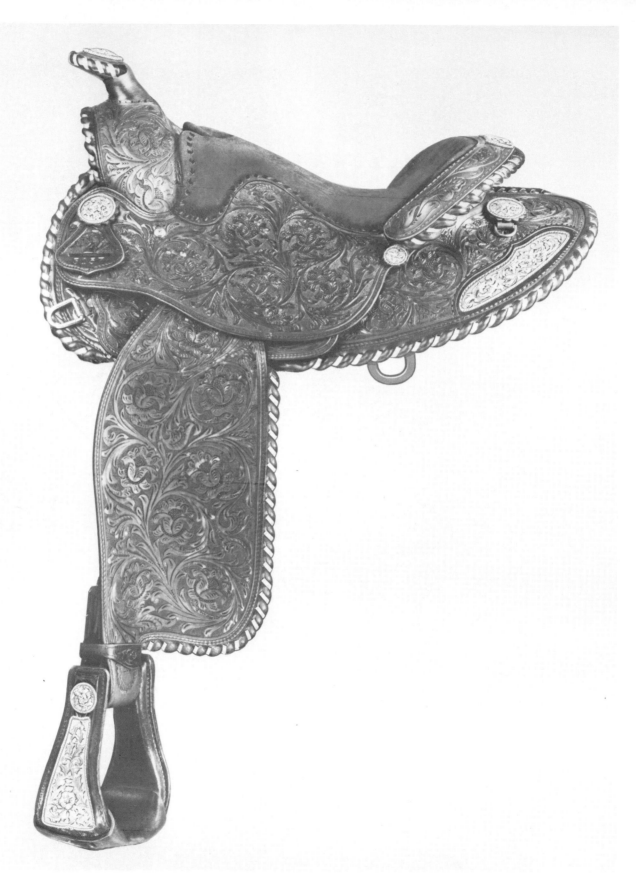

A

FIG. 28.9.   Show saddles with sterling-silver-laced trim. *(A)* California-style Arabian saddle with lacing on fork, horn, cantle, skirts, and both edges of the stirrup. Courtesy of Schneiders. Facing page: *(B)* Pleasure saddle with square skirts, laced on the fork, cantle, skirts, and center stirrup seam. Courtesy of Ryon's.

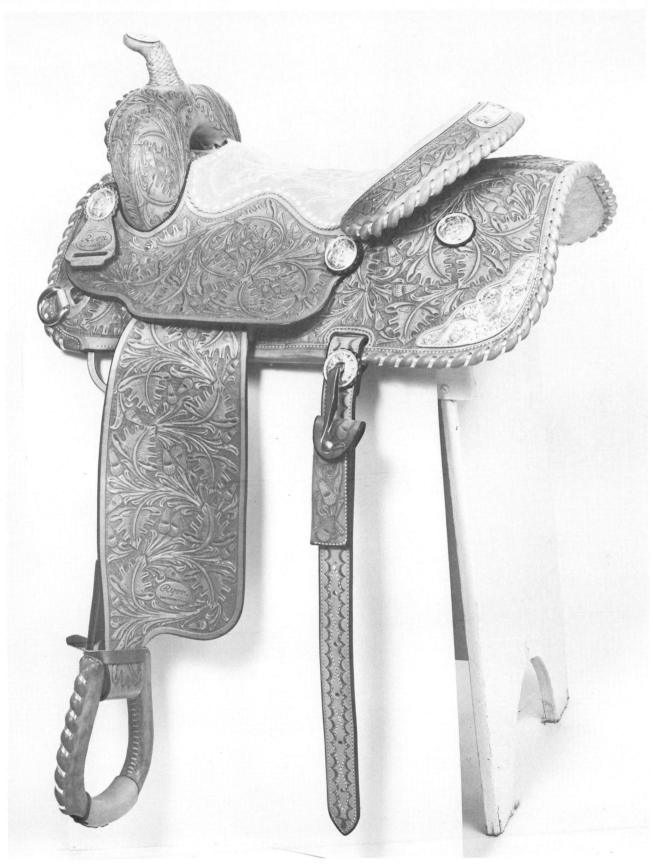

B

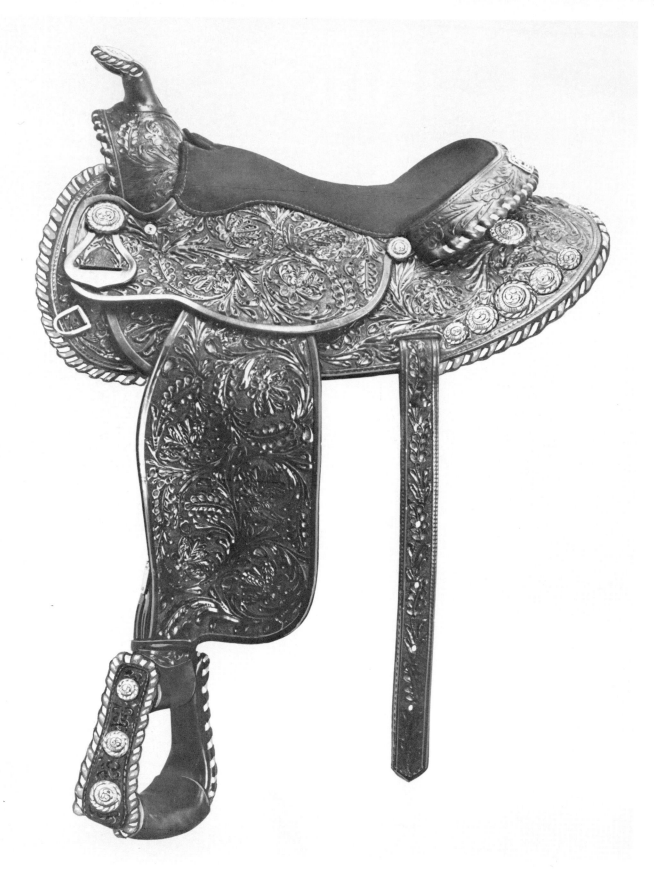

C

FIG. 28.9 *continued.* *(C)* Arabian saddle with maximum use of lacing on the fork, horn, cantle, skirts, and fenders. Courtesy of Schneiders.

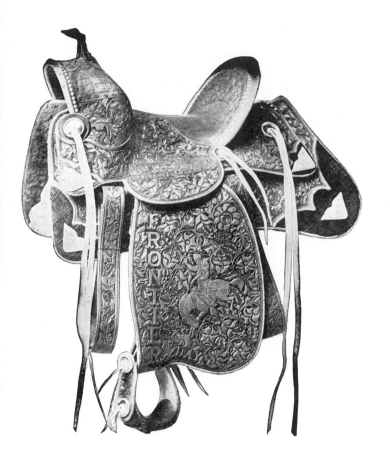

FIG. 28.10. Fine detailing work with elegant decorations of genuine alligator leather, snowflake leather, and silver mountings. The saddle is lined with llama skin. FIGS. 28.10–28.21 from Frazier, catalog no. 37, 1935.

FIG. 28.11. Early saddles often featured decorated cinch straps to match the saddle carving, plus extra-wide one-piece fenders to show off more of the leather carver's art.

FIG. 28.12.   Saddle with stirrup strap separate on top of the fender, as on most of the earlier western saddles. The addition and placement of the silver has remained the same over the years.

FIG. 28.13.   A top-of-the-line saddle, complete with a voluptuous dancing girl. For extra luxury, the saddle had angora saddle pockets.

FIG. 28.14.   A lower cantle featuring an early example of the quilted seat. The stirrup leathers on this saddle come through the lower part of the fenders. It has the still-popular decorated stirrups.

FIG. 28.15.   A working saddle of the era of large skirts, with partial stamping in geometric patterns.

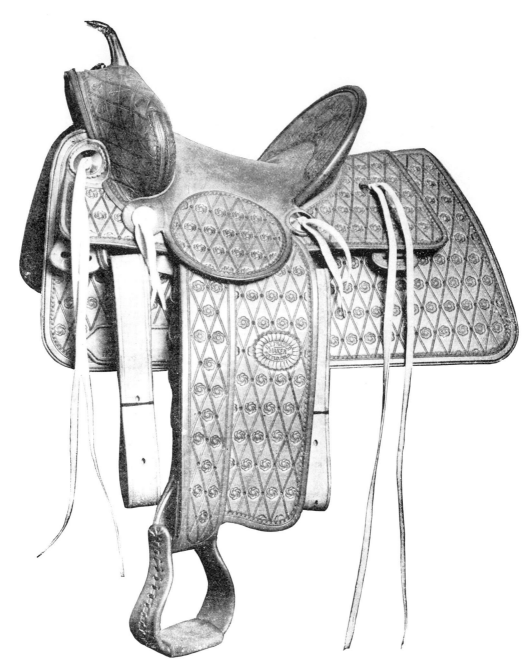

FIG. 28.16.   Another working saddle with a very unusual stamped pattern. The stirrups are the shaped kind, leather covered and laced.

FIG. 28.17.   Large-skirted saddle with silver corner pieces and conchas. The unusual stamp appears to be a combination of basket stamping and floral pattern in angled bands.

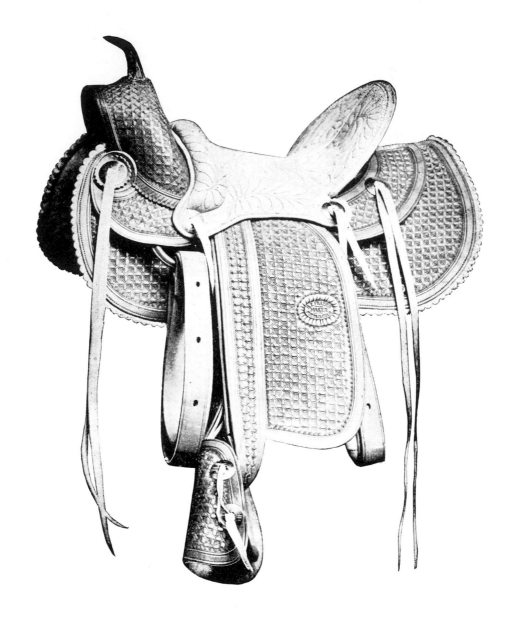

FIG. 28.18.   An excellent example of a very feminine ladies' astride saddle. The padding in front (called a "squaw roll") is similar to that on some of the early sidesaddles and plantation saddles. (see FIGS. 37.10, 38.18).

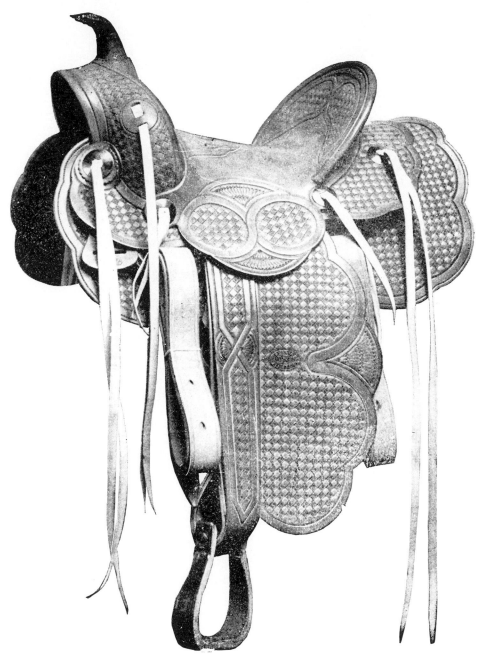

FIG. 28.19.   Ladies' thirteen-inch swell-fork saddle designed for rugged work. It includes a rope strap on the fork.

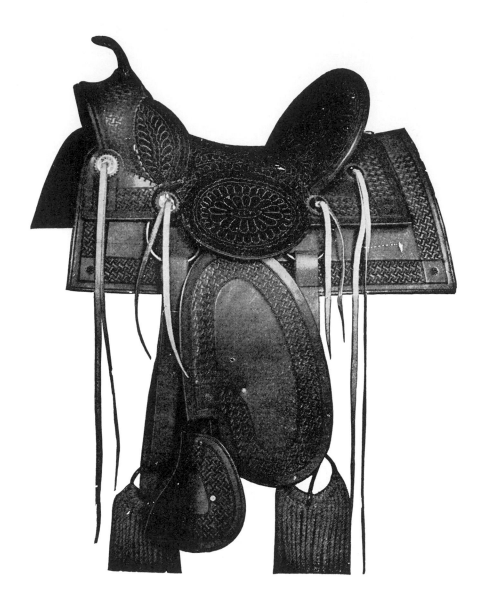

FIG. 28.20.   Saddle with artistically stitched quilting and wool lining in the tapaderos to protect the feet from bruises and keep them warm in cold weather.

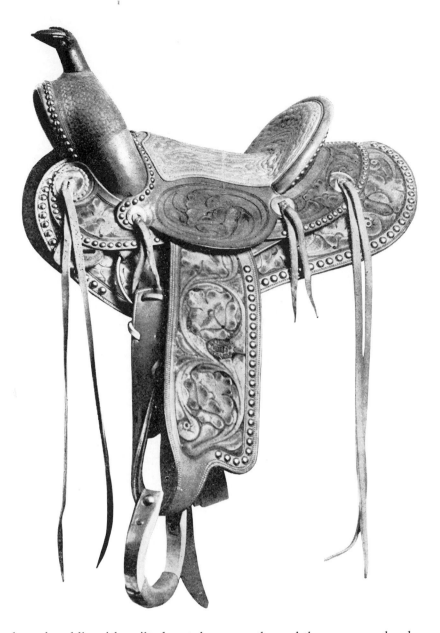

FIG. 28.21.   Typical youth saddle with quilted seat, lower cantle, and the very popular decorative metal spots.

FIG. 28.22.   Bronc-riding saddle with the popular acorn-and-oak-leaf pattern that is still seen on modern show saddles (see FIGS. 18.5*A* and 28.3*B*). FIGS. 28.22 to 28.29 from Hamley's, catalog no. 25, 1924.

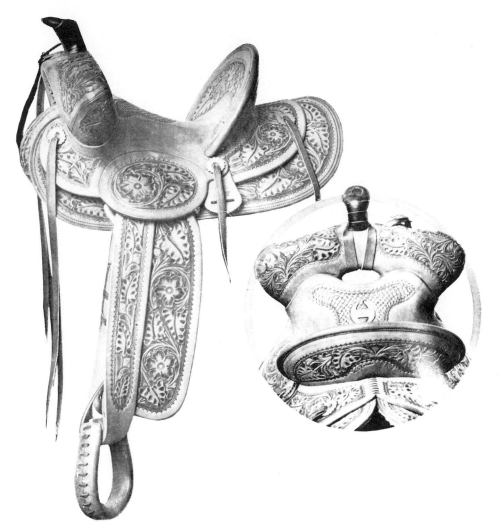

FIG. 28.23.   Rodeo saddle. The extrawide fork and the saddle name, "Lady Luck," undoubtedly helped make this a favorite in the days before the requirement for regulation saddles in bronc-riding events.

FIG. 28.24.   Saddle with stirrup leathers in loop position on the tree through the seat.

FIG. 28.25.   Saddle of the popular "Form-Fitter" style which features the shaped-back "beartrap" fork and the high cantle demanded for rugged bronc-busting and cattle work.

FIG. 28.26.   Saddle with an over-all floral pattern with basket stamping on the front of the seat and the back of the cantle. The pocket on the back of the cantle was handy for storing staples.

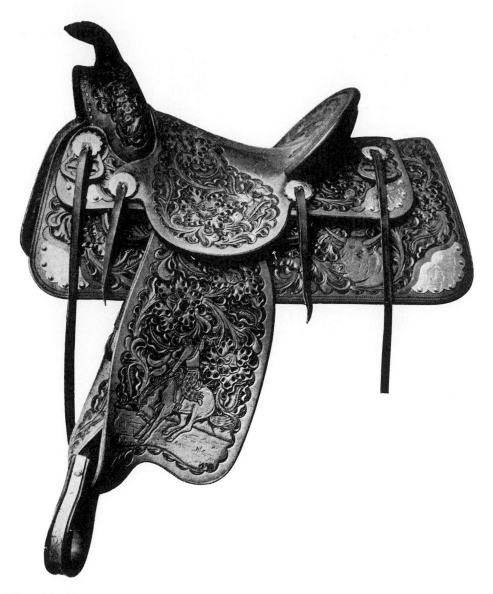

FIG. 28.27. Saddle with floral pattern with bucking-horse insert and silver trim. The bucking-horse motif changed to romantic wild West designs in the 1950s (FIG. 28.3A) and then to trained horses FIG. 36.20B).

FIG. 28.28.   An early trick-riding saddle, padded on the seat and jockeys like present-day models. The ornate carving and silver trim were not seen on trick-riding saddles in later years (Fig. 17.11).

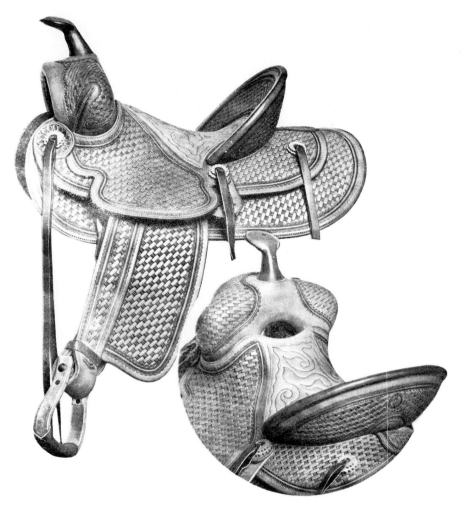

FIG. 28.29.   A full basket-stamped lightweight ladies' saddle with padded seat. Most present-day men's and women's saddles show no difference except seat size. FIGS. 28.29 to 28.32 from Visalia, catalog no. 18, 1917.

FIG. 28.30.   A low cantle, full-basket-stamped saddle with twisted stirrup leathers to position the
foot properly. The extralong tapaderos served as
protection in brush country.

FIG. 28.31.   Saddle with stirrup leathers showing
across the bars on top of the seat. The back half
of the seat is quilted. The twisted stirrup leathers
and the saddle are full-floral-stamped.

FIG. 28.32. The tame-rose pattern, still popular today (see Figs. 28.4A–C and 28.8A).

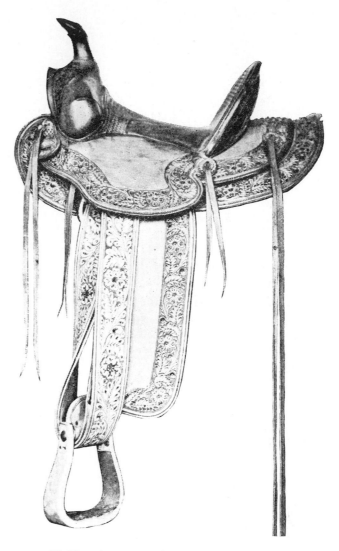

FIG. 28.33. An unusual ornate broad border with lines separating it, unlike the present free-form border patterns (Fig. 28.8B).

CHAPTER 29

Saddle Pads and Blankets

A *saddle pad* is a pad placed on the horse's back under the saddle. The pad protects the saddle, keeps the horse's sweat off the saddle, and helps protect the horse from an imperfectly fitted saddle. A *saddle blanket* serves the same purposes. One of the advantages of the blanket is that it can be folded in such a way as to make up for some conformation changes in the horse during long trail rides. It can also be folded to raise a saddle to protect sore areas on a horse's back and withers. A saddle blanket will not entirely make up for an ill-fitting saddle, but if the difficulties in fit are not too great, it can help. Corrective folding of a blanket requires that no fold be next to the horse (except the front half fold) and that extreme care must be taken to avoid injuring the back and withers. With narrow-withered horses an extra fold can be made over the withers.

Many saddle pads are quilted, with stitching across the pad to keep the stuffing in place (Fig. 29.1).

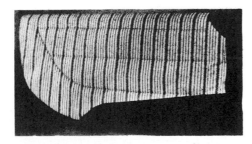

FIG. 29.1.   Hair-filled pad with wear leather. From Ruwart, catalog, 1963.

A recently developed pad is made of 100 percent Kodel Polyester pile (Fig. 29.5). There is an interesting story behind this pad. It was suggested by a doctor who was also a horseman. Knowing how effective pads of this material

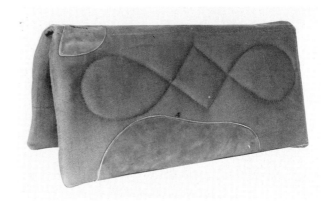

FIG. 29.2.   Flannel-covered pad with wear leather. Courtesy of Tex Tan.

were in relieving bedridden patients, it occurred to him that it might have the same effect when used as a saddle pad. Experiment proved that he was right. It adapts to the horse's back and seems to provide for better air circulation and over-all ventilation.

The saddle blanket is customarily doubled in use. It may have ornamental tassels on the ends. It can be made of several materials, including cotton, wool, mohair, and rayon. Whatever material is used in the blanket must be tolerable to the horse (Fig. 29.6).

For years *Navaho blankets* were favored by many riders. Though they are very expensive today the advantages of Navaho blankets are that they are extremely long-lived, soft, and absorbent. They are 100 percent wool, with

FIG. 29.3. Navaho blanket. From Hamleys, catalog no. 32, 1931.

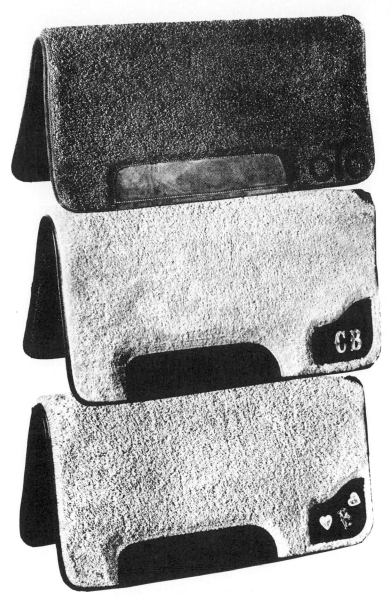

FIG. 29.4. Wyatt pad. From Ryon's, catalog no. 66, 1978.

the same heavy-textured yarn running both ways of the weaving, making the blankets durable. The imported or domestic look-alikes can be easily recognized by inner base threads with a very light-weight, stringlike appearance. With proper care a genuine Navaho blanket will give decades of good wear.

A *corona blanket* is a blanket cut to fit the outside of the skirt of the saddle, with a round, attractively fluffed edge that gives the appearance of a corona (Fig. 29.7).

After the pad or blanket is used, especially on warm days when the horse becomes sweaty and the underneath side of the blanket gets wet, it is necessary to air it out and let it dry completely before using it again. It should not be bundled up in such a way that it cannot air out and dry.

The size of the blanket or pad is important. When the blanket is on the horse, it should show at least an inch on all sides of the saddle. Thus the blanket should be ordered *at least* two inches longer than the length of the saddle skirt and at least two inches longer than the underneath surface of the saddle measured from the lower edge of one skirt up and over and down to the lower edge of the other skirt.

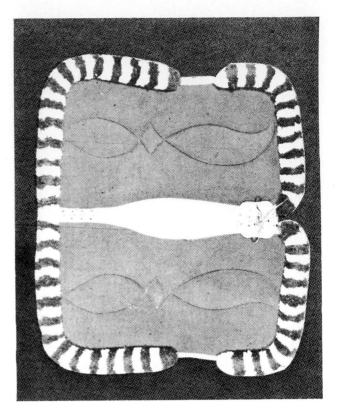

FIG. 29.7. Corona blanket with space for fender. From Tex Tan, catalog no. 82, 1973.

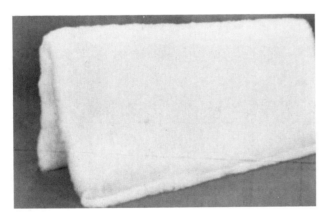

FIG. 29.5. Orthopedic saddle pad. From Tex Tan, catalog no. 87, 1977.

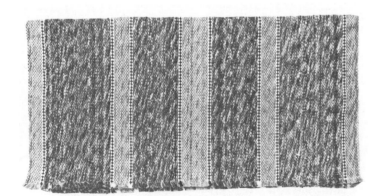

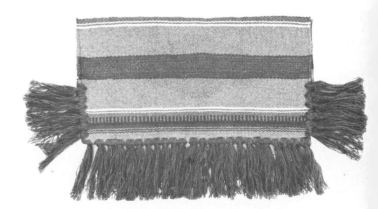

FIG. 29.6. Saddle blankets. Courtesy of Tex Tan.

CHAPTER 30

Saddle Care

A new saddle, like a new pair of boots, must be broken in and made to conform to the rider. That is not accomplished overnight. For example, on any new saddle the stirrup openings face each other. For the safety, comfort, and convenience of the rider the opening through the stirrup should face forward. There are two simple ways of accomplishing this shaping, which is called *setting the stirrup.*

Before setting the stirrups, the stirrup leathers should be adjusted to the proper length by putting the saddle on the horse, sitting correctly in the saddle (Fig. 36.8), and adjusting the stirrups to the proper fit. The legs should hang straight down naturally. Then each stirrup should be adjusted so that the tread is even with the anklebone. The proper stirrup-leather length has been achieved when the rider, sitting up straight and in the lowest part of the saddle seat with his knees bent slightly, can look past his knee and see just slightly ahead of the top of the toe of his boot when the ball of his foot is comfortably resting on the stirrup tread with the heel lower than the toe.

Another method of checking the correct length of the stirrup leathers is to stand in the stirrups. The rider should be able to slide his hand under his crotch in this standing position. Also, when sitting in the saddle with the stirrups properly adjusted, he should be able to push against the stirrups and rise out of the seat without rising up against the cantle. Stirrup leathers, especially on the mounting (near) side, stretch after they have been used for a period of time and need to be readjusted periodically.

When the stirrups are properly adjusted, they are ready to be set at the proper angle. With lukewarm water wet the back (flesh side) only of the stirrup leathers and fenders approx-imately halfway across the lower edge and farther up the front edge. Set the saddle flat on the floor, with the stirrup leathers extending out from each side. Turn the stirrup up so that the opening faces forward. Put a weight on the stirrup to keep it in this position while the leather dries slowly at a cool temperature (Fig. 26.19).

There is an alternate way of setting the stirrups. Follow the same procedure of wetting the back side of the stirrup leathers and fenders. Then place the saddle on a saddle rack while the leather is still wet and turn the stirrup leathers in the position described above. Run a broom handle through the stirrup on one side across to the stirrup on the other side. Leave the broom handle in this position until the leather has dried (Fig. 26.20). It helps to hang a weight from the center of the broom handle.

Sooner or later every rider finds it necessary to make additional holes in the leather of his saddle or bridle. Two tools are available for doing this easily and neatly. One is the *drive punch,* used to make larger holes (Fig. 30.1).

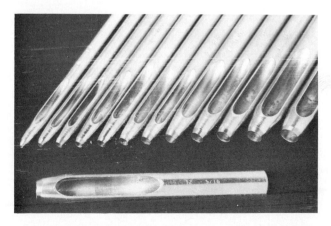

FIG. 30.1.　Drive punch. Courtesy of Tandy Crafts, Inc., Fort Worth, Texas.

Each drive punch makes only one size of hole; two or three drive punches will meet the needs of the average rider. The other is the *rotary punch,* which can be used to make small holes of six different sizes (Fig. 30.2). For use by

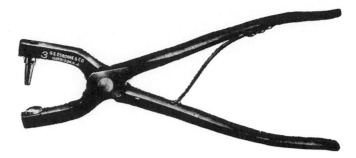

FIG. 30.3. Single-tube plier-type spring punch. From Osborne, catalog no. 56, 1977.

FIG. 30.2. Six-tube rotary punch. Courtesy of Tandy.

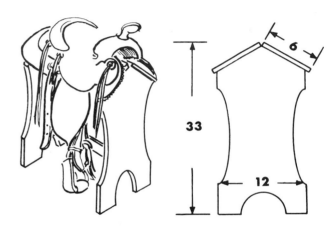

FIG. 30.4. Wooden saddle stand. Courtesy of Tex Tan.

strong hands, hand-operated plier-type punches are available. They look like rotary punches, but each punch makes only one size hole (Fig. 30.3).

Store the saddle in a dry place out of the sun on a wooden saddle stand (Fig. 30.4). The stand allows the saddle to dry and also helps it retain its shape. Do not allow the stirrups to touch the floor, or the fenders may be bent out of shape.

When the saddle is in storage, always cover it with canvas, a tarp, a plastic sheet, or even a newspaper to keep off dust. Over a period of time dust damages leather. The saddle blanket should be hung with the damp side out to dry.

A makeshift stand can be made from a steel drum with a 13-to-15-inch opening in the mouth, a small nail keg, or a large log. The keg or drum can be easily nailed to a wall. Plans, materials, and measurements for a serviceable homemade saddle stand are shown in Fig. 30.5. Stands can also be made from pipes (Fig. 30.6). Cover the top of the saddle rack with an old blanket, rug, or other soft material to prevent the underneath

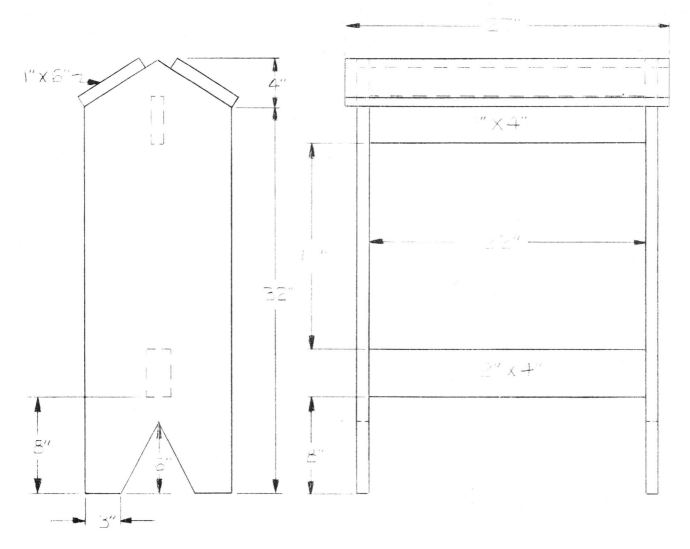

FIG. 30.5. Making a saddle stand. Materials needed, in the following sizes: two 1 by 12s, 36 inches long; two 1 by 6s, 27 inches long; one 1 by 4, 22 inches long; and one 2 by 4, 22 inches long; and 1 pound no. 8d tin-finishing or flathead screws.

side of the saddle from picking up dirt, dust, and splinters from the wood.

If no rack is available, the saddle can be suspended by a rope (Fig. 30.7A). Pull a rope through the hand hole on the back of the fork, forward and out the front side of the gullet, and up to the horn, tying it to the horn. The end of the rope that is used to suspend the saddle is the one that comes out the back of

the gullet through the hand hole. This will tend to hold the saddle in position. While it is not an ideal method of storage, it is better than laying the saddle on the ground. No saddle should be allowed to hang this way for very long, or the leather will take an incorrect set.

A saddle should never be laid on the ground. If it must be put on the ground briefly, lay it fork down on its nose. This allows it to rest on

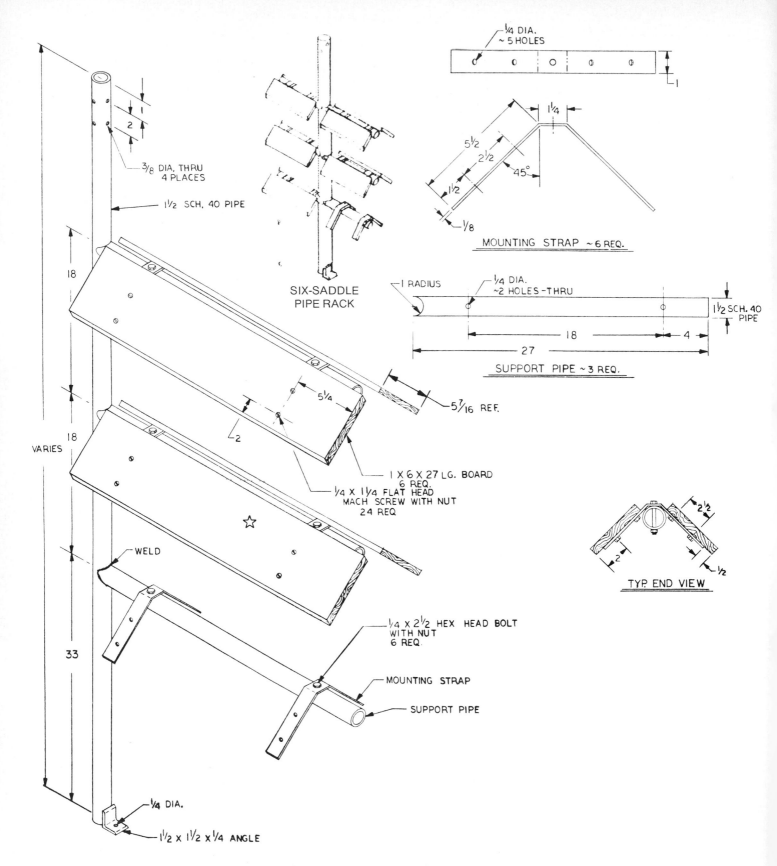

¼ DIA.
~ 5 HOLES

1

1¼

5½
2½
½
45°
⅛

MOUNTING STRAP ~ 6 REQ.

1 RADIUS

¼ DIA.
~ 2 HOLES – THRU

1½ SCH. 40 PIPE

18
4
27

SUPPORT PIPE ~ 3 REQ.

1

2

3/8 DIA, THRU
4 PLACES

1½ SCH. 40 PIPE

18

18

VARIES

SIX-SADDLE
PIPE RACK

5¼

2

5⁷/₁₆ REF.

1 X 6 X 27 LG. BOARD
6 REQ.

¼ X 1¼ FLAT HEAD
MACH SCREW WITH NUT
24 REQ

2½

2

½

TYP END VIEW

WELD

33

¼ X 2½ HEX HEAD BOLT
WITH NUT
6 REQ.

MOUNTING STRAP

SUPPORT PIPE

¼ DIA.

1½ X 1½ X ¼ ANGLE

FIG. 30.6.   Construction of a three-saddle pipe rack.

FIG. 30.7. Ways of resting a saddle. *(A)* Hanging by a rope. *(B)* Standing on the nose. *(C)* Laying a saddle on the side.

the front side of the skirt and either the horn or the fork binding. The saddle should not be left in this position for very long, or the front side of the skirt will take on an improper set (Fig. 30.7*B*). Another, even less satisfactory, way is to lay the saddle on its side (Fig. 30.7*C*). In short, do not leave a saddle for very long in a position where any of the leather is bent in an abnormal position. If it is left in such a position, the leather will take a set that will be hard to change.

If the sheepskin is allowed to touch the ground, it can pick up sticks, small stones,

burs, dirt, and dried grass, all of which are hard to clean off and, if overlooked, are hard on the horse's back.

Enclosed heat such as that in the trunk of a car on hot days dehydrates the leather, making it dry and brittle. Do not store a saddle in a car trunk for extended periods of time.

Saddle leather will remain in good condition for many years if it is given a reasonable amount of tender loving care. Proof of this is seen in many old saddles—some of them a hundred years old—that have their original leather and are still ridable. I have in my collection a beautiful 1911 R. T. Frazier saddle in perfect riding shape. The original leather is still intact. When I purchased it, all that was necessary was to polish the brass and clean and oil the saddle. The leather was as good as the day the saddle was made.

Salt from horse sweat, dust, and moisture are all detrimental to leather, and all of them are encountered daily by the saddle in use. A saddle given heavy, hard, daily use should be cleaned and oiled approximately every two to three months. If the saddle is used only occasionally, it should be cleaned and oiled two or three times a year. A good procedure for cleaning and oiling a saddle that has an oiled surface is as follows:

1. Wipe off dust and dirt with a dry cloth or soft brush. If mud is caked on the saddle use a stiff brush and a good grade of laundry soap, making plenty of suds. Rub in gently. Rinse off the soap with warm water. Dry slowly.

2. Using a good grade of saddle, Castile, or glycerin soap; lukewarm water; and a sponge or soft brush, work up a thick lather and wash the saddle. Give an extra washing to areas that have come in contact with sweat, such as the underside of the cinch strap, the fenders, the stirrup leathers, the flank cinch, and the flank billets. Rinse off the lather completely with clean, lukewarm water. Allow the saddle to dry at room temperature. Do not dry it in the sun.

3. Apply one light, even coat of slightly warmed neat's-foot oil using sheepskin or a soft cloth. Apply the oil evenly so that it does not spot. Neat's-foot oil darkens leather, and if it is applied unevenly, it will cause spotting. Apply a second coat of oil to sweaty areas. Use only genuine neat's-foot oil, not imitations (see Glossary). Do not use neat's-foot oil in tropical climates. Oil applied in extreme heat is damaging to leather.

4. After the neat's-foot oil is absorbed (thirty minutes or more), apply an *even* coat of saddle soap with a *damp* sponge. This gives the leather a hard, protective surface. Rub in the soap gently. Allow it to dry for at least two hours, and then polish with a soft rag.

5. If a glossy finish is desired, apply a coat of neutral wax shoe polish with a vigorous rub-down.

If the saddle is antiqued or has lacquered areas, the supplier should be consulted about techniques of care. Antique leather stain is available at tack stores for over-all darkening.

If the saddle is caught in the rain, wipe off as much of the moisture as possible. Allow the saddle to dry completely on a stand in a cool place. Oil it lightly.

When polishing metal conchas, rigging rings, and other ornamental metals on the saddle, do so before cleaning and oiling the saddle so that the metal polish left on the leather will be removed in the cleaning process. For silver, brass, and stainless steel a metal cleaner called Simichrome is the best and easiest to use, though it requires elbow grease.

While scratches on leather cannot be removed completely, they can be treated as follows: cover the scratched area with Goddard's Saddle Wax (which is about half Carnauba wax). Using a soft, dry cloth, rub down the waxed area vigorously with a lot of pressure. This should greatly improve the appearance of the scratched area.

Wash out the cloth cinch. This prevents it from becoming hard and causing irritation. Washing also prolongs its life. Washable cinch covers are popular and help preserve the cinch.

If you wish to do a really thorough job of saddle cleaning and oiling, strip the saddle down to the tree by loosening the saddle strings and removing both front jockeys, the back jockeys, and the skirts. The fork cover and cantle cover will not come off easily, and it is better to leave them on. Peel up the seat to expose the bars and the hard-to-get-to parts of the stirrup leathers.

Examine the rawhide covering of the tree.

Apply two or more coats of shellac or marine lacquer to reseal the surface. If any of the raw-hide seams have separated, replace them with waxed saddler's nylon. Olive oil, unsalted butter, or raw beef tallow can be used to oil the saddle parts, but genuine neat's-foot oil is the oil of preference today.

Jack Carroll adds the following suggestions:

If a saddle squeaks, use soft beef-fat trimmings, working the tallow well into the leather at that point.

Do not oil the cinch strap. It was tanned with chromate salts to resist salt and remain pliable. Clean with saddle soap.

Rusting iron rots leather. Replace any iron screws, plated conchas, etc., with brass or nickel ones.

One final note: if your horse has not worn a saddle for a long time, remember that his back and foreflank will be tender for a while.

CHAPTER 31

Selecting a Saddle

In selecting a saddle, the careful buyer has three requirements: (1) the saddle must fit the horse's conformation, (2) it must fit the rider's conformation, and (3) it must be the appropriate style for the type of riding or work to be done (Sabin, 1971).

The first step is to determine the size and conformation of the horse. A horse's height is measured from the ground to the highest point on the withers, the fifth vertebra (Fig. 31.1).

The measurement is easily taken with a quickly adjustable measuring stick or measuring tape (Fig. 31.2). It is also possible to get a reasonably accurate measurement without the use of a special measuring instrument. Stand the horse close to a wall and place a small board (1 by 2 inches) horizontally across the high point of the horse's withers, pushing the board against the wall to steady it. Measure from the underneath side of the board to the ground to obtain the

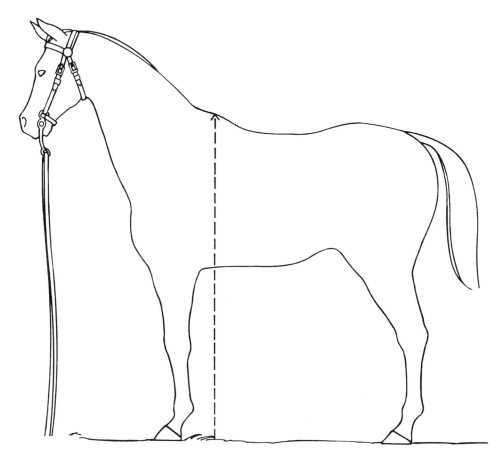

FIG. 31.1. Measuring a horse's height (from the ground to the highest point of the withers).

be impractical!). Far more important than the horse's height are the shape (height and width) of its withers (Fig. 31.3), the shape (flat or

FIG. 31.3.   Cross section of a horse's withers.

FIG. 31.4.   Cross section of a horse's back.

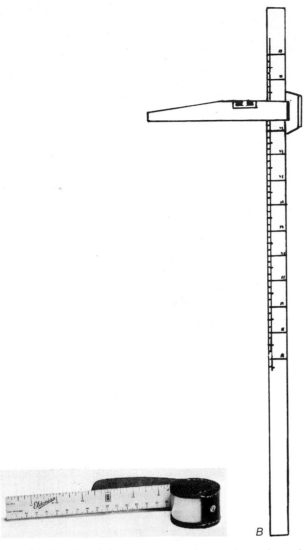

FIG. 31.2.   Special measures to determine a horse's height. *(A)* Folding measuring stick. Drawing adapted from Miller's, catalog no. 109, 1977. *(B)* Eldonian horse measure. Compact (2 by 1 1/4 inches) in leather case, extends to 18 hands. Courtesy of Miller's.

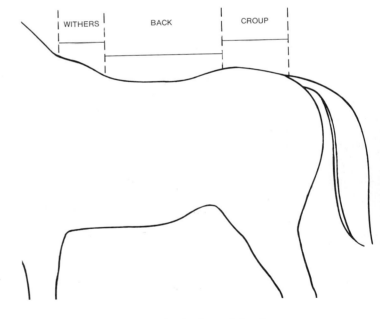

FIG. 31.5.   Length of a horse's back.

horse's height in inches. Divide by 4 to convert the inches to hands and count each inch left over as 1. Example: 58 inches ÷ 4 = 14 hands + 2 inches = 14.2 hands.

Actually, the height of the horse has only indirect bearing on the saddle measurements (though obviously it has a bearing on the size of some saddle accessories—22-inch tapaderos on a 14-hand horse ridden by a six-footer would

peaked) of its back (Fig. 31.4), and the length of its back (Fig. 31.5).

When selecting a saddle, it is most important

209

FIG. 31.6.   Horse shown in Fig. 31.5 with saddletree in position.

to have a proper fit at the withers (Fig. 31.6). Western saddles are available in designs to fit high, low, wide, and narrow withers. The saddle's gullet should clear the horse's withers at least two fingers edgewise; more clearance indicates that the tree is built wrong for the horse (Fig. 16.6A).

Long bars on a short-backed horse cause too much pressure over the loin and kidney area, injuring the horse or at the very least causing soreness in the area (Fig. 31.7).

It is necessary that the rider purchase a saddle with the most comfortable and most secure length of seat for himself. A seat that is too large is better than a seat that is too small, because a too-small seat limits the rider's free-

FIG. 31.7. Too-long saddletree bars on a short back.

dom of movement.

Because the stirrup leathers are usually suspended from the tree in stirrup-leather grooves directly behind the fork, there is no way to change their position back or forward. Therefore, the longer the seat the farther forward of the rider the stirrups will be. In other words, since the fork and the stirrup-leather grooves are in a fixed forward position, the only way to lengthen the seat is to move the cantle back on the bars.

In selecting a saddle, the shape of the rider, as well as the shape of the horse, must be considered. The seat sizes shown in Fig. 31.8 are for the average rider and are *suggestions only*. They are a place to start. It is important for the rider to try larger and smaller sizes until he finds the most comfortable seat length. If a foam-rubber-quilted or padded seat is being purchased, 1/2 inch should be added to the length of the seat.

Remember too that the method of measuring the seat size does not take into account variations in the pitches of the cantle and fork. A large-angled pitch to both the fork and cantle can make a small seat seem large, and a small-angled pitch to the fork and cantle can make a long seat feel short. The seat should keep the rider as close to the horse as is practical. In this way the rider gets the "feel" of the horse in somewhat the same way that early-day pilots flew "by the seat of their pants".

Make certain that the saddle has a flat seat, not one with an exaggerated slope upward toward the fork. It should also have fenders so shaped that when the rider is sitting properly, with knees slightly bent, the knees rest against the fender, not against the horse.

Another thing to remember is that the tooling or stamping on the leather is not there only to beautify the saddle. Its main purpose is to give the rider a better grip on his saddle and consequently a safer ride.

SEAT MEASUREMENT CHART

Rider's Height	Rider's Weight, Pounds	Average Pleasure Tree, Inches
5'1"–5'6"	100–130	14¾
5'4"–5'6"	120–150	14¾
5'5"–5'10"	135–65	15
5'8"–5'10"	170–200	15
5'10"–6'0"	150–60	15
5'10"–6'0"	170–200	15
5'10"–6'2"	200–220	15

FIG. 31.8. Saddle-selection chart. Adapted from Tex Tan, catalog no. 82, 1972.

In an interview with Jack Carroll, I learned about the following useful procedure for determining the correct cross-section outline of a horse at its withers and in the loin area. Carroll told me that for many years the English have used this procedure to obtain a correctly fitting saddle that is to be used on only one horse. If the saddle is to be used on several different horses, it is necessary to determine a middle-of-the-road composite of wither and back types. If the difference between horses seems too extreme, I recommend that you consult a veteran saddlemaker for advice.

To make a template at the horse's withers, buy heavy wire solder, double it, and twist a three-foot length. Bend this wire over the horse's back, over the withers, and press it down into the "pockets," or depressions, behind the shoulder blades into which the undersides of the burs of the saddletree bars fit. Carefully remove this form, place it on a sheet of cardboard, and trace an outline to give a template of the withers (a cross section of the horse at that point).

Carefully cut out the template with a pair of scissors. Put the top half of the template on the horse to double-check its accuracy. Take the lower section to the saddlemaker or check it with factory-made saddles to determine their fit on the horse.

Repeat this procedure about 14 to 17 inches behind the withers, depending on the rider's weight (see page 213). This gives a template for the cross section of the part of the back where the flared end of the bars take the rider's main weight at rest. Again place the top half of the template on the horse to check its accuracy and use the bottom half to check the flare of the saddletree bars at that point on the saddle.

The length behind the withers where the measurement for the back template is made is determined by the weight of the rider. A heavier rider requires a longer seat. For a rider weighing up to 140 pounds, the back measurement should be taken 14 inches behind the withers. For the rider weighing 150 to 180 pounds, the measurement should be taken at 15 inches. For the heavy rider, weighing 190

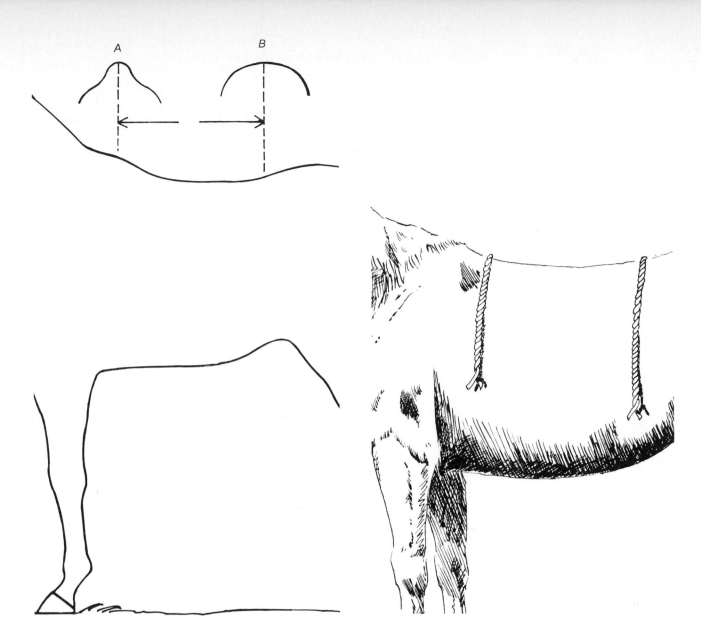

FIG. 31.9. Cross-section templates made at the points indicated. *(A)* Highest point of the withers. *(B)* Back (varies 14 to 17 inches, depending on the horse's size and the weight of the rider).

FIG. 31.10. Ropes on horse's back indicating points to fit. Drawing by Dick Foster. Courtesy of Jack Carroll.

to 250 pounds, the measurement should be taken at 16 to 17 inches. According to Carroll,

saddle seats should be ordered in 1/2-inch increments from 12 to 17 inches.

FIG. 31.11.   Saddletree with bars too close together or at a too-acute set angle.

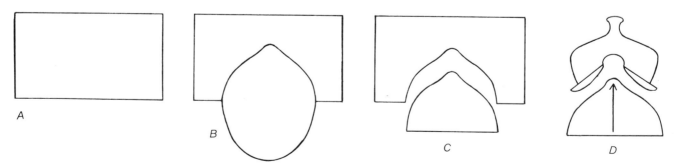

FIG. 31.12.   Withers template. *(A)* Blank template. *(B)* Template cut out. *(C)* Checking accuracy of template on horse's withers with female template. *(D)* Checking saddle with male template.

The following outline lists the information needed about horse or horses and rider in order to purchase a correctly fitting and appropriate western saddle.

HORSE

   Breed

   Wither measurement

   Back measurement

   Heart girth (circumference)

   Weight

   Height

RIDER

   Sex

   Height

   Weight

   Inseam leg length

TYPE OF SADDLE (western)

SADDLE USE

   Pleasure

   Ranch saddle (all-around)

   Rodeo (calf roping or bulldogging)

   Barrel racing

   Show

   Cutting

   Other

TREE

   Style

     A fork

     Narrow fork

     Swell fork

   Composition

     Wood

     Fiberglass

   Covering of tree

     Rawhide

     Canvas

     Other

   Length of bars

   Degrees from horizontal of bars at gullet (set angle)

   Flare of bars (angle)

   Seat length (add 1/2 inch if seat is padded)

FORK

   Slope

   Style

     Slick

     Round

     Swell (undercut or not undercut)

   Width

   Gullet

     Height

     Width

   Rope strap (yes or no; right or left)

     Leather strap

     D and string

HORN

   Type

     Ornamental

     Mexican

215

HORN, Continued

   Regular

   Roping

     Hard-and-fast-tie

     Dally

  Length of neck

  Cap

   Size

   Style

   Pitch

  Covering

CANTLE

  Height

  Width

  Shape

   Round

   Flat top

  Contour

   Flat

   Dished

  Slope (pitch)

  Binding type

   Bead (round)

   Roll

    Standard Cheyenne

     Plain

     Rope edge

    Elephant-ear Cheyenne

     Plain

     Rope edge

SKIRT

  Shape

Square

Round

Butterfly

Other

Dimensions

SADDLE STRINGS

  Number

  Conchas

   Leather

    German silver (nickel)

    Sterling silver

  No saddle strings (screw conchas only)

  Ds and strings

RIGGING

  Style

   Conventional

    Centerfire (California)

    Spanish (full)

    7/8 standard single

    3/4 standard single (Montana)

    5/8 single (Arizona)

   Double

    Full double standard

    Full double ("Sam Stagg")

    7/8 double

    3/4 double (rodeo saddles)

   In-skirt (built-in, built-on, or bulkless)

    Full double

    7/8 double

RIGGING RINGS OR SUBSTITUTES

  Round metal (wire)

Brass

  Circular

  D ring

Steel

  Circular (leather-covered or not)

  D ring

Flat metal

  Brass

  Steel

Ring built-in skirts

Plate rigging

  On tree

  In skirt

CINCH STRAPS

Near front side: strap only

Off front side: billet strap

Flank

  Billets

    Single

    Double

  Straps

STIRRUPS

Wood (outside metal-covered or not)

  Shape

    Oxbow

      Rodeo

      Standard

    Visalia

    Roper

    Bellbottom

    Overshoe

Tread leather-covered

All leather-covered

TAPADEROS

Length

Shape

  Leather hood

  Monkey nose

  Eagle bill

STIRRUP LEATHERS

Laced

Buckled

  Standard roller

  Quick-change

  Blevins (2- or 3-prong)

  Tackaberry

LEATHERS

Single

Double

Half double

STIRRUP LEATHER KEEPERS (yes or no)

FENDERS

Shape

Separate and attached to stirrup leathers

One piece with stirrup leathers

SEAT COVERING

Hard (unpadded)

Padded

  Quilted

SEAT COVERINGS, Continued

    Inlaid

    Overlaid

  Air foam

    Seat to top of cantle

    Jockeys and seat to top of cantle

LEATHERWORK

  Type of leather

    Smooth

    Roughout

  Tooled

    Hand-stamped

    Embossed

    Buckstitched

      Full

      Skirt

      Side jockey

      Fenders

      Stirrups

ACCESSORIES

  Cinch

    Material

      Mohair

      Cotton

      Length

      Width

    Rings

      Brass

      Cadmium-plated

    Buckles

      None (rings only)

      Buckle one end only

      Buckle both ends

      Ends covered by safe (yes or no)

    Shape

      Narrow

      Wide

      Roping

    Flank (rear)

      Style

      Buckles

        Brass

        Other

SADDLE FINISH

  Neat's-foot oil

  Saddle soap

  Natural

  Background dyed

  Antiqued

CHAPTER 32

Saddle Accessories

Of the many available saddle accessories several are very useful and some are necessary for the proper performance of the saddle.

BREAST COLLAR

The *breast collar,* or *breast harness,* is a wide strap (often 1 1/2 to 2 inches wide) that goes around the front of the horse in the breast area (Fig. 32.1). Its purpose is to prevent the backward movement of the saddle such as may occur with a mutton-withered horse or when a roping horse is making a fast start, or when a horse is going up a steep hill. It is usually anchored at the sides to small D rings or slots on the lower front side of the saddle skirt or around the cinch straps on the cinch. The smaller anchoring straps are called *rig straps.* The breast collar can be held in position horizontally with a shoulder strap that runs from the breast collar on one side of the horse, up and over the horse's shoulder, and down the other side, where it again attaches to the breast collar. The shoulder strap is seldom used today. On the lower side in the center of the breast collar (which is in the center front of the horse) is often a small D ring to which the tie-down of a martingale can be attached.

Breast collars dress up a horse and come in many ornate styles. For day-to-day flatland riding they are unnecessary unless the horse has extremely rounded withers that make it difficult to hold the saddle in place.

MARTINGALE

The purpose of the martingale is utilitarian, not ornamental. A *standing martingale* prevents the horse from throwing its head upward beyond a point determined by the length of the tie-down strap (Figs. 32.2 to 32.4). It consists of a tie-down strap that attaches at the front end of the cinch, either to a D ring on the cinch or around the cinch and at the front end by means of a snap to a D ring on a noseband or cavesson. If the saddle is equipped with a breast collar, the martingale tie-down strap is run through the D ring on the top center of the breast collar. If no breast collar is being used, the martingale must have a neck strap to hold the tie-down strap close enough to the horse that he will not put his hoof through the tie-down, even when he lowers his head to graze.

The standing martingale is used by ropers and barrel racers. In calf roping it gives the horse stability in stopping, according to Phil Livingston.

The *running martingale,* instead of having a single tie-down strap from the cinch to the bridle, has a single tie-down strap from the cinch two-thirds of the way up; the last third of the tie-down strap becomes two separate straps, each with a ring on the top end (Figs. 32.5 and 32.6). The bridle reins are put through these two rings, one ring to one rein. The purpose is to be able to keep the horse's head down when the rider wants it down and also to be able to set the proper carriage of the horse's head, using the rings on the tie-down as moving focal points.

Probably the best way of adjusting the running martingale properly is to take an imaginary line between the attachment point of the reins on the bit and the position of the rider's hands (assuming that he holds them in a low position, close to the withers). The rings on the martin-

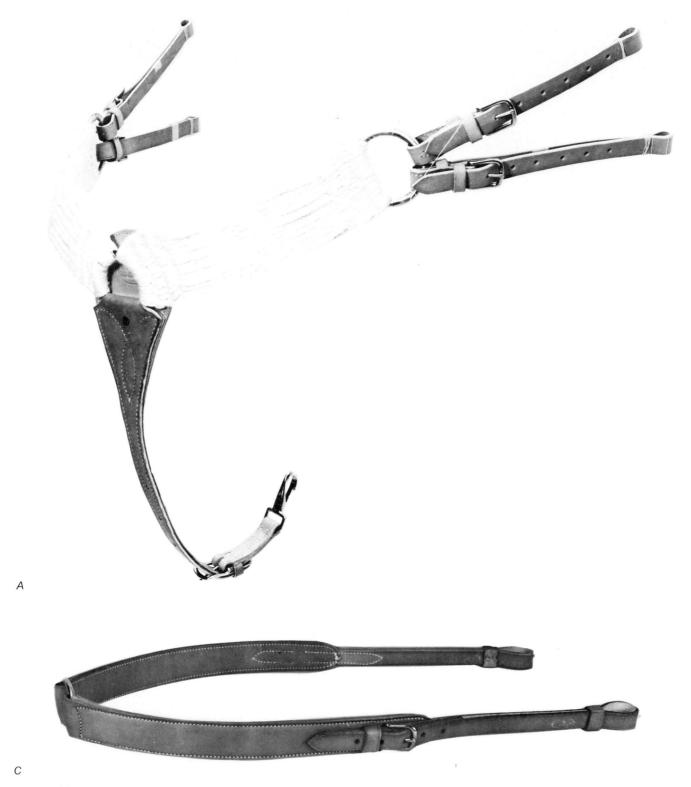

FIG. 32.1.   Breast collar. *(A)* Mohair roper's breast collar. Courtesy of Ryon's. *(B)* Carved-leather working breast collar. Courtesy of Ryon's. *(C)* Strap breast collar without cinch tie-down strap. Courtesy of Tex Tan. *(D)* Sterling-silver breast collar (matches cloverleaf saddle in Fig. 22.10*A*). Courtesy of Ryon's.

B

D

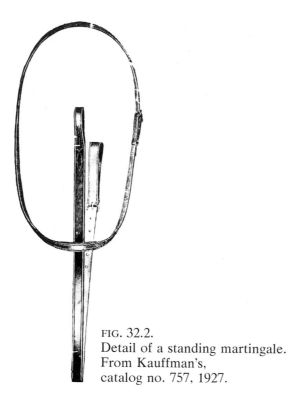

FIG. 32.2.
Detail of a standing martingale.
From Kauffman's,
catalog no. 757, 1927.

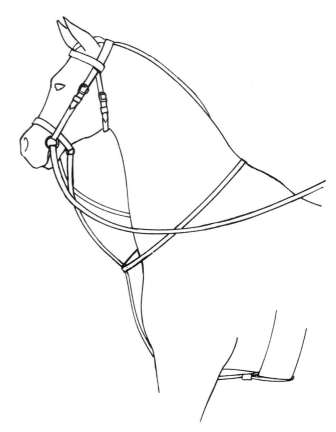

FIG. 32.4.   Standing martingale in position.

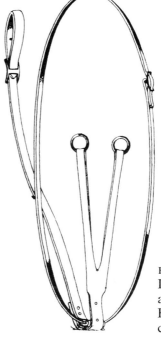

FIG. 32.3.   Standing-martingale tie-down strap to attach bridle cavesson to cinch. From Tex Tan, catalog no. 86, 1976.

gale should not come farther up than approximately two inches below this point. Another method is to adjust the length so that the rings reach the point of the horse's shoulder. This will give the rider adequate leverage when bringing the martingale into play but is not so low that a severe pull is automatically applied. It can be an excellent training aid.

FIG. 32.5.
Detail of
a running martingale.
From Carroll,
catalog no. 38, 1978.

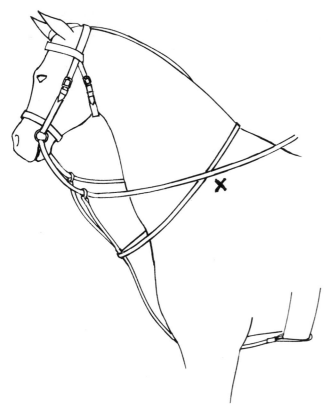

pose is to help keep the saddle from slipping forward. The crupper was almost universally used on military saddles in Europe but was not much used by the American cavalry. Most European cavalry saddles had a spoon at the rear of the cantle to which the crupper was attached (Fig. 32.8).

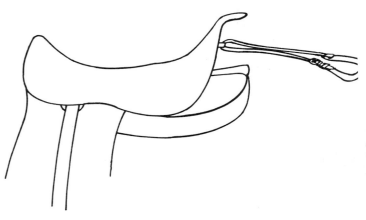

FIG. 32.8. Crupper attached to British military saddle.

FIG. 32.6. Running martingale in position. *X* is the point of the shoulder.

CRUPPER

A *crupper* is a strap running from the back of a saddle to the tail of a horse, underneath the tail, and back to the saddle (Fig. 32.7). Its pur-

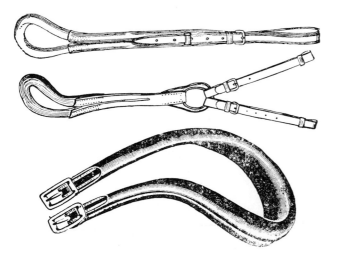

FIG. 32.7. Cruppers. *(A)* Complete riding-saddle cruppers. From L. D. Stone, catalog, ca. 1905. *(B)* Detail of crupper dock. From S. R. and I. C. McConnell Company, catalog, n.d.

BREECHING

The *breeching,* or *breech strap,* is a fairly heavy strap that extends around the rump of the horse well below the tail set point and attaches at its forward end at some point such as a D ring on the back of the saddle skirt. Its purpose too is to prevent forward movement of the saddle. The strap is held in position with a strap from one side up and over the croup of the horse and down the other side, where it is attached again to the breech strap. It is used mostly in mountainous country to prevent the saddle from shifting forward on a steep downhill grade. It is also used on packsaddles to keep the pack from shifting. It is very seldom used today in normal riding.

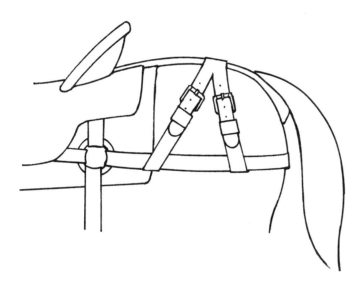

FIG. 32.9.   Breech strap in position.

SADDLEBAGS AND SADDLE POCKETS

Saddlebags are two storage bags, one on each side of the saddle (Fig. 32.10*A*). They are attached behind the cantle and to the rear jockeys or rear skirts. Sometimes they are an integral part of the rear jockeys or the skirt. They resemble old-fashioned strap-down portfolios. The size is determined by the size of the saddle and the horse and by what needs to be carried. They must never be uncomfortable to the horse or interfere with his movements.

A variation on the saddlebag is the *saddle pocket,* a small bag contoured in front to match the contour of the back of the cantle (Fig. 31.10*B*). It is pushed up against the back of the cantle and anchored to the number 4 saddle strings.

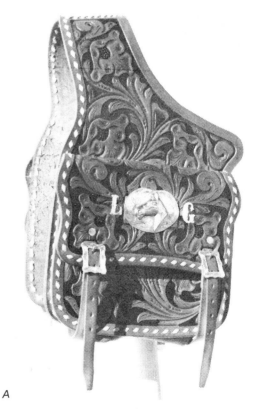

A

FIG. 32.10.   *(A)* Saddlebags. Courtesy of Tex Tan, and from Jack Carroll, catalog no. 38, 1978. *(B)* Saddle pocket. Courtesy of Tex Tan.

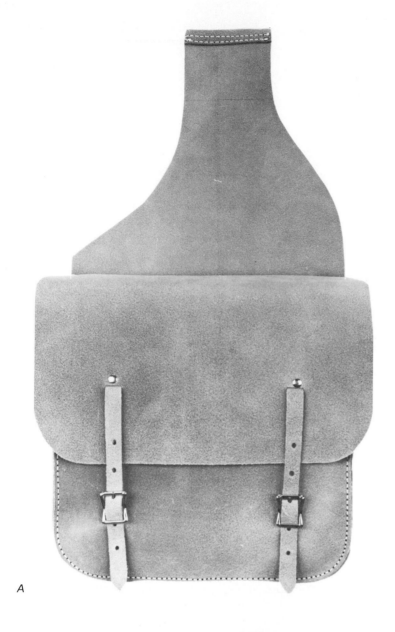

A

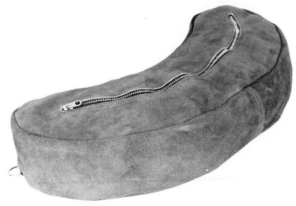

B

225

CHAPTER 33

Saddling a Horse

The first step in saddling a horse is to secure the horse, either with a ground tie or with a rope tied to a hitching rail or post. Then brush the horse's back, sides, and belly, brushing in the direction the hair lies. After shaking and checking the saddle blanket and removing any debris, place it on the horse's back so that the front edge is at least four inches forward of the position where the front of the saddle skirt will be placed. Pull the blanket *backward* to the correct position. Pull the blanket backward to be certain that the hair under the blanket lies flat; never pull the blanket forward. The sides of the blanket should be even on both sides.

Check the lining of the saddle to be certain that it is clean. Place the off-side stirrup, the front and flank cinches, and the saddle strings over the saddle to get them out of the way. Lift the saddle by the gullet and the cantle or rear skirt (Fig. 33.1). Place it gently and firmly

on the horse's back (Fig. 33.2). Shake the saddle backward (never forward) by the horn into the correct position. The correct position depends on how the saddle is rigged and the horse's conformation at the withers.

Walk around to the off side and gently let down the front and flank cinches and then the stirrup. Make certain that nothing is twisted and that the saddle strings are hanging down.

With an upward thrust of the hand raise the blanket slightly over the withers against the gullet to allow air to get underneath. Pull the mane free of the blanket. There should be a clearance of at least two fingers edgewise between the saddle blanket and the underneath side of the gullet over the withers, if the saddle fits the horse properly (Fig. 16.7). Sabin (1971) cautions: "Keep the blanket or pad from binding over the withers by raising the saddle and lifting the blanket into the gullet. Then set the saddle back down on the loosened blanket. Only the front of the saddle need be tipped up."

Put the near-side stirrup over the saddle or hook it onto the horn. Standing on the horse's near side near the front leg, reach underneath the horse and pull the front cinch toward you. Cinch up the horse at the front cinch so that three fingers flat can be placed between the horse and the cinch (Fig. 33.3).

If the cinch is too tight, it will be injurious to the horse, restricting breathing and causing galling. If it is too loose, you may lose yourself and the saddle at the first quick turn. Be certain that the cinch rings are not directly behind the horse's elbows; in that position they can hinder movement and easily cause bad sores. The ends of the cinch must be equal distances from the saddle (Fig. 25.16).

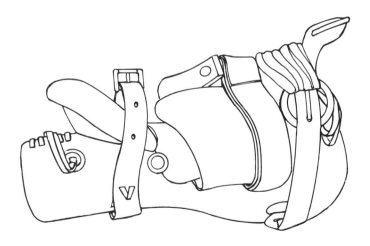

FIG. 33.1.   Off-side view of saddle ready to be lifted onto the horse.

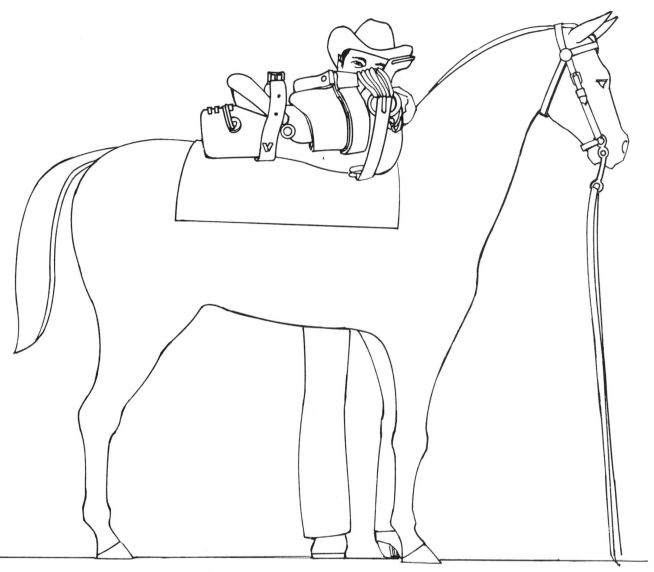

FIG. 33.2. Position of the saddle over the horse.

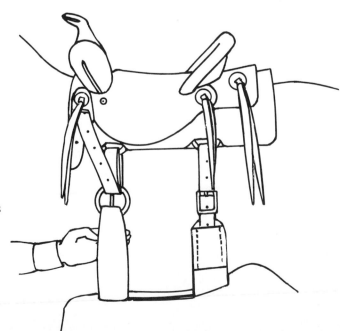

FIG. 33.3. Checking for proper tightness of front cinch.

Next cinch up the flank cinch so that there is a *maximum* distance of two or three fingers edgewise between the cinch and the horse's belly (Fig. 33.4). If it is too loose, it can catch

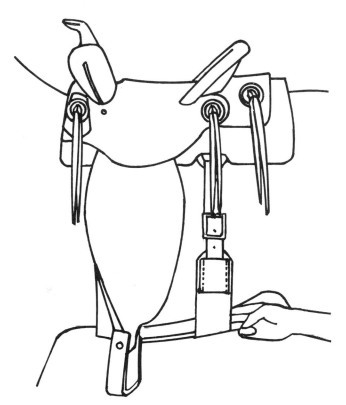

FIG. 33.4.   Checking for a properly tightened flank cinch.

on brush and other objects. Worse yet, the horse can catch his rear hoof in it when he tries to kick a fly off his underside. There should always be a connecting strap between the front and flank cinches to prevent the flank cinch from shifting back and interfering with the horse. *Never* cinch up the flank cinch first; and, when removing a saddle, *always* unbuckle the flank cinch first. If you do not do it in this order and the horse spooks away from you, the saddle could slip under his belly and be damaged severely by his hooves.

Now walk the horse twenty paces or so. Recheck the cinch for tightness. Many horses puff

up when they are being cinched up. When they release the air, the cinch may be so loose that the saddle will turn when you mount. Always reach down and check the cinch again when you have ridden a hundred yards or so.

When the saddle is secured, climb into the saddle (see below) and place your feet in the stirrups so that the stirrup tread is directly underneath the ball of each foot (Fig. 33.5).

FIG. 33.5.   Correct position of foot in stirrup.

The toe should be slightly higher than the heel. When you are in this position, you should be able to stand in the stirrups—on the ball of each foot, not on tiptoe—and place the palm of one hand between your crotch and the seat (Fig. 33.6).

When you are seated in the saddle in a normal, comfortable upright position, you should be able to look down across your knee and just see the tip of the toe of your boot (Fig. 36.8). If your position in the seat is correct (not too far back against the cantle), you should be able to push down on the stirrups without rising up against the cantle.

The length of the stirrup leathers must be the same on both sides. The quick-adjustable length adjusters are preferable to the older leathers that had to be laced (Figs. 26.7 to 26.14).

Equitation instructors teach the following procedure for mounting a horse: Take the reins

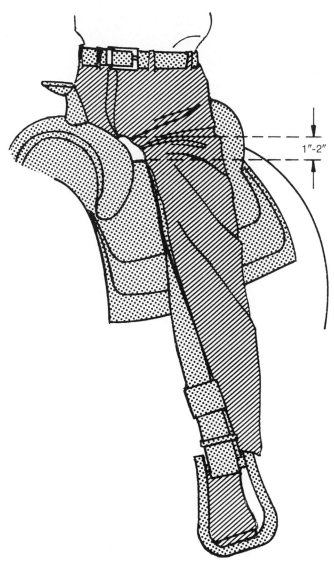

1"-2"

care not to gouge the horse's side with the toe of your boot. Apparently the logic in having the rider face the horse's hindquarters when mounting is that, should the horse move forward, the rider will be swung into the saddle.

Many horsemen mount facing the horse directly, with the foot in the stirrup facing slightly forward. This slight forward angle of the foot prevents the rider from gouging the horse's side with the toe of the boot during mounting.

There is a third acceptable way of mounting: Face forward toward the horse's head, put your left foot in the near side stirrup, take the reins in your left hand and place the left hand on the horse's mane approximately six inches in front of the saddle. Place your right hand on the horn. Mount with an even, swinging movement (Fig. 33.7).

When removing the saddle (unsaddling), unbuckle the flank cinch *first*. Release the front cinch. *Lift* the saddle off; do not drag it off.

FIG. 33.6. Checking stirrup-leather length when mounted by pushing against the stirrup. There should be 1 or 2 inches between the seat of the rider and the saddle.

in your left hand. Allowing the unused portion of the reins to fall on the near side, place your left hand (with reins) on the horse's mane approximately 6 inches ahead of the saddle. Place your right hand on the horn. You are facing almost to the horse's rear. Put your left foot properly in the stirrup. Mount with a rapid, even, swinging movement, not jumping. Take

FIG. 33.7. Mounting the horse.

PART III The Mechanics (Dynamics) of Riding

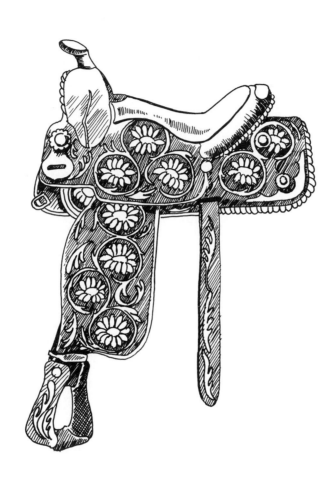

CHAPTER **34**

Horsemanship

The following discussion is included in this book to give readers a brief introduction to the dynamic forces involved in riding and to the "engineering structure" of the horse. It is not intended to be a manual of equitation. That is the province of a riding instructor. Readers interested in learning more about the development of the science and art of horsemanship will find *Masters of Equitation,* by W. Sidney Felton, a fascinating account, beginning with the time of Xenophon and moving to the present day. The author has also provided a helpful guide to those books most likely to be useful to today's horsemen, as well as to earlier classics that are primarily of historic interest. Another outstanding book is *Horseman's Progress,* by Vladimir Littauer. The book, by an author who combined scholarship with great ability as a horseman and a teacher of riding, relates the development of horsemanship to meet changing needs and describes the social and economic conditions that both caused and profoundly influenced that development.

Felton takes the reader through the evolution of the English saddle from an improperly designed "balanced seat" through the various changes that resulted in the forward-seat saddle in common use today. This type of saddle was the invention of Captain Federico Caprilli, an Italian cavalry officer. It is a balanced seat that placed the rider over the horse's center of gravity. It was not accepted at once; in fact, it had to overcome much resistance to change.

The ancient Parthians, Scythians, and Sarmatians, who were master horsemen, developed a style of riding that was so inherently correct that when the saddle and stirrup came into existence they too were designed to allow the rider to remain in balance with his horse. The Moors in Spain rode with a short stirrup and a forward seat, as did eastern European horsemen —note the forward seat shown in Rembrandt's *The Polish Rider,* painted in the seventeenth century (Fig. 34.1).

During the age of chivalry the knight, encumbered by heavy armor, lances, and swords and seated in big saddles, had developed a style of straight-legged riding that was diametrically opposed to balanced riding. This style spread throughout most of Europe after the demise of knighthood and was not really reversed until Caprilli entered the picture.

Many riders believe that "riding English" follows an entirely different set of rules from those followed in "riding western." That is, of course, incorrect. The horse is structurally the same whether he is under an English saddle or a western saddle. His balancing points are the same.

The Spanish war saddle that was brought to the Western Hemisphere by the conquistadors was changed through trial and error and finally evolved into the Mexican saddle, which, with its flat seat and stirrups nearly under the rider, was almost a balanced-seat saddle. So were the McClellan cavalry saddle (Fig. 39.12) and the Texas Trail saddle (Fig. 11.10). Many days, weeks, and months were spent in those saddles as the West was settled and developed. Unfortunately, from about 1930 the average western saddle began undergoing changes developed in the wrong direction. The seat was increasingly slanted up to the fork, making the rider a "cantle rider." That fad is now slowly being reversed.

FIG. 34.1. *The Polish Rider,* by Rembrandt. At a time when Western aristocracy was playing the elaborate game of dressage, the distance-covering horsemen of eastern Europe continued to go their traditional, relaxed, and practical way, using a position that foreshadowed the modern forward seat. Copyright by the Frick Collection, New York City.

CHAPTER 35

The Relationship Between the Horse and the Saddle

A careful examination of the side view of the horse given at the beginning of this book will give the reader a thorough understanding of the exterior parts of the horse. At this point we begin to be interested in the skeleton of the horse, the muscles on top of this skeleton on which the saddle will rest, and internal parts of the horse whose physiological function might be reduced or damaged by the presence of an improper, improperly adjusted, or improperly ridden saddle.

Of the horse's skeleton the main bones of interest to us are the backbone and the rib cage (Fig. 35.1).

The Horse's Backbone and Ribs

Spinal Column (backbone): 53 to 56 vertebrae
    Cervical (neck): 7
    Dorsal (thoracic, backbones): 18
        Withers: 1 to 8 or 10
        Back: 9 or 11 to 18
    Lumbar (loin bone): usually 6, sometimes 5
    Sacral (croup bone): 5
    Coccyx (tailbone): 17 to 20
Ribs: 18 on each side
    True ribs: first 8 on each side
    False ribs: next 10 on each side

The *backbone,* or *spinal column,* consists of 53 to 56 vertebrae. The variation occurs because there may be one fewer in the *lumbar (loin)* section in some breeds and several more or several fewer in the *coccyx,* or *tailbone* section.

The rib cage consists of eighteen ribs on each side of the horse attached in the *dorsal (back)* area. The first eight ribs are called *true ribs* because they are *articulated* (attached) at both the upper and to the backbone and at the lower end to the *sternum (chest bone).* The remaining ten ribs are called *false ribs* because they are articulated to the backbone only and are held in place by rods of cartilage to the sternum.

The horse breathes by expanding its chest mainly in the area of the true ribs, in the forward section. The false ribs overlay the small lobes of the lungs and contribute little to the act of breathing.

At the end of the back area of the horse, which is the end of the eighteenth vertebra, the horse runs out of ribs to support the saddle. If the saddle bars are so long that they extend into the loin (lumbar) area, there is no support except skin and muscle. Underneath the forward part of this area are the kidneys, which are suspended from, but not attached to, the back and whose function may be impaired by the constant jiggling of a poor horseman who rides the cantle (Fig. 35.2).

In the literature on riding writers often speak of damage to the kidneys caused by pressure of overlong bars. Admittedly there can be some damage; however, the horse's kidneys are suspended from the horse's back muscles and are not directly affected by the pressure of a saddle with long bars. Another point that is not often mentioned is the harmful effect on the horse's back of the rubbing of the back end of the bar fan against the rise of the back to the croup. This is especially noticeable in a short-backed horse on which a long-barred saddle is used.

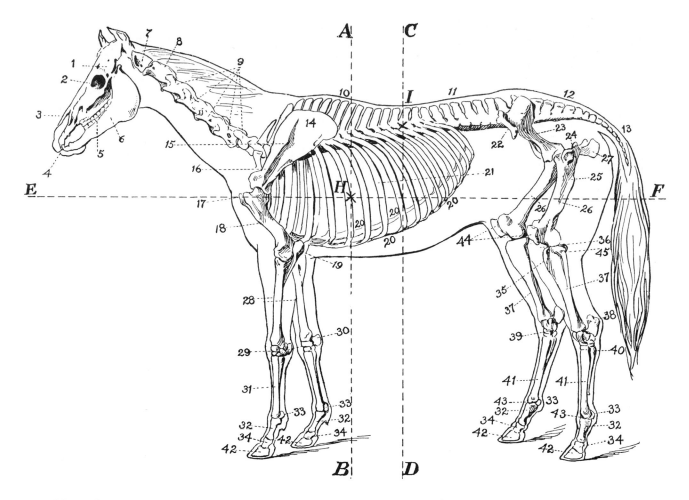

FIG. 35.1.   Backbone with vertebrae numbered. This is the skeleton of Eclipse, the greatest race horse of all time. From Carter, *Horses, Saddles, and Bridles.*

  1. Zygomatic arch.
  2. Eye cavity.
  3. Face bones.
  4. Incisor teeth.
  5. Molar teeth.
  6. Lower jaw.
  7. Atlas, 1st vertebra of neck.
  8. Axis, 2d vertebra of neck.
  9. Cervical vertebrae (5).
 10. Spinal processes of back.
 11. Dorsal and lumbar vertebrae.
 12. Sacrum.
 13. Tail bones.
 14. Shoulder blade.
 15. Acromion process.

 16. Hollow of shoulder blade.
 17. Upper end of arm bone.
 18. Arm bone or humerus.
 19. Elbow bone.
 20. Cartilages of the ribs.
 21. Ribs.
 22. Haunch.
 23. Haunch bone.
 24. Great trochanter.
 25. Small trochanter.
 26. Thigh bone.
 27. Ischium.
 28. Radius or forearm bone.
 29. Carpal or knee bones.
 30. Trapezium.

 31. Cannon bone.
 32. Pastern bone.
 33. Sesamoid bone.
 34. Small pastern bone.
 35. Upper end of leg bone.
 36. Stifle joint.
 37. Leg bone or tibia.
 38. Point of hock.
 39. Hock joint.
 40. Head of small metatarsal bone.
 41. Cannon or metatarsal bone.
 42. Coffin bone.
 43. Fetlock joint.
 44. Patella, or stifle.
 45. Fibula.

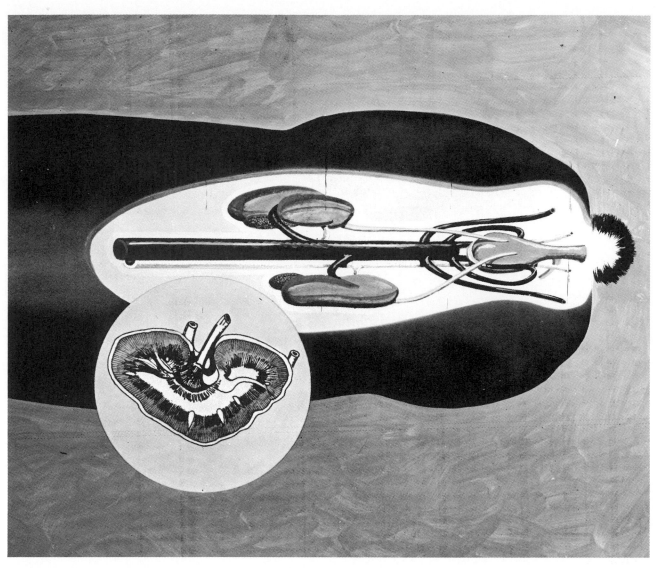

FIG. 35.2. Cross section of the top of the horse showing the position of the kidneys under the saddle area. Courtesy of Donald L. McDonald, *Know the Anatomy of the Horse,* Farnam Horse Library no. 107.

CHAPTER 36

The Mechanics of the Horse, Saddle, and Rider

The purpose of riding is to transport a person from one place to another faster than he can get there on foot, in as much comfort as possible. In order to accomplish this, the rider should understand the mechanics of weight distribution and its effect on the framework of the horse itself, the effect of the saddle and its various components on the horse, and the effect of the weight of the rider under different conditions and in various positions of the horse.

I have been able to find only one book (other than veterinary textbooks) that covers carefully and analytically the subject of *structural mechanics*. It is *Seats and Saddles; Bits and Bitting*, by Major Francis Dwyer, published in 1886. Although Major Dwyer made some errors, such as calling the fourteenth vertebra the "keystone or upright vertebra" (Romaszkan and veterinarians say that it is the sixteenth vertebra), he is still almost the only authority who analyzed the structural dynamics of the horse's bones, as well as the horse's center of gravity. Much of what follows is based on Dwyer's analysis.

THE FRAMEWORK OF THE HORSE CONSIDERED MECHANICALLY

As shown in Fig. 35.1, the backbone of the horse is in the form of an arch, which is the strongest mechanical means of supporting weight. The underline of the vertebrae (the backbone) is nearly straight, although not quite horizontal, inclining somewhat downward toward the front. The spinal processes *(fins)* of the first fifteen vertebrae of the back (the dorsal vertebrae) incline backward, whereas the fins of the seventeenth and eighteenth vertebrae and the six lum-

bar vertebrae incline forward. The sixteenth dorsal vertebra, with its process standing perfectly upright, forms the keystone of the arch. Dwyer wrote:

It is very obvious that this inclination of the processes [fins] toward the sixteenth is intended to and does limit the motion of the back downward and upward [i.e., vertically], so that in fact this sixteenth dorsal vertebra becomes the center of structural *motion* of the horse's body—the point about which the several *structural movements* of the front and hind legs are performed with various degrees of rapidity, either simultaneously or successively, and which constitute the paces of the horse.

Because of the forward projecting position of the head and neck, especially when the horse stands at ease, a somewhat greater proportion of its weight falls on the front legs than on the hind ones, and when it lowers its head, still more, as is represented in [Fig. 36.1].

In motion, the front legs are essentially bearers, and the hind legs of the horse, although chiefly propellers [impellers], are also to a certain extent, bearers.

A perpendicular line falling through the center of *gravity* of a horse, *xy* as represented in [Fig. 36.1] would lie nearer to the shoulder than the perpendicular *EF*, which falls through the center of *structural motion*—that is the sixteenth dorsal vertebra—and would probably cut the twelfth, or perhaps the eleventh, in some horses. [Dwyer]

R. H. Smythe states that when a horse weighing 1,000 pounds is standing in a normal position approximately 60 percent, or 600 pounds, of the horse's weight is carried by the front legs; the other 40 percent, or 400 pounds, is carried by the hind legs.

Jean Froissard, in his excellent book, *An Expert's Guide to Basic Dressage,* used a unique and very good method to determine the location of the horse's center of gravity. He accomplished this by having a horse stand with the front legs on one scale and the hind legs on another scale. With a horse weighing 768 pounds, holding his head and neck normally, the weight on the front legs was 420 pounds, 54.7 percent of the horse's weight. The weight on the scale under the back legs was 348 pounds. The same horse with his head and neck extended carried 436 pounds on his front legs, and the hind legs carried 332 pounds. This experiment illustrated the increases in weight on the forelegs as the head is extended. In this position the forelegs carry 57 percent of the horse's weight. When the head and neck were raised—as they are when a horse is in extreme collection—the weight on the front legs is decreased to 400 pounds, while that on the back legs increased to 368 pounds; 52 percent of the weight was carried on the front legs. The experiment proved that the center of gravity within the horse shifts in different postures. The reader must remember, of course, that these percentages are not absolute but vary somewhat with the conformation of the horse.

Dwyer's diagram (Fig. 36.1) shows that the center of *structural motion* of the framework of the horse is situated somewhere in the per-

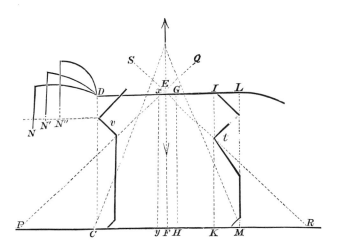

FIG. 36.1. Horse's center of gravity in various standing positions. From Dwyer, *Seats and Saddles, Bits and Bitting.*

pendicular line falling through the sixteenth dorsal vertebra *(EF)*. It can be shown from an analysis of all the mechanical information that in any state of rest or of action the sixteenth vertebra is constantly the center of *structural motion*. Because of the forward projection and the weight of the head and neck of the horse, however, the *center of gravity* falls through one or another of the vertebrae from the tenth to the thirteenth, which are closer to the neck. The horse's head and neck act as a lever; the farther forward the head, the more weight or pressure is put on point *D*, which tends to move the center of gravity forward. Thus, while the *center of structural motion* is the point around which the *framework* of the horse *moves,* the *center of gravity* is actually the point around which the horse must work (Fig. 36.3).

To me the above explanation is the most understandable means of demonstrating how the center of structural motion is tied to horse riding.

As shown in Fig. 36.1, when the head is in the position represented by *DN,* the *center of gravity* falls at approximately the line *xy,* which represents one of the dorsal vertebrae nearer to the neck than the sixteenth. Elevating the head to the position represented by *DN'* will bring the *center of gravity* back to the line *EF.* Bringing the head to the position represented by *DN'',* as the *manège* rider does, moves the *center of gravity* farther back, to the line represented by *GH.* See also Fig. 36.4, which illustrates externally the movement of the center of gravity forward and backward as the horse's motion and posture change.

THE RIDER AND HIS SADDLE

Riding, whether for pleasure, show, or work, is an athletic event, and the rider's muscles must be used enough to become accustomed to the action. No one who rides only once a month will attain sufficient muscular tone not to be sore after a long ride.

This section is addressed to the average rider

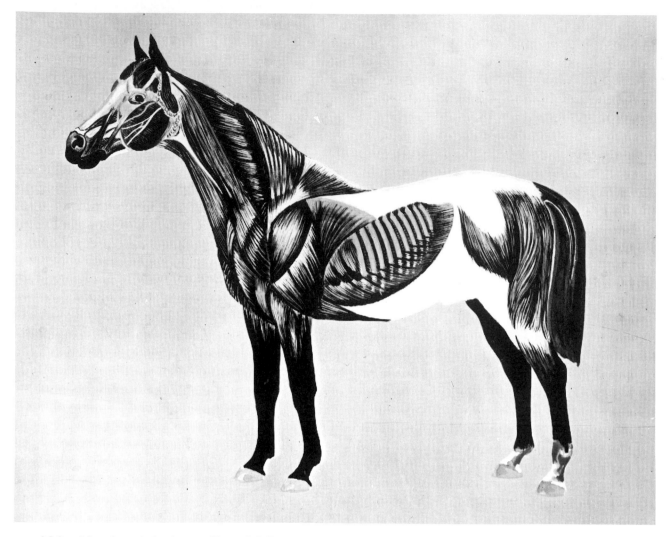

FIG. 36.2.   Muscles of the horse. From McDonald, *Know the Anatomy of the Horse*. Note the *Lumbodorsal fascia,* the large flat tendon covering much of the back of the horse. A tendon attaches muscles to bones. While this tendon has no ability to contract as a muscle does, it is elastic like a rubber band. Much of the saddle rides on it.

using a western saddle. The quotations will, I hope, be read with an open mind.

I am not here discussing a western saddle to be ridden on a horse in extreme collection in a show ring. The center of gravity of a horse in extreme collection is too far back for the usual western saddle. The following remarks pertain to a saddle to be used for western riding in western performance classes, pleasure riding,

trail riding, cross-country riding, roping, bull-dogging, and so on.

In these pages the terms *collect* and *horse in collection* are used according to the definition given in Bloodgood and Santini's *The Horseman's Dictionary:*

Collect (To); Collection: Loosely, to keep a horse in hand; to make it put more weight on its quarters

240

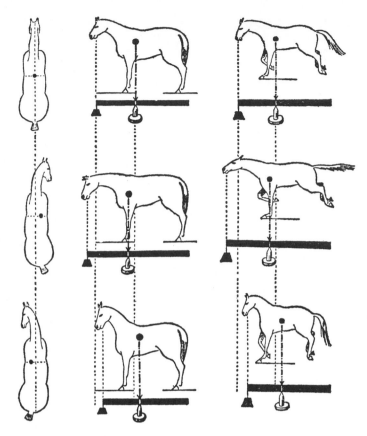

FIG. 36.3. The horse's center of gravity in various moving positions. From Gregor de Romaszkan, *The Horse and Rider in Equilibrium.*

than on the forehand. To "get his hocks under him." Specifically, to teach a horse by means of rein and leg to arch its neck and shift its balance backwards. In a position of extreme collection, usual in superior dressage and high school *(q.v.),* the horse's head is almost perpendicular to the ground.

Dwyer offered the following significant comments on the fit and shape of the saddle:

The under surface of the saddle—the portion coming in contact with the horse's back—has two principal points for consideration: its shape or form and its size or extent. One general mechanical principle applies to both—namely, that the larger the surface on which a given amount of pressure is equally spread or divided, the less will be the action on any given point of the under surface in contact.

The under surface should fit very closely and evenly all over the part of the back which it is intended to cover; however, it should never at any time contact that strip lying over the horse's backbone, which must remain altogether out of contact.

To put a large saddle on a horse's back, then place the rider's weight at one end, defeats the requirement of equal distribution of the weight. [Dwyer, 1886]

The last paragraph quoted above should be carefully noted. It points out the essential error in the construction of many modern-day western saddles. As Dwyer pointed out:

The rider's center of gravity must be placed over the center of the bearing surface of the saddle, for this is the only single point which, being loaded, transmits the pressure equally to the rest of the surface.

When a rider is sitting in the saddle seat, he should be nearly over the center of gravity of the horse. To attempt to stay out of the lowest place in the saddle is foolish because every action of the horse tends to move the rider towards this low point. [Dwyer, 1886]

A western saddle, properly placed on a horse, fits only one place: the burs at the front of the bars are contoured to fit slightly into the pockets on the horse's shoulders. The fork is over the horse's withers. The center of gravity of the horse is more or less under the area behind the back of the fork. If a saddle is placed on a horse's back and shaken a bit, it will usually fall into this position naturally.

The saddle seat should be long enough for the rider to shift his weight with the horse's shifting center of gravity. Unfortunately, the fork limits the ability of the rider in an upright position to shift forward at this point.

Where should the cinch be attached? From a *mechanical* point of view, the cinch should be attached in the center of a saddle to secure the saddle to the horse equally from the fork to the cantle; however, the position of the horse's diaphragm during inhalation and exhalation (Fig. 36.5) indicates that any cinch position from full rigged to centerfire is suitable as long as the

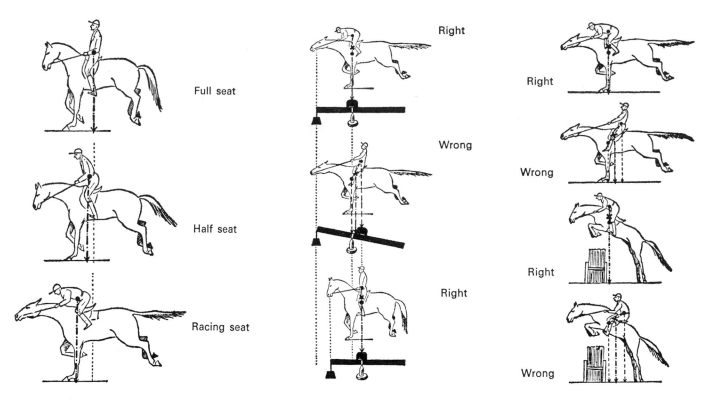

FIG. 36.4.   Center of gravity related to movement. From Romaszkan, *The Horse and Rider in Equilibrium.*

underline of the horse is such that it will allow the cinch to remain in its intended position.

In discussing stirrups, Dwyer commented that "the point from which the stirrup is suspended has nearly an equal influence on the stability of the saddle, and a much greater one on the form of the rider's seat (in the saddle) than the position of the cinch." Besides helping the rider mount the horse, what is the main purpose of the stirrups? It is to give the rider *lateral* support: to prevent him from slipping off to the right or left (see the section on inertia below). The stirrups should be so hung that when the rider is suspending almost all of his weight on them or is standing in them there is no change in the equilibrium of the horse.

For many years the stirrup leathers of western saddles have been attached to the saddletree just behind the fork. This position nearly coincides with the vertical center-of-gravity line through the horse. As the horse increases his speed of motion to a gallop, his head and neck automatically stretch forward, which moves his center of gravity slightly forward; however, the rider cannot move his body forward to get over the exact center of gravity because of the obstruction of the fork. He can, however, lean forward, which to some degree places him back in balance with the horse. That is the main reason for riding a flat-seated saddle: the rider can shift his weight farther forward in the flat saddle to remain over the center-of-gravity as the horse's speed and extension increase. With a built-up slanted-seat saddle this forward shift is difficult to impossible.

Because there are no frequent fast stops, riding English in a balanced seat can be accomplished with the stirrups more directly under the rider. The English saddle pommel is not as much a hindrance to the forward movement of the rider who is attempting to stay in balance with his horse. That explains the difference be-

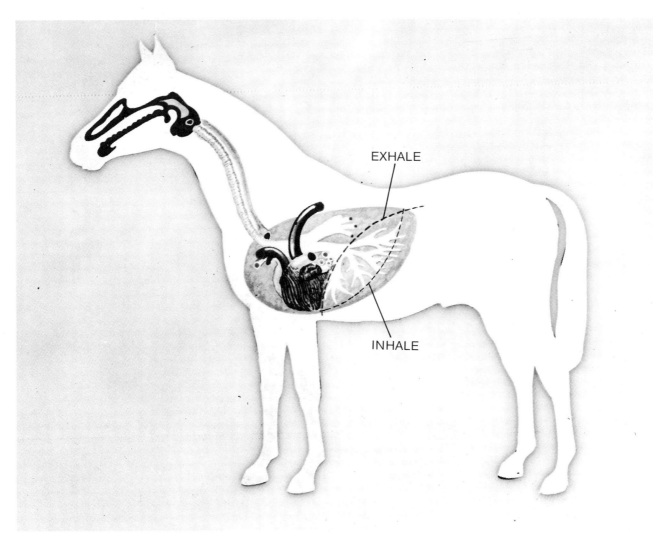

FIG. 36.5. Diaphragm of a horse. From McDonald, *Know the Anatomy of the Horse.*

tween the position of the stirrups on an English saddle and their position on a western saddle.

The stirrups on a western saddle should be slightly forward of the rider when the horse is standing still and should be capable of being swung forward to some degree to prevent a fast stop from catapulting the rider over the horse's head. This stirrup position also allows the rider to move over the horse's center of gravity when the horse is in motion, still keeping the stirrups under the rider. A stirrup should never be hung long enough to give the rider an insecure foot

on the tread. The stirrup leathers must be perpendicular, even when the rider's foot is in the stirrup, except during rapid deceleration or when riding up or down steep hills.

The exact location of the stirrups in relation to the rider's center of gravity is still a subject of controversy. According to Dwyer (1886), Caprilli, M. F. McTaggart (1925), and John Richard Young (1954) the suspension point of the stirrup should be directly over the center of gravity when the horse is standing and is collected. In a free-standing posture the horse's center of gravity will be in front of the rider's feet. Like many others I attach the stirrup leathers somewhat behind the backside of the fork so that the stirrups are over the center of gravity when the horse is in motion in an extended posture. Foreman, an excellent horseman and proponent of the "balanced ride," hangs his stirrup leathers even farther forward, more nearly under the fork.

THE RIDER

In the following discussion there is an intentional omission of discussion of two very important aspects of riding: the use of the reins and hands and bridles and bits. They have no direct bearing on this work, and both subjects are covered adequately elsewhere.

Most riding authorities agree that merely riding for many years does not necessarily make one a good horseman. It is said that practice does not make perfect—only perfect practice makes one perfect. By the same token, unless one rides properly for many years, he will not become an excellent horseman.

The principles of riding in relation to the horse's center of gravity are the same, whether riding English or riding western. The saddles differ in their over-all construction because of the differences in the requirements of horse and rider. English riding is largely made up of even starts and stops, whereas western riding contains more fast starts and fast stops in the course of riding. The most accomplished rider in either style is the one who is able to substitute balance for muscular action.

Let us go on from Major Dwyer's treatise to review the works of some other technicians in this field, who corroborate Dwyer's work and clarify some of his information.

After Dwyer, Federico Caprilli was the next horseman to analyze riding. From 1897 until his death in 1907, he was a proponent of forward-seat riding and advocated a riding style characterized by "noninterference with the horse's natural movements," which, translated, means

riding a balanced seat, or being in balance with the horse. After Caprilli came M. F. McTaggart, also a cavalryman, who stated that "the rider should be in balance (equilibrium) with his horse at all times." In his book *Mount and Man* he wrote:

There can be only three fulcra from which balance can be maintained in the saddle, namely, the seat bones, the knees and the feet. Each method has moments for use, and restriction at all times to only one of these cannot be correct.

When sitting in a saddle naturally, at both the stand still and the walk, it is necessary to have the seat bones as the fulcrum for the balance; not, however, because of any scientific rule of either statics or dynamics, but because most saddles today are built that way, and we cannot help ourselves. Perhaps, someday, saddles will be built on lines indicated later and we shall be able to bring the balance of the body, even when sitting without movement, into the realm of pure science.

Naturally, when we are riding at ease, much latitude can be allowed; but we must remember that the balance from the seat bones cannot be maintained beyond the walk. [McTaggart, 1925]

Dwyer had discussed balance as follows:

Now the seat on horseback is maintained either by balancing or by friction—that is to say, the greater or less amount of the rider's sitting parts which are brought into contact with the saddle—or by the support given by the knees and the stirrup. It is easy to perceive that such a combination of all three, which leaves each individual one its greatest amount of efficiency, will necessarily secure a much greater amount of stability than can be attained by depending on one to the neglect of the other two, or even depending on two in such a manner as to sacrifice the third. The best and safest seat will always be that which depends exclusively on no one means of support, but uses them all in the best manner. [Dwyer]

McTaggart wrote:

A point that is raised (by disbelievers) is that "the forward (or balanced) seat may be, and undoubtedly is, excellent for the show ring, but it is quite out of place in either the hunting field or the steeplechase." The answer to this is that there can be but

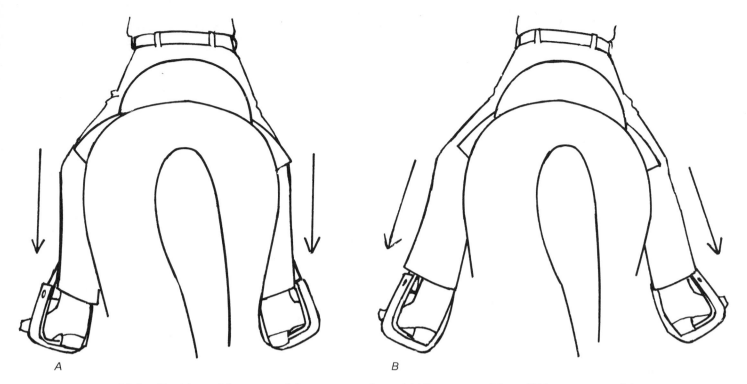

FIG. 36.6.   Position of leg around horse, rear view. *(A)* Correct position. *(B)* Incorrect position.

one right way. Three constants are to be found in all forms of horsemanship, no matter where we are or what we are doing. The three are: (1) the horse, which is still a horse, whether he canters in the show ring, extends himself in the steeplechase, or gallops in the hunting field; (2) gravitation, which applies to everything at all times without variation; (3) motion, propulsion, or dynamics (inertia), what you will. These laws must also be obeyed, always. These three are our constants, no matter what we are doing. The variation is only of degree. [McTaggart, 1925, p. 28]

McTaggart constantly reminded his readers that weight far back on the horse on the loin area not only is injurious to the horse but completely unbalances him, making it impossible to ride a balanced seat. He continued:

The rider's balance should be, normally, at all paces beyond the walk, from the feet. This is a matter of such importance in equitation that it can hardly be over-emphasized. Needless to say that as the balance is from the foot, the weight of the body must be largely borne upon the irons (stirrups) at all times."

McTaggart continued: "Although we cannot decrease our weight by leaning forward, we can reduce the jar by 'deferred impact,' or by absorbing the concussion in the muscles of the knee and ankle in a way the backward seat cannot do" (McTaggart, 1925, p. 30). As Romaszkan wrote, the rider can neither increase nor decrease his weight; he can only displace it.

There are three points in the rider's leg that can and should be used to absorb the shocks of the horse's movements: (1) the thigh joint, (2) the knee joint, and (3) the ankle joint. The area on a horse from the fetlock joint through the pastern to the hoof is not on a straight line with the horse's cannon bone. This structure allows the horse to absorb the shocks of movement. Compare this to the position of the rider's feet in the stirrups. If the feet are "all the way home" in the stirrup, the rider cannot absorb any of the shock of movement in the ankle. If the rider rides with the ball of the foot resting on the stirrup tread, then he has the same ability

FIG. 36.7.   Position of foot in the stirrup. *(A)* Toe down, incorrect. *(B)* Ball of foot on tread (heel down), correct. *(C)* Foot "all the way home" or "homed," comfortable, but unsafe.

through movement of the ankles to absorb shocks as does the horse in its fetlock-pastern-hoof area.

In 1950, Derring Davis wrote that the rider should let his legs hang down and adjust the stirrup so that the bottom of the stirrup will hit the ankle bones. With the foot in the stirrup a plumbline dropped from the rider's knee should touch the boot-toe area just *ahead* of the boot (Fig. 36.7). The rider should keep the heel *below* the level of the toes. According to Davis, the rider's entire weight rests on the front inner part of the crotch, thighs, and knees and on the stirrups. Davis added what anyone who studies western riding carefully knows: that most of the present-day cowboy's seats and saddles are wrong. The extremely built-up slanted seats force the rider to sit back on his buttocks against the cantle with his feet too far forward and almost no weight on the stirrups.

Also in 1950, D. Wilson wrote that a cowboy who lolls back in his saddle against the cantle with most of his weight on his seat wears a horse down with his dead weight. Weight in the stirrup helps his horse. It is live, springy weight. It is analogous to the difference between carrying an unconscious person and carrying a conscious one. It is incorrect to sit against the cantle, even though it may be natural to do so. There should be an open area between rider and cantle (Fig. 36.8). If one rides against the cantle, the centers of gravity of rider and horse are about one foot apart (Fig. 36.9).

Alex Grant Swaney summed up the rider's positions in a simple diagram and explanation, as shown in Fig. 36.10.

Let us return to McTaggart:

It is the ideal of all horsemen to be "one" with their horses. When this is effected it means simply that the rider's balance is working in conjunction with the horse's balance. To put it in other words, it implies that the rider's line of equipoise (center of gravity) passes vertically through the horse's center of gravity. [McTaggart, 1925]

This explanation corresponds to Caprilli's principle of "noninterference with the horse's natural movements."

To this point all the analyses of the relationship of the horse's center of gravity to the rider's center of gravity have referred to this relationship in a vertical plane. The rider's center of

FIG. 36.8.   Rider seated properly.

247

FIG. 36.9.   Rider seated too far back.

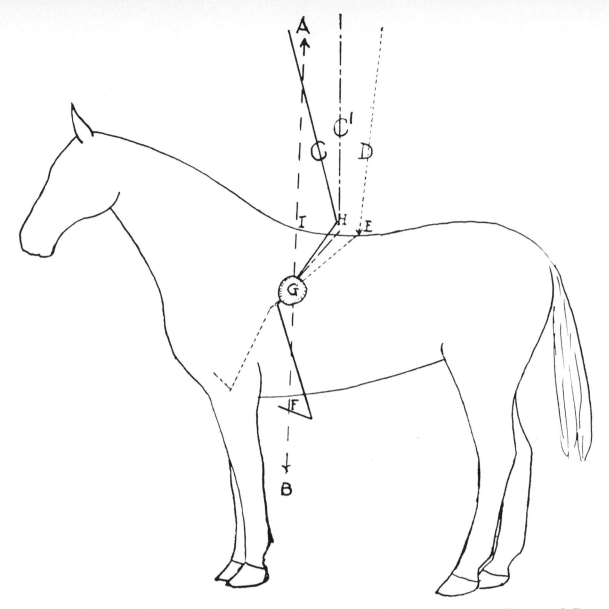

FIG. 36.10. Alex Grant Swaney's diagram and explanation of the balanced seat: *"(A)* The line *I–F* represents the line of the surcingle [cinch] on the near side of the horse. The natural center of balance of the horse lies within the area *G.* *(B)* The rider *C* (solid line) represents a balanced-seat rider at gaits faster than a walk or slow trot. Note that his weight is forward on the axis of balance, *A–B,* of the horse, and that it is carried principally by the stirrups at *F,* and that through the stirrup leathers it is distributed along the bars of the saddle in the vicinity of point *I,* which is immediately over the natural center of balance *G.* At a walk or slow trot rider *C*'s position would become *C*¹ (dot-dash line). Here more weight is in the saddle seat, and while the bottom of the buttocks constitute a part of the seat, the inner thighs, knees, and stirrups still play their part. It remains an alert and graceful position from which almost any emergency may be countered instantly.

"Rider *D* (dotted line) is a 'back' seat rider. Most of his weight is supported at point *E* on the horse's back near the loins, which is the weakest part. Rider *D*'s weight is behind the horse's natural center of balance and restricts his freedom of action, particularly behind. Rider *D* is balancing from the seat of his pants, whereas in every other form of action he balances from his feet. There are, of course, many variations in the positions of riders *C* and *D.* Rider *D*'s position may be more comfortable for him, and suitable for slow gaits, but it is not the most comfortable seat for the horse at any gait, for the reasons mentioned." From Alex Grant Swaney, "The Balanced Seat in the Stock Saddle," *Western Horseman,* May–June, 1943.

gravity is slightly below his diaphragm about midway through his body. At this point it is appropriate to consider the *force of inertia* on these centers of gravity. For our purposes this force is on a horizontal plane. Inertia is inactivity, expressed in riding as the force exerted by a body in motion (the rider) to continue its motion in a straight line at the same speed unless acted upon by an outside force, such as an immovable object (the horse's neck or the ground).

Dwyer, commenting that "the rider most generally falls laterally (sideways), not forward," explained the force of the rider's inertia during various actions of the horse, such as a quick turn. For example, the rider leans forward when the horse is increasing his speed to offset the force of propulsion (increased inertia) of the horse, leans somewhat backward as the horse slows down, and leans toward the inside when the horse is turning. McTaggart commented:

As the question is one of dynamics, it must be apparent to anyone who has even an elementary knowledge of this branch of mathmetics that, in order to overcome the force of propulsion, a balance in motion can only be attained by proportionately throwing the rider's weight in front of the statical balance. [McTaggart, 1925, p. 25]

The rider must by "noninterfering" actions allow his force of inertia to catch up with or slow down to that of the horse with the least interference with the horse's natural movements. When a horse accelerates his motion, he tends to leave the rider behind. McTaggart added that "the rider must keep his weight in front of the static balance (of a horse in motion) to overcome the force of propulsion (inertia)."

When a horse is decelerating rapidly, the rider's inertia tends to keep his body in motion, throwing him forward. At this point the rider's knees, feet, legs, and leg and back muscles are all used to create enough friction to overcome the rider's forward-movement inertia. In any riding this basic law of nature must be taken into account. The main objective is for the rider to offset his force of inertia while remaining in balance with the horse's center of gravity.

To express the principle much more technically, the rider's inertia can be referred to as *potential rectilinear* (straight-line) *kinetic energy*. Those who wish to calculate this energy into a quantity can use the following formula:

$$\text{Potential kinetic energy (in foot-pounds)} = \frac{1/2 \times \text{Rider's weight (in pounds)} \times \text{Rider's Velocity}^2 \text{ (in feet per second)}}{32}$$

A foot-pound is the energy required to raise one pound one foot off the ground. At a gallop (20 miles per hour, or 29 feet per second) a 160-pound rider has 2,103 foot-pounds of kinetic energy (inertia) to overcome by created friction when the horse stops suddenly. Fortunately for the rider (provided he is not riding the saddle's cantle, pressing on the loins, and behind the horse's center-of-gravity), when the horse stops suddenly, its natural movement is to bring its hind legs up under it, lowering its hindquarters, which helps dissipate the rider's inertia through the horse's body.

A study of the "triangle of forces" of the dynamics involved will explain this. *Centrifugal force* is the force necessary to change the straight-line force of inertia of a body when the body is going in a circle. A rider encounters centrifugal force when the horse turns rapidly, shies, or jumps. When the horse turns rapidly, it does so by using muscular effort to change its direction of movement. The rider's inertia will continue his motion in a straight line unless, by muscular effort and by balance (leaning), he is able to maintain his seat and thus change his own direction of movement. If the rider fails to maintain his seat, the two lines of motion separate, and the rider no longer has a horse under him. *He did not fall off.* The horse, by changing direction, just moved out from under him.

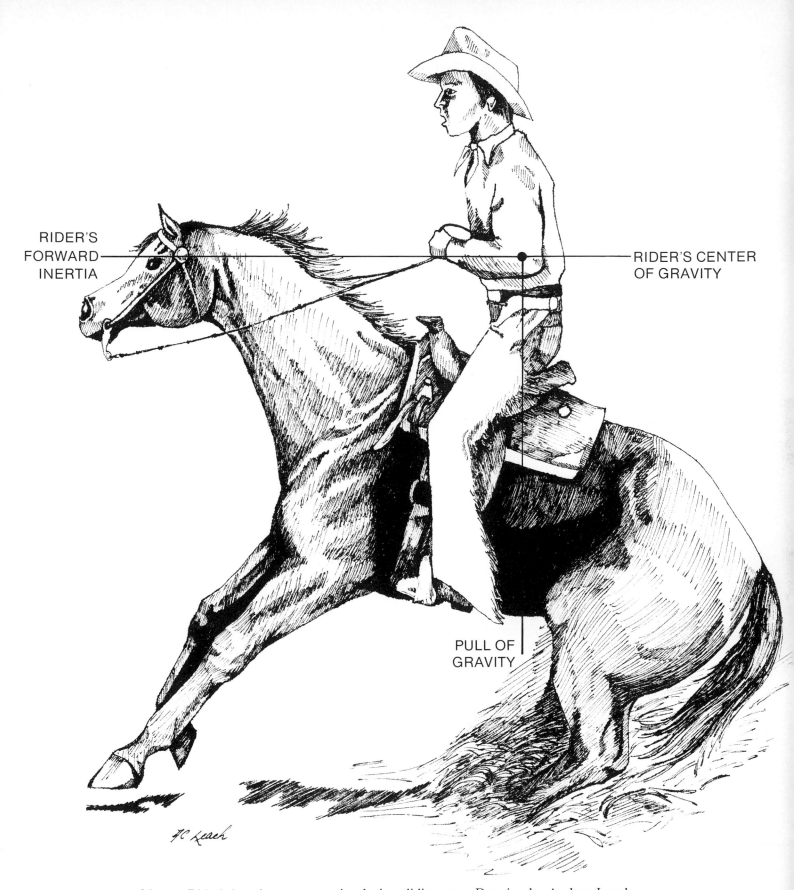

RIDER'S
FORWARD
INERTIA

RIDER'S CENTER
OF GRAVITY

PULL OF
GRAVITY

FIG. 36.11.   Rider's inertia versus gravity during sliding stop. Drawing by Andrea Leach.

THE SADDLE

In *Man and Mount,* McTaggart wrote:

We have grown up and lived with the saddle as we know it today, and we are so accustomed to its shape and appearance that criticism comes as rather a surprise. It is ridden in and seen so frequently that it is rare to hear discussion upon its merits or demerits. Almost every other point of riding, of horse mastery, of horse management, and of equipment is discussed daily, but the saddle is accepted as it is, without comment or controversy. [McTaggart, 1925, p. 95]

Unfortunately that is still true for western saddles. Dwyer also commented on this point:

It would be only reasonable, one should suppose, to accommodate our saddles to our seats, just as we do every other instrument to the purposes for which it is intended; but this is precisely what is very seldom done, and in the great majority of instances the rider sits his horse just in the fashion his saddle allows, or perhaps compels, him to do. [Dwyer, p. 55]

McTaggart wrote: "A horse's center of gravity is to be found within a spot varying within the circle shown [Fig. 36.12] . It is not a fixed point; it varies for several reasons. But it is sufficient to say that, generally speaking, it will always be found somewhere within this circle" (McTaggart, 1925).

The center of gravity of the average horse depends on its conformation and the way it is carrying itself (its posture) at the moment; however, when the horse is standing naturally, the center of gravity is three to four inches behind the withers according to John Richard Young (1954).

In Fig. 36.13 the line *AB* represents the natural line of the stirrup leather passing through the horse's center of gravity. *CD* represents the correct position of the rider's seat bones when the horse is standing still. *EF* represents the position of the improperly seated rider's seat bones. Note how much farther away from *AB* the line *EF* is than is *CD.*

John Richard Young published an excellent three-part series in *Western Horseman* in the late 1951s entitled "Is There a Right Seat?" In the third part he wrote:

The usual advice dished out by the professional wizards begins: "Sit on the lowest part of the seat." Unfortunately, the wizards never add: "But this is the chief thing you cannot easily do in almost all modern stock saddles and still maintain a balanced seat, because the average American stock saddle has a built-up slanted seat that is made to order for frustrating this nice balance we have been talking about."

This statement is also the contention of Monte Foreman in his excellent "Riding by Reasoning" articles.

The back-slanted western saddle seat is comparatively recent, starting in the 1940s. Of the forty-five old saddles (fifty to ninety years old) in my collection only one has a built-up, back-slanted seat.

McTaggart wrote:

The line *AB* [Fig. 36.13] represents his (the rider's) balancing line or line of equipoise. The line *CD* shows the position relative to the line of equipoise of his seat bones. These two lines are, as it will be seen, comparatively close together. But if we look at [Fig. 36.14] we shall see that in the modern saddle the lines are very much farther apart, proportionately. [McTaggart, 1925, p. 98]

The average modern western saddle has a built-up front on the seat near the fork, which automatically throws the rider back against the cantle, putting him out of balance with his horse. The best seat remains the flat seat. Why saddlemakers departed from this design is hard to understand.

The next question to be considered is, To what part of the saddle should the cinch be attached? Dwyer wrote:

Now it is very evident that, if the placing of the weight in the center of the saddle has the effect of transmitting an equal amount of pressure to all that part of the horse's back with which the latter is in contact, attaching the girths so as to act directly on the center of the saddle will have precisely the

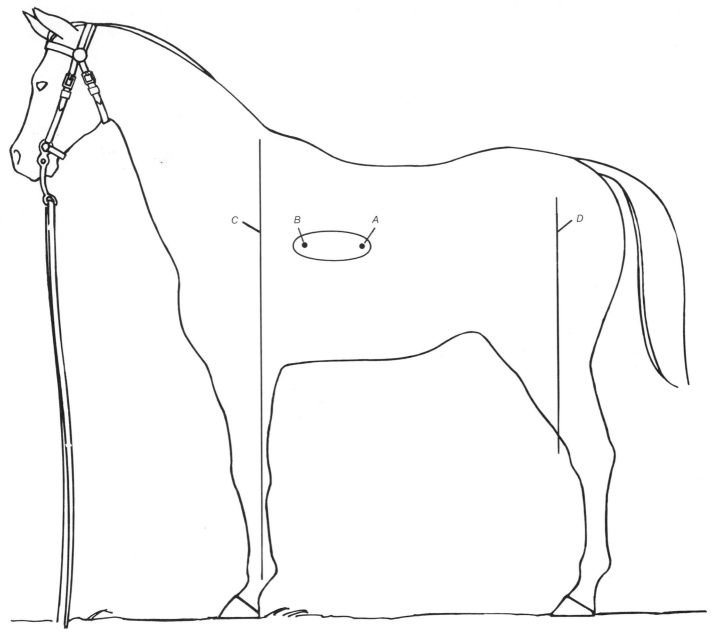

FIG. 36.12.   Horse's center of gravity. *(A)* Center of gravity of a horse standing in a collected posture, tenth vertebra. *(B)* Center of gravity of a horse at a gallop in an extended posture, seventh vertebra. *(C)* Suspension line of horse's front quarters. *(D)* Sus-pension line of horse's hindquarters. It is the horse's posture more than the speed of his movements that determines the position of his center of gravity. Redrawn from McTaggart (1925).

253

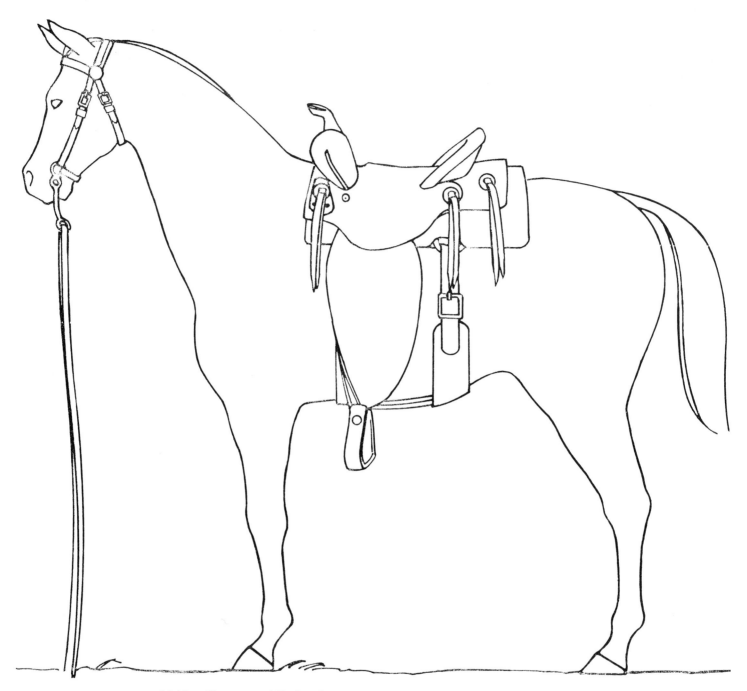

FIG. 36.13.   Correct saddle in place. Redrawn from M. F. McTaggart. *Mount and Man.*

same effect; and the friction that results—that is, the adhesiveness produced by pressure—will be equal throughout, and of course least likely to injure any one particular point. [Dwyer]

This principle accounts for the California centerfire position. It was also one of the strong points of the McClellan cavalry saddle (Fig. 19.2).

McTaggart's discussion of seat (as illustrated in Figs. 36.13 and 36.14) is as follows:

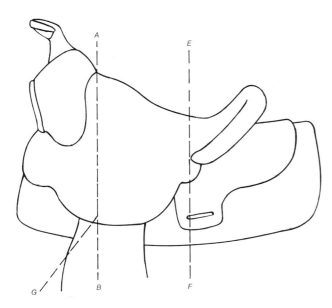

FIG. 36.14. Improper, back-slanted seat. *E–F* represents the most forward position possible for the seat bones, and is several inches behind line *A*. Consequently the feet tend to be too far forward for a true balance as shown by line *G*.

The line *AB* [Fig. 36.13] represents the line of the stirrup leathers, when hanging naturally. *E* represents the position into which the rider's seat is practically forced. Consequently, as the feet are so much in advance of the seat, when at the standstill and the walk, the tendency is always for the seat to keep slipping (or being pushed by the pressure of the feet) still farther back. As the seat slips back it brings the feet farther forward, and the normal position for them is on the line *G* [Fig. 36.14]. With saddles so made, it is rare to see a stirrup leather kept in a vertical position for this very reason [McTaggart, 1925, p. 96]

Back-slanted seats can be rectified on many saddles by a competent saddle repairman. He lowers the bar risers under the front of the seat to a point where the seat is almost flat.

Young, an expert on horsemanship, has maintained that the McClellan saddle (Fig. 36.15)

FIG. 36.15. McClellan cavalry saddle, 1904.

had the stirrup leathers in the best position for balance with the horse of almost any saddle he knew. The McClellan saddle was known as a "butt buster" by many of the cavalry people (including my commanding officer, Lieutenant Colonel Hilton H. Earle, Jr.). But even so, because of its flat seat, correct position of stirrup leathers, centerfire rigging, and other strong points, the McClellan managed to carry the American cavalry successfully on some notable long-distance, long-term campaigns. It has recently become popular again, this time among trail riders.

In a truly balanced seat the rider's center of gravity should be directly over the stirrups. "If a rider is to be truly balanced, i.e., from his feet, when sitting in the saddle, his seat bones should be almost in line with his heels," according to McTaggart (1925). The Mexican charro saddle approaches perfection in both seat and location of stirrup leathers (Fig. 36.13).

It is difficult to separate fact from fiction or fancy when discussing with riders ideas for

FIG. 36.16. Mexican charro saddle. Courtesy of Jack Carroll.

changes, because their minds are rigidly corraled by their own limited experience with other types of equipment or other ways of riding. It reminds me of a conversation I had with a customer regarding some equipment he was using. He told me that his equipment was the only kind that should be used on the domestic market. When I asked how many competitive items he had actually used, his response was, "None."

The average rider today thinks that the bronc rider's saddle, which is built for a specific purpose, looks like *the* saddle. This is not the case, and too many saddles are bought on this fallacious premise. Santini wrote:

I am aware that the inference that all saddles not of the variety recommended be discarded may appear somewhat drastic, especially to those who rightly value their beautiful mahogany coloured pigskins so pleasantly associated perhaps with memories of field and ring. Forward riding, whatever its detractors may assert, not being a passing fad limited to the show-ring, but having come to stay and spread, naturally exacts implements of design and build radically different from those heretofore employed. [Santini, p. 9]

Dwyer wrote:

Nothing can be more certain than this: that it is the saddler, and not the instructor of equitation, that can most effectually and certainly produce the uniformity of seat which is so desirable; but, unfortunately, few people ever think of this. [Dwyer, p. 68]

McTaggart philosophized: ". . . paper alone has never gained a victory; cogency in argument often vexes rather than convinces" (McTaggart, 1925, p. 30). All of them, it appears, had met with the attitude "Don't confuse me with facts."

Being a businessman, I can appreciate the problems of saddlemakers in producing the type of saddle the market demands. Yet when the demand is for an improperly built one, the only answer is education—proper education—and training of the new young horsemen and horsewomen who will be tomorrow's saddle buyers.

It would be a great service to the saddle industry if a panel of open-minded experts were gathered together to analyze all the findings on this subject, and to make recommendations for improvements in present-day saddles, particularly in the seat, which, as the reader has probably guessed by now, I believe is built wrong and fails to keep the rider in balance with his horse.

It is time to describe the western *balanced seat,* also known as the *forward seat.* Remember that the horse's center of gravity moves forward as his speed of motion and extension increase. The rider changes the position of his body with the change of motion of the horse, inclining the body forward as the motion increases until the ultimate is reached on a racing horse by the jockey in his Tod Sloan, crouched position over the withers. The *least* movement (the smoothest ride) is always near the center of gravity of the horse.

THE WESTERN BALANCED SEAT, OR FORWARD SEAT, SADDLE AND ITS RIDER

1. The seat of a balanced-seat western saddle is flat or nearly flat because the balanced rider is not supposed to sit with his rear against the cantle.

2. The seat is narrower at the throat to prevent bulk under the thighs.

3. The stirrup leather is vertical, straight down directly underneath its attachment point on the bar.

4. The fender extends ahead of the stirrup leather in the knee area.

5. The bar should not extend into the loin area.

6. The saddle may have on-tree plate rigging or in-skirt rigging for the forward cinch at least, to prevent bulk underneath the thighs of the rider.

THE RIDER'S POSITION

At stand still or walk

1. The rider's buttocks rest in the seat away

from the cantle. He sits erect with back caved in slightly and at ease, but he does not slouch. The bulk of his weight is on his buttocks.

2. The rider's knees are gently against the sides of the horse.

3. The stirrup leathers are vertical, even with the rider's foot in the stirrup.

4. The ball of the rider's foot rests on the stirrup tread. The heel is lower than the ball of the foot.

5. The knees are somewhat bent.

6. The toes are turned out 15 degrees or more. This makes the rider's calves face the horse's body, for use only when appropriate.

At the trot

1. The rider's weight has shifted from his buttocks to his crotch, thighs, knees, and feet.

2. Most of the rider's weight is supported by and cushioned on the stirrup.

3. The foot is positioned the same as at the stand still or walk.

4. The rider leans forward slightly with back slightly caved in to be over the horse's center of gravity, which has moved a little forward with the motion and the horse's extension, and also to overcome the force of propulsion (inertia).

5. The rider's knees are slightly bent and adhere to the fenders.

6. The stirrup leathers are vertical.

7. The toes are approximately below the knees or just behind.

At the extended gallop

1. The rider leans farther forward than he did at the trot for the same reasons. The buttocks are off the saddle.

2. The rider's back is slightly caved in.

3. The rider's knees are slightly bent and adhere to the saddle.

4. The foot is in the same position as at the walk and trot. Again, the balance is maintained from here.

5. Most of the rider's weight is supported by

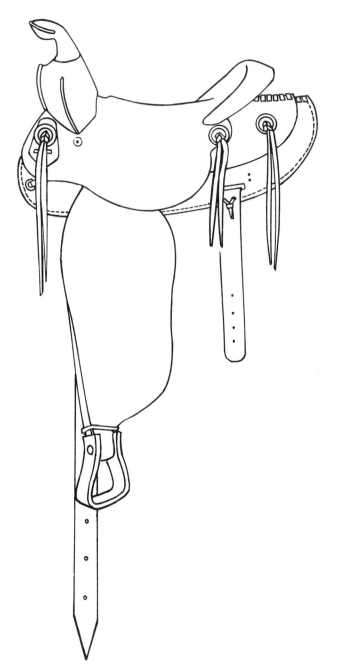

the stirrup; however, the knees, thighs, and crotch support some of his weight.

It must be emphasized that the balanced seat is applicable to pleasure riding, horsemanship, roping, and cutting. According to Monte Foreman, it does not apply to riding Tennessee Walking Horses or Saddlebreds. To these exceptions I would add another: a horse under extreme collection. One must keep in mind that certain saddles are built to be used for specific jobs and are correct for those jobs, even though they do not conform to the suggested construction of the balanced-seat saddle. One of the notable examples is the bronc rider's saddle.

It has been suggested that the "modern correct saddle" shown in Fig. 36.17 resembles the saddles popular between 1930 and 1950. This is somewhat correct. It has a flat seat so that

FIG. 36.17. Author's suggested design for western saddle with correct flat seat and proper fender design. Optional design features: rigging style, cantle and fork slope, skirt configurations, etc.

FIG. 36.18. Ed Connell's saddle. Courtesy of Jack Carroll.

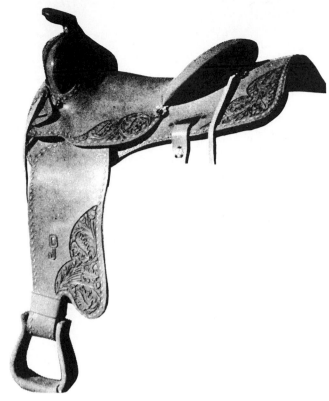

FIG. 36.20.   Dave Jones's forward saddle. From Carroll, catalog no. 32, 1971–72.

FIG. 36.19.   Charles O. Williamson's saddle. Courtesy of Jack Carroll.

the rider can change his position and posture to be with the changing center of gravity of the horse, and an upright cantle so that the cantle can do the work for which it was originally designed—prevent the rider from going off the back of the saddle, not serve as a backrest for the rider. I have been told that anyone who learns on, and continues to ride on, a badly slanted seat will never become an excellent horseman. Figs. 36.18 to 36.21 show some ex-

cellent examples of saddles with seats properly slanted to keep the rider in balance with the horse at all speeds.

The shape of the skirt, some of the rigging, the presence or absence of a Cheyenne roll, the shape of the fender (as long as it covers the area under the rider's knee), the type of horn, the type of stirrup, the presence or absence of strings—all are matters of preference and do not affect the dynamics of the horse.

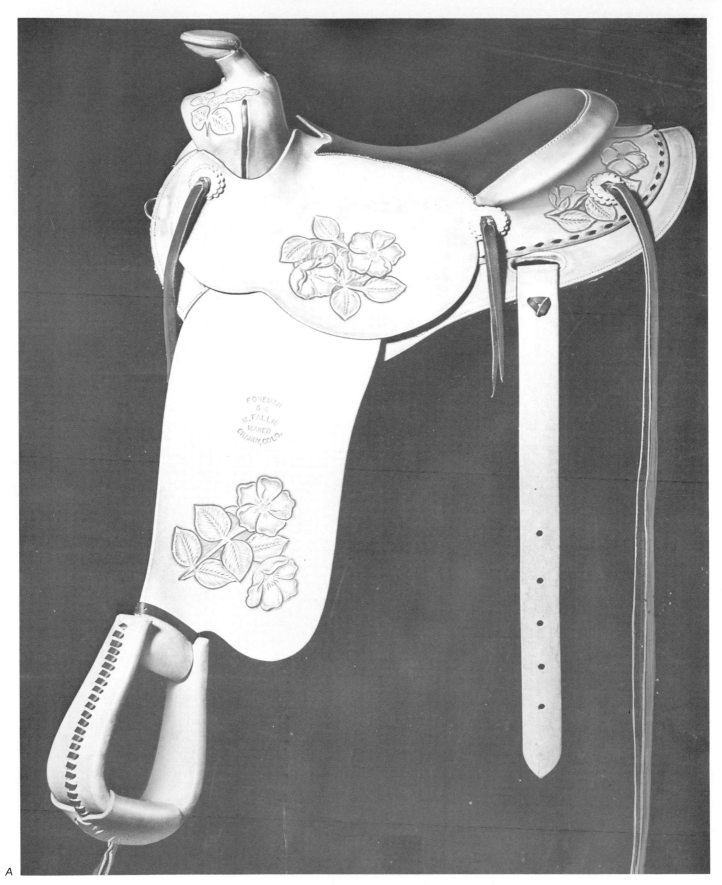

A

FIG. 36.21. Monte Foreman's Balanced Ride® saddle. *(A)* Original design,

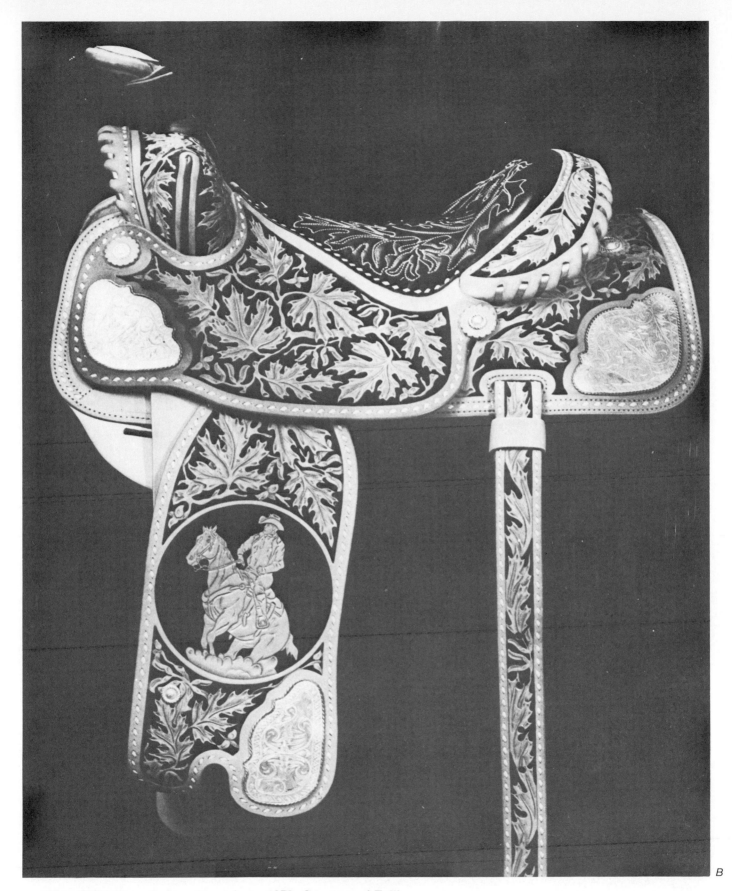

1954. *(B)* Modern design, dressed up. 1978. Courtesy of Fallis.

B

PART IV Sidesaddles

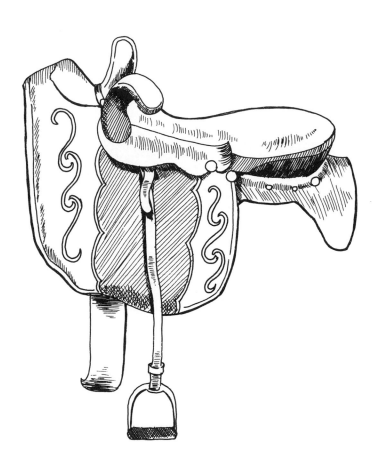

CHAPTER 37

Early-Day and Modern Sidesaddles

Some of the ancient peoples rode sidesaddle style (Fig. 4.3). They must have been accomplished horsemen indeed, for they had no saddles. From earliest times goddesses were portrayed riding sidesaddle style (Fig. 37.1). Before the advent of the sidesaddle, however, most women apparently rode astride or in horse-drawn vehicles.

The predecessor of the sidesaddle was a pannier, a large, heavy wicker basket mounted on a packsaddle frame. The woman rode sideways with her feet on a footrest on one side of the horse. From this device evolved a sidesaddle with a planchette, or footrest. The saddle was a stuffed, platformlike seat on the horse's back. There was often a railing or backing of some type opposite the open side. The woman sat

FIG. 37.1. Vase painting from antiquity showing goddess riding sidesaddle style. From Chenevix-Trench, *A History of Horsemanship.*

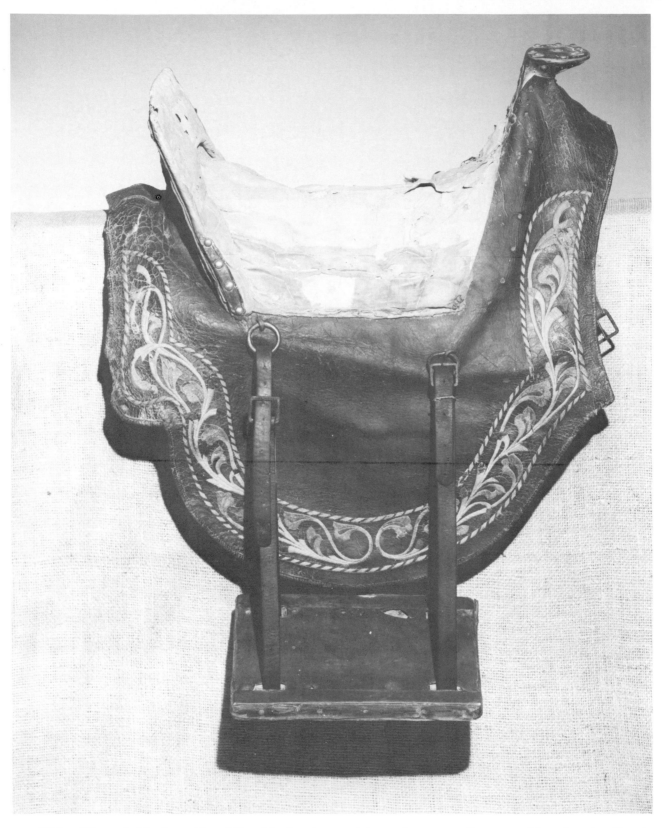

FIG. 37.2.   Woman's Mexican sidesaddle with planchette, eighteenth century. Courtesy of Los Angeles County Museum of Natural History.

FIG. 37.3. Incorrect posture on the sidesaddle. From S. Sidney, *Illustrated Book of the Horse.*

FIG. 37.4. Correct posture on the sidesaddle. From Sidney, *Illustrated Book of the Horse.*

sideways with her feet resting on the long flat planchette (Fig. 37.2).

The planchette is shown in many old pictures, engravings, and paintings, usually with the woman's legs on the near side of the horse, though several of the drawings show the women's legs on the off side. Because these old sidesaddles were not built to conform to the horse's back,

it has been suggested that the saddle with a planchette could be reversed from one side to the other to prevent sore-backing the horse.

Before the marriage of Richard II of England to Anne of Bohemia in 1382, Englishwomen rode astride. Anne introduced the sidesaddle and planchette into England, and from then on it was not considered ladylike to ride astride.

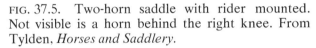

FIG. 37.5. Two-horn saddle with rider mounted. Not visible is a horn behind the right knee. From Tylden, *Horses and Saddlery.*

FIG. 37.6. Three-horn saddle with rider mounted. From Tylden, *Horses and Saddlery.*

Most women rode sidesaddle from that time until the early 1900s, when they began riding astride. Sometime around the early sixteenth century the sidesaddle began to evolve with the addition of a horn to the tree. The horn at this point was mainly a handhold. The woman began riding facing forward over the horse's head. The footrest was removed and replaced with a single stirrup. Because the rider had only the single horn to hold to, the seat was very unsteady. The infamous Catherine de Medicis (1519–89) added the second horn on the near side of the horse. The rider places her left leg over this horn to give her a good purchase on the saddle. On saddles designed for the legs on the near side, the rider's left leg is in the single stirrup, and the right leg is crooked over the horn, as shown in Fig. 37.5.

Over the years the front horn became smaller, sometimes only a small nubbin, but even so the saddle was known as a *two-horn sidesaddle* (Fig. 37.9).

In 1830 a third horn, called a *leaping horn,* was installed with a screw underneath the leg horn (Fig. 37.8). This innovation was the work of Jules Charles Pellier, a Frenchman, probably in collaboration with François Baucher, according to Bloodgood and Santini, though it has sometimes been attributed to Charles Goodnight, the famous early-day Texas rancher. The third horn, which goes over the thigh, just above the knee of the stirrup foot (the left knee) contributed greatly to the rider's stability in the saddle. (Figs. 37.6 and 37.8).

Sidesaddles can be built on an English saddletree or on a western saddletree. It is all but impossible to look at a sidesaddle from the side or top and tell on which tree it is built. That can be determined only by examining the underneath side.

Early in the twentieth century women at last began riding astride again, and today sidesaddles are seen only in shows, where sidesaddle classes are noted for their beauty and elegance.

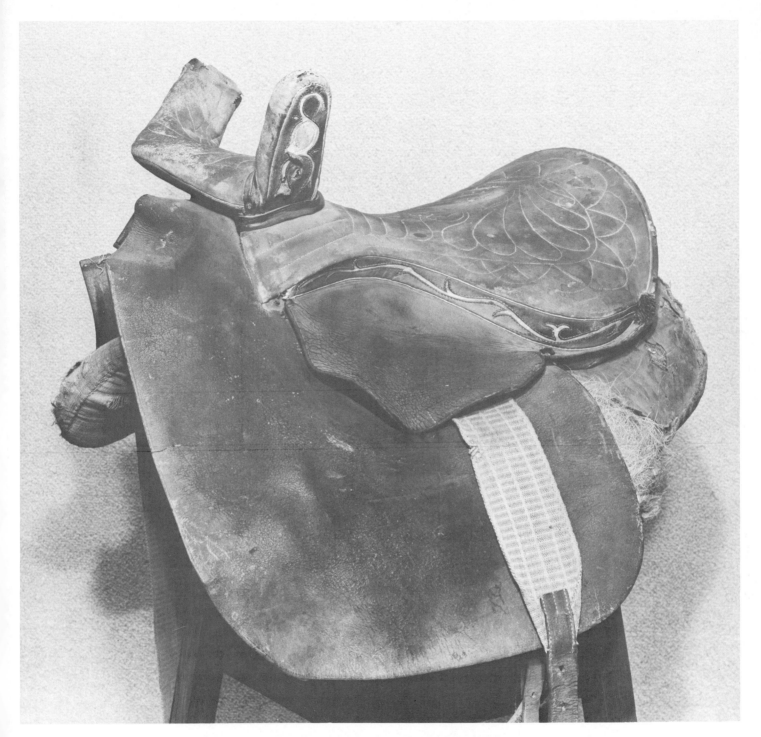

FIG. 37.7. The sidesaddle on which Lafayette, the famous French Revolutionary War hero, is said to have ridden during his visit to Rhode Island in 1824. Courtesy of Rhode Island Historical Society, Providence.

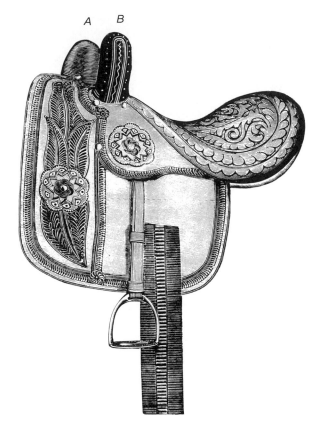

FIG. 37.8.   Three-horn sidesaddle. *(A)* First horn. *(B)* Second horn. *(C)* Third, or leaping, horn. From *Moseman's Illustrated Guide for Purchasers of Horse Furnishing Goods.*

FIG. 37.9.   Two-horn sidesaddle. From *Moseman's Illustrated Guide.*

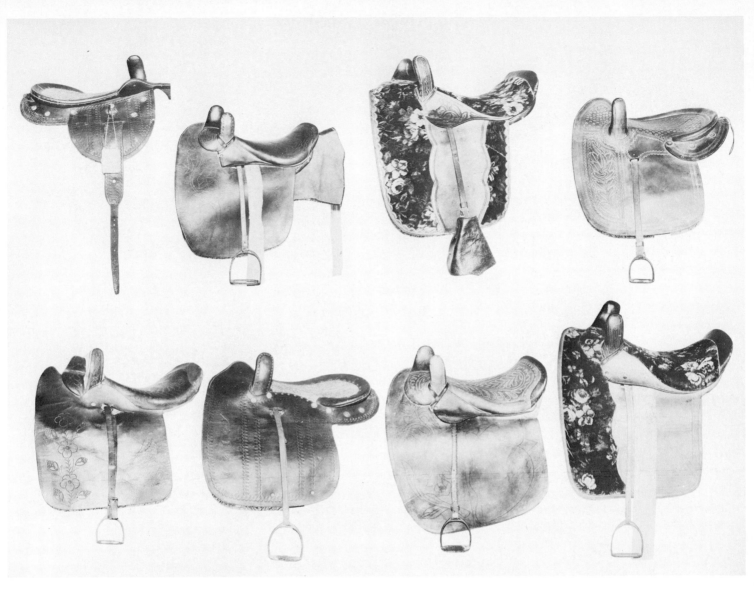

FIG. 37.10.   Different styles of two-horn sidesaddles. Courtesy of Ann Hall, Marthasville, Missouri, and *Hobbies Magazine,* November, 1964.

FIG. 37.11.   Sidesaddle of Mrs. Charles Goodnight, wife of the famous Texas cattle rancher, who accompanied him on some of his long cattle drives. Courtesy of Panhandle-Plains Museum, Canyon, Texas.

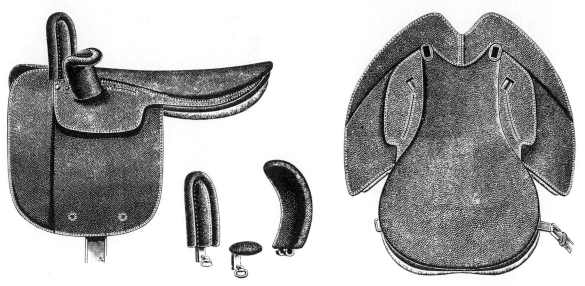

FIG. 37.12.   Three-horn "ladies' saddle" with interchangeable, reversible, right- or left-hand horns. From *Moseman's Illustrated Guide.*

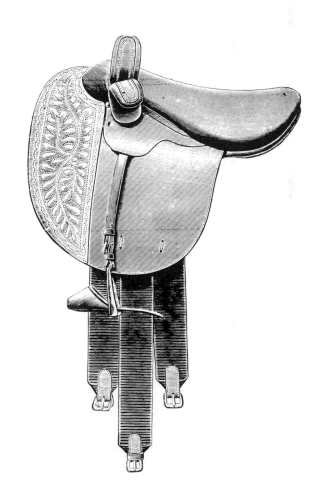

FIG. 37.13.   Elaborately stitched two-horn sidesaddle with slipper stirrup. From *Moseman's Illustrated Guide.*

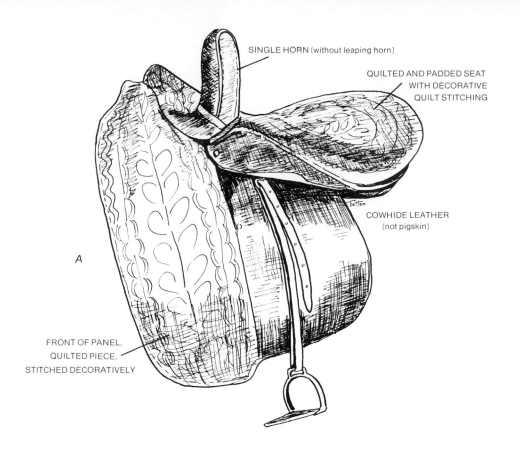

SINGLE HORN (without leaping horn)

QUILTED AND PADDED SEAT
WITH DECORATIVE
QUILT STITCHING

COWHIDE LEATHER
(not pigskin)

A

FRONT OF PANEL,
QUILTED PIECE,
STITCHED DECORATIVELY

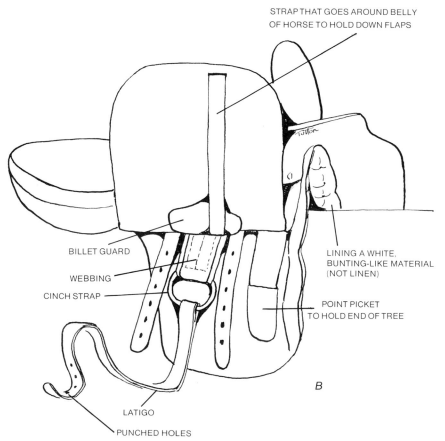

STRAP THAT GOES AROUND BELLY
OF HORSE TO HOLD DOWN FLAPS

BILLET GUARD

WEBBING

CINCH STRAP

LINING A WHITE,
BUNTING-LIKE MATERIAL
(NOT LINEN)

POINT PICKET
TO HOLD END OF TREE

B

LATIGO

PUNCHED HOLES

FIG. 37.14.   Sidesaddle from Spain, ca. 1850–70, found in an old castle in 1970. This saddle is unusual because it is designed without a balancing strap, but instead incorporates a cinch ring and cinch overdraw. It is used with Fitzwilliam-type girth-billet straps attached to outside buckles. The lining is a white bunting-like material (not linen). *(A)* Outside detail. *(B)* Rigging detail. Drawing by Jane Tutton.

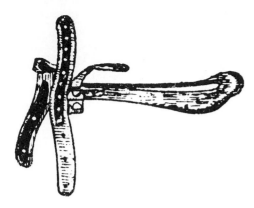

FIG. 37.15*A*. Three-horn English sidesaddle tree. From E. Hartley Edwards, *Saddlery*.

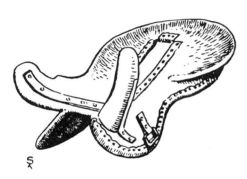

FIG. 37.15*B*. Western sidesaddle tree. From Randy Steffen, "The Sidesaddle Story," part 2, *Western Horseman,* December, 1963.

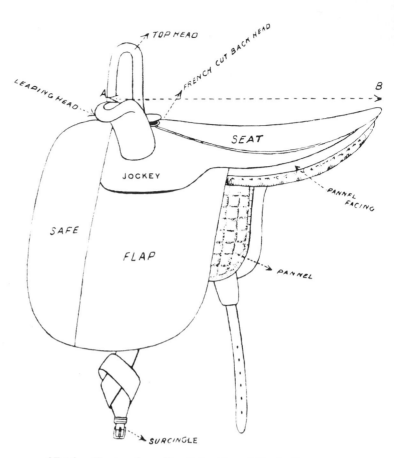

FIG. 37.16. Parts of an English sidesaddle built on an English tree, showing method of measuring the length of seat *(A-B).* From Smith-Worthington catalog, ca. 1905.

FIG. 37.17. Sidesaddle of the mid-eighteenth century with slipper stirrup. From Christian-H. Tavard, *L'Habit du Cheval: Selle et Bride.*

FIG. 37.18. Saddle of Marie-Antoinette with balconet and slipper stirrup, including a small covering over part of the stirrup leather. From the models by J. Pellier. From Tavard, *L'Habit du Cheval.*

275

PART V   English Saddles

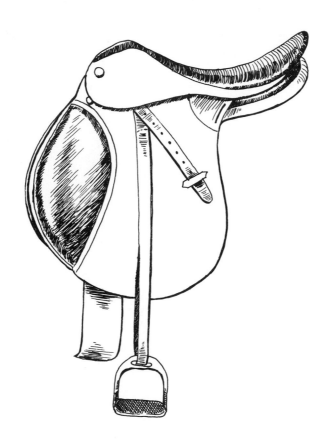

CHAPTER 38

Early and Modern English Saddles and Stirrups

The origin and evolution of the English saddle are unknown, and conjectures are undocumented and therefore questionable. Engravings and paintings surviving from the Middle Ages mostly depict knights with their large saddles. In the very few paintings showing commoners on horseback, the saddles cannot be clearly seen, though they are much smaller than those ridden by knights.

Though the origins of the English saddle are unknown, we do know that it underwent many refinements with the beginning of "educated riding" in the famous riding schools of Federico Grisoni and Giovan Battista Pignatelli in the mid-1500s (Figs. 38.3 and 38.4). The pictures of saddles in the books of Antoine de Pluvinel and the Duke of Newcastle bear no resemblance to the modern English saddle, but the style of riding they taught evolved into English riding as we know it, and the saddles must have been ancestors of the English saddle.

Antoine de Pluvinel was born in 1555 and died in 1620. In his early years he was a pupil of Pignatelli.

The basic English dressage saddle has changed but little in the past two centuries. Figure 38.6 shows the side view of the saddle Cornet Gape rode at the Battle of Waterloo in 1815. It is almost identical to a modern dressage saddle.

Of course, there have been many variations of the English saddle. The first basic change came after Caprilli's method of forward-seat, or balanced-seat, riding became widely accepted (Fig. 38.23). In spite of Caprilli's teachings, those who rode highly collected or dressage horses continued to use the older standard English saddle, and still do today.

FIG. 38.1. Eighteenth-century English fox hunters. From Littauer, *Horseman's Progress.*

MODERN ENGLISH SADDLES

The rider who rides only western saddles and looks down his nose at those who "ride English" on their small, flat saddles, betrays his lack of knowledge of horsemanship. Both styles of riding follow the same principles. The horse behaves the same way no matter which saddle is on him.

The pommels on modern English saddles (forks on western saddles) can be divided into two basic types: (1) the straight head and (2) the cut-back. There are many variations of both types. The tree of the English saddle is a basic tree, a spring tree (see Fig. 38.14), or a variation of either. Most trees are made of wood; other materials are used, but without wide acceptance.

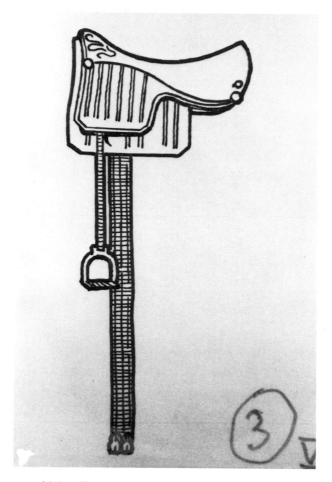

FIG. 38.2. English saddle shown by Chevalier de Harsault in the 1739 edition of his book *Le Nouveau Parfait Marechal.* From Tavard, *L'Habit du Cheval.*

Finished English saddles are grouped in the following classifications:

Lane-Fox Cut-Back show saddle (or saddle-seat equitation saddle)

Forward-seat saddle

Dressage saddle

Jumping saddle (or hunter-jumper saddle)

Polo saddle

All-purpose saddle

Exercise saddle

Racing saddle

There are many variations within each category. The rider preparing to buy an English saddle should purchase one to suit the type of riding in which he or she is interested. All-purpose saddles, as their name indicates, can be used for several purposes by the beginner.

The term *plantation saddle* is used for a variety of comfortable, padded saddles for easy riding (the Somerset saddle is an example). The term evidently came into use after the beginning of the twentieth century. It does not appear in any of the saddlemakers' catalogs available to me dating from the 1890s or early 1900s; in fact, the earliest reference to it that I could find is in H. Kauffman's 1927 catalog, though the term was used much earlier than that.

In the early part of the twentieth century the *Kentucky stitchdown,* a plantation saddle, was common, as was the *spring-seat* saddle, which had padding and a large roll over the front of the pommel and another over the rim of the cantle. (These types of rolls were also used on the ladies' astride western saddles made early in this century. On the western saddle they were called *squaw rolls.*)

The Buena Vista and the Wilbourn were popular plantation saddles of the early years of this century. According to Tom Matthews, Sr., of the B. T. Crump Company, they were made by Wilbourn at his Buena Vista Saddle Company in Buena Vista, Virginia.

The following information was furnished me by a friend, an accomplished rider who lives in Alabama. It provides a lot of useful detail about the distinguishing features of the various styles of English saddles:

Jumping models have the flaps out further forward, and on some brands the stirrup bars are also set further forward. Dressage models encourage the rider to sit down, not forward, and the flaps are quite straight, because the dressage rider uses a longer length of stirrup and a straighter leg than the jump rider (generally the difference in length of stirrups for jumping versus dressage is two to seven holes in the leathers). The all-purpose saddle is modified, halfway between, so that it can be used for both jumping and dressage. However, for high-level dressage, or for jumping over obstacles that are 5 feet high or higher, it is best to use a saddle designed especially for each use.

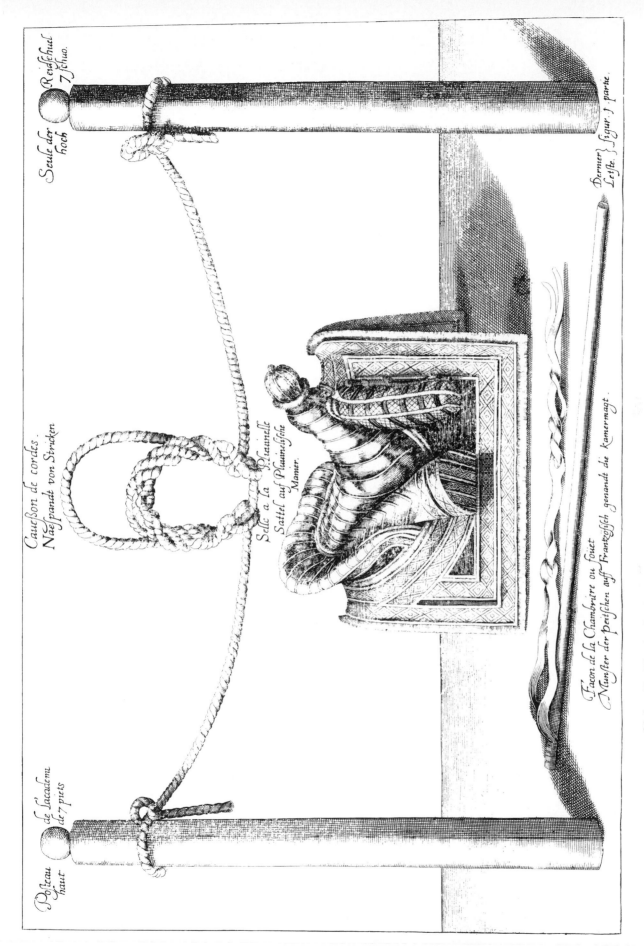

Seule der Reißschul
hoch.

7 schu.

Caueßon de cordes.
Naespandt von Stricken

Posteau
haut

de Sacademi
de 7 piets

Selle a la Pluuinelle
Sattel auf Pluuineißsche
Manier.

Facon de la Chambriere ou fouet
Munster der peitschen auff Frantzösich genandt die kamermagt.

Dernier figur. 5. parte.
Letste

FIG. 38.3. De Pluvinel's riding-instruction saddle. From Antoine de Pluvinel, *Le Manège royal.*

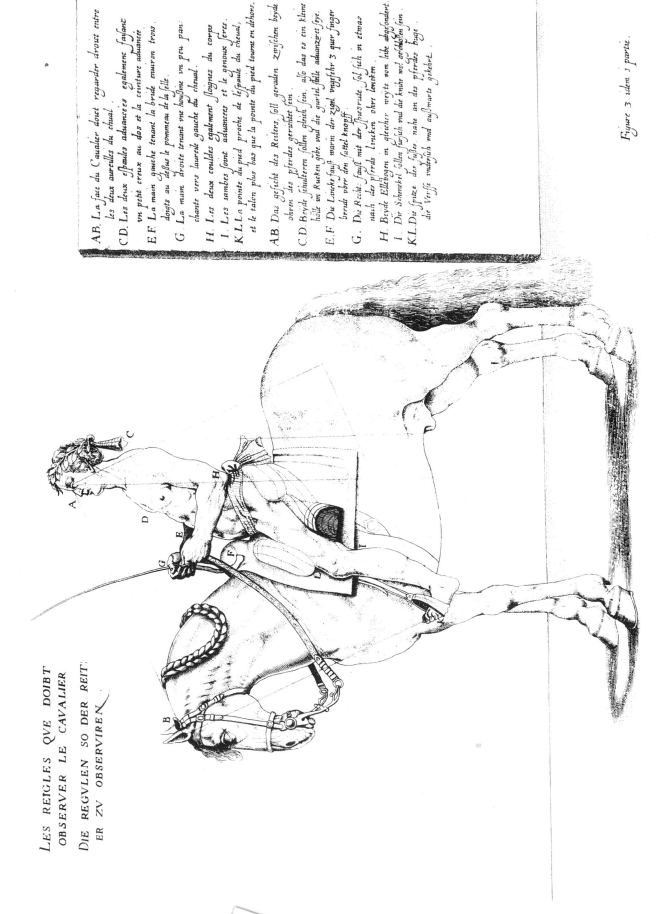

FIG. 38.4.   De Pluvinel's diagram of saddled horse with rider. From De Pluvinel, *Le Manège royal.*

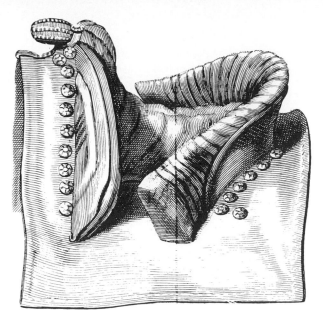

FIG. 38.5. Riding saddle of William Cavendish, Duke of Newcastle. From William Cavendish, Duke of Newcastle, *A General System of Horsemanship*.

FIG. 38.6. Saddle of Cornet Gape, Second Dragoons, used at Waterloo in 1815, showing bullet holes inflicted by enemy action. From Tylden, *Horses and Saddlery*.

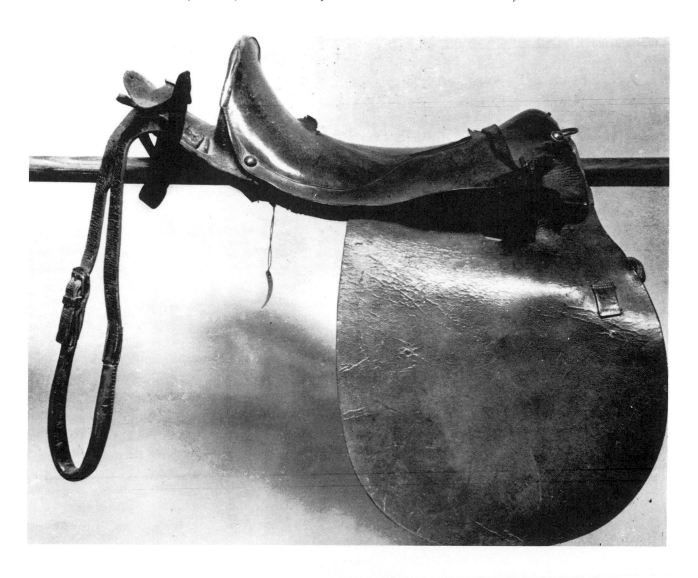

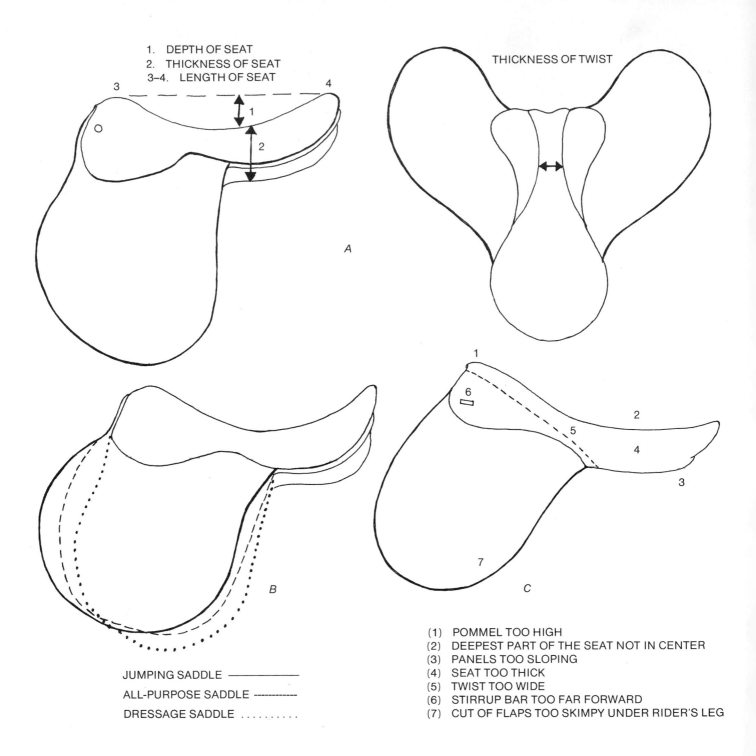

1. DEPTH OF SEAT
2. THICKNESS OF SEAT
3–4. LENGTH OF SEAT

THICKNESS OF TWIST

A

B

C

JUMPING SADDLE ————————

ALL-PURPOSE SADDLE ------------

DRESSAGE SADDLE . . . .

(1) POMMEL TOO HIGH
(2) DEEPEST PART OF THE SEAT NOT IN CENTER
(3) PANELS TOO SLOPING
(4) SEAT TOO THICK
(5) TWIST TOO WIDE
(6) STIRRUP BAR TOO FAR FORWARD
(7) CUT OF FLAPS TOO SKIMPY UNDER RIDER'S LEG

FIG. 38.7. Measurements, styles, and potential bad points of English saddles. *(A)* Points at which to measure an English saddle. *(B)* Flap shapes of different styles. *(C)* Weaknesses to be avoided. Drawings by Judy Osburn.

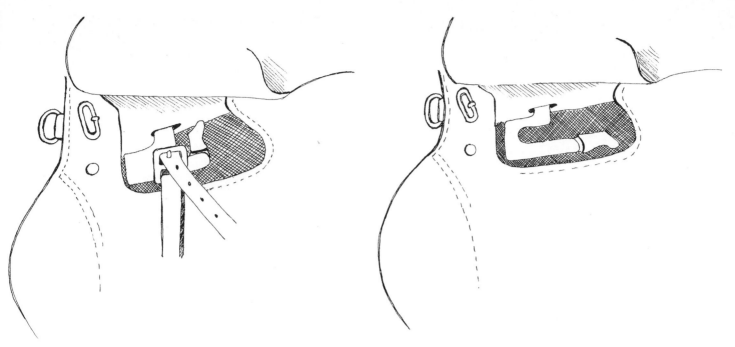

FIG. 38.8.   Stirrup-leather bar. *(A)* Closed. *(B)* Open.   Drawings by Judy Osburn.

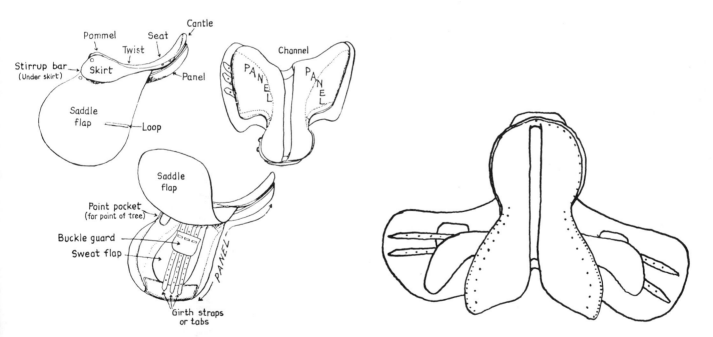

FIG. 38.9.   Parts of the modern English saddle. From E. Hartley Edwards, *Saddlery*.

FIG. 38.10.   Short panel. From Edwards, *Saddlery*.

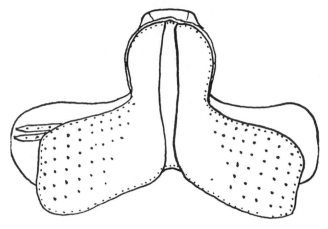

FIG. 38.11. Full panel. From Edwards, *Saddlery*.

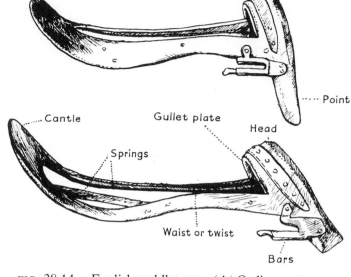

FIG. 38.14. English saddletrees. *(A)* Ordinary tree. *(B)* Spring tree. From Edwards, *Saddlery*.

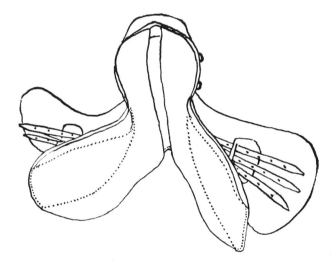

FIG. 38.12. Continental panel. From Edwards, *Saddlery*.

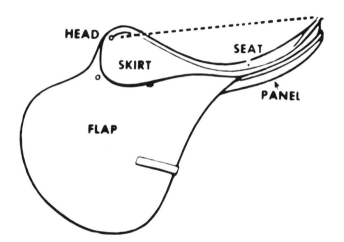

FIG. 38.15. Measuring a saddle. The length of the tree is measured from saddle nail at head to center of cantle. Always mention the rider's height and weight when ordering a saddle. Frequently a rider requires a larger seat size in one model and a smaller size in another. These variations are due to the differences in seat depths and widths. From Miller's, catalog no. 109, 1977.

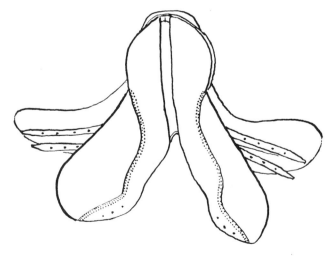

FIG. 38.13. Saumur panel. From Edwards, *Saddlery*.

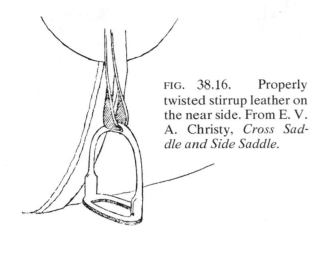

FIG. 38.16. Properly twisted stirrup leather on the near side. From E. V. A. Christy, *Cross Saddle and Side Saddle.*

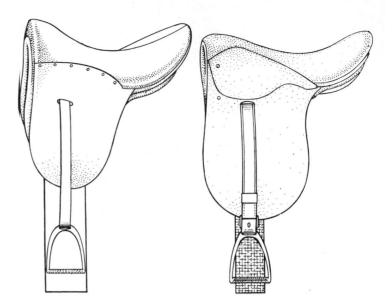

FIG. 38.18. Somerset plantation saddles. From Wyeth, catalog no. 220, 1939.

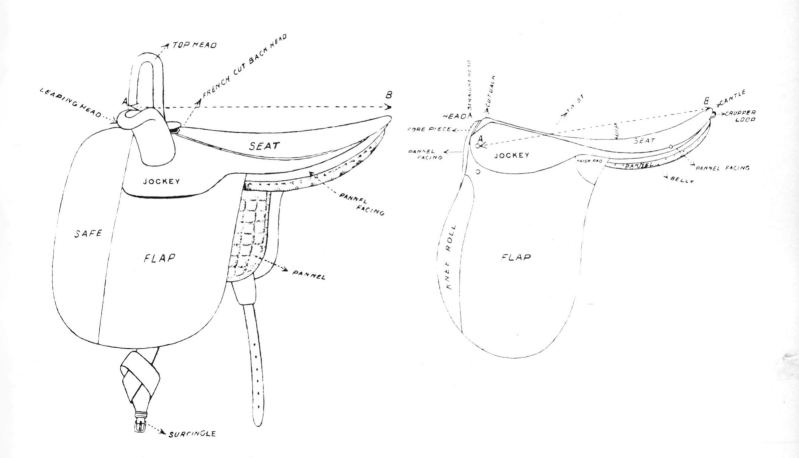

FIG. 38.17. English-saddle diagram. From Smith-Worthington catalog, ca. 1905.

287

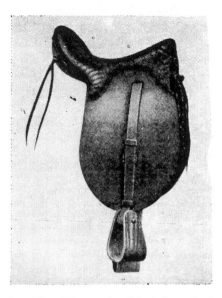

FIG. 38.19.   The "Kentucky Stitchdown" plantation saddle. From Kauffman's, catalog no. 757, 1927.

FIG. 38.21.   "Spring Seat" plantation saddle. From Kauffman's, catalog no. 757, 1927.

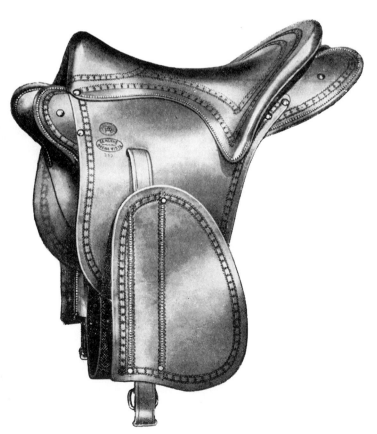

FIG. 38.20.   Buena Vista modern plantation saddle. Courtesy of Bona Allen, Inc., Buford, Georgia.

The twist is the part that is directly between the rider's thighs where they meet at the body. A wide twist, or a high one, not only will cause discomfort but will tend to push the rider back onto the cantle where he or she will end up banging away on the poor horse's kidneys—hardly a desirable situation. A wide twist also causes the legs to shoot forward, on top of the girth, where their application could not be effective unless crude kicking was used. So the narrowness of the twist is very important.

The pommel should be designed so that it will absolutely clear the withers, with not even a hint of touching them with the rider mounted. Involved in this is the width of the tree, for even a regular pommel will rub on a narrow horse, unless the saddle also has a narrow tree. The pommel must not be overly high because a high pommel usually goes along with a wide twist, and the sins rapidly multiply. If the rider gets a little low over a jump, or the horse jumps awkwardly and throws the rider onto the pommel, it is most unfortunate. If the pommel is cut back, or scooped, then not only is clearance of the withers assured but, in addition, the pommel can then be much lower and safer for the rider. Also, the modified cut-back types enable one rider to use the same saddle on a greater variety of wither types.

The stirrup bar *must* be of the safety type—any other kind is dangerous. The safety type has a catch that will open if the rider should fall and hang a foot in the stirrup. However, in order to be effective,

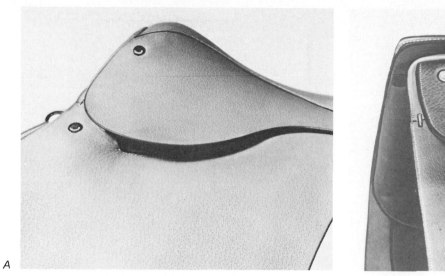
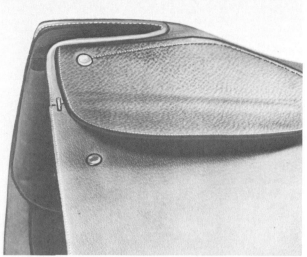

A

B

FIG. 38.22. Types of heads on English saddles. *(A)* Straight head. *(B)* Cut-back head. Courtesy of Miller's.

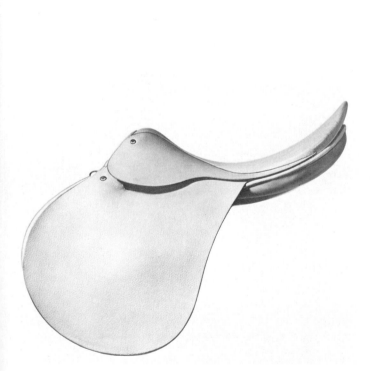

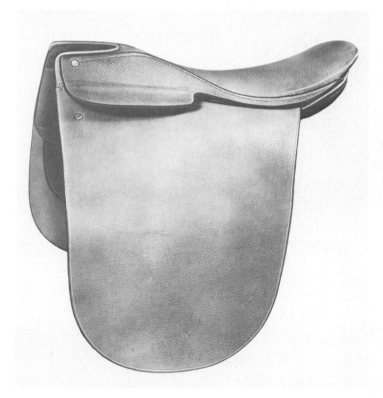

FIG. 38.23. Forward-seat saddle. Courtesy of Miller's.

FIG. 38.24. Lane-Fox cut-back show saddle. Courtesy of Miller's.

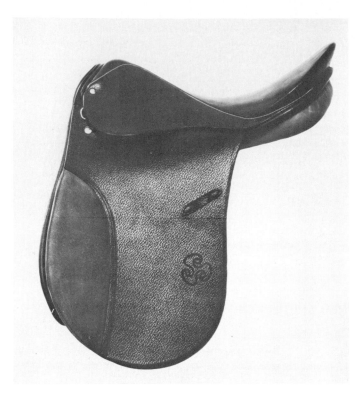

FIG. 38.25. Dressage saddle. Courtesy of H. Kauffman & Sons.

FIG. 38.26. Jumping saddle. Courtesy of H. Kauffman & Sons.

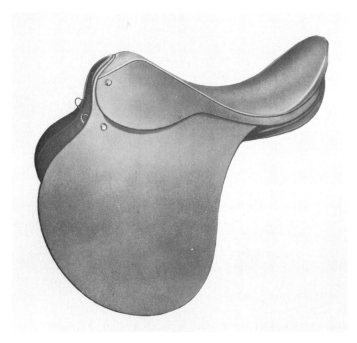

FIG. 38.27. Polo Saddle. Courtesy of H. Kauffman & Sons.

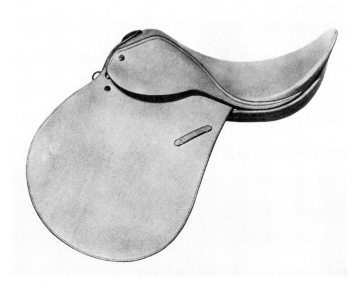

FIG. 38.28. All-purpose saddle. Courtesy of Miller's, New York.

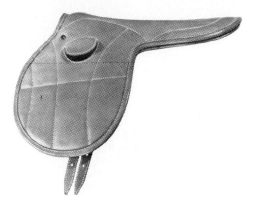

FIG. 38.29. Soft-back racing exercise saddle. Courtesy of Miller's, New York.

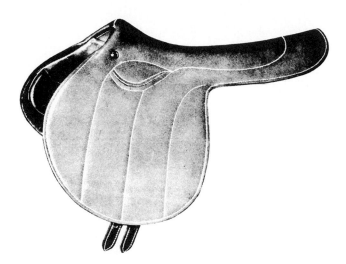

FIG. 38.30. Racing saddle. Total weight, 7 1/2 pounds, including stirrups and cinch. It is used on all major racing tracks in the United States, as well as in Mexico and four other countries. Courtesy of Mark's Turf Supply, Wichita, Kansas.

it must remain in the closed position at the start of the ride. If it is left open (and those who are proponents of this open position say it is for greater safety), and the rider should happen to have the leg slip too far back over an obstacle, then the stirrup will come off, even though the rider has not fallen. So the leg slips, which makes the rider insecure, and then the stirrup plops onto the ground, causing even more insecurity—and a fall can result from that alone. Evidently the members of our Olympic team consider it to be much more dangerous to have the stirrup come free by accident than to risk being dragged, for they *wire* the bars into the closed position during the steeplechase and cross-country rounds! This is not suggested for the average rider, as they are more apt to hang a foot than someone on the Olympic team. It would be unfortunate for some youngster to wire the bars and then hang a foot and be dragged to an early grave. An interesting sideline to this is that the *Pony Club Manual* states that the bars should be left open—despite that fact that they were *made* to open and close. Just recently at a Pony Club rally a rider left hers open. Her leg slipped back, and the stirrup came free, hit the horse in the knee, and shattered it. The look on her face when she realized what had happened was terribly sad—for she knew it was preventable. The horse had to be put down.

As for deep seats, they give security, better balance and more safety to the rider. They also make it slightly difficult to get out of the saddle for a high obstacle. For nearly all uses, they are excellent. But five feet or up, a somewhat flatter seat is better—for the rider can move about faster and stay with the horse better when going over big fences at high speeds.

Panels should be absolutely smooth to avoid sore backs, and firmly stuffed for long shape retention, not actually hard, but definitely not mushy. A recent development in panels is one that is inflatable so that it can be adjusted to exactly fit the back of the horse, or to give more support to the seat of the rider, as desired. The edge of the panel (under the cantle) should be moderate—a sharp edge digs into the kidney area, while one that is too sloping will cause the saddle to shift around because the base of support will be too small.

Cantles come in two styles—round and square. The square ones generally are found with a seat that is a bit wider, and chubby riders or those with large hips find them more comfortable.

The seat should be curved downward to fit the natural shape of a rider's bottom and *never* have projections at the edges—or the rider will feel as

291

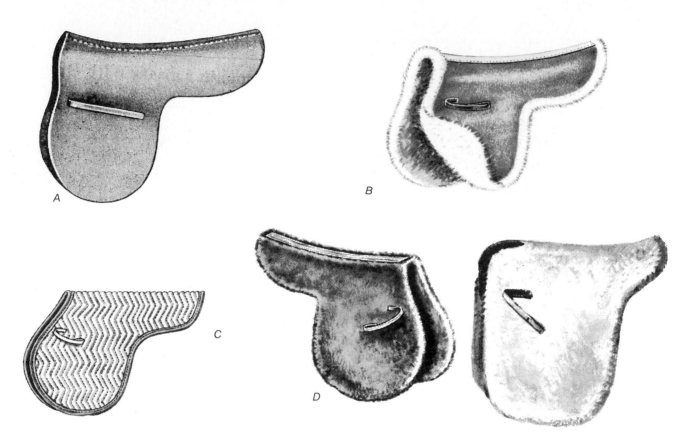

FIG. 38.31. English saddle pads *(A)* Felt numnah (pad). From Stockman-Farmer, catalog no. 41, 1932. *(B)* Merino sheepskin pad. *(C)* Quilted pad. *(D)* Double-faced Equi-Fleece pad. *(B–D)* from Miller's, catalog no. 109, 1977.

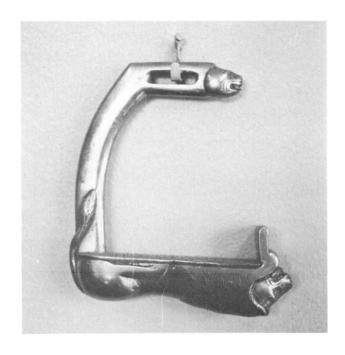

FIG. 38.32. French cavalry stirrup used during the time of Maximilian I of Mexico. This brass stirrup appeared in an old scene of Mexico City's main square with troops lined up for review by the emperor and the empress Carlotta. The right and left stirrups are mirror images of each other. The lion's tail is in front on each stirrup. Courtesy of Ford E. Smith.

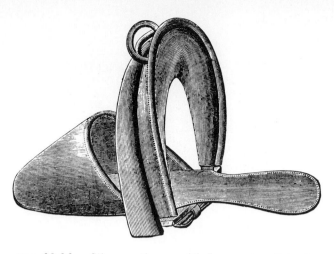

FIG. 38.33.   Cope's patented safety stirrups. *(A)* Open. *(B)* Closed. From *Moseman's Illustrated Guide.*

FIG. 38.36.   Slipper stirrup with Lennan's safety device. From *Moseman's Illustrated Guide.*

FIG. 38.34.   Spring side stirrup. From *Moseman's Illustrated Guide.*

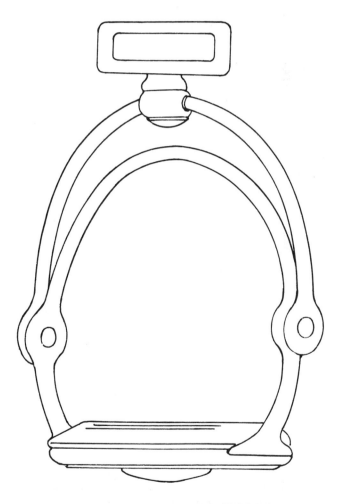

FIG. 38.35.   Lennan's patented safety stirrup, closed. From *Moseman's Illustrated Guide.*

FIG. 38.37.   Another version of Waggener's oscillating iron stirrup. Drawn from original, courtesy of Robert L. Kapuke.

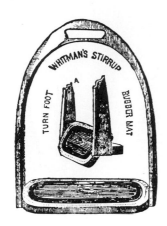

FIG. 38.38. Whitman turnfoot. From Stone, catalog, ca. 1905.

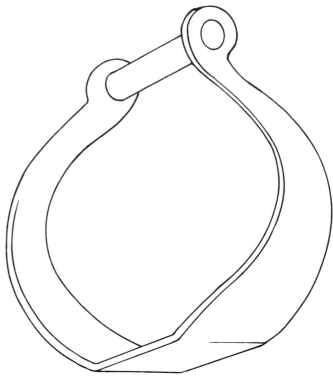

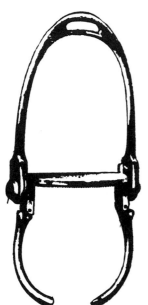

FIG. 38.39. Scott's safety stirrup. From Stone, catalog, ca. 1905.

FIG. 38.41. Kellner-type stirrup. Courtesy of Robert L. Kaupke.

FIG. 38.40. Latchford safety stirrup. From Sidney, *Book of the Horse*.

FIG. 38.42 Horton woman's safety stirrup. From Smith-Worthington, catalog, ca. 1905.

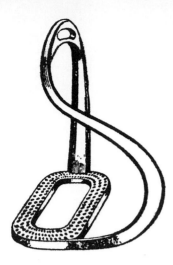

FIG. 38.43. Australian simplex-pattern safety stirrup. From R. M. Williams, Prospect, S.A., Australia, catalog, 1952.

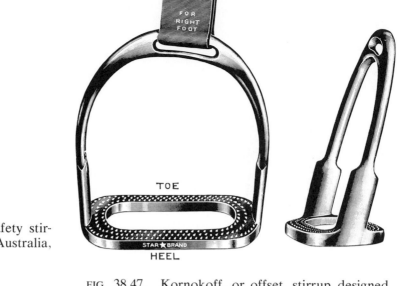

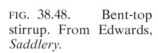

FIG. 38.47. Kornokoff, or offset, stirrup designed for the forward seat. From North & Judd catalog, no. 43.

FIG. 38.44. Four-bar stirrup iron. From Williams, catalog, 1952.

FIG. 38.48. Bent-top stirrup. From Edwards, *Saddlery*.

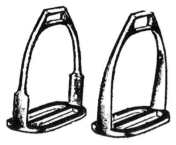

FIG. 38.45. Three-bar stirrup irons. Williams, catalog, 1952.

FIG. 38.46. Racing stirrup. From B. T. Crump Company.

FIG. 38.49. English hunting stirrup with Prussian sides and a two-bar stirrup iron. From North & Judd Manufacturing Co., New Britain, Connecitcut, catalog no. 43, 1968.

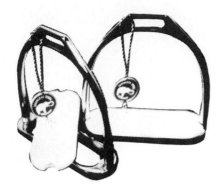

FIG. 38.50.   Stainless-steel Fillis stirrups. From B. T. Crump Company, Inc., Richmond, Virginia, catalog no. 96, ca. 1973.

FIG. 38.53.   Forerunner of Peacock safety stirrup. From *Moseman's Illustrated Guide.*

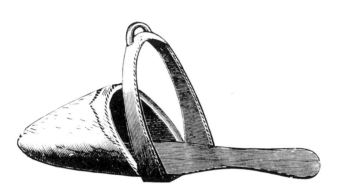

FIG. 38.51.   Slipper stirrup. From *Moseman's Illustrated Guide.*

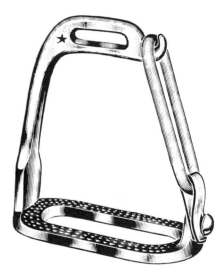

FIG. 38.54.   Peacock safety stirrup. From North & Judd, catalog no. 43, 1973.

FIG. 38.52.   Capped stirrup, leather-covered, also called children's clogs. From *Moseman's Illustrated Guide.*

FIG. 38.55.   Woman's toe stirrup, used on side-saddles. From Montgomery Ward, catalog no. 56.

if perched on a fence board. The edges should slope off smoothly.

Central depth of seat means that the deepest part is exactly halfway between the pommel and the cantle. Cheap saddles have the deepest part toward the rear, which causes the rider to sit on the kidneys of the horse, lean far forward to get balance, and also shove the legs forward. Without exception, saddles made in India and Argentina have this problem —and they made it very difficult for a rider to find his or her balance, and are, in addition, very hard on a horse's back. The reason they are constructed in this manner is that the horses in those countries do not have the heavy muscling in the wither area that our American horses do, and so the saddles are quite appropriate for the horses of those countries.

Close contact means that the rider feels that he is nearly bareback through the thigh area. Poorly constructed saddles are thick under the thigh, and also stiff, and cut down on sensitivity between the horse and rider. . . . Another enemy of good contact is a *thick* seat, which forces the rider to jab with the legs and yank on the reins, because the horse cannot feel the seat and weight aids through all that padding and heavy leather.

Stirrup bars should be inset for comfort—if they are not, the stirrup leathers will bulge out and either raise hob with the rider's contact, or else raise welts on the thighs.

The size of the saddle is very important for comfort and ease of handling the horse. Children's saddles are 15- and 16-inch, measured from the center edge of the cantle to the nail head at the side of the pommel. Sometimes a 14-inch or 13-inch can be found.

The most common mistake people make when buying a saddle is to get it in too large a size—it should fit like a glove; snug, but not binding anywhere. All too often I have seen slender young teenagers sliding around in a 17 1/2, and they simply can't *ride* in so large a saddle. The size for English saddles is much more important than for western saddles, as the fit is snugger. For people with slender hips but long legs, some are available in an extra-forward model, with the flaps out farther to the front, for more room for a lengthy thigh (opposite of a child's model). Stout riders with ample hips and short thighs must get one specially made, which can take up to a year to consummate when a person orders direct from Germany. If a horse has a very unusual back (not just very high or very wide withers), an exact description, accompanied by measurements and a photo, can be sent and a saddle specially made.

PART VI American Cavalry Saddles

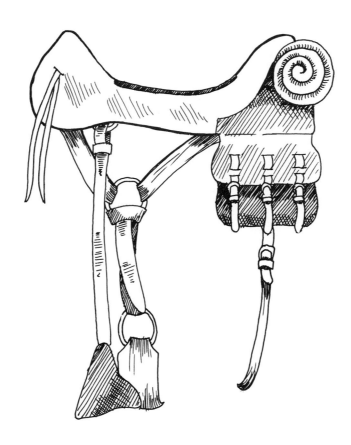

CHAPTER 39

Saddles in War and Westering, 1812-1936

The reader wanting complete information on United States military saddles should consult Randy Steffen's *United States Military Saddles* (see Bibliography). Steffen's research on this subject was thorough and documented, and his drawings are incomparable in their meticulous detail.

Following is a list, abstracted from Steffen, of all the standard military-issue saddles, and the dates of first issue or model:

James Walker saddle, 1812
Hussar-style dragoon saddle, 1812
Dragoon saddle, 1814–16
Artillery driver's saddle, 1832
Dragoon saddle, 1833–44
Dragoon saddle, 1841
Ringgold dragoon saddle, 1844
Grimsley dragoon saddle, 1847
Hope saddle (Texas saddle), 1857
Grimsley artillery driver's saddle, 1859
Daniel Campbell saddle, 1855
Driver's saddle, 1859
McClellan saddle, 1859
W. H. Jenifer cavalry saddle, 1860
McClellan saddle, 1868
McClellan saddle, 1874
Whitman saddle, 1879
McClellan saddle, 1885
McClellan saddle, 1893
McClellan saddle, 1896
McClellan saddle, 1904
Experimental cavalry saddle, 1912
Mule riding saddle, 1913
Experimental cavalry saddle, 1916
Officer's training saddle, 1916
Officer's field saddle, 1917
Training saddle (French Saumur type), 1926
McClellan saddle, 1928
Phillips officer's cross-country saddle, 1936

Several other saddles are known to have been used by military personnel; however, they were privately purchased, personal saddles and were not military issue. I have often been told of the existence of an officer's horned saddle. With the possible exception of the brass eagle's-head horned saddle (Fig. 10.1), there has never been a military-issue horned officer's saddle.

It appears that the United States military saddles of the first half of the nineteenth century were copies of European military saddles, especially the Hungarian hussar saddle (see Fig. 18.1). The first deviation from that tradition came with the issuance of the Hope, or Texas, saddle in 1857 (see Fig. 10.5). The second was the McClellan saddle. It was designed by George B. McClellan when he was a cavalry captain. He had been an attaché in Europe, and he claimed that his saddle was derived from a Hungarian and a Mexican saddle. Steffen, however, after much research through old military records, concluded that it was more likely that the McClellan design was derived from the best features of two American saddles, the Campbell and the Grimsley, which had previously been submitted to the army. The army accepted the McClellan saddle in 1858.

The original McClellan (Fig. 39.12) had a rawhide-covered tree with the seams on the upper inside of the tree slot. The first tree was not leather-covered; however, ten years later, in 1869, the tree was fully covered with black leather. The 1859 McClellan had a single black-leather skirt under the quarter straps. The skirt was removed in 1872 and was not put back on the saddle until 1928.

The lower outside edge of the saddletree was a straight line. Two quarter straps (one over the pommel and one over the bars behind the cantle) attached to an exposed round stock metal D ring hung below the approximate center of the tree (the centerfire) and buckled to a cinch on each side. Sweat leathers were issued but were not always used. The sweat leathers were removed in 1866, added again in 1874, and finally removed in 1928. Cinch straps were attached to the flat side of each D ring. The metal on these first McClellans was iron. The D ring at the lower end of the quarter straps tended to shift position. In 1874 the D rings were cast with a small plate, shaped like an inverted trapezoid, which extended upward between the lower ends of the quarter straps. This prevented the D ring from shifting. Billets replaced the cinch straps sometime during this period. Also in 1874 a heart-shaped leather chape was put behind the D ring. About 1885 the D-ring assembly was replaced with a round ring on top of a square chape. Cinch straps replaced billets. About 1904 a round ring was put on top of a round leather chape with sheepskin underneath.

The cavalry consistently used wooden stirrups. The original McClellan had leather-hooded wooden stirrups. The hoods were removed and put back several times throughout the life of the saddle.

The artillery McClellans had brass stirrups during the Civil War. In 1912 a nickel-steel stirrup was issued; then came the steel stirrup. On the underneath side of the footrest of a regulation steel McClellan stirrup appears "B.M. Co." (the manufacturer's initials), with "U.S." underneath.

In the 1904 issue the two-piece adjustable quarter straps over the cantle and pommel were each equipped with a brass rectangle at the lower edge of the tree. The lower quarter straps then attached to a circular ring on a circular leather chape. This assembly, called a *safe,* had sheepskin covering the back side next to the horse. The lower outside edge of the bars on the 1904 tree had a light indentation in them. A D-shaped metal loop for attaching breast harness and breeching was provided on the cantle and pommel on the artillery McClellans.

McClellans came in three seat sizes: 11, 11 1/2, and 12 inches. Measured on the flat seat itself, the size was shown on an embossed brass plate on the rider's side of the pommel.

All leather on the McClellans was dyed black until the Army adopted olive drab as its official color about 1902. The saddle leather from then on was russet-colored.

In 1928 the quarter straps were removed, the skirt was put back on, and double girth billets were added.

The cavalry several times experimented with English-style saddles that to some degree copied foreign cavalry saddles, but each of them lost out to the old tried and proven McClellan. The McClellan, the mainstay of the United States cavalry, lasted almost one hundred years, from 1858 to 1942, when the cavalry was mechanized.

The McClellan is still used by many riders today, especially trail and endurance riders. It was and is a remarkable saddle.

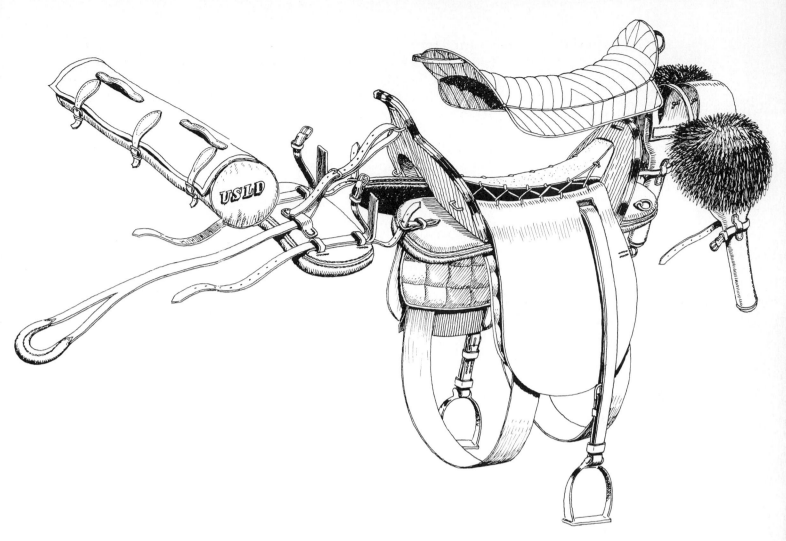

FIG. 39.1.   James Walker saddle, 1812. From Randy Steffen, *United States Military Saddles, 1812–1943*.

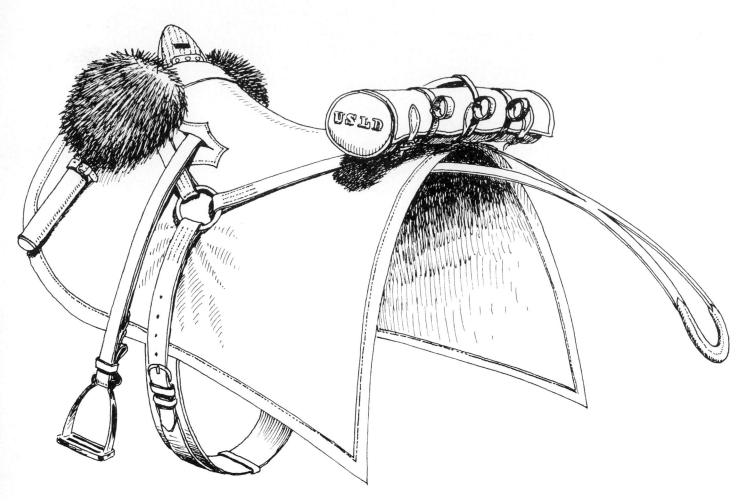

FIG. 39.2.   Hussar-style dragoon saddle, 1812. From Steffen, *United States Military Saddles.*

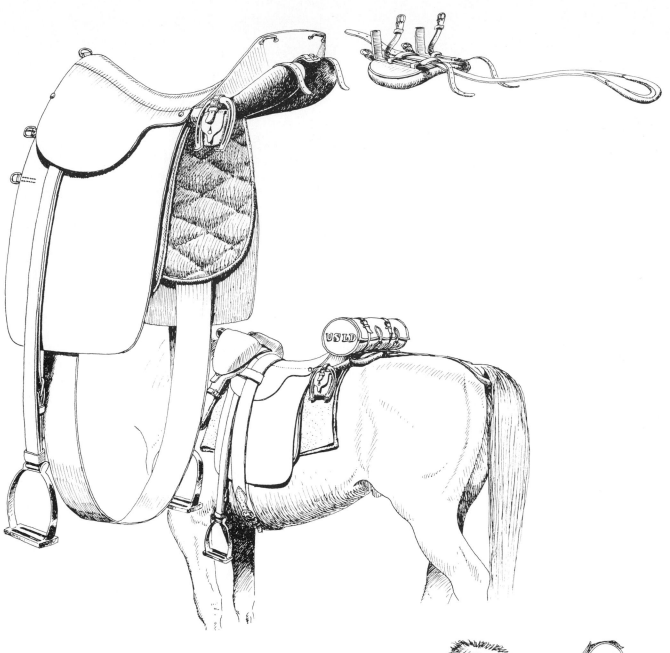

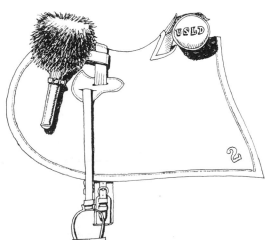

FIG. 39.3.   Dragoon saddle, 1814–16. From Steffen,
United States Military Saddles.

FIG. 39.4.   Artillery driver's saddle, 1832–44. From Steffen, *United States Military Saddles.*

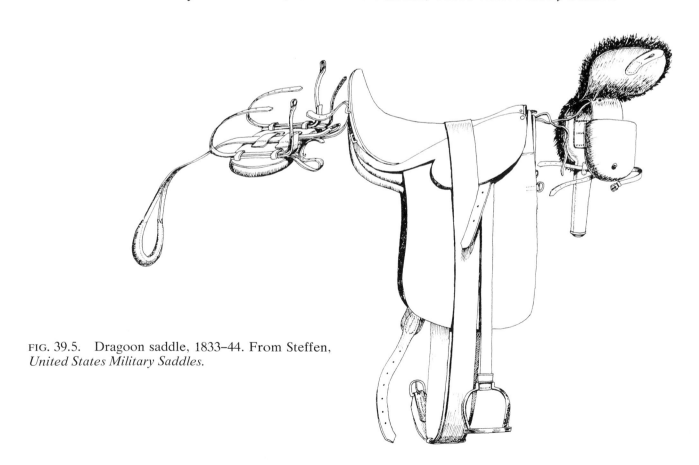

FIG. 39.5.   Dragoon saddle, 1833–44. From Steffen,
United States Military Saddles.

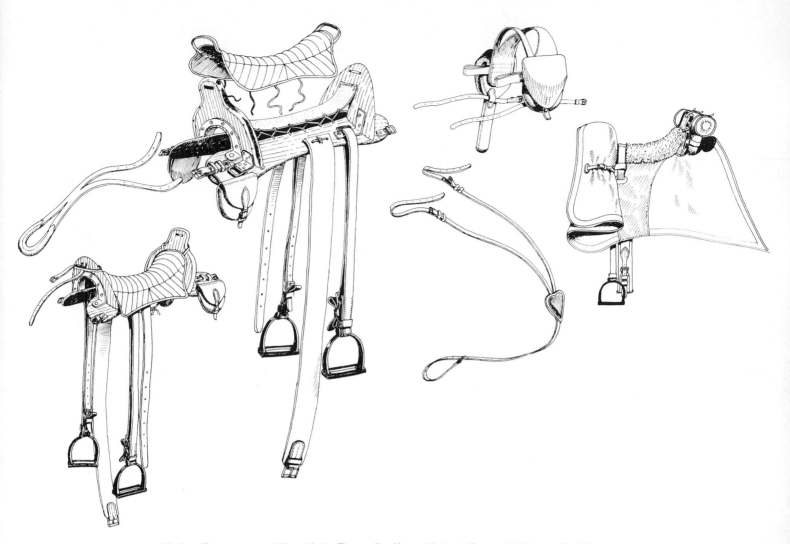

FIG. 39.6.   Dragoon saddle, 1841. From Steffen, *United States Military Saddles.*

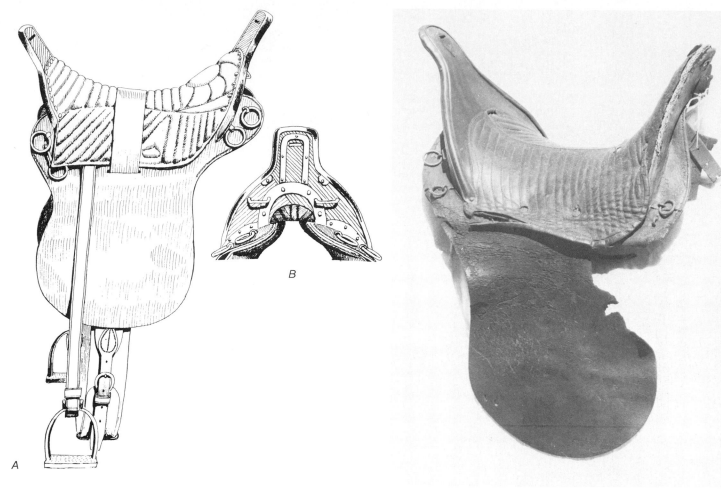

FIG. 39.7.   Ringgold dragoon saddle, 1844. (A) Side
view. (B) Front view. From Steffen, *United States
Military Saddles.*

FIG. 39.8.   Grimsley dragoon saddle, 1847. Courtesy
of Fort Sill Museum.

308

FIG. 39.9. Grimsley artillery driver's saddle, 1859–80. Courtesy of Fort Sill Museum.

FIG. 39.10. Daniel Campbell saddle, 1855. From Steffen, *United States Military Saddles.*

FIG. 39.11. Six-mule jerkline driver's saddle. From Nick Eggenhofer, *Wagons, Mules, and Men.*

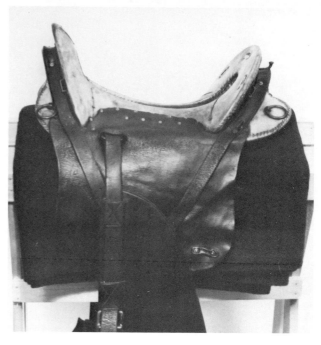

FIG. 39.12. McClellan saddle, 1859. Courtesy of D. W. Freeborn.

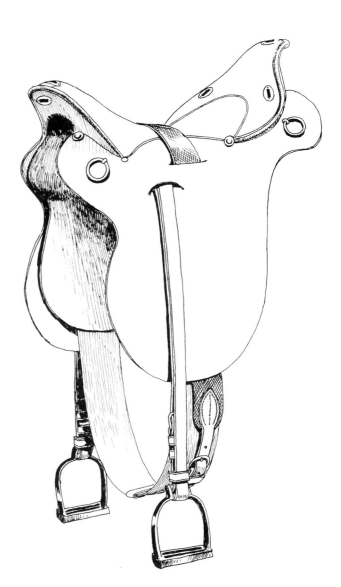

FIG. 39.13. W. H. Jenifer cavalry saddle, 1860. From Steffen, *United States Military Saddles.*

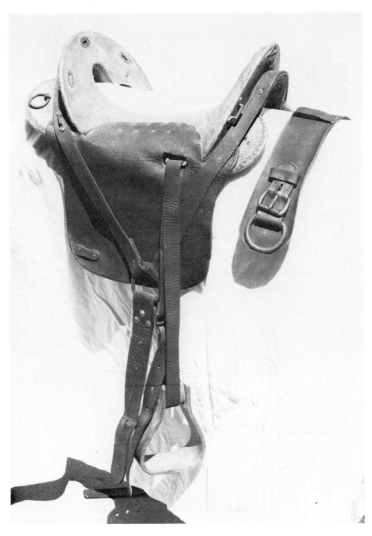

FIG. 39.14. McClellan saddle, 1868. Courtesy of Fort Sill Museum.

FIG. 39.15. McClellan saddle, 1874. Courtesy of Fort Sill Museum.

311

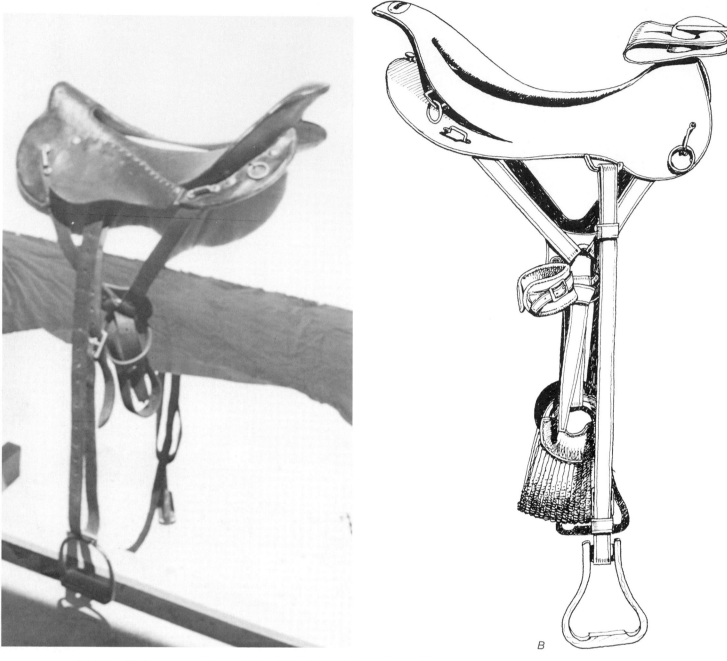

FIG. 39.16.   Whitman cavalry saddles, 189. *(A)* Without horn. Courtesy of Fort Sill Museum. *(B)* With horn. From Steffen, *United States Military Saddles.*

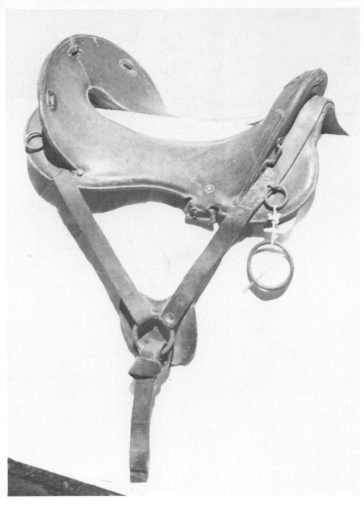

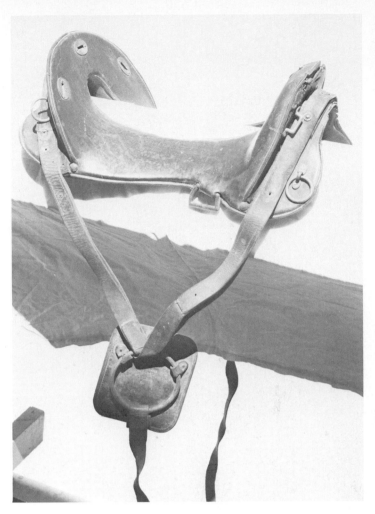

FIG. 39.17. McClellan saddle, 1885. Courtesy of Fort Sill Museum.

FIG. 39.18. McClellan saddle, 1896. Courtesy of Fort Sill Museum.

FIG. 39.19. Hooded wooden cavalry stirrup. *(A)* Front view. *(B)* Side view. Drawings by Nancy Kay Niles.

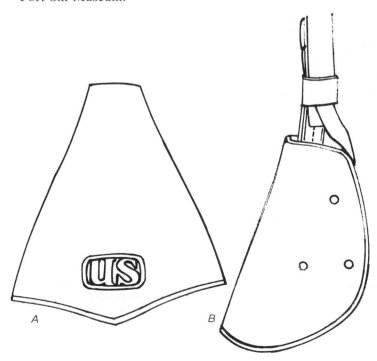

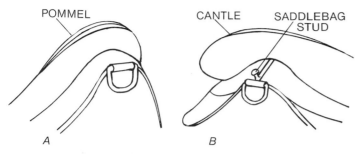

FIG. 39.20. D rings on McClellan artillery saddle. *(A)* On pommel. *(B)* On fan under saddlebag stud.

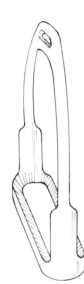

FIG. 39.21.
Steel artillery stirrup.

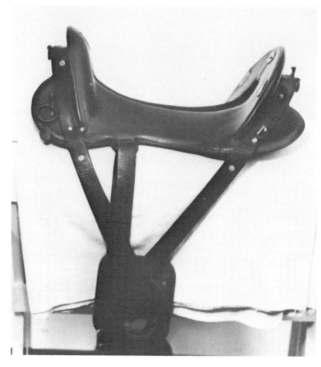

FIG. 39.23. McClellan artillery saddle, 1896. Courtesy of D. W. Freeborn.

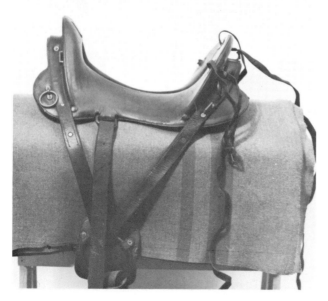

FIG. 39.22. McClellan cavalry saddle, 1896. Courtesy of D. W. Freeborn.

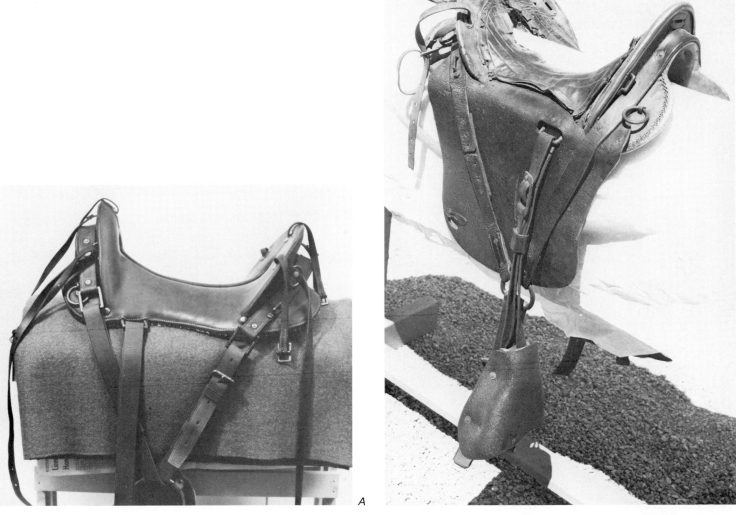

FIG. 39.24. McClellan cavalry saddles, 1904. *(A)* Near side. Courtesy of D. W. Freeborn. *(B)* Off side. Courtesy of Fort Sill Museum.

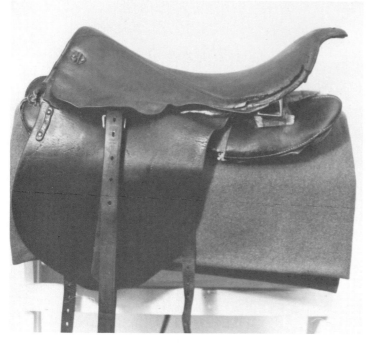

FIG. 39.25. Model 1912 experimental saddle, 1912. Courtesy of D. W. Freeborn.

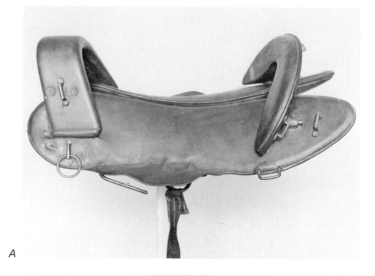

A

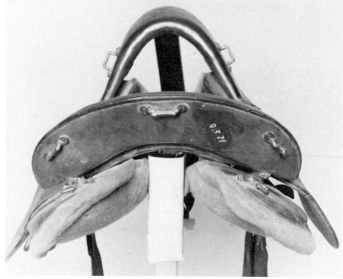

B

FIG. 39.27. Experimental cavalry saddle, ca. 1916. (A) Near side. (B) Back. Courtesy of Fort Sill Museum.

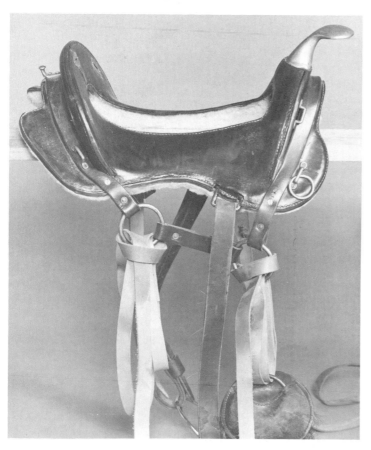

FIG. 39.26. Mule-riding saddle, 1913. Courtesy of D. W. Freeborn.

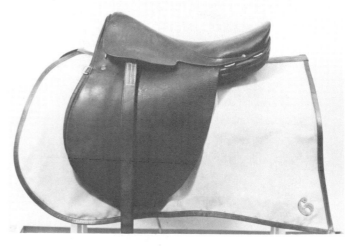

FIG. 39.28. Officer's training saddle, 1916. Courtesy of D. W. Freeborn.

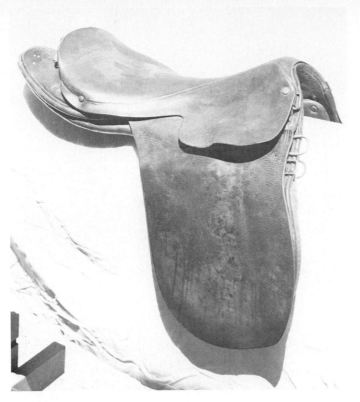

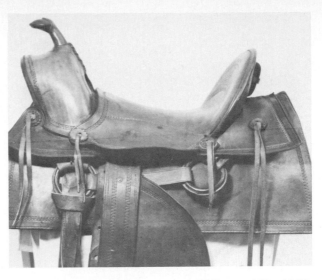

FIG. 39.30. Full-rigged packer's riding saddle, 1917. Courtesy of D. W. Freeborn.

FIG. 39.29. Officer's field saddle, 1917. Courtesy of Fort Sill Museum.

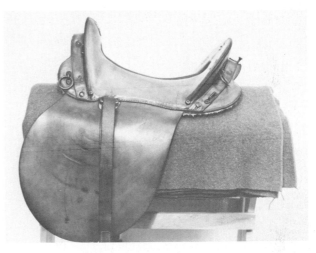

FIG. 39.32. Modified McClellan saddle, 1928, the last model issued by the United States Cavalry. Courtesy of D. W. Freeborn.

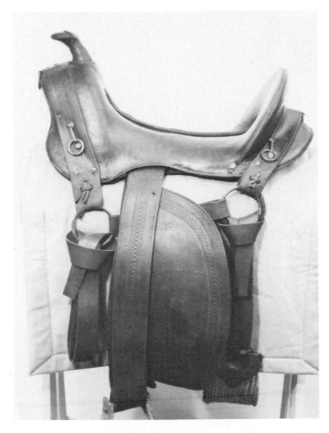

FIG. 39.31. Skeleton-rigged packer's riding saddle, 1917. Courtesy of D. W. Freeborn.

FIG. 39.33. Phillips officer's cross-country saddle, 1936. Courtesy of D. W. Freeborn.

PART VII   Famous Saddles

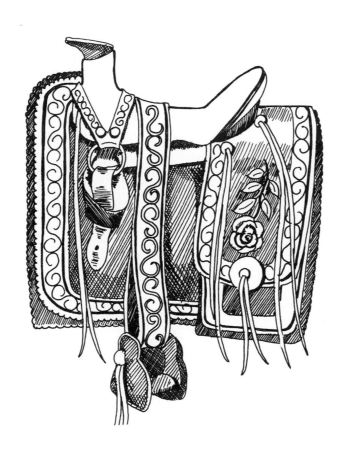

CHAPTER 40

Saddles as History and Art

This chapter contains pictures and information on saddles that for one reason or another are often encountered in the literature and are of historical note. Some are of special interest to saddle buffs; still others are included because of their reputation for performance under stress; others are included simply because they are beautiful examples of the saddlemaker's and the silversmith's artistry. The jade saddle, for example, is unique, as far as I can determine. Many of these saddles are extremely valuable, because of the jewels and silver on them, because of their makers, and sometimes because of their owners.

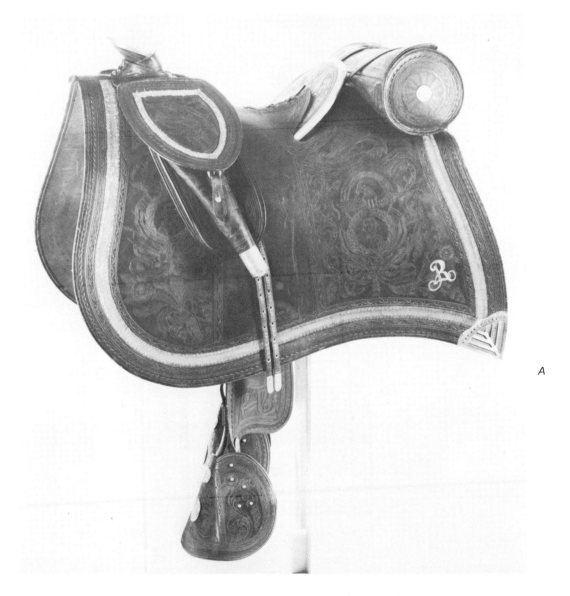

A

B

FIG. 40.1.   Colonel Henry Leavenworth's saddle. *(A)* With mochila. *(B)* Without mochila. The saddle was made in 1862 by Edward L. Gallatin, of Denver, and purchased for $350 in Denver City by friends and officers of Leavenworth's command, the Second Colorado Volunteers. It was presented to him at Camp Weld on December 4, 1862. The gift aroused the jealousy of the officers of Colonel J. M. Chivington and his First Colorado Volunteers. They purchased a $550 saddle for Colonel Chivington. His saddle, reportedly more elaborate than Leavenworth's, has not been found. Colonel Leavenworth's saddle is the property of the Colorado State Historical Museum, where it was displayed for several years, and is now on loan for display in the Smithsonian Institution, Washington, D.C. Courtesy of Colorado State Historical Society.

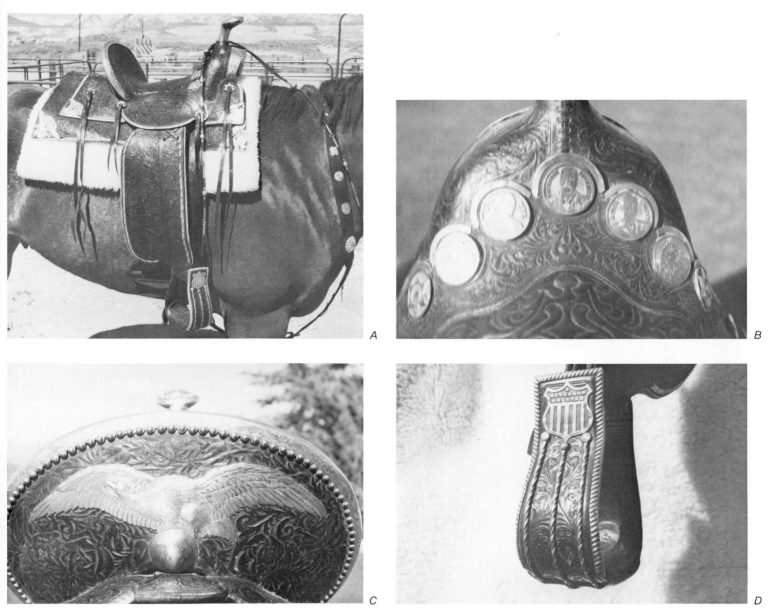

FIG. 40.2.   G. S. Garcia's gold-and-silver show saddle. *(A)* Side view. *(B)* Back of the fork. *(C)* Back of the cantle. *(D)* Stirrup. The saddle originally valued at $5,000, was two years in the making. It won first prize at the Saint Louis World's Fair in 1904 and first prize at the Lewis and Clark Centennial Exposition of Portland, Oregon, in 1905. For many years this goldsmith-turned-saddlemaker's prize work was stored in a vault. Then a niece inherited it, and in 1975 the saddle and matching bridle and breast collar were offered for sale for $275,000. Courtesy of the Garcia family and C. R. Larom, Hutchinson, Kansas.

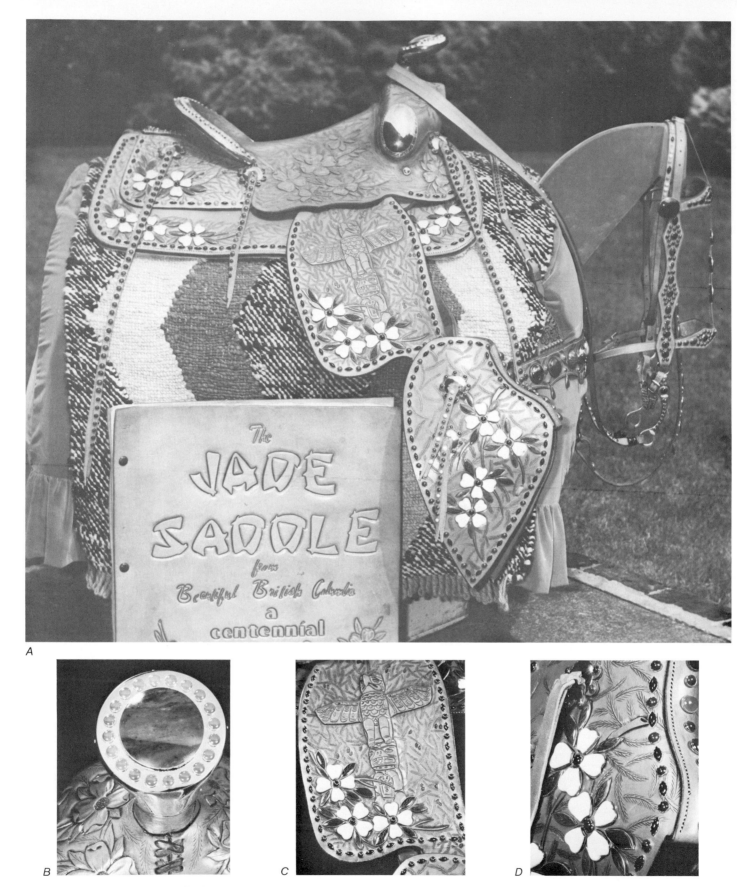

FIG. 40.3. The Jade Saddle, a leather-and-gem portrayal of the history of British Columbia, symbolizing the western outdoors. *(A)* Off side view. Note jade in saddle strings. *(B)* Top of horn. *(C)* Detail of fender. *(D)* Detail of tapadero. Collecting the rough gems for this work took fifteen years. The saddle was created and is owned by Peter A. White, British Columbia, Canada. Photograph courtesy of Les Ashe, Toronto.

"$10,000.00 saddle made for J. C. Miller of the 101 Wild West Show by S. D. Myers Sweetwater, Texas. This saddle contains 166 diamonds, 120 sapphires, 17 rubies, 4 garnets and 15 pounds of sterling silver and gold."

FIG. 40.4. 101 Ranch saddle. The saddle was made about 1913 by S. D. Myres in his Sweetwater, Texas, saddle shop. It is said that J. C. Miller, of the Miller Brothers 101 Ranch, had seen an expensive saddle in France while touring with his wild West show and determined then to own the world's finest saddle. When the show train went through Sweetwater, Miller went to Myres and contracted for the saddle at a cost of $10,000. The saddle contained 166 diamonds, 120 sapphires, 17 rubies, and 4 garnets and 15 pounds of sterling silver and gold. Courtesy of Jack Harney, Ponca City, Oklahoma.

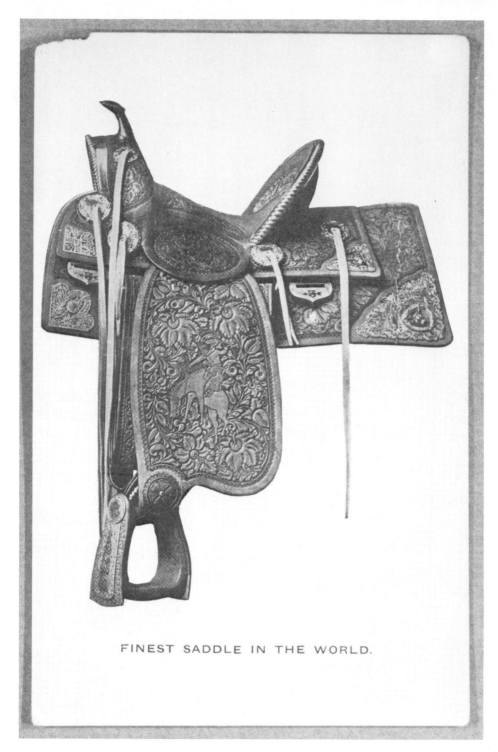

FINEST SADDLE IN THE WORLD.

FIG. 40.5.   101 Ranch saddle. There is no record when this saddle, made by Wyeth, was completed, but R. Charles Mape, advertising manager of the Wyeth Company, Saint Joseph, Missouri, determined from old-time employees that it was completed probably in 1914 and at a cost of $5,800. The saddle has diamonds, rubies, and sapphires set in the different ornaments. On the cantle is spelled out "Joseph C. Miller, 101 Ranch," in 168 cut diamonds embedded in raised gold letters. Eighteen pounds of solid gold and silver were used in making it. The saddle, owned by Zack Miller, Jr., the son of one of the Miller brothers, is now on loan to the Texas Rangers Hall of Fame, Waco, Texas. Courtesy of Jack Harney, Ponca City, Oklahoma.

FIG. 40.6.   Edward H. Bohlin's personal parade saddle. The seventy-pound saddle required fourteen years to build, and was finished in the early 1940s. The gold-relief carvings depict in detail western life and the game animals of the Pacific Slope. Mr. Bohlin died May 28, 1980, at the age of eighty-five. Courtesy of Bohlin Saddlery, Hollywood, California.

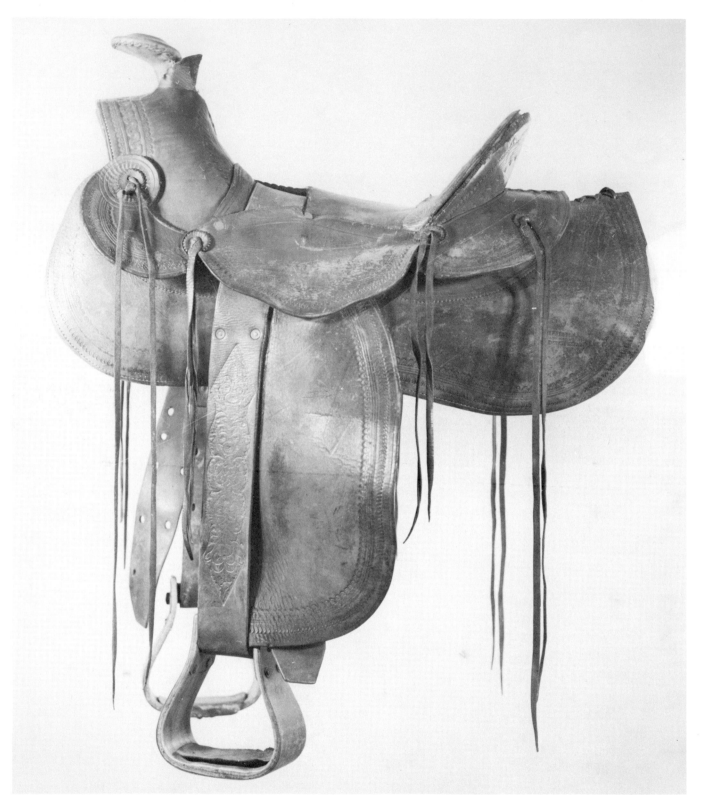

FIG. 40.7.   Tom Mix's early saddle, which legend says the famous motion-picture actor used when he was a member of Teddy Roosevelt's Rough Riders during the Spanish-American War. Mix also used it in his early movies. Courtesy of Woolaroc Museum.

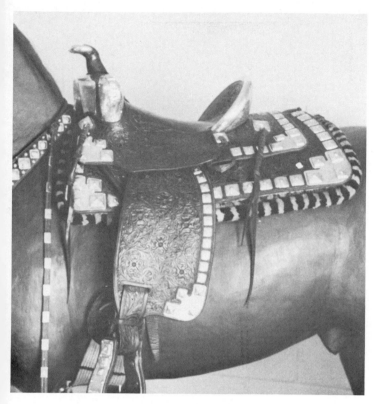

FIG. 40.8. Tom Mix's Bohlin-made show saddle, which he used in most of his later movies and personal appearances. Courtesy of Tom Mix Museum, Dewey, Oklahoma. Photographer Charles Beam.

FIG. 40.9. Bohlin parade saddle on Thousands Cheered, three times World's Champion Parade Horse, owned by Emerald View Stables, O'Fallon, Missouri, and ridden by Dan Breakbill. The saddle was purchased by the stable in 1953 for $15,000. Courtesy of Emerald View Stables, O'Fallon, Missouri.

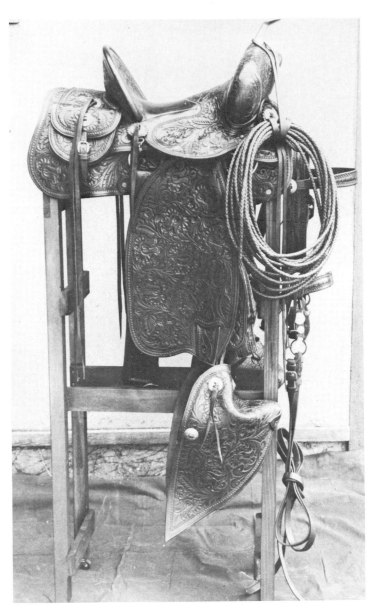

FIG. 40.10. Edward Larocque Tinker's personal saddle, made to order about 1911. Tinker, a teacher and researcher, wrote a book on riders, *Centaurs of Many Lands.* Courtesy of Will Rogers Memorial Museum, Claremore, Oklahoma.

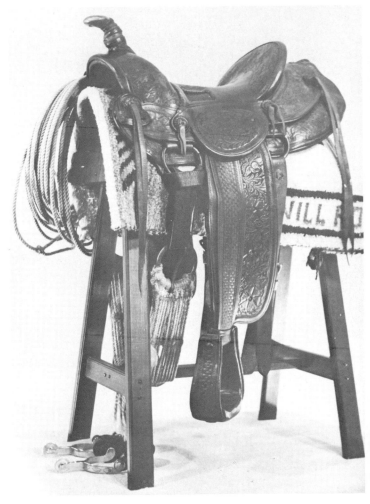

FIG. 40.11. Will Rogers's favorite saddle, typical of the kind he used on the vaudeville stage. It was made by the famous G. S. Garcia, of Elko, Nevada, about 1909. It originally had tapaderos on the stirrups. Courtesy of Will Rogers Memorial Museum.

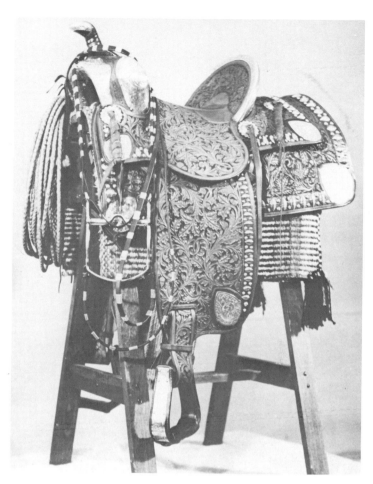

FIG. 40.12. Will Rogers's Fred Stone saddle, made by Brydon Brothers, Los Angeles, California. Rogers and Stone, a famous character actor on stage and in films, became friends in New York after Will began his career in vaudeville. On the back of the high cantle is a silver plate inscribed "From Fred to Will." Courtesy of Will Rogers Memorial Museum.

FIG. 40.13. Saddle of Jim Rogers, Will Rogers's younger son. The Bohlin-made saddle was given to Jim by his father on his sixteenth birthday. Will rode this saddle when he played the leading role in the 1931 movie version of Mark Twain's *The Connecticut Yankee.* Courtesy of Will Rogers Memorial Museum.

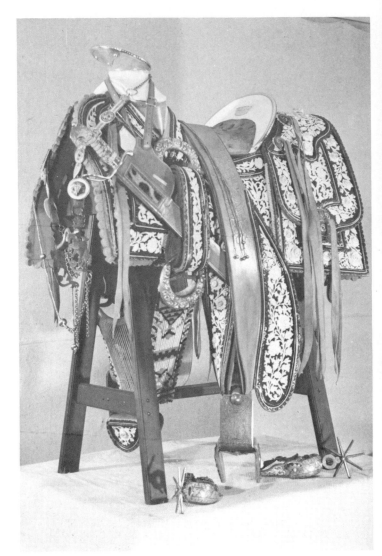

FIG. 40.14. Jack Carroll custom-fitted-tree saddle ridden by Ms. Mary Ellen Eckelberg in 1975 on her 6,400-mile ride from Winnipeg, Manitoba, to New Orleans, Louisiana, and back. Ms. Eckelberg made the ride without sorebacking her horse. It is claimed that half the distance was at speed and in hot weather. The journey began the first of June, 1975, and ended a few days before Christmas, 1976. Photograph taken in December, 1975, by Port Sulphur Photographers, Port Arthur, Louisiana.

FIG. 40.15. Will Rogers's fancy charro saddle, an elaborate variation of the Mexican saddle. It features a wooden tree, large square skirts, a wide horn cap and Spanish rigging. It was made to order for Rogers by J. Jesús Pérez y Hijos. Courtesy of Will Rogers Memorial Museum.

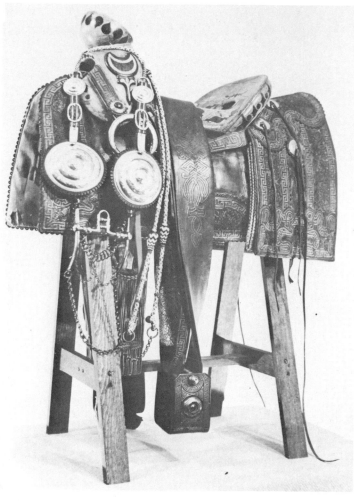

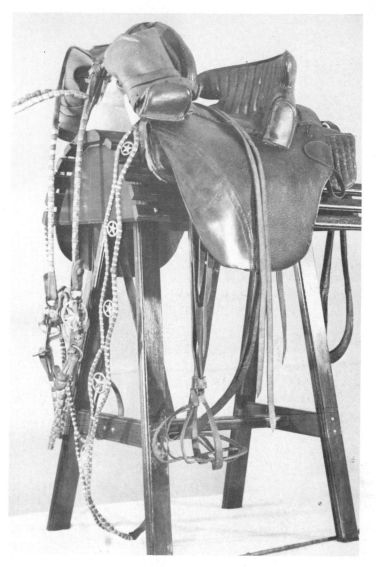

FIG. 40.16.   Will Rogers's Mexican saddle, the type used by the early Spaniards and Mexicans. Its uncovered tree is decorated with darker wood inlays on the broad fork, horn, and rolled cantle. This saddle was taken to Texas by a band of Mexicans who fled across the Rio Grande about 1912. Joe Miller of the 101 Ranch bought all the Mexicans' saddles and equipment, and Will Rogers obtained this one from him. Courtesy of Will Rogers Memorial Museum.

FIG. 40.17.   Will Rogers's Camargue saddle from southern France, one of the oldest kinds used by French "cowboys." It is descended from the old jousting saddle that almost locked the rider in the seat. This saddle was made entirely by hand. The leather was tanned by an early-day process, and the iron stirrups were forged and riveted. This saddle has no horn because the French cowboy ropes with a noose fastened to the end of a long pole and carries his rope in a leather bag slung over his shoulder. Courtesy of Will Rogers Memorial Museum.

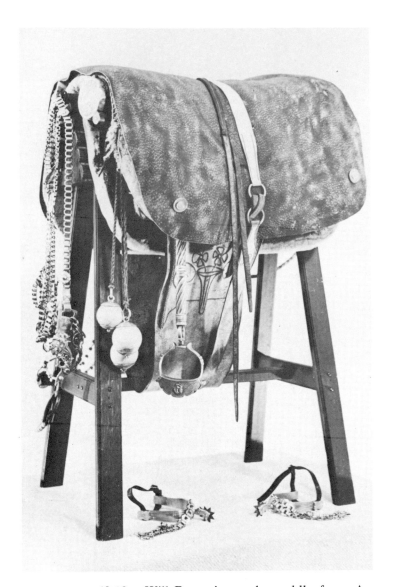

FIG. 40.18. Will Rogers's gaucho saddle from Argentina, home of the best-known cowboys of South America. This silver-mounted saddle is built on a light tree made of two bundles of reeds. The heavy wool padding is held in place with conchas. The silver stirrups are attached to silver instead of leather rods and are so small that the rider who used this saddle must have been a "toe rider." He did not thrust his feet deep into the stirrups but rested them lightly, a posture giving him a graceful seat in the saddle. Courtesy of Will Rogers Memorial Museum.

FIG. 40.19. Mongolian saddle purchased by Will Rogers when he was in Manchuria in 1931. It is perhaps the most unusual one in his collection. The saddle is double-rigged with woven-wool cinches about two inches wide trimmed in blue and white. Note the high fork and short stirrups. The saddle, matching martingale, bridle, and stirrups are ornately decorated with inlaid cloisonné pieces in bright colors. The workmanship on the saddle and blanket is an outstanding example of handicraft. Courtesy of Will Rogers Memorial Museum.

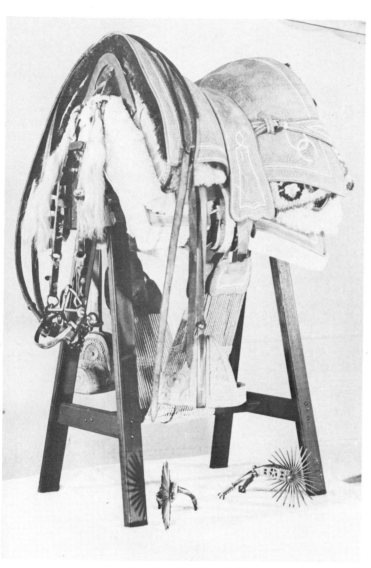

FIG. 40.20. Will Rogers's Chilean saddle, much like the one used by the gauchos in Argentina. The tree is built up to an iron fork, and the cantle is small. Layers of wool padding topped by the handsome leather give comfort to the rider. The carved-wood stirrups with closed toes were probably copied from the earlier Spanish type of engraved metal and are counterparts of today's leather tapadero stirrup coverings. Courtesy of Will Rogers Memorial Museum.

FIG. 40.21. Will Rogers's Venezuelan rawhide saddle. This type of saddle is used in heavy brush country on small ponies or burros. The wide skirts protect the animal and the rider. Courtesy of Will Rogers Memorial Museum.

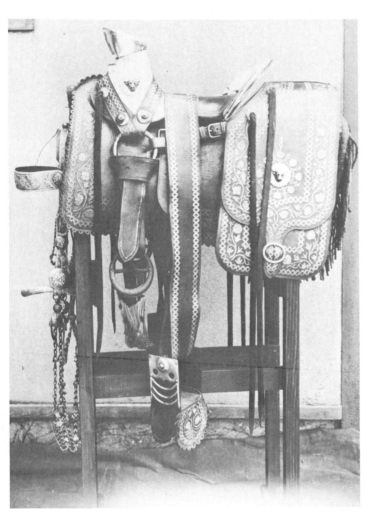

FIG. 40.22. Charro saddle bought in Guadalajara by Edward Larocque Tinker while he was traveling in Pancho Villa's private railroad car at the time of the Battle of Celaya. Courtesy of Will Rogers Memorial Museum.

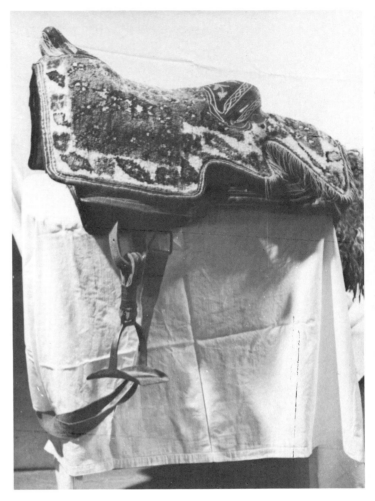

FIG. 40.23A. Turkish saddle made in the mid-1920s. This beautiful saddle, in the author's collection, is stitched with fine copper wire. The Persian rug covering was woven to fit the saddle exactly. It has maroon fringe on the backside. The brass stirrups are hand-hammered.

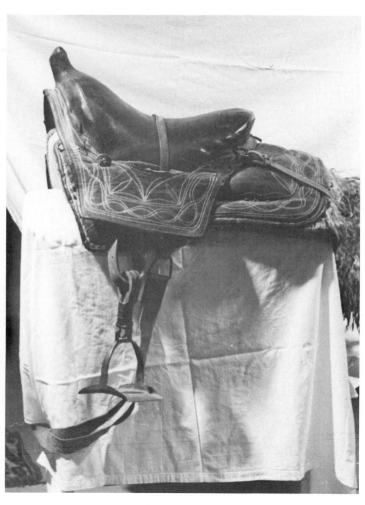

FIG. 40.23*B*.   Turkish saddle shown in FIG. 40.23*A* with rug covering removed.

FIG. 40.24.   Saddle presented to Yakima Canutt in 1923 by the Union Pacific Railway System (note the silver-trim emblems on the skirts and tapaderos). Canutt earned the saddle by winning the World's Championship Bucking Contest at the Pendleton (Oregon) Roundup. Made by Hamley and Company, the saddle was valued then at $350. From Hamley's, catalog no. 25, 1924.

Yakima Canutt went on to become legendary in stunt work in Hollywood. He doubled for most of the famous western stars and developed the "stage-coach drag," in which he dropped to the ground between the wheelhorses and then grabbed the back of the stagecoach as it rolled over him to pull himself up and overcome the "bad guys." The great chariot race in the film *Ben Hur* was also one of his projects. During the film his son followed in his footsteps, doubling for the hero, played by Charleton Heston.

337

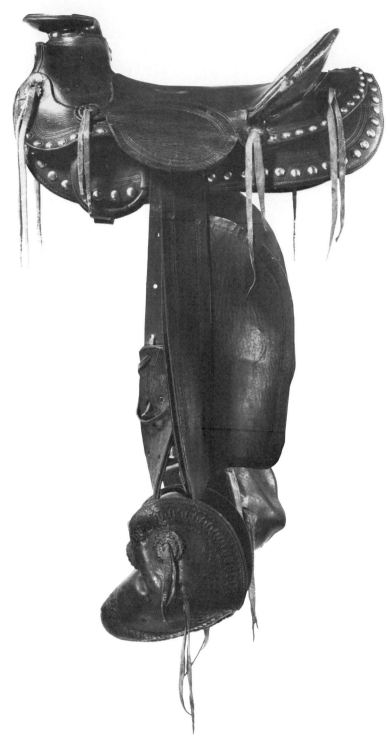

FIG. 40.25.   Saddle used on the 101 Ranch. Courtesy of National Cowboy Hall of Fame Collection.

Saddles Cast in Bronze

Paul A. Rossi, the noted sculptor-historian of Woodland Park, Colorado, has created with consummate craftmanship twelve saddle miniatures in bronze. Only twenty-five sets of these miniatures are in existence. The proud possessors of one of the sets are Bartlett F. and Nancy Crawford, of the Southern Valley (Arabian) Farms, Tulsa, Oklahoma, whose set is pictured here. These miniature bronzes were cast by the Graves Art Foundry of Woodland Park, Colorado. The photographs were made by Crawford.

Rossi was formerly director of the Thomas Gilcrease Institute of American History and Art, Tulsa, Oklahoma. An authority on western art and frontier military history, he has many paintings, sculptures, and publications to his credit.

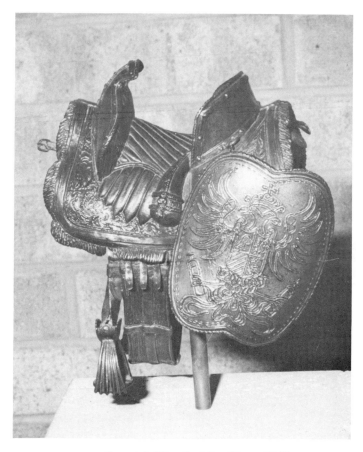

Spanish War Saddle, Circa 1540.

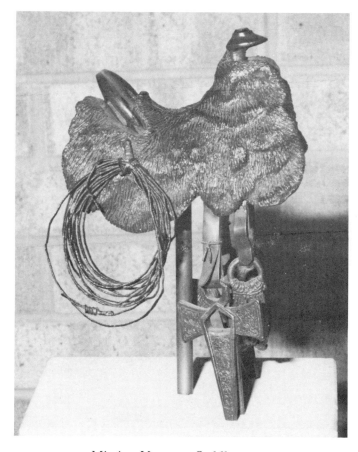

Mission Vaquero Saddle.

FIG. 41.1. "Great Saddles of the West." Miniature saddles depicting the development and history of the West, cast in bronze by Paul A. Rossi, sculptor-historian of Woodland Park, Colorado. Reproduced courtesy of Paul A. Rossi and of Bartlett F. Crawford and Nancy Crawford, owners of the set shown on pages 339 to 344. Photographs by Bartlett F. Crawford.

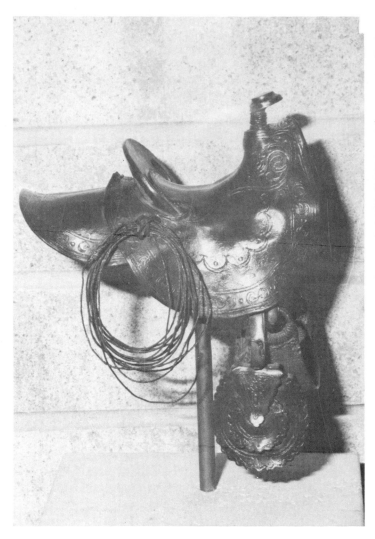

Cheyenne Indian Saddle, Circa 1820.

California Ranchero Saddle, Circa 1830.

340

Santa Fe (Mountain Man's) Saddle.

Texas Stock Saddle.

Mother Hubbard Saddle.   *Great Plains Stock Saddle, Circa 1880 or 1885.*

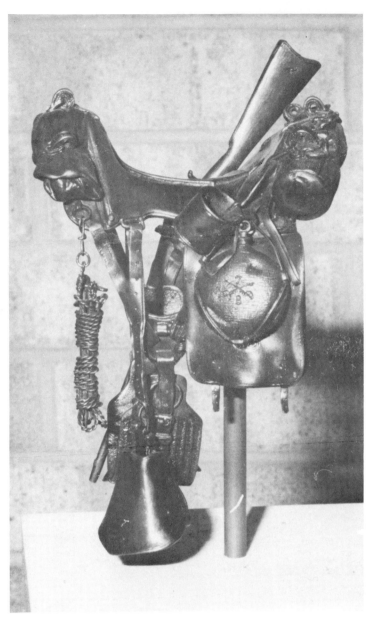

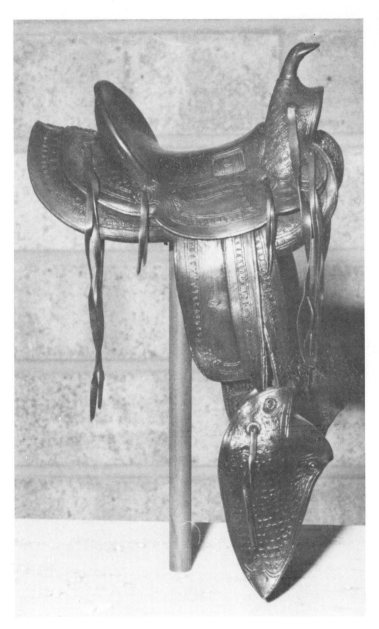

McClellan Cavalry Saddle, Circa 1885.

California Classic Stock Saddle, Circa 1890 or 1900.

343

Woman's Side Saddle, Circa 1895.

Stock Saddle, Swell Fork, Circa 1910.

Appendix

Early Saddlemakers

The information in this section has been compiled from many sources, chief of which are the many articles by Lee M. Rice that appeared over the years in *Western Horseman.*

The listing is not complete. There were hundreds of good itinerant saddlemakers whose names are forever lost to us. Modern-day saddle manufacturers founded in early days are included. Those listed without dates are included because they are mentioned in the literature. No other information is available about them.

The dates given are as accurate as I can make them with the sources at hand, and some were established by interpolation.

ARIZONA

N(ewton) Porter Saddlery, Phoenix. Founded 1875 at Tharall, Texas; moved to Taylor, then Abilene, Texas; moved to Seattle, Washington, 1885, then to Phoenix, 1895.

CALIFORNIA

Arana Saddlery, San Luis Obispo. In business, 1883. G. S. Garcia apprenticed there.

Edward H. Bohlin, Hollywood, 1922–78. At one time in Cody, Wyoming.

W. Davis & Son, Bought by Keyston Brothers in 1917. Davis name dropped in 1927.

(G. S.) Garcia and Brewster, Santa Margarita. 1882–83. Garcia moved to Elko, Nevada.

Goldberg's Saddlery.

Walt Goldsmith Saddlery, San Francisco. Now in Novato. Learned about trees from Vernal Newton, apprenticed to Visalia Saddlery.

James Keyston, San Francisco. 1868–72. Also manufactured whips. Father, Samuel, was leather worker from England. See Keyston Brothers.

Keyston Brothers (James and William), San Francisco, 1872–.

Main & Winchester, San Francisco. 1849. Bought by Keyston Brothers, 1912. See also L. D. Stone.

Juan Martarel, Visalia. 1869–70. Started in Hornitos in 1860s. Joined Shuhan & Walker, 1870. See Shuhan & Walker.

Clarence J. Nelson, Sacramento. Sold to Goldberg's Saddlery about 1890.

Olsen (Al) Nolte Saddle Shop, Nolte learned trade in Main & Winchester.

T. Salazar. 1860–ca. 1890. Salazar had had a saddle shop in Hornitos.

(Henry Gust) Shuhan & (David E.) Walker, Visalia. 1870. Both partners had been with Main & Winchester. Shuhan bought out Walker in 1877. Walker bought out Shuhan in 1879. See D. E. Walker.

(Rockwell) Stone & (Peter) Hayden. In business, 1877. Lucius D. Stone was a salesman for them in 1881.

Clarence Stone, Sacramento. 1873–?

Lucius D. Stone & Co., San Francisco. 1852. Consolidated with Main & Winchester in 1905, becoming Main, Winchester & Stone. Sold out to Keyston in 1911.

H. Thornwaldsen, Fresno. 1898–1912.

Van Voorhies, Sacramento from early days. Ceased making saddles a few years ago. Had previously been with T. Salazar. Tony Ladesma worked for this shop.

Visalia Stock Saddle Co. 1902–. Still in business. Edmund Walker Weeks inherited D. E. Walker's share and bought Henry Wegner's from his widow. Sold to Kenway (Canada) in 1958.

Wade & Co., Visalia. In business in the 1880s.

D(avid) E. Walker, Visalia. 1877–87. Opened shop with partner Wade, in San Francisco. See Walker & Wade.

(D. E.) Walker & Wade, San Francisco. 1887–92. Wade sold interest to Henry Wegner. See Walker and Wegner.

(D. E.) Walker & (Henry) Wegner, Visalia. 1892–ca. 1902. Edmund Walker Weeks, D. E. Walker's

nephew, had joined the firm. See Visalia Stock Saddle Co.

COLORADO

W. D. Allison, Montrose. Founded 1911. Allison learned trade in Fred Mantey's shop. Worked with Wyeth, Askew Brothers, Shipley, and K. C. Saddlery. In 1911 bought out M. E. French, who had been operator in Swope's shop after its purchase by French. In business in the early 1970s but no longer.

Peter Becker, Leadville. In business by late 1870s. Moved from Glenwood Springs (or was in Glenwood Springs with partner in 1882).

(Peter) Becker & Leonard. 1882–?

Ike Cherry, Durango. 1887–?

T(homas) Flynn Saddlery, Pueblo. 1892–1932. In 1880 at Silver Cliff, then at Trinidad.

R(obert) T(hompson) Frazier, Pueblo. 1876–1945. Robert Thompson Frazier was born in New Philadelphia, Ohio, October 3, 1850, and died in Pueblo, July 27, 1931. He fought in the Civil War. He learned saddlemaking under his father. He went to Leadville in the 1870s, where he had a saddle shop and was also deputy sheriff. He went to Durango, then to Pueblo. His first job in Pueblo was with the Gallup Saddlery. He married Katherine Henley in 1892. In 1881 he joined Gallup in a partnership and in 1898 bought out Gallup and Frazier, which became R. T. Frazier Saddlery. He was assisted by Earl Dunlap, who in 1931 was undersheriff in Pueblo. (The above information was obtained by Arthur Woodward in an interview with Mrs. Frazier in July, 1955, and from information in the *Pueblo Chieftain* of July 28, 1931. Woodward gave this information to Lou Cherbeneau on Feb. 28, 1975.)

E. L. Gallatin. Apprenticed under Thornton Grimsley, of pre–Civil War fame. He also worked with John Landis, of Missouri. See E. L. Gallatin & Co.

E. L. Gallatin & Co., Denver. 1860–63. It was Gallatin & Landis in 1863. Gallatin & Gallup started in 1863. See Gallup & Gallatin.

(John) Landis & F. Gallatin. 1859–63.

S. C(ollie) Gallup Saddlery Company, Denver. 1870; Pueblo, 1898–ca. 1924. Bankrupted by flood.

Gallup & Frazier, Pueblo. 1870–98. See R. T. Frazier.

(Francis) Gallup & (E. L.) Gallatin, Denver and Cheyenne. 1865–73. Gallatin sold out to Gallup. See Gallup. Francis was a brother of S. C. Gallup.

George Hamburger Saddle Co., Denver. 1880–?

Charles Hammond, Delta. 1885 (or 1884)–1900. Sold to George Wilson, who operated it until 1910.

Hartkey & Sheets. 1889–91. Sold to John Daugan. See W. R. Thompson.

H(erman) H. Heiser, Denver. Established, 1858, in Central City. Moved to Denver. Bought by Keyston, 1950.

Barney Johns, Denver, 1924–? Worked in Meanea's shop, 1884–1924. He was a nephew of Frank Meanea.

Fred Mantey, Grand Junction. 1885–? W. D. Allison learned trade from Mantey.

Theodore E. Meanea, Denver. Brother of Frank Meanea. Made saddletrees in 1870s and 1880s. Shop acquired by Henry Ruwart, Sr., in 1913.

Blake Miller, Denver. Moved to Denver from Cheyenne in 1927.

Fred Mueller, Inc., Denver. 1891–1960s.

C. H. Nelson, Grand Junction(?). 1920s–early 1930s.

Ruwart Saddle Tree Co., Denver. 1913–68.

O. J. Snyder, Denver. Early 1900s–1930.

Charles Swope, Montrose. 1883–1911. Sold to M. E. French, who sold to W. D. Allison in 1911. See Allison.

W. R. Thompson, Rifle. 1888–1931. Learned trade with Becker & Leonard. Sold to John Daugan, 1916. Ed C. Webb bought from Daugan, 1931, and operated, 1931–41.

E. Wagoner, Hayden.

Wells Saddlery, Denver.

Western Saddle Manufacturing Co., Denver. Orville L. ("Doc") Ostrander bought the J. H. Wilson Saddle Co. in 1920 (or 1921) and changed the name. Produced fine saddles for many years.

Wilson Saddlery, Denver. ?–1920. See Western Saddle Manufacturing Co.

CONNECTICUT

Smith-Worthington Saddlery Co., 287 Homestead Ave., Hartford. Established 1794.

GEORGIA

Bona Allen, Buford. 1873. Still in business at this writing.

IDAHO

Bannock Saddle Co., Pocatello.

ILLINOIS

(Eli A.) Collins & Grant, Galena. Collins was the father of John S. and George H. Collins. Started business with sons in Nebraska, 1864. See Nebraska.

INDIANA

Ben Schroeder Saddle Tree Co., Madison. 1850. In business in 1931.

KANSAS

Coad Saddlery (Clifford P. Coad), Cawker City. Still in business at this writing.
Adolph Roenigk, Lincoln.

MARYLAND

Walter H. Jenifer, Baltimore. Designed Jenifer saddle for the army in 1860.

MISSOURI

Paul Askew. 1868(?)–ca. 1890. See Askew Brothers Saddlery.
Askew Bros. Saddlery, Kansas City. Ca. 1890–ca. 1910. Reorganized as Kansas City Saddlery, ca. 1900.
John Chandler & Co. 1812–?
Thornton Grimsley, St. Louis. It was Grimsley & Stark in 1820, then Grimsley alone in 1825, then Grimsley & Spaulding in 1835. The Grimsley saddle was accepted by the U.S. Army in 1848. Grimsley made both military and domestic saddles.
John Jacoby. 1816–?
Israel Landis, St. Joseph. 1844–? (not listed in 1873 directory).
John C. Landis, St. Joseph. 1860–? Son of Israel Landis.
Charles P. Shipley Saddlery, Kansas City. 1884–1967.
J. B. Sickles Saddler, St. Louis. 1834–? Sold business in 1972; however, had not made saddles for a few years.
J. S. Sullivan Saddle Tree Co., Jefferson City. Their Catalog no. 16 was issued in 1912. They called themselves "the Largest Manufacturer of Saddle Trees in the World." Many of the trees have wide-swell forks, 14–17 inches wide, with small horns and slots in the sidebars for attaching the stirrup leathers.

Veatch's (Monroe) Saddlery Co., Trenton. 1919–present.
Wyeth (Saddlery and) Hardware, St. Joseph. 1859–1954, when quit manufacturing saddles. Still in business.

MONTANA

Ario & Moreland, Great Falls. 1897–1903.
Victor Ario Saddlery, Great Falls. 1903–?
Charles E. Coggshall Saddlery, Miles City. 1893–1909. Coggshall worked for Furstnow, then bought out Moran.
John S. Collins (Branch of Omaha), Billings. 1883–98.
Connolly Brothers (Jack, Andy, and Pat), Butte. 1907–? Andy was left in charge in 1912. Jack and Pat operated saddlery in Billings, 1912–29.
Connolly Saddlery Co., Billings. 1950–.
Jack Connolly Saddlery, Livingston. 1929–46. Sold to Miles City Saddlery.
Pat Connolly Saddlery, Billings. 1929–50.
Al Furstnow, Miles City. 1884–. Furstnow had worked for Goettlich.
E. Goettlich, Miles City. Early 1880s–1887. Bought by Al Furstnow.
Miles City Saddlery, Miles City. 1909–? In 1909, Coggshall sold out to three men: Clem Kathmann, his foreman; Frank Jelinek, a saddler from Forsyth, Mont.; and Bert Coleman. They formed Miles City Saddlery Co.
Hugh Moran, Miles City. ?–1893.
Robbins & Lenoir, Miles City. Early 1800s–?
J. B. Steffen Saddlery, Great Falls. ?–1897.

NEBRASKA

Collins Brothers (John S. and George H.) Saddlery, Omaha. 1864–96. See Collins & Morrison.
(John S.) Collins & Morrison, Omaha. 1890–1912. Wholesale only. See Alfred Cornish.
Alfred Cornish, Omaha. Successor to Collins & Morrison. 1896–? He bought retail business of Collins Brothers and later bought Collins & Morrison.

NEVADA

Books & Butler, Reno.
Goldberg & Stanton, Winnemucca.
G(uadalupe) S. Garcia, Elko. 1896–1940. His first shop was in Santa Margarita, Calif., with a partner.

OHIO

Strecker Brothers (Charles F. & Benjamin F.) Co., Marietta. 1884–1970.

OKLAHOMA

Hughes-Bozarth-Anderson, Oklahoma City. 1911–?
T. M. Lumley, Cushing.

OREGON

Andy Connolly Saddlery, Klamath Falls.
J. P. Cullen, John Day.
T. W. Farrell, Ellensburg. In business in 1892. Ellensburg tree invented by him.
Hamley & Company, Pendleton. Ashton, S.Dak. 1883–90; Kendrich, Idaho, 1890–1904; Pendleton, Oreg., 1905–present. Operated today by David Hamley.
George Lawrence Co., Portland. Founded by Samuel Sherlock, 1857. Lawrence, Sherlock's brother-in-law, joined him in 1874. Sherlock died in 1876. In 1893 business was reorganized and named George Lawrence Co.
Victor Marden, The Dalles. 1890–?
George Noble, Sr. Began making saddles, 1865. Moved to Heppner, opened shop, 1886.
Noble Brothers (George & Eugene), Heppner.
Noble, Horner, Herrington, Heppner. 1886–? George, Sr., opened shop. Sons Eugene and George worked with him.

PENNSYLVANIA

James Walker, Philadelphia. Manufactured military saddles in 1812.

SOUTH DAKOTA

Peter Duhamel, Rapid City. In business in 1921.
Emmett C. Lee Company, Pierre. In business in 1921.
J. E. Streeter, Buffalo Gap. In business in 1921.

TEXAS

C. C. Blandford, Colorado. In business in 1887.
Edelbrock & Dougherty (Joe B.). In business in 1882.
Joe Edelbrock & Sons, Forth Worth. 1876–1944. Don Ryan took over in 1944.
J. C. Higgins. Manufactured saddles for Sears Roebuck & Co.
Leddy Brothers (Frank, Silas, and O. C.), Fort Worth. 1941–?
M. L. Leddy Boot Shop, Brady, to San Angelo. 1922–?
S(amuel) D(ale) Myres, Sweetwater. Founded in 1881. In Sweetwater, 1893. Moved to El Paso, 1920.
Padgitt Brothers Co. (Jesse D. and W. C.), Dallas. 1869–?
Tom Padgitt & Co., Waco. 1867–? Started in Bryan, moved several times, finally settling in Waco. Padgitt died in 1926.
N. Porter, Taylor. 1875–95. In Phoenix, 1895–. See under Arizona.
Rice & Childress, San Antonio. In business in 1857. Made Hope military saddles for U.S. Army.
O. J. Schneider Saddle Co., Wichita Falls.
(G. H.) Schoellkopf Company, Dallas. 1869–. Ceased making saddles in 1970. Bought by Tandy Corporation.
Stelzig Saddlery, Houston. 1887–.
Robert F. Tackaberry, Fort Worth. In business in 1882.

UTAH

Cornish & Walton Saddlery, Ogden. In business in 1872. See Hodgman Saddlery.
Hodgman Saddlery, Ogden. ?–1883. Succeeded Cornish & Walton in late 1870s. See J. C. Read Brothers Co.
J. W. Jenkins, Salt Lake City. 1855–90.
J. W. Jenkins & Sons (J. W. II, S. J., and C. H.). 1890–? (still in business in 1948).
Newton Brothers Saddlery, Vernal.
J. C. Read Brothers Co., Ogden. Succeeded Hodgman Saddlery. 1883–?

VIRGINIA

B. T. Crump Co., Richmond. 1875–. In business in 1980.

WASHINGTON

T. W. Farrell Saddlery, Ellensburg. 1892–?

WISCONSIN

Hamley, William, Ripon. Founded ca. 1856. Father founder of Hamley & Company. See Hamley & Company under Oregon.
Young, Benjamin, Milwaukee. Sold to a Mr. Campbell before 1906.

WYOMING

John S. Collins, Cheyenne (branch office of Omaha firm). 1874–96.

Otto F. Ernst, Inc., Sheridan. 1921–.

Gallatin & Gallup, Cheyenne (branch office of Denver firm). Sold out to Frank A. Meanea, who was Gallatin's nephew. See Frank A. Meanea. Meanea had managed this shop from its start, when he was nineteen.

Robert (Bobbie) Gardner, Laramie. 1880–? Listed as harness maker.

J. T. Irick, Casper.

Knox & Tanner, Rawlins. 1905–33.

Laramie Grocery Co., Laramie. 1900–50.

Laramie Saddlery Co. (Joseph Lohlein and Gus N. Sigwart), Laramie. In business, 1892–1908.

Frank A. Meanea, Cheyenne. 1873–1928, when Frank died. Shop given to Tom Cobry, who later closed it.

Blake Miller, Cheyenne. 1915–26. Moved to Denver, 1927. Learned saddlemaking in Meanea's shop.

LOCATION UNKNOWN

Daniel Campbell. Around 1855 patented a military saddle.

CANADA

Alberta:

(Felmar) Eamor's Leather Works, High River. Bought out C. B. Mills. 1942–?

Lower's Saddlery. 1903–?

C. B. Mills Saddle Shop. ?–1942.

Calgary:

Kenway Saddle & Leather Co. (Kenneth R. Coppock). ?–present. Bought Visalia Stock Saddle Co. in 1958.

Riley & McCormick, Ltd. 1901. In business, 1940.

Glossary of Saddle and Horse Terms

A fork (slick fork): A narrow saddle fork with no swell, shaped like the letter A, peaking at the base of the horn.

A la brida: A style of riding using long stirrup leathers. The legs are kept straight and somewhat forward. Term used when referring to light cavalry.

A la estradiota: A style of riding using essentially the same riding position as *a la brida.* Term used when referring to heavily armored knights.

A la jineta: A style of riding with rather short stirrup leathers, the knees bent, and the stirrup nearly under the rider, similar to the style of a jockey.

All the way home: See *home.*

Anquera: "A rumble seat" or "mother-in-law's seat" attached to the back skirt of a Mexican saddle, enabling a passenger to ride double.

Applehorn: An almost round horn cap the size of a small hen's egg.

Appointments: Equipment and clothing used in show riding.

Association saddle (Committee saddle): The standard saddle design approved in 1919 by the management of four large western rodeos in a meeting at Hamley & Company in Pendleton, Oregon, for use by all bucking-horse riders. Its use eliminated the various "freak" saddles ridden earlier.

Astride, riding: Riding with one leg on each side of the horse.

Back, horse's: The flat backbone area of a horse between the withers and the loin. Technically, the area from the ninth or eleventh vertebra including the eighteenth dorsal vertebra.

Back bulge (swell): A fork with a puffed-out shape on its backside, designed in an attempt to make a popular bronc-riding saddle.

Back jockey (back housing or rear jockey): Leather flaps that cover and protect the fans of the tree bars from the back of the cantle to the rear of the bars.

Barrel: A cross section of the horse about the middle of the back, below the backbone and behind the withers, that resembles the cross section of a barrel.

Bar risers: Strips of wood or leather placed on top of the bars behind the fork to shape the contour of the seat.

Bars, saddletree (sidebars or sideboards): Two long horizontal tree bars that rest on the back of the horse, one on each side of the spine, supporting and anchoring the fork and cantle.

Bead, cantle and fork: See *cantle binding.*

Bear-trap saddle: A short-seated, wide-swelled saddle with a high cantle. A true bear-trap saddle has the wide-swelled fork V'd backward from the center. It is excellent for bronc busting but dangerous if a horse falls because it is almost impossible for the rider to get out of it.

Beef hide: Secondary grade of rawhide tree covering. See *rawhide.*

Belly: The soft underneath side of the horse's barrel behind the rib cage.

Billet, cinch (tug): A short leather cinch strap that attaches to the rigging device or skirt slots on the off side of the saddle and to the cinch. It is used only with a buckle-type cinch, both front and rear. It is also used on the near side on the rear rigging ring.

Binding: See *cantle* and *fork.*

Blanket: Any padding or blanket placed between the horse and the saddle to ease the pressure of the saddletree bars on the horse and also to absorb perspiration and prevent it from getting on the saddle. A blanket (as opposed to a pad) may be refolded in various ways on long rides to lessen pressure on sore spots on the horse's back.

Blind-stitched: See *seam.*

Border-stamped saddle: A saddle with the full edge trim stamped with a design, or often just the corner of the fenders and skirts.

Breast collar (breast harness or breast strap): A leather strap going around the shoulder point of the horse, attaching at each end to the rigging rings, small D rings, or slots on the front of the saddle skirt. It may also have a D in the middle for attaching a tiedown strap to the noseband and the breast collar to the cinch between the front legs. It prevents the saddle from moving backward during roping or climbing. It is also necessary with many mutton-withered horses. The English term for breast collar is *breastplate*.

Breeching (breech strap): A leather strap that passes around the breech (buttocks) of a horse to prevent the saddle from slipping forward. It is seldom used today except in packing.

Bronc-busting saddle: A loose designation for any wide-swell, high-backed, short-seated saddle designed to keep the rider in the saddle on a gyrating bronc.

Bucking roll (saddle roll): A roll made with a slicker, blanket, etc., attached to the back of the fork to help wedge in the rider and make it harder for the horse to buck him off.

Buckle guard: A protective leather covering over a buckle on one or both sides. See *safe, chape*.

Buckstitch: A contrasting thong of leather or vinyl, usually white, woven in and out of a piece of leather for decoration or to bind the leather together.

Buck strap: A leather loop attached to the saddle horn or around the fork to provide a handhold when riding a bucking horse. Used only by a novice. Also called *fraidy strap*.

Bulge (on fork): The swell formed when the outer edges of the fork *curve back* to the bar. See *swell*.

Bulldog tapadero: A short tapadero closed at the bottom.

Bull hide: The best grade of rawhide tree covering. See *rawhide*.

Bur: The part of the bar that extends forward in front of the fork.

California saddle: A saddle, developed in the late 1800s, characterized by rounded skirts, long tapaderos, and a small horn.

California skirts: Round skirts, so called because of their popularity in California.

Cantle (hindbow): The up-curved back of a saddle. The rear, scooped-out section of the saddletree, separate from and attached to the bars. It determines the depth of the seat and the amount of back support.

Cantle binding: Rolled leather "bead-stitched" over the perimeter of the cantle. It can be narrow,

round, and upright (bead) or wide and flattened, as in the Cheyenne-roll style.

Cantle drop: The outside of the back of the cantle.

Cantle rider: One who rides pressing against the cantle because of badly slanted seat or stirrups too far forward. Also called *dashboarder*.

Cantle roll: A long welt protruding a third of an inch or more from the front face of the cantle just under its top rim. Designed to prevent the rider from sliding backward out of the saddle or from moving skyward when riding a bucking horse.

Carleitas: A solid-color (generally white) wool Mexican blanket used as a saddle blanket, similar to a Navajo blanket.

Castile soap: Fine, hard soap made from olive oil and caustic soda.

Center-bar cinch ring: A cinch ring with a bar across the center to which the buckle tongue is attached.

Centerfire (California rig, single rig, single-fire rig, or single-barreled rig): A western saddle with a single rigging ring suspended halfway between the fork and the cantle on each side.

Chape (cavalry): A leather plate which attaches the metal cinch-strap ring of a McClellan saddle to the *safe*.

Chape (Western): A covering or pocket that encloses the cinch ring to prevent it from galling the horse.

Channel (slot or chamber): The long, narrow area between the bars of the tree. It was uncovered on the McClellan saddle but in the stock saddle is usually covered with the seat leather and a metal plate. It allows some air to circulate above the horse's spine.

Channel keeper (tunnel keeper): A stationary keeper, 3 or more inches long, used on a flank cinch to keep the flank billets from flapping and ropes from catching on the loose billet.

Charro saddle: A "gentleman rider's" ornate Mexican saddle. Many such saddles are used in parades and shows.

Chest, horse's: The part of the horse between and in front of the upper portion of the horse's front legs, behind the base of the neck.

Cheyenne roll: A wide, flat, backward extension of the cantle binding. It was strictly ornamental and was added to saddles by Frank Meanea in his Miles City, Montana, saddlery in the early 1870s. It is almost universally on saddles today. See *cantle binding*.

Cheyenne saddle: See *Texas Trail saddle.*

Cinch (cincha or girth): A wide band, usually more than 22 inches long, made of parallel strands of cotton, mohair, or tough webbing material, and in some cases of folded leather, that goes underneath the horse from the off side to the near side. Its purpose is to hold the saddle firmly on the horse. In western equipment it has a large ring at each end, sometimes with a buckle tongue. In English tack it is equipped with buckles and is almost double the length of the western cinch. It is tightened from the rigging D on the near side of the horse so that it fits firmly around the horse's belly. The flank cinch is equipped with buckles for attaching it to the billet on each side of the saddle. The use of the word *girth* is incorrect in referring to the western saddle (the Texans pronounce it "girt").

Cinch connector strap (cinch hobble): The strap connecting the center of the front cinch to the center of the flank cinch on the horse's belly, to give stability of position to the flank cinch and to keep it from sliding back and causing the horse discomfort, which could induce bucking.

Cinch crossbar (cinch bar): The band crosswise of the center of the cinch whose purpose is to hold the strands together and keep the cinch straight.

Cinched up: Said of a horse with the cinch properly tightened so that the saddle is secured to the horse. One should be able to get three or four fingers between the cinch and the horse's belly or ribs.

Cinch hitch (cinch tie, necktie knot, or buntline hitch): A hitch made on the rigging ring when the cinch has no buckle tongue in its end ring on the near side. It is made the same as the Windsor knot in a man's tie—a four-in-hand knot.

Cinch-ring leathers (cinch-ring protector, chape, guard, or rub guard): A piece of leather covering the back of the cinch ring to prevent the ring from galling the horse. There may also be a cover over half the front on a center-bar cinch ring. See *chape.*

Cinch strap (latigo or tie strap): The leather strap used to hold the saddle in place. It is 6 feet long and 1, 1 1/2, or 2 inches wide, attached permanently to the bottom of the rigging ring on the near side. The other, loose, end goes through the cinch ring and back through the rigging ring and ties at the lower part of the rigging ring. It is usually made of a special tan of cowhide called *latigo,* but is also made of skirting leather.

Cinch strap, off-side: A complete cinch strap attached to the off-side rigging ring that is the same as the one on the near side. It is different from the *off strap.*

Cinch-strap hitch: See *cinch hitch.*

Cinch-strap holder: A small, bell-shaped leather flap slotted at the bottom, usually near the base of the fork or cantle, used only to hold the long free end of the cinch strap when the saddle is cinched up with a cinch-ring buckle. It is not used when the saddle is cinched up with a cinch-strap hitch.

Cinchy: Said of a horse that is touchy when being cinched up and bites or kicks.

Cold-backed: Said of a horse that tends to hump his back when a saddle is placed on him or to buck after he is first mounted.

Collect: To bring a horse into complete balance between the hands and legs by the use of rein aids and leg cues.

Committee saddle: See *Association saddle.*

Concha: A silver or other metal coin-size decorative piece with two slots or a screw base placed on top of the rosette or rosettes through which the saddle strings are passed and tied (slit braid), holding the skirts and jockeys to the saddletree.

Connector, back jockey: A leather plate sewed to and on top of the back jockeys to connect them.

Connector strap, rigging ring: The strap that connects the front and rear rigging rings just under the skirts. It adds stability and strength to the rigging assembly when the horse is in action.

Corona blanket: A saddle pad cut to fit the shape of the saddle skirt with a large roll around the edge, usually two-colored.

Corus rig (corse): A rig with leather completely covering the rawhide covering of the tree—a *mochila* covering. Originally it was made in two pieces laced together with a slot for the cantle and buckled or laced in front of the horn.

Cross saddle: Any saddle ridden astride, with the legs across the horse, as distinguished from *side-saddle.*

Crupper: A leather strap attached to the rear of the saddle, extending to the horse's tail. A round leather at the posterior end circles underneath the horse's dock (the bony part of the tail) to prevent the saddle from sliding forward. It is now being used only by mule riders and on pack rigs.

Cutting saddle: A saddle with a flat seat or a seat built up with an upright cantle. It often features a built-up front to give the rider a secure seat during the quick movements and quick reverses made by a well-trained cutting horse.

Dally horn: A type of horn used by the *dally (dally welta* or *dale welta)* ropers. There must be enough room (height) on the horn's neck for the lariat to be wrapped around it counterclockwise one or two times so that the dally roper can play out his lariat to absorb the shock when the roped animal reaches the end of the rope. To secure the rope, a clove hitch is made.

Dinner plate: Large, round, flat horn cap on a Mexican saddle, often several inches in diameter.

Dish: The degree of horizontal rounding of the cantle to conform to the rider's outline. A *deep-dished* cantle is a well-rounded, scooped cantle.

Doghouse stirrup: The old, wide, bent wooden stirrup, so called because "it had enough wood in it to build a doghouse."

Double-rigged (double-fire or double-barreled saddle): A saddle with two cinches, full-rigged with one rigging ring directly below the fork and one directly below the cantle. Double rigs may also be 7/8-rigged or 3/4-rigged. The 5/8 and center-fire rigs are not doubled. The old Spanish rig had only one rigging ring beneath and a little in front of the fork. It was single-rigged.

Dressage: The French term for the training of horses (and dogs), the purpose of which, according to the Fédération Equestre Internationale is "to make an animal keen and obedient." There are three stages of dressage: elementary, secondary (medium), and superior (advanced).

D ring (dee ring): A D-shaped metal ring. Large rings are usually used as rigging rings; small rings are used in breast collars, on the concha tie for snapping on a rifle scabbard or quirt, and on both sides of the center of the cinch.

Dutchman: See *sudadero.*

Ears: The circular pieces at the corners of the seat and the jockeys through which the saddle strings are passed. The purpose of the ears is for anchorage.

Eight-string-seat: A saddle with a front jockey separate from the side jockey requiring four saddle strings on each side to anchor all the leather parts, instead of the three or less customarily used today.

Elephant-eared Cheyenne roll (squaw cheeks): A Cheyenne roll with enlarged ends where the cantle attaches to the bar.

Ellensburg tree: The basic saddletree modified to become the official bucking-contest tree.

English saddle (flat saddle): A saddle distinguished from a western (stock) saddle by its small, flat shape; absence of skirt and horn; and large, rounded fenders, or flaps. It features a single wide cinch (called a *girth*), usually made of leather or canvas, and light, open steel stirrups.

Ephippium: A Greek saddle-pad-type saddle.

Equine: Of or pertaining to a horse.

Equus caballus: The scientific name of the horse.

Escutcheon (cavalry): A slotted brass plate covering the mortise (slot) on a McClellan saddle.

Fan: The part of the sidebar that extends backward behind the cantle.

Far side: See *off side.*

Fender (seat leather, sweat flap or rosadero): The part of a saddle attached on each side to the stirrup leathers that protects the legs of the rider from the horse's body and the rigging. It may be one piece with the stirrup leathers. It also keeps the horse's sweat off the rider's legs. Sometimes incorrectly called *sudadero.*

Five-eighths-rigged: Said of a saddle rigged with the rigging ring halfway between the 3/4 and the centerfire position.

Flank: The area on the horse's body just in front of the upper part of the rear leg, usually very sensitive.

Flank cinch (rear cinch or rear girth): The back cinch on a double-rigged saddle, used to prevent the saddle from tipping up and flipping forward during roping.

Flank-cinch billet: A leather strap attached to each rear rigging ring to which the buckles on the ends of the flank cinch are buckled.

Flap, saddle (English): A large, flat piece of leather placed under the rider's legs to increase grip and prevent the horse's sweat from getting on the rider. It corresponds to the fender on a western saddle.

Flare (of bar): The contour of the bar as it follows the contour of the horse's back. The angle (across the back of the bar) difference between the front and the back of the bar is a measurement of the amount of twist (or flare), called the *twist angle.*

Flat saddle (postage stamp, pimple, or kidney pad): Slang for *English saddle.*

Forebow: See *fork.*

Forehand: The front legs, chest, shoulders, and head of a horse.

Fork (forebow): The front, vertical portion of the saddletree that is dovetailed and grooved into connection with the two bars. The swell provides a contact position for the lower thighs of the rider not experienced with the A fork. It supports the horn for roping and mounting. It was so named because riders who made their own saddles used a forked branch from a tree or a forked antler. The term *pommel* should be used only in reference to an English saddle, not to a western saddle.

Fork binding (gullet roll): Roll binding that ties together the fork cover and the gullet cover. If it is not used, the fork cover is pulled under the gullet in front and nailed with tacks.

Form-Fitter Saddle: A bronc-riding saddle with the outside lower rear part of the fork cut out to conform to the rider's thighs. The name was copyrighted in 1929 by Hamley & Company, Pendleton, Oregon.

Forward-seat (balanced-seat) saddle: A saddle constructed so that the rider is able to move his body forward and backward to stay over the horse's center of gravity. It has a flat seat, stirrup leathers essentially underneath the horse's center of gravity, and fenders in the knee area that extend forward of the stirrup leathers, because the rider rides with fairly short stirrup leathers, causing the knees to bend slightly.

Four-string seat: A seat that has no saddle strings at the base of the fork or the base of the cantle but instead has a screw-and-ferrule or a screw-and-concha arrangement.

Front-horn rigging strap, back-fork rigging strap (if there are two): A strap that circles the horn and attaches at the lower end to the front rigging ring. It is called the *Sam Stagg rigging.*

Full-extended seat: A seat entirely covered with leather.

Full-stamped saddle: A saddle covered with stamped designs.

Gelding smacker: Cowboy slang for *saddle.*

Girth: The measure of the circumference of a horse's body behind the withers (also called *heart girth):* 1. The only technically correct usage of the word *girth* when discussing western riding (pronounced "girt" by cowboys). 2. A leather, canvas, or corded piece around the belly of the horse to secure the saddle. See *cinch.* 3. The cinch of an English saddle.

Gourd horn: The standard wooden horn on a Mexican saddle, shaped much like a small gourd, flattened diagonally on one side.

Great saddle: A large, heavy saddle (weighing about 60 pounds), used for *manège* or riding-school work on great horses. It had a high, upright cantle; a large, protective fork; and a very narrow seat. It was well padded and was ridden *a la brida.*

Ground seat (ground work): Layers of leather on top of the tree between the tree and the seat, used to form the seat into the desired shape with the strainer.

Gullet: The opening through the fork and above the bars that sits over the horse's withers, including, underneath, the curved portion of the underside of the fork.

Gullet roll: See *fork binding.*

Gusset: See *seam.*

Halfbreed: An off cinch strap or billet doubled over through the cinch ring and then looped over the rigging ring or D and run back down and through the buckle ring inside to outside and buckled, as opposed to the permanently stitched or fastened near-side cinch strap.

Half-rigged saddle: A saddle with only a triangle of leather tacked to the tree for a seat.

Half-twist: A method of lacing the stirrup leathers together so that the stirrup automatically faces forward. The top stirrup leather is given a 180-degree turn to the right and then laced.

Halter squares: Brass rectangles at the lower sides of the bars on the McClellan saddle quarter strap.

Hand: A unit of measure used in giving the height of a horse. One hand equals four inches. The horse's height is measured vertically from the ground to the highest point (the sixth vertebra) of the withers. A horse 14.3 hands high would be 14 hands, 3 inches high (59 inches). It would be spoken "fourteen three."

Hand hole: The rear hole of the gullet on the back side of the fork. The seat may have a semicircle cut out of the front side to leave the hole more open. The hole is used as a handhold to pick up the saddle and to carry it.

Heart girth: See *girth.*

High-back saddle: An old-fashioned western saddle with a 5- or 6-inch-high cantle.

High-school horse: A highly trained horse, schooled

in specific maneuvers often based on dressage. It is ridden in extreme collection and is also known as a *trick horse.*

Hindbow: See *cantle.*

Hobble-strap: To hobble a horse or connect together the stirrups underneath the horse's belly for greater stability. The term should not be used for *stirrup leather keepers.* The term *cinch hobble strap* can refer to the strap between the front and rear cinches.

Home (homed): A term referring to the position of the rider's foot in the stirrup. When the foot of the rider's boot is in the stirrup so that the back of the stirrup tread is touching the front of the boot heel, the foot is said to be *home, homed,* or *all the way home* in the stirrup.

Horn (pommel): The knob on the upper side in the middle of a western saddle. The name was probably derived from antlers or horns used by Indians and mountain men for the forks of their "homemade" saddles. Horns were originally wooden; afterward came steel, brass, and nickel horns.

Horn cap (head): The enlarged top of the saddle horn. Its principal purpose is to keep the lariat from slipping off the top of the horn.

Horn neck: The thin neck between the horn cap and the saddle fork around which the lariat is wrapped by the dally roper or to which the lariat is tied by the "hard-and-fast-tie" roper.

Housing: See *jockey* and *mochila.*

Hull: Cowboy slang for *saddle.*

In-skirt rigging: Rigging in which the rigging rings, Ds or plates are anchored to the skirt, not the tree. This type of rigging has no rigging leathers.

Jockey (housing): The leather panel that covers and protects the exposed upper side of the bars and fits firmly against the cantle in the rear end, the fork in the front of the saddle, and the bars between the fork and the cantle, flat down on the skirt, protecting the connecting leather thongs (saddle strings) that hold the skirt in place.

Kak: Cowboy slang for *saddle.*

Keeper, free (loop): A piece of leather seamed together at the ends in the shape of a rectangle that encircles two or more straps of leather. Its purpose is to keep the straps together neatly and yet allow any movement necessary between them. It slides into the desired position. See also *stirrup leather keeper.*

Keeper, stationary: A keeper is stitched to one strap in a fixed position. The second strap is in-

serted through the stationary keeper and is held in place. See *channel keeper.*

Kidney pad: A cowboy's derisive term for an English saddle.

Kip: The undressed hide of a young steer, cow, or horse, the cheapest form of rawhide tree covering.

Laced seam: See *seam.*

Lace strings: See *saddle strings.*

Latigo: 1. A cinch strap. For the sake of uniformity and because *latigo* has several other meanings, the preferable term is *cinch strap.* 2. A Spanish word meaning literally "the end of every strap that must be passed through a buckle" (Adams, 1968). 3. A special kind of leather used for saddle strings. 4. A chemical tan. See also *cinch strap.*

Leaping horn: The lower horn on the near side of a sidesaddle.

Leather-hooded stirrup: A leather stirrup-cover panel extending around the front and sides of the stirrup and attached to the outer sides of the stirrup. It extends a maximum of 2 inches below the stirrup tread. It is used to protect the rider's boots from brush, grass, cold, etc. See also *tapadero.*

Leather roll binding: An early name for the *Cheyenne roll.*

Left-hand saddle: A saddle with the rope strap on the near side of the fork.

Leg roll (English): A padded roll on the forward side of the saddle flap on an English saddle and on some spring-seat saddles.

Light rider: A rider who rides not only in balance *on* the horse but in balance *with* the horse.

Loop seat: A full seat, common in the early 1900s, with squares or rectangles of leather cut out of the seat just over the area where the stirrup leathers fit over the tree in the stirrup-leather grooves. Changing stirrup leathers was easy on such a saddle. It also allowed easy application of neat's-foot oil to an area on the stirrup leather otherwise often neglected because of the difficulty in reaching it. The style was originated because of the stiffness of the stirrup leather of that day.

Martingale, standing: A strap running from the cinch between the front legs through the breast collar to the bridle noseband to prevent the horse from throwing its head too high.

Martingale, running: A Y-shaped strap with rings on the ends through which the reins pass. It is attached to the cinch in the same manner as the standing martingale.

Mexican saddle: A saddle characterized by a rawhide-covered tree with no leather covering except at the rear of the seat and slightly up the cantle; Spanish (single) rigging in the full-rigged position; ornate tapaderos; either a large, flat horn cap or a gourd horn for dallying; and small square skirts rounded on the corners and lined with felt.

Mochila (housing): An early one-piece removable leather covering that fitted over the saddletree and covered the entire saddle from in front of the horn to behind the cantle. It was put in place after the horse was saddled. It had cutouts through which the horn and cantle protruded. Also called *machere* or *macheer.*

Mortise (cavalry): A slot through the cantle or pommel of a McClellan saddle. Leather straps passed through the mortises were used to anchor the cavalryman's equipment.

Mother Hubbard saddle: A mochila-like covered saddle on which the mochila is permanently attached to the tree.

Muley saddle: A western saddle without a horn or with the horn removed.

Mutton-withered: Said of a horse with very low, round withers; a horse with very little bone definition at the withers.

Narrow fork: A fork whose sides do not extend outward beyond their outside attachment point to the bar.

Near (near side): The left side of the horse when the rider is seated; the side which a horse is customarily mounted.

Neat's-foot oil: Oil used to soften, condition, and preserve leather. Its continued use darkens the leather permanently. It consists of a pale-yellow fixed synovial oil made by boiling the feet, shinbones, and suet of neat (bovine) cattle. *Pure neat's-foot oil* (100 percent neat's-foot—no other oils added) is used for leather articles under heavy usage and those exposed to weather. *Prime neat's-foot oil* (oil after the first pressing) is used for softening and lubricating leather. *Neat's-foot-oil compound* is a blend of pure neat's-foot oil and leather-process oil (a petroleum-paraffin oil). Most compound neat's-foot oils are 10 to 20 percent pure neat's-foot oil with the remainder paraffin oil. This mixture is widely used to protect leather from drying and becoming brittle. Excessive use of neat's-foot-oil compound on saddles can cause deterioration of stitching.

Numnah (cavalry): A thick woolen or felt pad used under the saddle.

Off (off side or far side): 1. The right side of the horse when the rider is seated.

2. The side of the saddle opposite the mounting side of the horse.

Off billet: A billet on the off side of the horse. See *billet.* The opposite of *near billet,* which is the back (flank) billet on the near (left) side.

Off strap: A leather strap doubled over the off-side front rigging ring to which the cinch buckle is buckled; the front off billet.

On-tree rigging: A type of rigging in which the leathers are anchored to the saddletree, as opposed to *in-skirt rigging.*

Open stirrup: A stirrup with no leather hood or tapadero.

Oxbow stirrup: A wooden stirrup with the wood tread rounded so that the rider's foot has a grip at all angles.

Padded seat, inlaid: A seat on which the seat leather is cut out underneath the padded area and the pad covering at its joint is flush with the remaining portion of the seat. The padding rests on the ground seat.

Padded seat, overlaid: A seat on which the padding rests on the seat leather and the pad covering is stitched to the seat leather.

Pad saddle (bareback pad): A pad with stirrups and a cinch, used for exercising the horse. It is popular with young riders.

Panels (cavalry): Heavy coverings for the underneath side of the bars, made of felt, horsehair, etc. They replaced the blanket or saddle pad.

Panels (English): A cushion on the underneath surface of the bars. It gives clearance to the horse's backbone, between the horse's back and the saddletree.

Pelican horn: An early horn on which the top of the cap was flat and the underneath side was shaped like the lower jaw of a pelican's bill.

Pergamino: Parchment-thin leather rawhide used by Mexican saddlemakers for many years.

Pilch (cavalry): A loose seat covering.

Pillion: A small pad behind the saddle on which a second rider or pack is carried.

Pimple: A cowboy's derisive term for an English saddle.

Pique (cavalry): A high pommel arch.

Points (English): The part of the pommel arch on an English saddle that extends below the bars. Its purpose is to reduce rolling, or sideways movement of the saddle.

Split seam: See *seam.*

Spoon (cavalry): A spoon-shaped protrusion from the upper side of the cantle or pommel of a cavalry saddle. There is a slot in the center of the spoon, used to attach the crupper or equipment.

Spring-seat saddle (spring-bar saddle or ladies' astride saddle): A saddle with a heavily padded seat and a large, soft, round cantle bead and pommel roll.

Squaw roll: A large, soft, protective roll across the back of the fork on a western spring-seat saddle.

Staple pocket: A small leather pocket stitched to the back of the cantle.

Staples, foot (cavalry): Staples used on McClellan saddles to hold the 1 1/4-inch brass rings or as anchors for straps.

Steel fork: 1. A cast-steel fork with a steel horn on the top. 2. A wooden fork reinforced with a steel strap countersunk in the gullet and a steel horn on top bolted to the steel strap. 3. A reinforcing rod, approximately 5/16 to 3/8 inch in diameter, inserted in a hole drilled diagonally in the fork from the base of the horn to the bar. It had no tap on either end.

Stirrup: A foot support or footrest, one on each side, hanging down from the saddletree, used to support the rider laterally.

Stirrup, open: A stirrup without a front leather hood, shield, or tapadero.

Stirrup bolt (stirrup roller bar): A bolt through the upper part of the stirrup, used to suspend it from the stirrup leather; also known as *cross bar* at the upper end of the stirrup. It is the stirrup's point of suspension in the stirrup leather.

Stirrup-leather keeper: A narrow strap that holds the doubled stirrup leathers close together just above the stirrup.

Stirrup leathers: Long leather straps that support the stirrups. At the upper end each stirrup leather usually circles a notch in the tree bar.

Stirrup tread: See *tread.*

Stirrup wear leathers: A leather cover over the stirrup tread to reduce wear. It is laced or stitched on the underneath side of the tread.

Stock saddle: See *western saddle.*

Strainer: A thin piece of galvanized iron covering the sidebars in the seat area underneath the seat leather and on top of the bars. Its purpose is to cover the channel between the bars and the openings for the stirrup leathers and to prevent the seat from sagging in these areas.

Strainer leather: A piece of leather cut the same shape as the strainer and placed between the strainer and the tree.

Sudadero (Dutchman): The leather lining of the skirt; often improperly used to refer to the fender.

Surcingle (roller): A broad strap completely encircling the horse to hold the blanket or saddle in place. It goes over the saddle seat, as on a race saddle, not under it. A roller has two swells built in on the sides to discourage a horse from rolling when wearing a stable blanket. Often improperly used to refer to the cinch.

Sweat leather (sweat flap): See *fender.*

Swell (bulge): The portion of the fork that bulges on each side from a line perpendicular to the point where the fork attaches to the bars of the tree. Sometimes used interchangeably, but incorrectly, with *fork.* See *bulge.*

Tack: Items of saddlery and horse equipment.

Tack room: A storage room for tack.

Tapadero (tap or toe fender): A leather hoodlike cover over the front and sides of the stirrup, open at the back, to protect the booted foot in brush and high grass and against cold and wet. It also serves as a safety device to prevent the foot from sliding through the stirrup and getting hung up. It may be as long as 28 inches or as short as the bottom of the stirrup and is often named to describe the appearance of the outline: monkey face, hog snout, eagle bill, bulldog, etc.

Texas skirt: A square skirt so named because of its popularity in early-day Texas.

Texas Trail (Plains) saddle: A saddle popular around the 1880s to 1900. It was characterized by its 3/4 seat, high cantle with a roll, separate side jockey, eight-string seat, and full double rigging. It was rather lightweight and extremely comfortable. See also *three-quarter seat.*

Three-quarter rigging: Rigging in which the front rigging ring is placed halfway between the center-fire rig and the full double rig.

Three-quarter seat (solid or half-covered seat): A seat on which the leather extends forward to the rear edge of the stirrup-leather grooves in the tree, common from 1870 to 1905. It originally had a separate side jockey. Later, when the side jockey and the seat of the saddle became one piece of leather, it was called a *short seat.*

Throat (twist): The portion of the saddle seat under and just in front of the rider's crotch.

Tie-down: A strap connecting the noseband on the

bridle to the cinch. It prevents the horse from throwing his head up.

Tie-strap: See *cinch-strap holder.*

Tie strings: See *saddle strings.*

Tread (of stirrup): The bottom of the stirrup, the resting and support place for the foot when riding.

Tree: 1. The wooden, plastic, or fiber-glass structure forming the foundation of the saddle. It is the form on which the saddle is built, consisting of a fork, two bars, and a cantle. Wooden trees are usually covered with wet rawhide sewed tightly, which shrinks as it dries, forming a very strong tree. Lightweight trees are usually covered with canvas. 2. Cowboy slang for *saddle.*

Tug: See *billet* and *cinch.*

Tunnel keeper: See *channel keeper.*

Turned welt: See *welt.*

Twist (English): See *throat.*

Two-string seat: A saddle on which there are only two saddle strings, one on each back jockey of the saddle.

Wear leather: A piece of leather on a saddle posi-tioned to reduce wear between leathers and other materials.

Welt: A piece of leather stitched into the outer seam in the leather covering of swell forks, up the sides of the swells. This seam is necessary to make the leather fork covering conform to the shape of the fork. There are two types of welts. 1. *Single welt:* A single piece of leather between the stitched-together pieces of leather of the seam. 2. *Turned welt:* A doubled piece of leather between the stitched-together pieces of leather of the seam. See also *seam, laced.*

Western (stock) saddle: A saddle distinguished by a large, noticeable fork on which is some form of horn, a high cantle, and large skirts.

Whang strings: See *saddle strings.*

Withers: The convex prominence at the front of a horse's back above the rear part of the horse's shoulder blades.

Wood: Cowboy slang for *saddle.*

XC finish: A type of surface finish on malleable iron stirrups, an extrabright cadmium plating used in place of galvanizing.

Bibliography

GENERAL

Books

Adams, Ramon F.
  1936. *Cowboy Lingo.* Boston: Houghton Mifflin Co.
  1944. *Western Words: A Dictionary of the Range, Cow Camp, and Trail.* Norman: University of Oklahoma Press.
  1968. *Western Words: A Dictionary of the American West.* Norman: University of Oklahoma Press.
Anderson, J. K.
  1961. *Ancient Greek Horsemanship.* Berkeley: University of California Press.
Apsley, Lady Viola (Meeking) Bathurst
  1936. *Bridleways Through History.* London: Hutchinson & Co.
Back, Joe
  1959. *Horses, Hitches, and Rocky Trails.* Chicago: Swallow Press.
Baird, P. O.
  1946. *Leather Art.* Los Angeles: Arner Handicrafts Co.
Bancroft, Hubert Howe
  1888. *California Pastoral, 1769–1848.* San Francisco: History Co.
Banulos y de la Cerda, Luis de
  1877. *Libro de la jineta.* Madrid: Society of Spanish Book Lovers.
Baranowski, Zdzislaw
  1955. *The International Horseman's Dictionary.* Cranbury, N.J.: A. S. Barnes & Co.
Beck, John H.
  1950. *Saddle Making.* Phoenix, Ariz.: Privately printed. 2d ed., 1955.
Beck, Warren A., and Ynez D. Haase
  1974. *Historical Atlas of California.* Norman: University of Oklahoma Press.

Beckman, John
  1846. *History of Inventions, Discoveries, and Origins.* Vol. 1, "Saddles," "Stirrups." London.
Beebe, Lucius, and Charles Clegg
  1955. *American West.* New York: Crown Publishing Co., Bonanza Books.
Benoist, Jacques Mechin
  1966. *Alexander the Great.* New York: Hawthorn Books.
Berjeau, Philibert Charles
  1864. *Horses of Antiquity, Middle Ages, and Renaissance from the Monuments Down to the Sixteenth Century.* London: Dulau & Co.
Bloodgood, Lida Fleitman, and Piero Santini
  1964. *The Horseman's Dictionary.* New York: E. P. Dutton & Co.
Boyd, Robert T.
  1969. *Tells, Tombs, and Treasure.* New York: Crown Publishing Co., Bonanza Books.
Brayer, Herbert O., and M. Garret
  1952. *American Cattle Trails, 1540–1900.* Denver, Colo.: Smith-Brooks Printing Co.
Broderick, A. Houghton
  1972. *Animals in Archaeology.* New York Praeger Publishers.
Brown, Mark H., and W. R. Felton
  1953. *The Frontier Years.* New York: Bramhall House.

Carter, William H.
  1906. *Horses, Saddles, and Bridles.* Baltimore: Lord Baltimore Press.
Chamberlin, Harry D.
  1947. *Riding and Schooling Horses.* London: Hurst & Blackett.
Chapman, Arthur
  1932. *The Pony Express.* New York: G. P. Putnam's Sons.

Chenevix-Trench, Charles
  1970. *A History of Horsemanship.* Garden City, N.Y.: Doubleday & Co.

Cheney, Sheldon
  1962. *A New World History of Art.* New York: Viking Press.

Childe, V. Gordon
  1939. *Man Makes Himself.* New York: Oxford University Press.

Christy, E. V. A.
  1952. *Cross Saddle and Side Saddle.* 2d ed. London: Hutchinson & Co.

Cossar, J., and E. Prisse D'Avennes
  1967. *The Multiple Origin of Horses and Ponies and Egyptian and Arabian Horses.* Seattle, Wash.: Shorey Book Store.

Daremberg, Charles Victor, and Edmond Saglio, eds.
  1892. *Dictionnaire des antiquités grecques et romaines.* Paris. [See "Ephippium Sella Equestris," by Georges LaFaye.]

Daumas, E.
  1863. *The Horses of the Sahara and Manners of the Desert.* London: W. H. Allen & Co.

Davis, A.
  1867. *A Treatise on Harness, Saddles, and Bridles: Their History and Manufacture from the Earliest Times Down to the Present Period.* London: Horace Cox.

Demmin, Auguste Frederic
  1877. *A History of Arms and Armor (with a Section on the Saddle and the Stirrup).* London: William Clovis & Sons. Originally published by M. A. Bell and Sons, 1823.

Denhardt, Robert Moorman
  1948. *The Horse of the Americas.* Norman: University of Oklahoma Press. New ed., 1975.

Denison, George T.
  1913. *A History of Cavalry.* 2d ed. London: Macmillan & Co.

Dent, Anthony
  1974. *The Horse Through Fifty Centuries of Civilization.* London: Phaidon Press.

de Pluvinel, Antoine
  1626. *Le Manège royal.* London: J. A. Allen & Co.

des Noëttes, R. Lefebvre
  1931. *L'Attelage: Le Cheval de selle à travers les ages.* Paris: A. Picard.

Díaz del Castillo, Bernal
  1927. *The True History of the Conquest of Mexico.* New York: Robert M. McBride & Co. Written in 1568.

Dobie, J. Frank
  1952. *The Mustangs.* New York: Bramhall House.

Dodge, Theodore Ayrault
  1894. *Riders of Many Lands.* New York: Harper & Brothers.

Dulaney, George
  1972. *Know All About Tack.* Title 117. Omaha, Nebr.: Farnam Horse Library.

Dwyer, Francis
  1886. *Seats and Saddles; Bits and Bitting.* London: W. B. Whittingham & Co. 4th ed., New.York: Lovell, Coryell & Co.

Edwards, E. Hartley
  1963. *Saddlery.* Cranbury, N.J.: A. S. Barnes & Co.

Eggenhofer, Nick
  1961. *Wagons, Mules, and Men.* New York: Hastings House.

Felton, W. Sidney
  1962. *Masters of Equitation.* London: J. A. Allen & Co.
  1968. *The Literature of Equitation (One Man's Opinion).* London: V. S. Pony Clubs and J. A. Allen & Co.

Fillis, James
  1902. *Breaking and Riding.* London: J. A. Allen & Co. Reprinted 1963.

Fletcher, Sidney
  1951. *The Cowboy and His Horse.* New York: Grosset & Dunlap.

French, E. G.
  1951. *Goodbye to Boots and Saddle.* London: n.p.

Frink, Maurice
  1954. *Cow Country Cavalcade.* Denver, Colo.: n.p., 1954.

Froissard, Jean
  1974. *An Expert's Guide to Basic Dressage.* North Hollywood, Calif.: Wilshire Book Co.

Gallardo, D. Carlos Rincón, and Romero de Terreros
  1960. *El Libro del charro mexicano.* Mexico City: Editorial Porrua.

Gallatin, E. L.
  1900. *What Life Has Taught Me.* n.p.: John Frederic, Printer.

Galluci, Alfred D., and Mary McClennon Galluci
1958. *Birch, James E. (Pioneer California Transportation).* Sacramento, Calif.: Sacramento County Historical Society.

Garst, Shannon
1947. *Three Conquistadors: Cortez, Coronado, Pizzaro.* New York: Julian Messner.

Gianoli, Luigi
1969. *Horses and Horsemanship Through the Ages.* New York: Crown Publishers.

Graham, Robert B. Cunninghame
1949. *The Horses of the Conquest.* Norman: University of Oklahoma Press.

Grancsay, Stephen W.
1955. *Medieval and Renaissance Arms and Armor.* Hagerstown, Md.: Washington County Museum of Fine Arts.

Grant, Bruce
1951. *The Cowboy Encyclopedia.* New York: Rand, McNally & Co.
1953. *How to Make Cowboy Horse Gear.* Cambridge, Md.: Cornell Maritime Press.
————, and Lee M. Rice
1956. *How to Make Cowboy Horse Gear, with a Section on How to Make a Western Saddle.* Cambridge, Md.: Cornell Maritime Press.

Grigson, Geoffrey
1950. *Horse and Rider.* New York: Thames & Hudson.

Grousset, Réné
1970. *The Empire of the Steppes: A History of Central Asia.* New Brunswick, N.J.: Rutgers University Press.

Guldbeck, Per E.
1972. *The Care of Historical Collections.* Nashville, Tenn.: American Association for State and Local History.

Hasluck, Paul Nooncree
1962. *Saddlery and Harnessmaking.* London: J. A. Allen & Co.

Hassrick, Peter
1975. *Frederic Remington.* Fort Worth, Texas: Amon Carter Museum of Western Art.

Hitchcock, F. C.
1935. *Saddle Up.* New York: Charles Scribner's Sons.

Holling, Holling C.
1936. *The Book of Cowboys.* New York: Platt & Munk Co.

Horan, James D.
1959. *The Great American West.* New York: Crown Publishing Co., Bonanza Books.

Jackson, Marta
1970. *The Illustrations of Frederic Remington.* New York: Crown Publishers.

Janer, Don Florencia
N.d. *Of the Saddles.* N.p. [Janer was a member of the Academy of Archaeology of Belgium.]

Jankovich, Miklos
1971. *They Rode into Europe.* London: George G. Harrap and Company.

Jeschko, Kurt, and Harold Lange
1972. *The Horse Today—and Tomorrow.* London: Kaye & Ward.

Jettmar, Karl
1964. *The Art of the Steppes.* Translated by Ann E. Keep. Baden-Baden: Holle Verlag English translation, 1967.

Jones, William E.
1972. *Anatomy of the Horse.* East Lansing, Mich.: Caballus Publishers.

Kent, William
1937. *An Encyclopedia of London: Companies of the City of London.* London: J. M. Dent & Sons.

Lacroix, Paul
1875. *The Arts in the Middle Ages.* London: Chapman & Hall.

Laking, Sir Guy Francis
1920. *European Armour and Arms.* London: G. Bell & Sons.

Lamb, Harold.
1930. *Genghis Kahn: Emperor of All Men.* New York: Robert M. McBride & Co.
1940. *The March of the Barbarians.* Garden City, N.Y.: Country Life Press.

Lavender, David
1964. *The American Heritage History of the Great West.* New York: American Heritage Publishing Co.

Le Duc, E. Viollet, ed.
1877. *Dictionnaire raisonné due mobilier français.* Vol. 6, "Harnois," by Ernest Grund. Paris.

Lepé, José I.
1951. *Diccionario de asuntos hípicos y ecuestres.* Mexico City.

Littauer, Vladimir S.
1945a.   *The Forward Seat.* London: Hurst & Blackett. Reprint.
1945b.   *More About the Forward Seat.* London: Hurst & Blackett.
1962.   *Horseman's Progress.* New York: D. Van Nostrand Co.

Livingston, Phil
N.d.   *Cavalcade of American Saddles.* Yoakum, Texas: Tex-Tan Western Leather Company.

Loving, Mabel
1961.   *The Pony Express Rides On.* St. Joseph, Mo.: Robidoux Printing Company.

McAlester, A. Lee
1968.   *The History of Life.* Englewood Cliffs, N.J.: Prentice-Hall, Inc.

McCallum, Henry D., and Frances T. McCallum.
1965.   *The Wire That Fenced the West.* Norman: University of Oklahoma Press.

McDonald, Donald L.
1971.   *Know the Anatomy of the Horse.* Title 107. Omaha, Nebr.: Farnam Horse Library.

McDowell, Bart
1972.   *The American Cowboy in Life and Legend.* Washington, D.C.: National Geographic Society.

McGovern, William M.
1939.   *The Early Empires of Central Asia.* Chapel Hill, N.C.: University of North Carolina Press.

McTaggart, M.F.
1925.   *Mount and Man.* London: Country Life, Ltd.
1930.   *Stable and Saddle.* New York: Charles Scribner's Sons.

Marcy, Randolph B.
1859.   *The Prairie Traveler.* New York: Harper & Brothers.

Markham, Gervase
1975.   *The Complete Horseman.* Boston: Houghton Mifflin Co. Originally published in 1614.

Martin, C. C.
1891.   *The Harness-Maker's Complete Guide.* Chicago: Jefferson-Jackson.

Matthews, W. D.
1913.   *Evolution of the Horse in Nature.* Publication no. 36. Washington, D.C.: American Museum of Natural History.

Mellin, Jeanne
1953.   *Horses Across America.* New York: E. P. Dutton & Co.

Mohr, Erna
1971.   *The Asiatic Wild Horse.* London: J. A. Allen & Co.

Monaghan, Jay
1963.   *The Book of the American West.* New York: Crown Publishing Co., Bonanza Books.

Mora, Jo
1946.   *Trail Dust and Saddle Leather.* New York: Charles Scribner's Sons.
1949.   *Californios.* New York: Doubleday & Co., Inc.

Morison, Samuel Eliot
1942.   *Admiral of the Ocean Sea: A Life of Christopher Columbus.* Boston: Little, Brown and Co.

Muller, Hans
1969.   *The Pocket Dictionary of Horseman's Terms.* London: Hamlyn Publishing Group.

Myres, Sandra L.
1961.   *S. D. Myres: Saddlemaker.* Kerrville, Texas: privately printed.

Neihardt, John G.
1953.   *The Mountain Men* [poetry] Lincoln: University of Nebraska Press.

Norman, Vesey
1964.   *Arms and Armor.* New York: G. P. Putnam's Sons.

Osborne, Walter D., and Patricia H. Johnson
1966.   *A Treasury of Horses.* New York: Golden Press.

Paden, Irene D.
1953.   *The Wake of the Prairie Schooner.* New York: Macmillan Co.

Parrot, André
1961.   *The Arts of Assyria.* New York: Golden Press.

Paxson, Frederick L.
1924a.   *History of the American Frontier.* Cambridge, Mass.: Riverside Press.
1924b.   *The Last American Frontier.* New York: Macmillan Co.

Pennoyer, A. Sheldon
1938.   *This Was California.* New York: G. P. Putnam's Sons.

Perkins, J. B. Ward
1940.   *London Museum, Medieval Catalogue.*

London: H. M. Stationery Office.

Pocock, Roger
1917.   *Horses.* London: John Murray.

Reid, William
1976.   *Arms Through the Ages.* New York: Harper & Row.

Rice, Lee M., and Glenn R. Vernam
1975.   *They Saddled the West.* Cambridge, Md.: Cornell Maritime Press.

Riegel, Robert Edgar
1926.   *The Story of the Western Railroads.* New York: Macmillan Co.

Rienits, Rex, and Thea Rienits
1970.   *The Voyages of Columbus.* New York: Hamlyn Publishing Group.

Robertson, M. S.
1961.   *Rodeo: Standard Guide to the Cowboy Sport.* North Berkeley, Calif.: Howell.

Rojas, Arnold R.
1960.   *The Last of the Vaqueros.* Fresno, Calif.: Academy Library Guild.

Rolland, H.
1969.   *Le Mausolée de Glanum (Saint-Remy-de-Provence).* Paris: Editions du Centre National de la Recherche Scientifique.

Rollins, Phillip Aston
1936.   *The Cowboy.* New York: Charles Scribner's Sons.

Romaszkan, Gregor de
1967.   *Horse and Rider in Equilibrium.* Brattleboro, Vt.: Stephen Greene Press.

Rossi, Paul A.
N.d.   "The Vaquero," *American Scene,* vol. 11, no. 4. Tulsa: Thomas Gilcrease Institute of American History and Art.
———, and David C. Hunt
1971.   *The Art of the Old West.* New ·York: Alfred A. Knopf.

Rudenko, Sergei I.
1970.   *The Frozen Tombs of Siberia: The Pazyryk Burials of Iron Age Horsemen.* Berkeley: University of California Press.

Rudorff, Raymond
1974.   *Knights and the Age of Chivalry.* New York: Viking Press.

Russell, Charles M.
1929.   *Good Medicine: Memories of the Real West.* Garden City, N.Y.: Doubleday Book Co.

Santini, Piero
1933.   *Riding Reflections.* London: Country

Press.
1942.   *Learning to Ride.* New York: World Publishing Co.
1967.   *The Caprilli Papers.* London: J. A. Allen & Co.

Saubidet, Tito
1948.   *Vocabulario.* Buenos Aires: Guillermo Kraft.

Schmalenbach, Werner
1962.   *The Noble Horse.* London: J. A. Allen & Co.

Self, Margaret Cabell
1946.   *The Horseman's Encyclopedia.* New York: A. S. Barnes & Co.

Settle, Mary Lund, and Raymond W. Settle
1955.   *Saddles and Spurs.* New York: Crown Publishers.

Shumway, George, and Howard C. Frey
1968.   *Conestoga Wagon 1750–1850.* 3d ed. York, Pa.: George Shumway.

Sidney, Samuel
1875.   *Illustrated Book of the Horse.* London: Cassell. Reprinted by Wilshire Book Co., North Hollywood, Calif., 1974.

Simpson, George Gaylord
1951.   *Horses: The Story of the Horse Family in the Modern World and Through Sixty Million Years of History.* New York: Oxford University Press.

Sisson, Septimus, and James Daniels Grossman
1953.   *Anatomy of the Domestic Animals.* 4th ed. Philadelphia: W. B. Saunders Co.

Smith, R. N.
1971.   *An Anatomy of the Horse.* London: Quartilles International.

Smythe, R. H.
1967.   *The Horse Structure and Movement.* London: J. A. Allen & Co. Revised ed., 1972.

Steffen, Randy
1967.   *Horsemen Through Civilization.* Colorado Springs, Colo.: Western Horseman.

Stewart, Dwight
1973.   *Western Equitation, Horsemanship, and Showmanship.* New York: Vantage Press.

Stocking, Hobart E.
1971.   *The Road to Santa Fe.* New York: Hastings House.

Stone, George Cameron
1931.   *A Glossary of the Construction, Decora-*

369

tion, and Use of Arms and Armor. Portland, Me.: Southworth Press.

Suárez de Peralta, Juan
1580.   *Treatise of the Horseman a la Jineta y de la Brida.*

Summerhays, R. S.
1952.   *Encyclopedia for Horsemen.* London: Frederick Warne and Co.

Tavard, Christian-H.
1975.   *L'Habit du cheval: selle et bride.* Fribourg, Switzerland: Office du Livre.

Tex-Tan Company
1973a.   *Tree Talk.* Yoakum, Texas: Tex-Tan Western Leather Co.
1973b.   *Your Saddle and Its Care.* Yoakum, Texas: Tex-Tan Western Leather Co.

Tozer, Basil
1903.   *The Horse in History.* London: Methuen & Co.

Trew, Cecil G.
1951.   *The Accoutrements of the Riding Horse.* Plymouth, England: Browning Press.
1960.   *The Horse Through the Ages.* New York: Roy Publishers.

Tylden, G.
1965.   *Horses and Saddlery.* London: J. A. Allen & Co.
1971.   *Discovering Harness and Saddlery.* Tring, England: Shine Publications.

Vernam, Glenn R.
1964.   *Man on Horseback.* New York: Harper & Row.

Vernon, Arthur
1939.   *The History and Romance of the Horse.* Garden City, N.Y.: Halcyon House.

Volbach, W. F.
N.d.   *Early Christian Art.* New York: Harry N. Abrams, Inc.

Ward, Fay E.
1958.   *The Cowboy at Work.* New York: Hastings House.

Warner, Rex
1972.   *Men of Athens.* New York: Viking Press.

Waterer, John W.
1950.   *Leather Craftsmanship.* London: Faber and Faber.
1972.   *A Guide to the Conservation and Restoration of Objects Made Wholly or in Part of Leather.* New York: Drake Publishers.

Weber, David J.
1971.   *The Taos Trappers: The Fur Trade in the Far Southwest.* Norman: University of Oklahoma Press.

Williamson, Charles O.
1973.   *Breaking and Training the Stock Horse.* Caldwell, Idaho: Caxton Printers.

Willoughby, David P.
1974.   *The Empire of Equus.* Cranbury, N.J.: A. S. Barnes & Co.

Xenophon
1962a.   *Xenophon's Anabasis.* Edited by Maurice W. Mather and Joseph William Hewitt. Norman: University of Oklahoma Press.
1962b.   *The Art of Horsemanship.* Translated by M. H. Morgan. London: J. A. Allen & Co.

Yadin, Yigoel
1963.   *The Art of Warfare in Biblical Lands.* 2 vols. New York: McGraw-Hill Book Company.

Young, John Richard
1954.   *The Schooling of the Western Horse.* 1st ed. Norman: University of Oklahoma Press.

Articles

Adams, Ramon F.
1947.   "Western Words and Cowboy Lingo." *Western Horseman,* September–December.
1948.   "Western Words and Cowboy Lingo." *Western Horseman,* January–June, September–October.
1949.   "Western Words and Cowboy Lingo." *Western Horseman,* August.

Ahlefeld, Dick
1971.   "Two Old Timers." *Horse Lover's Magazine,* November–December.

Albert, Paul
1936.   "Romance of the American Stock Horse." *Western Horseman,* January, April, July, October.
1937.   "Romance of the American Stock Horse." *Western Horseman,* July–December.
1938.   "Romance of the American Stock Horse." *Western Horseman,* January–December.

1939. "Romance of the American Stock Horse." *Western Horseman,* January–December.

1940. "Romance of the American Stock Horse." *Western Horseman,* January–June, September–December.

1941. "Romance of the American Stock Horse." *Western Horseman,* January–December.

1942. "Romance of the American Stock Horse." *Western Horseman,* March–April.

1943. "Romance of the American Stock Horse." *Western Horseman,* January–February.

Amaral, Anthony

1965. "Martingales." *Western Horseman,* January.

1967a. "La Jineta, the Riding Style of the New World." *Horse Lover's Magazine,* March–April.

1967b. "Wonders of the Stirrup." *Western Horseman,* June.

1973. "Master Saddlemaker, G. S. Garcia." *Nevada Highways and Parks,* Summer.

Ammerman, Paul

1972a. "How a Saddle Should Suit a Horse." *Western Outfitter,* February.

1972b. "Saddles That Suit Their Riders." *Western Outfitter,* April.

Anonymous

1937a. "An Early Sculptured Saddle." *Bulletin of the Metropolitan Museum of Art,* April.

1937b. "History of Saddlery & Harness." *Horse* (England) vol. 9, no. 33 (Michaelmas).

1941a. "Fifth Year Anniversary." *Western Horseman,* July–August.

1941b. "Historical Development of the Saddle." *Cattleman,* September.

1941c. "A Medieval Sculptured Saddle." *Bulletin of the Metropolitan Museum of Arts,* April.

1942. "It's Time to Saddle Up." *The Westerner,* May.

1945. "A Saddle for 'Bull' Halsey." *Western Horseman,* September–October.

1952. "Jo Mora's 'Horsemen of the West.'" *Arizona Highways,* September.

1960. "World's Lightest Western Saddle, 14–17 lbs." *Horse Lover's Magazine,* February–March.

1962a. "New Taping Technique Makes Leather Amazingly Strong." *Horse Lover's Magazine,* May.

1962b. "Saddles—From Then Til Now." *Western Horseman,* May.

1964. "Randy Steffen's 'Old West'—The Pony Express." *Horse Lover's Magazine,* August–September.

1965. "Fiberglass Saddle Tree." *Western Horseman,* November.

1966. "Space Age Materials and the Saddler's Art." *Western Horseman,* January.

1967a. "History of the Horse in Asia." *Horse Lover's Magazine,* November–December.

1967b. "Meanea Saddle Shop—Magic City of the Plains, Cheyenne, 1867–1967." *Centennial Historical Committee,* July.

1968. "Wrapping the Saddlehorn." *Western Horseman,* September.

1969a. "How Should You Rig a Saddle." *Western Outfitter,* December.

1969b. "Saddlemaker: Ray Holes." *Western Outfitter,* December.

1970. "Wyoming Saddle School?" *Wyoming Rural Electric News,* July.

1971a. "100 Years of Saddle Making." *Hoofs and Horns* [Australia], April.

1971b. "Saddles in Bronze." *Western Horseman,* August.

1971c. "Texas Trail Saddle (100 Years Old)." *Horse and Rider,* May.

1973. "School for Saddlemakers." *Western Horseman,* July.

1974. "Frontier Past: The Story of a Saddle." *Frontier Times,* March.

Ashton, John

1942. "Horses and Mules Are Brought to the Americas." *Cattleman,* September.

1943. "Cortez and His Steeds." *Cattleman,* September.

1944. "How the Horse Came to the Americas." *Cattleman,* September.

Austin, G. A.

1960. "Saga of the Saddle." *New Mexico Magazine,* May.

Baker, Calvin

1960. "A Visit to Panhandle-Plains Historical

Museum." *Quarter Horse Journal,* March.

Baker, Fred
1965.   "Riding on Glass." *Empire Magazine of the Denver Post,* Nov. 7.

Barnett, R. D.
1953.   "World's Oldest Persian Carpet, 2,400 Years in Perpetual Ice." *Illustrated London News,* July 11.

Bell, James G.
1932.   "A Log of the Texas-California Cattle Trail." *Southwestern Historical Quarterly* (3 pts.), January, April, July.

Bergan, Yvonne
1940.   "The Saddlemaker's Corner." *Western Horseman,* March–April.

Bigler, Alexander B.
1968.   "The Western McClellan." *Western Horseman,* June, 1968.

Bivar, A. D. H.
1955.   "The Stirrup and Its Origins." *Oriental Art,* n.s., 1, no. 2.

Blair, Neal L.
1968.   "Saddles and Saddle Makers." *Wyoming Wildlife,* June.

Bosley, Lucia
1943.   "Saddles: Their History and Romance." *Cattleman,* September.

Boyd, Bob
1974.   "Saddles, Good and Bad." *American Horseman,* March.

Bracho, Miguel E.
1950.   "Schools of Riding in the New World —La Jineta." *Western Horseman,* September.

Brand, Franklin B., and Lee M. Rice
1958.   "Kenway-Visalia Saddlery." *Western Horseman,* November.

Burnett, Edward
1940.   "The Cowboy Saddle." *Cattleman,* September.

Bush, Doreen
1974.   "Those Amazing Stirrups." *Horseman,* April.

Carmichael, Joe M.
1949.   "Your Best Saddle Is 1,500 Years Old." *Cattleman,* September.

Carroll, Jack
1971.   "A Saddlemaker Looks at the Forward Seat." *Horse and Rider,* January.

1973.   "Back and the Saddle." *Horse and Rider,* December.

1974.   "Saddle-saving Savvy." *Horse and Rider,* November.

1977.   "The Western Saddle." *Horse, Illustrated,* vol. 1.

Casement, Jack
1951.   "Tall in the Saddle." *Western Horseman,* May.

Cathey, James
1957.   "Leddy—A Big Name in Western Goods." *Western Horseman,* May.

Cheney, F. Dexter
1962.   "Eighty-Year-Old Saddle, Still Going Strong." *Western Horseman,* November.

Clevenger, Barbara
1972.   "Harlan Webb, Saddle Maker." *Quarter Horse Journal,* September.

Close, Pat
1969.   "A Guide to Buying a Saddle." *Western Horseman,* July.

Connell, Ed
1973.   "The A-Fork Saddle." *Horse and Rider,* January.

Copeland, Luther
1974.   "Don't Abuse That Saddle." *Horseman,* April.

Cunningham, Eugene
1951.   "Tío Sam—Saddle Man." *Horse Lover's Magazine,* February–March.

Curley, Cal
1949.   "The Origin of the Association Saddle." *Western Horseman,* January.

1952.   "Pages of the Past." *Western Horseman,* March.

Davis, Deering
1950.   "The Balanced Seat and Its History." *Western Horseman,* June.

1952.   "The Balance of Horse and Rider." *Horse Lover's Magazine,* October–November.

1962.   "The Heavy Saddle Handicap." *Horse Lover's Magazine,* August–September.

1969.   "The Balance of Horse and Rider." *Horse Lover's Magazine,* May–June.

Davy, Marguerite Ross
1946.   "Pictures in Leather." *Popular Home Craft,* April.

Dean, Frank
1976.   "The $125,000 Saddle." *Western Horse-*

man, July–August.

Denhardt, Robert M.
1938a.   "The Western Saddle: From Moslem Spain to Modern California." *Westways,* February.
1938b.   "The Mexican Saddle." *Western Horseman,* July–August.
1938–39. "The Southwestern Cow-Horse" (4 pts.). *Cattleman,* December, January–March.

Dick, Everett
1926–28. "The Long Drive." *Journal of the Kansas State Historical Society,* vol. 17.

Diespecker, Dick
1968.   "The Keyston Story." *Western Horseman,* August.

Dobie, J. Frank
1951.   "Up the Trail to Wyoming." *Western Horseman,* March.

Dunn, Nora
1954.   "Frank A. Meanea, Pioneer Saddler." *Annals of Wyoming,* vol. 26, no. 1 (January).

Eastwood, Douglas
1966.   "Return of the Tarpan." *Western Horseman,* March.

Eckelberg, Mary Ellen
1969.   "Julius Caesar on Horseback." *Horse Lover's Magazine,* July–August.

Edwards, Gladys Brown
1971.   "Baubles, Bangles, and Beads." *Arabian Horse World,* December.
1973.   "The Arabian Connection" (2 pts.). *Horse and Rider,* September–October.

Ensign, Arthur
1941.   "The Western Saddle." *Arizona Highways,* February.

Evans, Edna H.
1968.   "Sixteen Horses That Conquered a Nation" (2 pts.). *Western Horseman,* November, December.

Fellows, Fred R.
1966a.   "The People's Pillion: A Study of Western Saddles." *Montana: The Magazine of Western History,* vol. 16, no. 1 (January).
1966b.   "The Santa Fe Saddle." *Western Horseman,* March.

Fletcher, Curley
1950.   "The Origin of the Swelled Fork Saddle." *Western Livestock Magazine,* July.

Foreman, Monte
1951.   "Tall in the Saddle." *Western Horseman,* March.
1953–56. "Riding by Reasoning." *Western Horseman,* March–June, 1953; May, June, August, October–December, 1954; January–May, July, October, 1955; January, February, 1956.
1959.   "Stand to Get On." *Horse Lover's Magazine,* October–November.
1960.   "The Balanced Stop." *Horse Lover's Magazine,* April–May.
1960–61. "Horse Training." *Horse Lover's Magazine,* December–January.
1965a.   "The Balanced Stop." *Horse Lover's Magazine,* June–July.
1965b.   "The Head in Relation to Balance." *Horse Lover's Magazine,* August–September.
1965c.   "Head Balancing for Accurate Control." *Horse Lover's Magazine,* October–November.
1966.   "Saddling Up." *Horse Lover's Magazine,* November–December.

Francis, Noel
1944.   "Stirrups." *Hobbies,* January.

Fuqua, Carl
1950.   "Ideas on Saddlemaking." *Western Horseman,* November.

George, Leo
1942.   "Saddles Through the Ages." *Western Livestock Journal,* Sept. 15.

Gillespie, A. S. ("Bud")
1962.   "Saddles." *Annals of Wyoming,* vol. 34, no. 2 (October).

Grancsay, Stephen V.
1938.   "A Gift of Mexican 'Conquistador' Stirrups." *Bulletin of the Metropolitan Museum of Art,* vol. 33, pp. 73–76.

Grant, Bruce
1966.   "How to Make a Braided Cincha." *Western Horseman,* March.

Gray, Bill
1955.   "The Stelzig Saddlery." *Western Horseman,* September.

Greene, Nora Lou
1967.   "Mecca for Saddles: The Cowboy Hall of Fame." *Cattleman,* September.

Griffin, Bert
1976.   "Miles City Saddlery." *Persimmon Hill,*

vol. 6, no. 2 (Spring).

Griffin, Ken, and Bert Griffin
1958.   "Miles City Saddlery, Makers of Cogshall Saddle." *Western Horseman,* March.
1962.   "Saddlemaker to the Stars." *Western Horseman,* May.

Griffin, Randi
1969.   "Equus Przewalski." *Western Horseman,* January.

Grover, Dorys C.
1963.   "Przewalski: The Little Horse with a Big Name." *Western Horseman,* October.

Haley, J. Evetts
1938.   "Texian Saddles." *Cattleman,* June.

Halliday, Dick
1947.   "Early Day Saddles." *Cattleman,* September.

Harris, Fredie Steve
1972.   "Dally vs. Tie-Fast." *Horseman,* January.

Harris, Leo D.
1950.   "Art on the Ranch." *Western Livestock,* February.

Hartung, A. M.
1943.   "Famous War Horses." *Western Horseman,* March–April.

Hartwell, Lee M.
1958.   "Western Saddles." *Denver Westerners Monthly Roundup,* vol. 14, no. 9 (September).

Harvey, Patricia
1959.   "How the Horse Spread in America." *Western Horseman,* October.

Hawley, Don
1965.   "Tamerlane's Horses." *Western Horseman,* March.

Hedges, Mac, and Ernest Morris
1976.   "Hard and Fast Roping." *Horse and Rider,* November.

Hemphill, Robert
1971.   "Cowpuncher's Saddle." *Western Horseman,* May.

Hervey, John
1941.   "Prehistoric Horse Discovered Intact." *National Horseman,* June.

Hesse, Curtis J.
1940.   "Where Did the Horse Come From?" *Cattleman,* September.

Hewitt, Bob
1971.   "Spanish Exploration in the West." *Western Horseman,* August.

1975.   "Taps." *Western Horseman,* January.

Holes, Ray
1949.   "Rigging." *Western Horseman,* April.
1950.   "Choosing a Saddle." *Western Horseman,* July.

Holmes, Hallie
1954.   "Leo Leonard, Leather Artist." *Western Horseman,* December.

Hoppe, Paul
1956.   "Evolution and Use of the Western Stock Saddle." *Chicago Westerners Brand Book,* vol. 13, no. 5 (July).

Horn, Paul W.
1971.   "Three Generations of Saddlemaking." *Cattleman,* April.

Howard, Virginia
1952:   "The Navajo Saddle Blanket." *Western Horseman,* August.

Hughes, Pollyanna B.
1955.   "Empty Saddles." *Western Horseman,* February.
1957.   "Stirrups Rate a Second Look." *Western Horseman,* September.

Hutchinson, W. H.
1957.   "Pastoral California." *Western Horseman,* September.

Ingraham, H. C.
1960.   "The Saddles They Left." *Western Horseman,* January.

Irving, Ralph
1943.   "The Case of the Dale Vuelta vs. the Texas Tie." *Western Horseman,* January–February.

Jary, William E.
1959.   "Leddy Bros. 'So-Fa Ride' Saddle." *Western Horseman,* May.

Johansen, Ulla
1965.   "Der Reistsattel bei den Altaischen Völkern." *Central Asiatic Journal,* vol. 10, nos. 3–4 (December).

Jones, Dave
1954.   "Rigs for the Problem Horse." *Western Horseman,* January.

Kester, W. O.
1953.   "Sore Backs Are Man Made." *Horse Lover's Magazine,* October–November.
1962.   "Sore Backs Are Man Made." *Horse Lover's Magazine,* September.

King, Chuck
1963.   "The Dally Horn." *Western Horseman,* November.

1977. "Cinches, Rings, and Latigoes." *Western Horseman,* March.

King, Ferne E.
1966. "Legend of the Veach Saddlery — Twenty Years in Tulsa." *Ranchman,* April.

King, Patricia A.
1971. "The Remains of Eohippus." *Quarter Horse of the Pacific,* November.

Kirk, C. N.
1952. "Cowboy Saddlemaker; Lee M. Rice." *Western Horseman,* November.

Klaue, Lola Shelton
1963. "Ario's Saddlery." *Western Horseman,* August.

Knowles-Peterson
1964. "'Tio' Sam Myres — King of the Frontier Saddlemakers." *Quarter Horse Journal,* November.

Krenmayr, Janice
1957. "Stirrups with Stories." *Western Horseman,* April.

Laurence, Vic
1971. "Saddlemakers: Endangered Species." *American Horseman,* March.

Leftwich, Bill
1959. "Estribos Españoles." *Western Horseman,* September.
1960. "Saddler of Big Bend." *Quarter Horse Journal,* March.

Lewis, Jack
1975. "Search for a Saddle." *Horse and Horseman,* January.

Lindgren, Carl H.
1955. "Balance in Riding." *Horse Lover's Magazine,* December.
1956a. "How's Your Balance?" *Horse Lover's Magazine,* January.
1956b. "Balance in Riding." *Horse Lover's Magazine,* February–March.
1956c. "Balance in Riding." *Horse Lover's Magazine,* August–September.
1956d. "Balance in Riding." *Horse Lover's Magazine,* October–November.
1958–59. "Saddle Up." *Horse Lover's Magazine,* December–January.

Livingston, Phil
1970. "Take Care of Your Saddle." *Quarter Horse Journal,* September.
1971. "For War and Wear." *Horse and Rider,* May.
1972a. "Cavalcade of American Saddles." *Ap-*

paloosa News, January.
1972b. "Emil Anders — Tree Maker." *Western Horseman,* December.
1973. "Catch as Catch Can." *American Horseman,* January.

Lloyd, Bob
1955. "Prehistoric Horses Discovered." *Western Horseman,* November.

Long, Bill
1969. "Snubbing Post Dally Horn." *Western Horseman,* June.

Long, Paul V., Jr.
1971. "Saddles in Bronze." *Western Horseman,* August.

Louaillier, Al
1954. "Story of the Saddle." *Quarter Horse Journal,* December.

Love, Paula McSpadden
1953. "Will Rogers' Saddles." *Western Horseman,* May.

Luiten, Bina G.
1960. "Harness Maker." *Western Horseman,* September.

Luña de la Fuente, Carlos
1971a. "Saddles of the World (the Persian Saddle)." *Hoofs and Horns* [Australia], November.
1971b. "Saddles of the World (the Peruvian Saddle)." *Hoofs and Horns* [Australia], November.

Lutz, Aleta
1964. "The Fabulous 101 Ranch." *Western Horseman,* November.

Lynch, Dick
1962. "Harry Rowell: A Famous Name in Rodeos, Saddles, Saddle Trees, and Silver Work." *Horse Lover's Magazine,* October–November.

McCurry, Lee
1953. "Saddle Wise." *Western Horseman,* February.

McMechen, Edgar C.
1944. "The Gallatin Saddle." *Colorado Magazine,* March.

McMillin, Mark
1965. "Famous Horsemen of the Early West." *Horse Lover's Magazine,* January–February.

McNeal, W. H.
1951. "The Pony Express." *Western Horseman,* December.

Manning, Douglas
1962.   "Tips on Selecting the Correct Saddle for You." *Horse Lover's Magazine,* November.

Meyers, Robert
1959.   "What to Look for in a Custom Made Saddle." *Western Horseman,* May.

Mitchell, Annie R.
1959.   "Visalia Stock Saddle." *Los Tulares Quarterly Bulletin* (Tulare County Historical Society), vol. 41 (September).

Mizwa, Tad S.
1976.   "Edward Bohlin—Saddler in Silver." *Western Outfitter,* May.

Mizwa, Tad S., and William N. Porter
1972.   "Removing Bulk Between Horse and Rider." *Western Outfitter,* November.
———, and Harlan Webb
1973.   "Selling Saddles." *Western Outfitter,* April.

Morris, Ernest, and Mac Hedges
1976.   "Dally Roping." *Horse and Rider,* November.

Myres, Sandra L.
1960.   "S. D. Myres and the Myres Saddle Company of Sweetwater." *West Texas Historical Association Yearbook,* vol. 36 (October).

Napoletano, Al M.
1964.   "Tarpan, Wild Horse of Asia." *Horse Lover's Magazine,* June–July.

Necer, George M.
1971a.   "Saddles of the World (the Camargue Stock Saddle)." *Hoofs and Horns* [Australia], January.
1971b.   "Saddles of the World (North Africa)." *Hoofs and Horns* [Australia], April.
1975a.   "Saddles of Old Mexico." *Horse and Rider,* March.
1975b.   "Evolution of the Stock Saddle." *Horse and Rider,* April.

Nolte, Lawrence W.
1963.   "Principles of Saddle Design," *Horse Lover's Magazine,* February–March.

O'Brien, Mary A.
1975.   "Indian Acquisition of the Horse." *Western Horseman,* September–October.

Oliphant, J. Orin
1946.   "The Eastward Movement of Cattle from the Oregon Country." *Agricultural History* [Bucknell University] vol. 20 (January).

O'Malley, Jeanne
1973.   "Evolution of the Stock Saddle." *Horse and Rider,* December.
1975.   "Selecting Western Saddles." *American Horseman,* January.

Ortega, Luis B.
1944.   "The California Centerfire." *Western Horseman,* March–April, May–June, September–October.
1946.   "Adding Life to Riding Gear." *Western Horseman,* March–April.
1953.   "Los Latigos de Cuero (the Rawhide Latigos)." *Western Horseman,* November.

Osmer, Norman A.
1972.   "Evolution of the Western Saddle." *Hoofs and Horns* [United States], January–February.

Padgitt, James T.
1953.   "The Padgitts and Saddle Leather." *West Texas Historical Association Year Book,* vol. 29 (October).

Pattie, Jane
1968.   "Just Call Windy." *Quarter Horse Journal,* August.
1971.   "Cinch 'Em Right." *Horse and Rider,* May.
1973.   "Little Aubrey, the Human Racehorse." *Horseman,* December.

Porter, Fred S., Sr.
1959.   "Porter's Is Part of the West." *Western Horseman,* May.

Porter, Willard
1956.   "Keep Your Cinches Tight." *Western Horseman,* April.

Probert, Alan
1976.   "Cruciform Stirrups." *Western Horseman,* January.

Ray, Phil
1968.   "Selecting a Stock Saddle." *Western Horseman,* January.

Read, Dennis R.
1966.   "Noblest of Them All." *Western Horseman,* May.

Reames, Wallace
1948.   "Trends of the Stock Saddle." *Western Horseman,* May–June.

Reed, Charles A.

1959. "Animal Domestication in the Prehistoric Near East." *Science,* Dec. 11.

Reynolds, Franklin
1958. "Can He Wear a Saddle?" *Quarter Horse Journal,* February.

Rice, Lee M.
1942. "The Mother Hubbard Saddle." *Western Horseman,* January–February.

1943a. "An Outline of the Western Saddle." *Western Horseman,* January–February.

1943b. "The Famous Collins Saddles." *Western Horseman,* May–June.

1943c. "The Famous Hamley Saddle." *Western Horseman,* November–December.

1944a. "The Famous Meanea Saddles." *Western Horseman,* January–February.

1944b. "Olsen-Nolte Saddles." *Western Horseman,* March–April.

1944c. "Ray Holes Saddles." *Western Horseman,* July–August.

1944d. "The Famous Garcia Saddles." *Western Horseman,* October.

1944e. "The Famous Myres Saddles." *Western Horseman,* January–February.

1945. "Lawrence Saddles." *Western Horseman,* January–February.

1947. "The Sickles Saddles of St. Louis." *Western Horseman,* December.

1948a. "E. L. Gallatin, Pioneer Saddle Maker." *Western Horseman,* January–February.

1948b. "The Early Saddle Houses of Utah." *Western Horseman,* May, June.

1948c. "The T. Flynn Saddlery of Pueblo." *Western Horseman,* September–October.

1949. "The Gallup and Frazier Saddles." *Western Horseman,* July.

1950a. "Saddle Trees, Then and Now." *Western Horseman,* April.

1950b. "Western Colorado Saddles." *Western Horseman,* December.

1953. "Fred Mueller, Inc., of Larimer Street." *Western Horseman,* October.

1954a. "American Built Arabian Saddle." *Western Horseman,* April.

1954b. "Porter's." *Western Horseman,* May.

1954c. "What's New in Saddlery." *Western Horseman,* June.

1955a. "The Hamley Story." *Western Horseman,* May.

1955b. "The Story of the Keyston Brothers." *Western Horseman,* August.

1956a. "The Veach Saddlery Company." *Western Horseman,* May.

1956b. "The Slim Pickens Saddle." *Western Horseman,* December.

1957a. "The Eamor Saddlery of Alberta." *Western Horseman,* April.

1957b. "Old Goettlich Saddle." *Western Horseman,* April.

1957c. "An Old Porter Saddle." *Western Horseman,* September.

1960. "Montana and the Connolly Saddles." *Western Horseman,* March.

1961a. "Backtrailing the Western Saddle Tree." *Western Horseman,* April.

1961b. "Saddles by Rowell." *Western Horseman,* June.

1969. "The Visalia Stock Saddle Company." *Western Horseman,* December.

1974. "A Bit About Old Saddles" (2 pts.). *Western Horseman,* February–March.

———, and Florence Morgan
1943. "The Famous Porter Saddles." *Western Horseman,* September–October.

Rideout, Leana
1972. "McClellans for Mule Skinners." *Mr. Longears,* Summer.

Riordan, Marguerite
1952. "Uncle Jimmy Deam, Old Time Saddlemaker." *Cattleman,* September.

Robertson, Bob
1957. "Saddle Trees." *Los Angeles Corral.*

Rosa, Joseph B.
1969. "The Saga of a Saddle." *Relics,* Summer.

Rossan, Charles G.
1959–60. "The Museum of Western History (Panhandle-Plains Historical Museum)" (2 pts.). *Horse Lover's Magazine,* December–January.

Rossi, Paul A.
1966. "The Western Stock Saddle." *American West,* Summer.

1974. "Makers of the Forty Dollar Saddle." *Persimmon Hill,* vol. 4, no. 2.

Saare, Sharon
1973. "Saddle Selection Thoughts—A Case for the 3/4 Rigging." *Appaloosa News,* May.

Sabin, Samuel W.
1971. "Saddles and Saddling: Selection and Adjustment." *Bulletin of the New York State College of Agriculture and Life Sciences* [Cornell University], August.
1973. "Selecting a Saddle." *Bulletin of the Columbia Extension Division,* University of Missouri [Horse Short Course Series], April.

Schipman, Henry, Jr.
1962. "Baja, California—Where the Wild West Still Lives." *Western Horseman,* April.
1964. "The Stock Saddles of Hawaii" (2 pts.). *Western Horseman,* March–April.
1970. "Saddles of the World (Hawaiian Stock Saddles)." *Hoofs and Horns* [Australia], November.

Schulman, A. R.
1957. "Egyptian Representation of Horseman Riding in the New Kingdom." *Journal of Near Eastern Studies,* vol. 16.

Serven, James E.
1970. "Cattle, Guns, and Cowboys." *Arizona Highways,* October.
1972. "Horses of the West." *Arizona Highways,* March.

Sheldon, W. M.
1943. "The Saddle—A History of the Evolution of the Western Saddle." *Hoofs and Horns* [Australia], November.

Shope, Irvin
1943. "How the Spanish Saddle Came to Montana." *Western Horseman,* May–June.

Shuessler, Raymond
1971. "Saga of the Saddle." *Quarter Horse of the Pacific Coast,* November.

Simpson, George Gaylord
1940. "Resurrection of the Dawn Horse." *Natural History,* November.

Sisco, Sammy
1947. "Types and Kinds of Stirrups." *Western Horseman,* December.
1948. "Sidelights on Saddles." *Quarter Horse Journal,* October.
1949. "What to Look for in a Saddle Tree." *Quarter Horse Journal,* May.
1950. "Have Quarter Horses Changed Saddle Trees?" *Quarter Horse Journal,* March.

Slykhouse, John
1940. "Saddlemaker's Corner: Muley Saddles," *Western Horseman,* November–December.

Smillie, Jack
1969. "My Deep Seat." *Western Horseman,* July.

Smith, Lewis
1976. "Celebrity Saddles." *Horse and Rider,* November.

Spencer, Dick, III
1954. "The Ruwart Saddle Trees." *Western Horseman,* August.
1957. "Porters at Buffalo Ranch." *Western Horseman,* December.
1958. "Saddle Up." *Western Horseman,* July.
1959. "Equipment Care." *Western Horseman,* December.
1969. "Stirrups That Tell a Story of the West." *Western Horseman,* June.

Spencer, Rick
1967. "The Mountain Man." *Western Horseman,* August.

Spring, Agnes Wright
1970. "More on the Garcia Saddle." *True West,* December.

Stalter, Marcile Weist
1945. *Western Horseman,* July–August.
1946a. "The Mexican T-shaped Stirrup." *Western Horseman,* January–February.
1946b. "Some Early American Saddles." *Western Horseman,* May–June.

Stangl, Mrs. Linda
1971. "Homemade Running Martingale." *Western Horseman,* October.

Starnes, Luke
1972. "The Panhandle Past." *Horse and Rider,* July.

Steffen, Randy
1953–54. "Saddles of the West." *Horse Lover's Magazine,* December, January.
1955. "Horsemen Through Civilization." *Western Horseman,* January–December.
1956. "Horsemen Through Civilization." *Western Horseman,* January–May, August–December.
1957. "Horsemen Through Civilization." *Western Horseman,* March–May, September, December.
1958a. "Horsemen Through Civilization." *Western Horseman,* January, March, April, June, September, November.

1958b. "Dally Roper Hint." *Western Horseman,* October.

1959. "Horse Through Civilization." *Western Horseman,* April, May.

1961. "Saddles Through History" (5 pts.). *Western Horseman,* June–October.

1963a. "Randy Steffen's Old West—The Mountain Man." *Horse Lover's Magazine,* July.

1963b. "Randy Steffen's Old West—California Vaquero." *Horse Lover's Magazine,* September.

1964. "The Story of the Cowboy's Stock Saddle" (2 pts.). *Quarter Horse Journal,* February–March.

1967a. "Randy Steffen's Old West: Texas Trail Drives." *Horse Lover's Magazine,* September–October.

1967b. "Randy Steffen's Old West: The Stock Saddle." *Horse Lover's Magazine,* November–December.

1968. "Horse Equipment of the Middle Ages." (3 pts.). *Western Horseman,* April–June.

1971. "The American Stock Saddle (3 pts.). *Western Horseman,* April–June.
(See also under "Military Saddles.")

Stinson, Byron
1960. "The Yankee Saddle." *Western Horseman,* December.

Swaney, Alex Grant
1943. "The Balanced Seat in the Stock Saddle." *Western Horseman,* May–June.

Terrett, Courtenay
1949. "Miles City Saddles." *Western Horseman,* September.

Thomas, Jim
1947. "Sailor to Saddlemaker." *Western Livestock Journal,* May.

Tidwell, Derl
1974. "Make Sure That Saddle Fits." *Horseman,* April.

Tutton, James S.
1973. "Choose a Saddle That Fits." *American Horseman,* December.

Tyler, Chuck
1967. "Eddie Bohlin, Michelangelo of Saddle Craft." *Western Life,* August.

1969. "The Last Saddle." *Horse and Rider,* February.

Vandervelde, Marjorie
1940. "The Pony Express." *Western Horseman,* April.

Ward, Fay
1975. "Old-Time Bronc Saddles." *Western Horseman,* May.

Waterston, Barbara
1974. "Toe-Holds, Toe-Rings, and Stirrups." *Field,* April 18.

Werham, Edward
1930. "Spanish American Saddlery in California." *International Studio,* vol. 97, no. 400 (September).

Whitmore, Eugene
1955. "A Century of Saddlemaking (Tex-Tan)." *Western Horseman,* March.

Williamson, Charles O.
1962. "Hoss Talk: Principles of Horsemanship." *Horse Lover's Magazine,* April–May.

Wilson, Brownlow
1950. "Effect of Weight on Horses." *Western Horseman,* August.

Wolfgang, Otto
1968. "History of the Saddle." *Real West,* May.

1969. "Saga of the Saddle." *Canadian Cattleman,* March.

Woodson, Weldon D.
1966. "Leather Artist—Al Shelton." *Western Horseman,* March.

Woodward, Arthur
1949. "La Mochila: A Saddle Trapping of the Old West." *Magazine of Los Angeles County Historical Museum,* Autumn.

1961. "Saddles in the New World." *Horse Lover's Magazine,* November.

Wyland, E. E.
1959. "The Westernaires and Their Museum of Horse History." *Western Horseman,* July.

Young, John Richard
1951a. "Is There a 'Right' Seat?" (2 pts.). *Western Horseman,* August–December.

1951b. "Regarding 'Tall in the Saddle.'" *Western Horseman,* July.

1951c. "What Is a 'Good' Seat?" *Western Horseman,* September.

Catalogs

Anderson Saddlery, Houston, Texas
    1966.   Catalog.
Carroll Saddle Co., McNeal, Ariz.
    1971–72. Catalog no. 32.
    1977.   Catalog no. 37.
Casa Zea, Juárez, Mexico
    1973.   Catalog no. 1.
B. T. Crump Company, Inc., Richmond, Va.
    Ca. 1973. Catalog no. 96.
Denver Dry Goods Co., Denver, Colo.
    1936–37. Fall–Winter Catalog.
    1937.   Spring–Summer Catalog.
Fallis Custom Made Saddlery, Inc., Granby (later Elbert), Colo.
    1954.   Catalog no. 1.
    1965.   Catalog no. 4.
R. T. Frazier Saddlery, Pueblo, Colo.
    Ca. 1906. Catalog.
    Ca. 1935. Catalog no. 37.
Hamley's, Pendleton, Oreg.
    1924.   Catalog no. 25.
    1931.   Catalog no. 32.
    1953.   Catalog no. 53.
    1974.   Catalog no. 77.
H. Kauffman & Sons, New York
    1927.   Catalog no. 757.
Kopf Manufacturing Co., Inc., New York
    Ca. 1920. Catalog no. 21.
S. R. and I. C. McConnell Co., Burlington, Iowa
    N.d.   Catalog.
H. R. Miller Saddle Company, Kansas City, Mo.
    1952.   Catalog no. 11.
Miller's, Inc., New York
    1977.   Catalog no. 109.
Miller-Stockman, Denver, Colo.
    1947–48. Catalog no. 74, Fall–Winter.
    N.d.   Catalog no. 79.
Montgomery Ward & Company
    1894–95. Catalog. Reprinted, Northfield, Ill.: Grin Digest Company.
Moseman's Illustrated Guide for Purchasers of Horse Goods
    1892.   Reprinted, New York: Arco Publishing, Co., Inc.
Muellers Stockmen's Supplies, Denver, Colo.
    1950.   Catalog no. 88.
C. S. Osborne & Company, Harrison, N.J.
    1977.   Catalog no. 56.
North & Judd Manufacturing Co., New Britain, Conn.
    1968.   Catalog no. 43.

N. Porter's, Phoenix, Ariz.
    Ca. 1959. Catalog no. 37.
Potts Longhorn Leather, Dallas, Texas
    1972.   Catalog.
Riley & McCormick, Calgary, Alberta, Canada
    N.d.   Supplementary Catalog no. 1.
    1940.   November, 1940, Catalog.
Ruwart Manufacturing Company, Denver, Colo.
    1958.   May, 1958, Catalog.
    1963.   May, 1963, Catalog.
Ryon's Saddle and Ranch Supplies, Inc., Fort Worth, Texas
    1977.   Spring and Summer, 1977. Catalog no. 63.
    1978.   Fall, 1978, Catalog no. 66.
Schneiders, Cleveland, Ohio
    1978.   Catalog no. 7800.
Smith-Worthington Company, New York
    Ca. 1905. Catalog.
Stockman-Farmer Supply Company, Denver, Colo.
    1927–28. Catalog no. 31.
    1932.   Catalog no. 41.
    1933.   Catalog no. 43, Fall–Winter, 1933.
    1934.   Catalog no. 44, Spring–Summer, 1934.
L. D. Stone Company, San Francisco, Calif.
    Ca. 1905. Catalog.
Tandy Crafts, Inc., Tandy Center, Fort Worth, Texas
    1977.   Catalog no. 116.
Tex Tan Western Leather Company, Yoakum, Texas
    1973.   Catalog no. 82.
    1974.   Catalog no. 84.
    1976.   Catalog no. 86.
    1977.   Catalog no. 87.
Visalia Stock Saddle Company, San Francisco, Calif.
    1917.   Catalog no. 18.
    1940.   Catalog no. 32.
    1974.   Catalog no. 101.
Western Saddle Manufacturing Co., Denver, Colo.
    1951.   Catalog, December, 1951.
R. M. Williams, Prospect, S.A., Australia
    1952.   Catalog.
J. V. Wilson Leather Company, Bellefontaine, Miss.
    1973.   Catalog no. 73.
Wyeth Hardware & Manufacturing Company, Saint Joseph, Mo.
    1916.   Catalog no. 119.
    1930.   Catalog no. 207.
    1939.   Catalog no. 220.

Unpublished Materials

Anderson, E. L.
  N.d.   "Early History of Horsemanship." Manuscript.
Anderson, J. K.
  1976–78. Letters to author, Feb. 20, 1976; March 11, 1976; April 6, 1976; June 24, 1976; Nov. 18, 1978.
Carroll, Jack
  N.d.   Letter to author.
Haley, J. Evetts
  N.d.   Personal files.
Littauer, Mary Aiken
  1977.   Letter to author, Dec. 18.
Nickel, Helmut
  N.d.   Letter to author.

MILITARY SADDLES

Books

Anonymous
  1912.   *The History of Company A, Second Illinois Cavalry.* Chicago.
Boniface, John J.
  1903.   *The Cavalry Horse and His Pack.* Kansas City, Mo.: Franklin Hudson Publishing Co.
Miller, Francis Trevelyan, ed.
  Ca. 1865. *The Photographic History of the Civil War.* Vol. 4 (photographs by Mathew Brady). N.p.
Carter, William H.
  1895.   *Horses, Saddles, and Bridles.* Leavenworth, Kans.: Ketcheson & Reeves.
Confederate States of America, Ordnance Office
  1863.   *The Ordnance Manual for the Use of Officers of the Confederate States Army.* Charleston, S.C.: Evans & Cogswell. [See esp. pp. 149–52, plate 22.]
Great Britain, War Office, Veterinary Department
  1908.   *Animal Management, 1908.* Chap. 7. London: H.M. Stationery Office.
Herrie, Col.
  1811.   *Abstract of Colonel Herrie's Instructions for Volunteer Corps of Cavalry, Adapted to the Use of the Volunteer and Militia Cavalry of the United States.* Philadelphia; Anthony Finley.

Hoyt, Epaphras
  1798.   *A Treatise on the Military Art.* Brattleboro, Vt.: Benjamin Smeed.
  1813.   *Rules and Regulations for Cavalry.* Greenfield, Mass.
Lord, Francis A.
  N.d.   *Civil War Collector's Encyclopedia.* N.p.
Merrill, James M.
  1966.   *Spurs to Glory.* New York: Rand McNally & Co.
Miller, Francis T.
  1911.   *The Photographic History of the Civil War.* Vol. 4, frontispiece, p. 311. New York. [Illustrates a padded seat cinched down.]
Nott, Charles
  1865.   *Sketches of the War.* New York.
Peterson, Harold L.
  1968.   *Book of the Continental Soldier.* Harrisburg, Pa.: Stackpole Books.
Scott, Sibbald
  1867.   *The British Army: Its Origins, Progress, and Equipment.* 2 vols. N.p.
Selby, John
  1972.   *U.S. Cavalry.* Berks., England: Osprey Publishing.
Smith, F.
  1897.   *A Manual of Saddles and Collars, Sore Backs, and Sore Shoulders.* London: H. M. Stationery Office.
Steffen, Randy
  1973.   *United States Military Saddles, 1812–1943.* Norman: University of Oklahoma Press.
  1975–79. *The Horse Soldier.* Norman: University of Oklahoma Press.
Tone, William Theobald Wolfe
  1824.   *School of Cavalry.* Georgetown, D.C.: James Thomas.
Tylden, G.
  1965.   *Horses and Saddlery of the British Army.* London: J. A. Allen & Co.
Whitman, S. E.
  1962.   *The Troopers: An Informal History of the Plains Cavalry, 1865–1890.* New York: Hastings House.
Whittaker, Frederick
  1871.   *Volunteer Cavalry: Lessons of the Decade.* New York, 1871.

U.S. War Department Publications

(Unless otherwise noted, all published by U.S. Government Printing Office, Washington, D.C.)

U.S. War Department
1834. *A System of Tactics . . . of the Cavalry and Light Infantry and Rifleman of the United States.* pp. 9–13, plates 2, 3.
1841. *Cavalry Tactics.*
1845. *Instruction for Field Artillery, Horse, and Foot.* Plate 11.
1861. *Cavalry Tactics: Uniform, Dress, and Horse Equipments of the Army.* General Order no. 6. March 13.
1863. *Revised U.S. Army Regulations for 1861.* Pp. 477–79.
1872. General Order no. 60.
1879. General Order no. 76.
————, Cavalry Equipment Board
1911. *Directions for Use of Experimental Equipment Originated by Cavalry Equipment Board, 1911.* Rock Island, Ill.: Rock Island Arsenal.
————, Cavalry School
1862. *Revised Regulations for the Army of the United States, 1861.* Philadelphia: George W. Childs. [See also later editions of army regulations.]
1896. *Drill Regulations for Cavalry.* [See also earlier and later editions of cavalry-tactics manuals.]
1942. *The Saddler.* Training Manual no. 10-430, March 27.
————, Ordnance Department [Bureau]
1861a. *The Ordnance for the Use of Officers of the United States Army.* Philadelphia: J. B. Lippincott & Co. [See also the manuals of 1841 and 1850.]
1861b. *Revised U.S. Army Regulations.* Ordnance Manual. Article 51.
1862. Ordnance Manual. Plate 21.
1868. Ordnance Memoranda, no. 9.
1870. Ordnance Memoranda, no. 10.
1874. *Cavalry Outfit: Proceedings of the Board of Officers.* Ordnance Memoranda, no. 18. Facsimile ed.: Glendale, N.Y.: S & S Firearms.
1885. *Horse Equipments and Cavalry Accoutrements.* Ordnance Memoranda, no. 29.
1905. *Horse Equipments and Equipments for Officers and Enlisted Men.* Ordnance Memoranda, no. 1719. May 10; revised July 3, 1905 [or 1908].
1914. *Description and Directions for Use and Care of Cavalry Equipment, Model of 1912, October 5, 1914.* Ordnance Manual no. 1715.

Articles

Anonymous
1922. "The Battle Abbey." *Confederate Veteran,* vol. 30.
Cantwell, Robert
1973. "They Led the Life of Riley." *Sports Illustrated.* Nov. 19.
Cavalry Journal
1923. *Cavalry Journal,* vol. 32, no. 132 (July), plate opp. p. 302.
George, Alexander R.
1946. "Machines and Atom Bombs Doom Cavalry to Boneyard." *Denver Post,* May 5.
Glendenning, Marcia
1964. "Military Saddles." *Western Horseman,* August.
Granfelt, Carl-Erick
1973. "McClellan Saddle Modification of 1893 and the McClellan Saddle, 1896." *Military Collector and Historian,* vol. 25, no. 2 (Summer).
Griffith, Perry B.
1972. "That, Sir, Is Leather." *Horse and Rider,* December.
Hutchins, James S.
1956. "Variations in the M1858 McClellan Saddle." *Military Collector and Historian,* vol. 8, no. 2 (Summer).
Keenan, Jerry
1965. "Mounting the Union Cavalry." *Western Horseman,* May.
Olsen, Stanley J.
1955. "The Development of the U.S. Army Saddle." *Military Collector and Historian,* vol. 7, no. 6 (Spring).
1956. "Variations in the 1858 McClellan Saddle." *Military Collector and Historian,* vol. 8, no. 2 (Summer).
Rice, Lee M.
1852. "The McClellan Saddle." *Western Horseman,* November.

Smithers, W. D.
  1960–61. "The U.S. Cavalry." *Western Horse-
          man,* November–December, 1960; Jan-
          uary–April, 1961.
Steffen, Randy
  1960.   "Cavalry in Ancient History." *Western
          Horseman,* September.
  1962.   "The Civil War Soldier." *Western Horse-
          man,* January–March.
  1963c.   "Indian-fighting Cavalryman." *Western
          Horseman,* March–July.
  1963d.   "Randy Steffen's Old West: Frontier
          Cavalryman." *Horse Lover's Magazine,*
          October–November.
  1966a.   "Randy Steffen's Old West: Frontier
          Dragoon." *Horse Lover's Magazine,*
          April–May.
  1966b.   "Randy Steffen's Old West: U.S. Mil-
          itary Saddles." *Horse Lover's Magazine,*
          September–October.
  1971–72. "U.S. Military Saddles." *Western Horse-
          man,* November, 1971–April, 1972. [See
          also under "Military Saddles—Books."]
Swaney, Alex Grant
  1954.   "March to Glory: The Cavalry Horse
          in the Sioux Campaign of 1876." *West-
          ern Horseman,* January–February.
Wedge, Lucille
  1967.   "A Century-Old Saddle." *Western Horse-
          man,* May.
Whiting, Edgar M.
  1931.   "The McClellan Saddle and Its Proposed
          Modifications." *Military Collector and
          Historian,* November–December.
Wischnowski,Edgar A.
  1958.   "U.S. Army Uniform Regulations of
          1851 [or 50?]." *Journal of Company of
          Military Historians,* vol. 10, no. 2 (Sum-
          mer).

                SIDESADDLES

                  Books

Apsley, Lady Viola, and Lady Diana Shedden
  1930.   *To Whom the Goddess.* London: Hutch-
          inson & Co.
Beach, Belle
  1912.   *Riding and Driving for Women.* New
          York: Charles Scribner's Sons.

Bloodgood, Lida Fleitman
  1921.   *Comments on Hacks and Hunters.* New
          York: Charles Scribner's Sons.
  1959.   *The Saddle of Queens.* London: J. A.
          Allen & Co.
Christy, E. V. A.
  N.d.   *Cross-Saddle and Side-Saddle: Modern
          Riding for Men and Women.* Philadel-
          phia: J. B. Lippincott Co.
Clarke, Mrs. J. Stirling
  1857.   *The Habit and the Horse.* N.p.
De Hurst, C.
  1892.   *How Women Should Ride.* N.p.
de Sousa, Baretto
  1925.   *Principles of Equitation.* New York:
          E. P. Dutton & Co.
Faulkner, Nancy
  N.d.   *Sidesaddle for Dandy.* N.p.
Fawcett, William
  1943.   *The Young Horseman.* N.p.
Hance, J. E.
  1932.   *School for Horse and Rider.* N.p.
Hayes, Mrs. Alice M.
  1903.   *The Horsewoman.* London: Hurst &
          Blackett.
Houblon, Doreen Archer
  1938.   *Side-Saddle.* London: Country Life.
Kneeland, Charlotte
  N.d.   *Side-Saddle News.* Mount Holly, N.J.
O'Donoghue, Mrs. Power (Nannie Lambert)
  1881.   *Ladies on Horseback.* London: W. H.
          Allen & Co.
Self, Margaret Cabell
  1968.   *The Complete Book of Horses and
          Ponies.* New York: McGraw-Hill Book
          Company.
Sidney, Samuel
  1875–98. *Book of the Horse.* London: Cassell.
Summerhays, R. S.
  1892.   *How to Ride.* N.p.: Mark W. Cross & Co.
  1939.   *Riding for All.* London: G. Bell & Sons.

                  Articles

Buttrel, Maggie
  1969.   "Side, of Course." *Western Horseman,*
          September.
Edwards, Gladys Brown
  1974.   "The Amazones." *Arabian Horse World,*
          March.

Haley, J. Evetts
1927.   "Historic Saddle Is Saved." *Cattleman,* January.

Hall, Ann
1964a. "Grandma's Side-Saddle and the Quarter Horse." *Quarter Horse Journal,* March.
1964b. "Victorian Side-Saddles." *Hobbies,* November.

Hansen, Sandra
1975.   "Sidesaddle Fever." *Western Horseman,* December.

Lewis, Margaret
1973.   "Pain in the Side (Saddle)." *Horse and Rider,* February.

McCulloch, Vi
1972.   "Side-Saddle Riding and Dress: History of the Side-Saddle." *Canadian Arabian News,* August–September.

McLean, Catherine
1974.   "A Lady to Ride." *Western Horseman,* November.

Marra, Marti
1977.   "Tips on Riding Sidesaddle." *Western Horseman,* December.

Montali, Patty
1973.   "Side-Saddle." *Horse Play,* October–November.

Nyegaard, Carl A.
1891.   "Horseback-Riding for Women." *Ladies' Home Journal,* June.

O'Malley, Jeanne T.
1972.   "Addled Saddle." *Horse Lover's Magazine,* March–April.

Rogers, Georgia M.
1974.   "The Side-Saddle Returns." *American Horseman,* February.

ENGLISH SADDLES

(See also under "General")

Books

Cavendish, William, Duke of Newcastle
1743.   *A General System of Horsemanship.* London: J. A. Allen & Co. Originally published in 1658 in French.

Tuke, Diana R.
1970.   *Stitch by Stitch.* London: J. A. Allen & Co.

Articles

Anzer, Bill
1973.   "Winscher's Saddled with Work, but Master of Ancient Craft." *Ohio Thoroughbred,* July.

Havill, Barbara
1971.   "Hunt Seat Versus Saddle Seat." *Horse and Rider,* May

Rankin, Bob
1973.   "Saddle Making's a Lost Art." *Ohio Thoroughbred,* January.

Tuke, Diana R.
1971.   "Selecting a Saddle." *Pennsylvania Horse,* November.

Index